SNAPSHOTS

HOWARD L. CHAPMAN

WingSpan Press

Copyright © 2014 by Howard L. Chapman

All rights reserved.

No part of this book may be reproduced or transmitted in any form or by any means, electronic or mechanical, including photocopying, recording or by any information storage and retrieval system, without written permission from the author, except for the inclusion of brief quotations in review.

Published in the United States and the United Kingdom by WingSpan Press, Livermore, CA

The WingSpan name, logo and colophon are the trademarks of WingSpan Publishing.
www.wingspanpress.com

First edition 2014

Printed in the United States of America

Publisher's Cataloging-in-Publication Data
Chapman, Howard L.
   Snapshots / Howard L. Chapman.
      pages cm
   ISBN: 978-1-59594-681-2 (hardcover)
   ISBN: 978-1-59594-520-4 (pbk.)
   ISBN: 978-1-59594-859-5 (e-book)
   1. Travelers—Biography. 2. Voyages and travels.
3. Voyages around the world. I. Title.
      G154.5.C53 A3 2014
      910.4`092—dc23
                    2014934013

1 2 3 4 5 6 7 8 9 10

This book is dedicated with great affection
to our three grandsons:

Stephen Donahue Chapman,
James Howard Chapman,
and
Daniel Patrick Chapman.

Also by Howard Chapman

The Wisdom of Howard:
The Collected Columns of Howard L. Chapman

PROLOGUE

Is it necessary to have a reason to write a book? Perhaps, so I will say a few words about the motivations for this one.

Over the past several years we, that is, my wife Betsy and I, have enjoyed traveling. On some of those trips I kept a log of events and, in some of those cases, I transcribed the notes from my log into a journal after we had returned home. As I have reviewed those journals, it has occurred to me that, at some time in the future, these reminiscences may be of interest to our progeny, and to the progeny of our various traveling companions who were essential to the success of so many of our adventures.

In addition, there may be some who will be interested in the historical value of these accounts that relate what it was like to travel "back in the day." I have been surprised, in re-reading them, how much has already changed. For instance, while driving to Canada in 2000, we searched for a gas station or other place where we could find a public pay telephone. Today, most people, even children, have cell phones. It has been only a few years, and the pay phone has almost become extinct!

Nearly all of our experiences have been immeasurably enhanced by the company of good friends who shared them with us. Most of them are people we have known for many years in Fort Wayne, Indiana, such as Mac and Pat Parker, Bill and Suzanne Hall, Ron and Patti Gettel, Max and Holley Hobbs, Cliff and Elaine Shultz, Dick and Marcia Adams, and Gene and Marcia Laker. Some are relatives, such as Dick and Marni Waterfield and Fran Le May. And some are overseas friends such as John and Jean Campion, who live in the United Kingdom.

In some cases we have made friends from the United States and abroad through the travel experience, and have been in communication with them since, such as Patsy Malone, who has given us two extraordinary excursions in and about Ireland.

There have been some travels that I failed to properly record, including Egypt with the Gettels, Russia with the Parkers, and an extraordinary two weeks in Vienna, Austria, with my brother Bruce and his family while they were living there. Unhappily (or happily, depending on your point of view) they cannot be represented now - the memory dims. But because the memory dims, it is important to preserve what has been written. And so, I hope you will enjoy this book.

TABLE OF CONTENTS

CHAPTER 1 – THE FORTUNE COOKIE CRUMBLES 1

CHAPTER 2 - THE GREAT SAIL 14

CHAPTER 3 - ON BOARD THE PHOENIX 31

CHAPTER 4 - DOWN UNDER... 51

CHAPTER 5 – ENGLAND, WEST COUNTRY AND LONDON........ 82

CHAPTER 6 - BERMUDA SHORTS 96

CHAPTER 7 - KENYA - THE AFRICAN SURPRISE 111

CHAPTER 8 - TURKEY.. 136

CHAPTER 9 - YORKSHIRE PUDDING.. 164

CHAPTER 10 - TAKAOKA: 20 YEARS... 184

CHAPTER 11 - WALES & SAILS 222

CHAPTER 12 - TEPID WATERS 247

CHAPTER 13 - RED WINE AND PASTA 258

CHAPTER 14 - OH, CANADA!... 281

CHAPTER 15 - A STIRLING EXPERIENCE 290

CHAPTER 16 - SHAMROCKS 316

CHAPTER 17 – TAKAOKA REDUX..350

Chapter 1

The Fortune Cookie Crumbles

I

Shanghai. The day begins with a telephone call to our room at 4:23 a.m. "Good Morning" says the pleasant Chinese woman. I thank her, even though the call is a mistake, and we do not have to get up for three more hours. Naturally, neither my wife, Betsy, nor I are able to go back to sleep, and as I lie there I wonder who was supposed to get the call. I hope that they had an alarm of their own.

It is September 14, 1983, and we are quartered at the Cypress Hotel, opened by the Chinese in 1982 to serve as a "Western Style" resort hotel for the benefit of business visitors. It is only twenty minutes from the Shanghai Airport but, unfortunately for us, is a long way from the main part of Shanghai. Although it is inconvenient to the sights, it does have the advantage of being quiet.

Our room is twelve feet by fifteen feet, with a carpet that has never been vacuumed. When the bathroom was built, marble tile was put around the walls, but the mortar and tar used in cementing them has never been cleaned or removed. The walls are covered with expensive-looking wall fabric, but it has been poorly applied, and no effort has been made to remove the numerous grease spots and scuff marks around the room.

For the first time since we arrived in China, our room has a television set, a twelve-inch color "National" brand. We are able to receive three channels, each with an excellent picture. The room is also equipped with a radio, and we try it out in an effort to get Voice of America. I had been told by our Chinese guide in Guilin that he listens to it often, but we have no luck.

Snapshots

We are delighted to find that the bathroom has a 110 A.C. electric outlet, meaning I can re-charge my Norelco razor, and we can use our electric hairdryer.

It is easy to have laundry done at Chinese hotels, and inexpensive. We decide to send out laundry, with the assurance that we will get it back by 6:00 o'clock that evening.

One does not drink the tap water in China. In our hotel room, the ubiquitous thermos of hot water is available, together with glasses. We have become spoiled by being provided with fine porcelain cups at other hotels, but here we will have to get along with glasses. It occurs to me that there must be a mattress-aging factory somewhere in China. The mattresses in our room have only been there for a year, but feel like they are at least twenty years old. One of our traveling companions, Henry Moses, has commented that the hotel is beautiful, but that there appears to have been no maintenance upon it since it was built.

As we go to breakfast, we walk along glass-lined corridors which allow us to admire the beautiful gardens and pool that have been constructed all around this hotel. The weather is gray, and it has been raining, but now shows signs of drying up.

We are pleased by the excellent breakfast served in the dining room. Each of us receives a good omelet, pseudo orange juice, fresh coffee, toast, butter and jam. The table is equipped with a lazy susan in the middle, so that the family-style plates can be sent around (or pulled around) to whoever needs them. There are chopsticks, of course, but the hotel has also thoughtfully provided us with silverware. Luxury. At breakfast we discover that most of our group also received the 4:30 "wake up" calls.

The Chinese seem determined that we will all become exhausted, and the national tourist agency, CITS, is making every effort to deprive us of sleep. At breakfast our leader, Marcia Adams, announces the absurd schedule that we have been given for the day. We will all get on a tour bus promptly after breakfast at 8:30 a.m., and will be sightseeing through dinner _and_ a performance of Chinese acrobats, returning late to the hotel. Our luggage is to be packed and outside our door by 10:00 p.m. tonight and we will leave the hotel tomorrow morning for Xian at 6:30 a.m. I ask if there are any flights to Hong Kong. I am ready to go home.

Our group has been joined by Primrose Friend. Friend is her married name, and she often uses her maiden name, Gigliesi. She tells me that she is Italian, and is fluent in French, English and Chinese. A remarkable woman, she is also reputed to be an expert on Chinese art. She will share a room

Howard L. Chapman

with Helene Foellinger. Primrose lives with her husband in Beijing, and is an editor of the Italian edition of "China Pictorial."

As the daily tour begins, it is starting to rain again. We have the first chance to really meet and talk to our local guide whose name is Zhou Kwo Ping. In China, the "family" name is stated first, so that her "first name" is "Kwo Ping." She explains that her family name, Zhou, is the same as former Chairman Zhou En Lai, although they are "not related." She is a young lady with thick glasses and hair in pigtails. She speaks good English, but not in the same class as Robert Li, our local guide in Guilin, who was exceptional. Kwo Ping seems a little stiff at first, but as the day wears on she becomes rather pleasant and easy to talk to.

Kwo Ping uses the microphone on the bus to explain to us that we will have a very, very heavy day, and will have to go hard all day, through dinner, and through the acrobatic show, because there is just too much to see in Shanghai, and we only have one full day there. *In fact*, she intends that we spend most of the day at various "arts and crafts" factories, institutes, and stores, all of which are in reality designed to encourage tourists to buy local ceramics, woodwork, fabrics, and similar items. The Chinese need and want hard currency.

Driving into Shanghai I notice that, as usual, there are no private automobiles, only work vehicles and public buses. None of these seem to have brakes, and rely entirely on horns to get them through traffic. The landscape is lush and green, and there are more bicycles than I have ever seen. Apparently, China is the place where bicycles come to spawn.

Kwo Ping tells us that Chinese holidays are staggered, so that one group of workers has Sunday off, while another group has Tuesday, another Friday, and so on. Accordingly, the city is always jammed with people who are not working. I suspect that a good number of these are people who don't have anything to do seven days a week. There are over 8,600 factories in Shanghai, and the air pollution is terrible. The Chinese are attempting to deal with the problem by planting trees, and by moving some of the factories to the suburbs.

The air conditioner on the bus is not working, so Dick Adams has opened a window. The fresh air is cool enough, but the "fragrance" from the street also comes in. Even though a light rain continues, I notice that people are hanging laundry out to dry.

The Chinese children are beautiful and are always lots of fun. There are no diapers in China, and the little ones have split pants, and they go about their business as and when the occasion demands.

Kwo Ping says there are a lot of temples in Shanghai but we will not be able to see them because of our "busy schedule" and limited time. Too bad,

Snapshots

in the few days that we have been in China, we have only seen about 5,000 temples.

The most impressive thing about Shanghai is the number of people. The place is absolutely mobbed everywhere you look. Every neighborhood street corner looks like Fifth Avenue at rush hour. The place is a veritable anthill - worse than the HUD headquarters in Washington, D.C.

We pass the new sports stadium with 18,000 seats. Shanghai is about to host a national sports festival, so lots of athletes are in town, and there is a strain on hotel space, and also on train and airplane accommodations. Driving near the stadium, someone reports seeing a man holding a rat by the tail and banging it against the sidewalk. Why he does this is anybody's guess.

All of the sights are exotic. We see men on bicycles pulling two-wheel carts with huge loads of vegetables, baskets, tiles, straw, and other material, sometimes not identifiable. Other, similar carts are also being pulled by men and women who are on foot. Many people carry their bundles using "shoulder poles," which stretch across their shoulders and have a large basket tied at each end. Occasionally the bus passes through a market, and thousands of people are thronging around areas where produce is being sold, including live animals, and also various other consumer products. Although the Chinese don't have the variety of food that we have, nor the high quality of food to which we are accustomed, there does seem to be enough for everybody to eat. At least none of the people we see appear to be hungry.

Shanghai has thousands of Sycamore trees. They grow well here, and more are being planted all the time. Several streets are lined with them, and they are beautiful.

We learn that the average wage of a worker in Shanghai is $35.00 per month. In each family, everybody works, except children in school. The Chinese unit of currency is the Yuan, and the official exchange rate is two Yuan per U.S. dollar. This is entirely artificial, of course, and outside the borders of China, the Yuan is not worth anything at all.

The cost of living is very cheap, and a family pays only two or three dollars a month for rent. Furthermore, the Chinese now have the "responsibility system" which is another way of saying that workers are paid more if they are more productive. They know that this is capitalism, but they just can't bring themselves to say it. Kwo Ping tells us that about 80% of the people in Shanghai now have TV, nearly all black and white. Sewing machines are also a big item here, but hardly anyone has a washer, dryer or refrigerator. You need to keep in mind that the average Chinese apartment is very small, and apart from the cost of these appliances, they also require space. In the countryside, we often see women washing clothes on rocks along the sides of rivers or irrigation ditches.

The guide points out that we are driving through the former French Concession, meaning an area that was given over to the French for their diplomatic and commercial people to live in. It was obviously beautiful when it was built, but now looks ramshackle and dirty, like all of the other buildings we have seen. It appears that nothing is spent for aesthetics, except in the case of original construction.

We pass a policeman who is criticizing a bicyclist for some infraction. The scene immediately draws a huge crowd of on-lookers. We also pass a movie theater and learn that movies are very popular in China. Usually, the first feature begins at 8:00 a.m., and shows are continuous until 10:00 o'clock at night. In the summertime, when there is more daylight, the features begin at 5:00 a.m., and every performance is always completely sold out.

In the city, everyone lives in an apartment. All, of course, are owned by the government. With regard to apartments built since the sixties, each apartment has its own kitchen and bath. In pre-sixties buildings, a kitchen and bath is shared among three or four families. The government provides retirement for men at age sixty and for women at age fifty, except that women doing "mental work" cannot retire until age fifty-five. Once a person retires, he draws from seventy percent to eight-five percent of his former pay. Many of these retired people volunteer to work as a public service at such jobs as traffic control, school wardens, or street cleaning. They are identified by red arm bands, and draw a supplement to their retirement pay. There is, however, no obligation for anyone to do anything after retirement.

Kwo Ping is unable to explain to me why retirement is structured in such a way that it discriminates in favor of women. When Mao came to power he declared that "Half the sky in China is supported by women," which meant that there was to be complete equality between the sexes from then on. Somehow, this hasn't worked out yet as to retirement - but then, it also doesn't seem to have worked out with regard to the more influential, powerful or desirable Communist Party positions, which still are dominated by men.

II

We arrive at the entrance to the Yu Yuan Garden. To get there, we must walk through the Yu Yuan Bazaar, which is a large public market, filled with ancient buildings, a lake, street vendors, stores, restaurants, and a zillion people. One of the restaurants specializes in Dim Sum, a Chinese dish in which something, usually meat, is cooked in a dumpling. People in the restaurant are elbow to elbow.

Snapshots

We wedge our way through and across the "nine turning bridge," and past the "mid-lake pavilion," and enter the garden. It was built about 400 years ago by the emperor's treasurer. He did not build it as a residence, but went there to pray for a good corn crop and for "pleasure." Kwo Ping points out that there are two corridors, a wide one, close to the garden, to be used only by men, and a much narrower, parallel corridor to be used by women. The gardens are beautiful and the architecture and style of the old buildings is fascinating. The place is enormously popular, and there are so many people in, around and through it that we have trouble staying together. In fact, several of us become lost from time to time, but always manage to get back together.

By eleven o'clock we have left the Yu Yuan Gardens and headed for the Shanghai Harbor area, located on the Huangpu River. We drive along the broad avenue that adjoins the harbor, formerly known as the "Bund," and the bus stops opposite the Heping (Peace) Hotel, so that we can walk about, look at the harbor, and have thirty minutes to see what commercial Shanghai used to be like.

Most of us head across the street to the Hotel in order to use the bathroom facilities. Happily, they are Western style. I am amazed that I am able to buy a three-day old copy of the Asian Wall Street Journal. In addition, we buy candy, instant coffee, and greeting cards from the "bookstore." The Hotel was obviously once grand, but now shows the effects of many years of neglect. The Chinese always seem to underlight everything, so that every building seems dim when you go in, and this hotel is no exception. The lobby is filled with unattractive glass display cases behind which uninterested clerks are stationed for the purpose of selling cloisonné vases, silks, or other items to tourists. It is remarkable how ugly these glass cases are.

We go to the eighth floor to see the famous lunchroom which overlooks Shanghai Harbor and, indeed, the view is magnificent. There is no one eating there at the time, and the restaurant workers don't seem to mind when we walk over to the windows, open them, and snap pictures.

Back on the bus, we drive by the Shanghai Mansions Hotel, which is located near the river. Today it is entirely turned over to athletes and others who are in town in connection with the current sports event.

In Shanghai, as in all Chinese cities, there is at least one traffic policeman at every busy corner, even though there is also a traffic light. No one pays any attention, either to the lights or to the policemen, who stand quite erect and manage to look very official. They wear a white cap and jacket with a red collar and a gold star, and blue trousers. Quite natty. When they go to lunch, no one replaces them, and they are not missed.

Howard L. Chapman

We turn on to Nanking Road, which is the main shopping street in Shanghai and is three miles long. The government owns all of the shops here, but there are some private shops now allowed in Shanghai. At this time, however, they are relegated to back streets or other relatively undesirable locations. Many people are walking in the streets because there is no room on the sidewalks. Buses are so full that it does not appear that one more person could be put on, even if you used a crowbar.

Kwo Ping tells us that there are four movie studios in Shanghai, and that the city is now a major production center for motion pictures. She also tells us that they receive two local T.V. channels and one from Beijing. She says that they also receive radio BBC and VOA, both in English and Chinese.

We arrive at the Shanghai Arts and Crafts Center, built in 1954. It houses a permanent industrial exhibition, and we are to have thirty minutes to shop before going to lunch. On the wall is a Chinese sports slogan, "Friendship first, competition second."

Shopping at the Arts and Crafts Center turns up some bargains and a wide array of typical tourist goods. A fine cashmere sweater for a man costs $40.00, $35.00 for women's sizes. We also found some nice porcelain jewelry. If someone were interested, they could buy all sorts of clothing, electronics goods, and consumer items not available to the average Chinese.

We, as tourists, exchange our American dollars for Scrip which our Chinese guides call "funny money." A One Yuan Scrip Note is equivalent in purchasing power to a One Yuan Note; however, only foreigners and high Communist officials can obtain the Scrip, and only the Scrip, not Chinese money, can be used to buy goods at stores like this. This serves the purpose of allowing foreigners and high-ranking officials to enjoy the privilege of buying many things that are not available to the Chinese common man.

After shopping, we move to another building, to a roof-top restaurant. I sit next to Primrose Friend, and enjoy talking with her about China. She assures me that the ice that is served with the drinks is safe, made with boiled water, but she also cautions me to peel the apples before we eat them. Like all meals, lunch is served in a wave of family-style dishes, which then are passed around among us. Typically, there are eight people at a table. We start with *hors d'oeuvres* including chicken, ham, salami, and possible fish. Shrimp and vegetables are good, as are the buns. We have a dish of vegetable greens that remind me of spinach, and two fish cooked and served whole which, as usual, go around the table untouched and are taken away at the end of the meal in the same condition as when they arrived. Unfortunately, nearly everything, including the dishes, is very greasy.

Snapshots

There is always warm beer to drink, and the heavy, sweet orange soda pop which is sold under the trade name "Vita." A visiting tennis player once quipped that, if you drink too much of it, you develop a syndrome known as "Vitasgerulitis." The meals always finish with soup. Chinese traditionally do not serve any beverages at their meals, so soup is served last to provide liquid to aid in digestion. With rice, we have in all about ten courses. Each of us has started with one tiny plate in front of us, and that serves for the entire meal, except for the soup, which has its own bowl and spoon. Everyone is using their chopsticks with some dexterity by now. At least, we are not starving.

III

As we get back on the bus, Grace Schultz is taking notes and says she will write a poem about our experiences. Carl Keck has loaded up on cashmere sweaters, which he and his wife, Betty, will use for Christmas presents. (Carl is an ophthalmologist. His office is a site for sore eyes).

Every Chinese bus driver likes to see how close he can come to the bicycles. The bicycle riders play chicken with those in motorized vehicles, but nobody seems to get mad. Still, the accident statistics must be staggering.

We pass a school, and learn that school starts at 7:30 in the morning, exercises are at 7:45, and study begins at 8:00. Kwo Ping says that the kids go home for lunch, but I can't see how that could be true since their parents are all working. She does say that lunch is available at school for those who don't go home. The school day is over at 3:30, and then most children go to a "children's palace" to engage in activities until their parents are home from work.

Every tour in China has a "National Guide" who stays with it from start to finish. Our national guide is a twenty-three year old, good-looking young man named Li ZhongJi. At the beginning of the trip he told us that we could call him "Charlie," but in a private conversation I asked him what his given name is, and he told me "ZhongJi." I asked if it would be all right if I call him that and he said it would be "more friendly," so I do. ZhongJi has some problems with his English, although he seems to have learned every cliché and slang expression in the language. He is extremely good natured and easy to get along with, and seems willing to talk about anything.

While waiting at one of the numerous "arts and crafts institutes," I ask ZhongJi about lawyers in China. He says that they all work for the government, and there are no private attorneys. He says that lawyers make the same as everybody else, that is, about $40.00 a month, but that is not surprising since their job is very easy. All they have to do in defending a criminal, for instance, is argue about what his sentence ought to be.

Lawyers are not involved prior to arrest and, once the person is arrested, conviction is certain. I ask ZhongJi if this didn't sometimes cause problems for an accused who feels that he is innocent, but he assures me that the government does not arrest anybody unless he is guilty. I ask ZhongJi if I might talk to a lawyer while we are in Xian, but he is very dubious and, in fact, resists the idea. He says he is sure he can answer all my questions. I ask him why our local guide in Canton said that we were free to wander about the city, but not beyond, as the area outside Canton is "restricted." ZhongJi looks genuinely puzzled, and says that he does not know why that guide had made that statement.

I have eaten the last of my canned Sunsweet prunes, and have opened a box of dried prunes brought from home. Anyone going to China should plan to eat prunes or bring a laxative, just in case. Don Keltsch has been well supplied with all types of pharmaceutical items, including a laxative called Senokot. I found that it has amazing qualities, in that it worked for me by simply carrying the bottle into my hotel room.

Betsy and I each have a plastic flask loaned to us by Fort Wayne friends Mac and Pat Parker, and they are invaluable. Each morning we fill them with boiled water from the thermos in our room, and use them throughout the day. Mac had also loaned me a transformer and a set of electrical adapters, which have been essential in using our electrical appliances.

IV

We proceed to the "Shanghai Arts and Crafts Research Institute." As usual, the proceedings begin with all of us sitting around a table, having tea, while the local chief cadre tells us about the Institute. Since the cadre purportedly speaks no English, our guide translates everything that she says. We are then treated to a demonstration of how Chinese miniature dolls are made from dough, watch the making of paper cut into pretty patterns, and observe the making of lacquerware. All of this, of course, is simply a prelude to directing us into a shop where all of these things can be purchased, and we spend one and one-half hours at it. Dick Adams and I manage to slip away and walk around the streets outside taking pictures.

After the Institute, Marcia Adams asks for a vote as to what the crowd prefers - either a visit to a Buddhist temple, or to see the Shanghai Museum of Art. The vote goes for the latter. Americans are traditionally hard to regiment, and at this point some of the members of the group are tired, and begin to bail out. The bus stops at the Jin Jiang Hotel, where taxis are available. It is very difficult to get a taxi in China. They cannot be hailed, and in some cities don't exist at all. Shanghai, however, is big enough that there are a few around at major hotels or by telephone if you call one-half hour in advance.

Using her Chinese, Primrose Friend arranges a taxi to take me, Carl Keck and Jim Reffeitt back to our hotel for a nap, and then she went by cab with Don and Jane Keltsch to the Friendship Store so that they can shop for silk products. The remaining group went to the Shanghai Museum of Art and History for an hour and reportedly saw some beautiful scrolls and other examples of Chinese art, after which they went to the Peace Hotel for cocktails. They had their cocktails in the first-floor coffee shop which, unfortunately, has no view. By pre-arrangement, all of us are to converge at a restaurant at 5:30.

All of the stores, hotels, restaurants and other public buildings (including hospitals) have spittoons. Most Chinese, men and women, seem to like to hack and spit. One source reports that this is a problem in winter in the northern cities because the hockers freeze on the sidewalks and present a hazard to pedestrians, who tend to slip on them and fall. In such cases, they are known as "Beijing Land Mines."

It seems that we never eat at a restaurant located on the ground floor. The one for this evening is no exception and we climb the stairs by dim light, sufficient to notice that much of the plaster is missing, windows are broken, and wires are hanging out of the walls. There is no evidence of any maintenance, and only minimum evidence of sanitation. In other words, it is typical. After all, the government owns all of these places, so who is going to spend any money on them? The food is greasy, as usual, but otherwise not too bad.

The best part of the meal is the celebration of Helen Hill's birthday. We all sing "Happy Birthday," and Helen stands up and gets a big hand from the crowd in the restaurant. There are birthday cards, and a Guilin landscape drawn by Henry Moses and signed by all of us, and later, on the bus, Grace Schultz read a poem to Helen that she had written, and delivered a card to her from Helen's daughter.

ZhongJi has brought moon cakes for the occasion. The autumnal equinox is celebrated as a holiday by the Chinese, and on that evening they traditionally gather in family groups, eat moon cakes, and gaze at the moon. Moon cakes are six to eight inches in diameter and about two inches thick, filled with rather sweet pastry, and almonds or walnuts. Some of them are okay. ZhongJi has brought candles and each of us has a piece of moon cake with a lighted candle in it.

By this time we have grown accustomed to the Chinese fare. Everything seems to be prepared in heavy grease, even dishes consisting entirely of vegetables. There is no lazy susan here, and soon the serving plates are stacked one on top of another, and the table is a mess. Gratefully, we leave early because we are going on a cruise of the harbor.

V

All morning we had been told that we were to see a troop of Chinese acrobats this evening, but to our great relief this has been changed to a boat cruise on the harbor. The ship is a large one docked near the Peace Hotel. The entire area is brightly lit and there is a gay, exciting atmosphere about the place. It seems that all of the people in the world have gathered around the docks to form a pulsing mass of humanity, and it does not look as though there is any possible way that we can get through to the ship. Nonetheless, as if by magic, a path opens and we pass through and around the crowd by means of a separate gate.

Kwo Ping instructs us to go to the third deck, the top of the ship, and to enter an area which is marked "Special Class." None of us misses the irony of the existence of a "Special Class" area in the Peoples Republic. (In an airport in Hangchow we saw a restaurant clearly marked "Foreign Visitors and Overseas Chinese.") Most of the ship is a disaster area, but our "Special Class" is plush. Girls in white jackets serve orange juice, moon cakes and apples. I notice that even the Chinese peel the apples. Our group occupied half of the "Special Class" section, and the other half is taken up by a group of Japanese tourists. Dick Adams gives one of them a balloon and takes his picture.

Shanghai's harbor is enormous, thirty-five miles long, and has more visible shipping tonnage than I have ever seen in any one place. It is located entirely on the Huangpu River, which flows to the Yangtze and thence into the ocean. There are countless ocean-going ships and many more tugs, barges, service boats and ferries. The night scene is gorgeous. A spectacle. Our boat leaves the dock at 7:00 p.m., and we are to be gone nearly three hours. Obviously, it is going to be difficult to "have the bags outside the door by 10:00."

Shortly after leaving the dock, a loudspeaker begins to blare American rock and roll. We ask if it can be turned down, but it can't, and accordingly most of us go on deck where it is very pleasant. Later, the wind got a little stiff and most of us came back in.

I have been able to secure a current copy of China Daily, a newspaper published in English by the Chinese government. Most of the articles and stories come from Xinhua, which is the official Chinese news agency, although many of them are acknowledged reprints from AP, UPI or Reuters. Among other things, we get current American baseball scores. According to Xinhua, each month the average Chinese consumes twice his own weight in grease.

I have a cold, and so do Grace Schultz and Bill Hall. Carl Keck and Suzanne Hall report that they are "feeling a little funny," and Jim Reffeitt says he thinks he may have a cold coming on. Eventually, of course, all of us will be sick, one way or another. How can you avoid it? You are exhausted, exposed to countless types of germs you've never encountered in your life, eaten from common plates, and used dishes and glasses that would give an American board of health officer apoplexy.

Kwo Ping now also wants to talk about lawyers. Like all Chinese girls, she has been brought up in pants, and now seems somewhat ill at ease in her wool skirt. In China, she says, people can get a government lawyer to draw a will or to work out a contract. In a civil dispute, each side can get a government lawyer and, if necessary, they have "two trials" and then the judge decides. All of this seems rather vague to me, but I wasn't able to get much clarification.

About 8:30 Kwo Ping invites all of us to come below deck (the middle deck) to see a live show. The place is absolutely jammed, but the first three rows are empty for us and the Japanese tourists who share our "Special Class" facility. None of the Japanese show up for the show. There is a live band consisting of one trumpet, one drum and two saxophones. They aren't bad. When they play "Cherry Pink and Apple Blossom White," one saxophone switches to maracas.

The first act is a juggler. He juggles balls, eggs, glasses of water, and so forth, and seems very good to me - but each time he does a stunt, only the Americans applaud. For some reason, the Chinese just sit there and look. Later ZhongJi says that this is because the Chinese are used to seeing this stuff, and anyway, this guy is not too good. Meanwhile, he works very hard, and sweat pours off his forehead, so that he frequently has to interrupt his act to towel off. A large sign printed on the wall behind him says "Touring the Huangpu River."

As the juggling goes on and on, the Americans begin to leave, one or two at a time. By the time the magician begins his act, only a few remain. Marcia Adams has been visiting with Primrose, discussing peasant art in Xian. We hope we will get to visit the best location, a village called Huxian, but it is very uncertain, depending on what ZhongJi and CITS will let us do. Carl Keck has his camera out and is trying to take night shots of the harbor. Dick Adams is keeping him company, and I join them for a while. It is getting cool now, although still very hot in the city. The boat finally returns at 10:00 p.m., and rigor mortis is setting in. Everyone gets on the bus and crashes.

The bus ride to the hotel takes thirty minutes and we are told that our luggage must be put outside the room before we go to bed.

Kwo Ping reminds us that the bus will leave the hotel tomorrow morning at 6:30 a.m. to go to the airport to catch our flight to Xian. She asks if we will want wake-up calls, and is greeted by a chorus of very loud "No's."

Quote of the day: ZhongJi, on hearing complaints about our exhausting schedule: "You are in China. Now you will have to face the music."

Howard and Betsy Chapman at the Great Wall of China.

Chapter 2

THE GREAT SAIL

This is a "ship's log," more or less, about our week of sailing on Lake Michigan. The sailors were Max and Holley Hobbs, Bill and Suzanne Hall, my wife, Betsy, and me. With two lawyers and a doctor on board, as well as three excellent cooks, how could we possibly ever get into trouble?

The three women had gone from Fort Wayne, Indiana, to Traverse City, Michigan, on Thursday, August 15, 1985, a day before we were to get the boat, so that they could acquire a week's provisions and start putting them on the boat on Friday.

I arranged to pick up Max at 9 a.m. on Friday. As I surveyed our family room I was dismayed at all of the gear that I was bringing. Two large duffels, a large "carry-on bag," a plastic "lawn bag" full of pillows and towels, two sleeping bags, a portable television set, and two life jackets, and this did not even include the two duffel bags that Betsy had with her. I felt pretty embarrassed about it until I got to Max's house and found that he had at least twice as much stuff as I did (including an inflatable dinghy). Max said that he also wanted to take his outboard motor to attach to the dinghy, but that the outboard was at North Harbor Marine on Main Street to be serviced, and we would have to stop and pick it up.

When we got to North Harbor Marine it turned out that they had not yet worked on Max's motor, and Max got pretty sore at them. His anger was tempered when they went back and looked at the motor and discovered that its only problem was that Max had not put gas in it.

We got to Bill's house at 10:30, which was about one hour later than he had expected us, and found that he had packed as much stuff as Max.

His main excuse was that he was responsible for acquiring and bringing the beverage supply for the trip, and this required two large boxes and a couple of large sacks.

Fortunately, I had been able to obtain the use of a van for this trip, and it was full to the brim, leaving barely enough room for Max, Bill and me to ride in it. I drove the first leg to Marshall, Michigan, where we stopped at Schuler's Restaurant for lunch, absorbing one and a half hours. Max offered to drive the next leg and I sat in the back reading. When we got to Lansing I found that I was seeing the same scenery more than once and learned that Max was lost and that we were going back and forth on some freeway. I went back to reading and Max apparently got it straightened out.

Later on Bill took over the driving and I reminded him that Michigan has a seatbelt law. Bill grudgingly put on the seatbelt, but takes a dim view of such laws.

By the time we got to Grayling, Michigan, we were supposed to be in Traverse City, more than an hour away, so we called ahead to alert our wives that we would be late. They were staying at the home of Yvonne (Von) Johnson, Holley's sister-in-law, who lives in Traverse City. They had already ordered pizza, so by the time we got there, it was cold.

After eating we drove the van and also Hall's car (which the women had used) to the West Harbor Marina where our boat was located. Max had arranged to "bare-boat" charter a 41-foot Morgan from Bay Breeze Charters, and it was waiting for us. The moment was not quite as exciting for me as it might have been because I noticed that the van was acting funny. The transmission did not seem to want to engage, and I was worried about it. But, it was after dark on a Friday evening, we were going to leave on a one-week sail, and there was nothing I could do about it, so we parked the van at the Harbor and loaded everything onto the boat.

Loading the boat was no easy task, even though the women had already stowed a lot of the food on board. When we finally did get everything loaded, it came time to choose cabins. Nobody wanted to say which cabin they preferred, but eventually it was decided that Max and Holley would use the aft cabin, Bill and Suzanne the forward cabin, and Betsy and I would be in the middle. The middle cabin is also the main "living area" on the boat, and I would be obliged to adjust the table each night to become a part of my bunk. Additional cushions to cover the table were found in the forward cabin.

Max gave us all a lesson on how to use the heads on a sailboat. (In nautical terms, a toilet is called a "head.") Every marina has permanent bathroom facilities built at the ends of the docks, and we were encouraged to use those

Snapshots

whenever possible; however, the heads on the boat would do when it was "inconvenient" to use the permanent facilities.

Our boat is called the "Cindy Lee" and looked enormous to me. It has a diesel engine which allows it to proceed under power if there is no wind, when docking or leaving the harbor, or otherwise when it might seem desirable. It really is a beautiful ship, and we all decided to lie out in the cockpit and on the deck and enjoy the beautiful evening. We were joined by Von and her son Eric Johnson and his wife Debbie, and their boy Brett. Eric is an experienced sailor and we invited him and Debbie to sail with us the next day to Northport. They seemed to be happy to accept.

Watching the northern sky was great. We put a cardboard box over the light on the dock near the boat so that we could see the stars better. Max explained to me how to find the North Star (you first find the Big Dipper, find the star that is the far end of the bucket, then draw a line from that star through the star below it and you will find the North Star. Or maybe you draw the line in the other direction. Or maybe you draw a line from the star above the end of the bucket. Or something).

Front: Bill Hall and Max Hobbs. Rear: Suzanne Hall, Holley Hobbs, Betsy Chapman, Howard Chapman.

Getting to bed the first night was an interesting time. Everybody was congenial and in good spirits, and it all seemed to go okay. I was tired but didn't sleep. At 1 a.m. my alarm clock went off (by accident). Also, I discovered that when anyone runs any water, it activates a water pump which was about one foot from my head. In addition, there are a lot of ducks swimming about in the harbor, and they like to come up to the boat, peck on the hull and quack. At 4:15 a.m. Betsy and I both decided to take a sleeping pill, and went to sleep.

Max was up early and the water pump got me up too, at 6:15. An hour later Holley banged on the hatches and told us all to get up and get ready to sail. Breakfast consisted of fresh fruit and grapenuts cereal. A man named Skip who works for the charter company came around at 9 a.m. to "check us out." This included collecting a certified check for $250 from each of us which the charter company will hold as a "damage deposit." While Skip was checking us out we watched the "Phoenix," a 46-footer moored two slips down from us, as it prepared to sail with 22 college kids on board. They apparently have chartered the boat and a skipper for the day, and they are now perched all over it drinking beer and otherwise acting collegiate.

The Cast Off

Eric and Debbie arrived at about 9:30 and we cast off. Max started up the engine and we pulled out into Grand Traverse Bay. Although Eric has sailed a lot, he said that this is the biggest boat he has sailed on.

It was good sailing weather, with a steady wind. The only problem was that the wind was behind us. I always thought that it was good to have the wind behind you, but I learned that, for sailing, it is better if the wind is coming toward you. If the wind is coming toward you, it allows you to "tack" which is the preferable way for maneuvering a sailboat. When the wind is behind you, you have to "jibe," and this can be a difficult procedure. Nonetheless, we did jibe the boat on several occasions during the day and it seemed to perform very well.

There are gauges in front of the cockpit which show our boat's speed and the water depth. We were making five to seven knots, and were often in water that is more than 300 feet deep. The boat is steered with a wheel, not a tiller, and there is a large compass on the post to which the wheel is attached, which helps the helmsman follow his course.

We had been getting some instructions from Max about hoisting sail, and we got the sails up with no trouble. Eric was a big help and was busy all day trying to adjust the sails this way and that in order to get a little more speed out of the boat.

We all took turns at the helm, sailing the boat. Betsy and Suzanne both seemed like natural sailors. Despite the brisk wind, the weather was good with lots of sunshine and smooth water. Max and Holley had brought along charts and maps and we spent a lot of time picking out various landmarks. There are red and green buoys here and there on the lake, which are navigational aids. Red ones mean you should keep them on your right when going into the harbor. Eric's rule is "don't go between a buoy and the land." Unfortunately, some of the buoys are equal distant from land on both sides.

Holley set up lunch below buffet style. We still had some pizza from last night. Some of us made bologna sandwiches, others deviled ham sandwiches, and there were chips and fruit. I had seen to it that we had some Classic Coke on board.

By late afternoon we were east of Northport, a tiny community on the peninsula of land between the two forks of Grand Traverse Bay. Because of the direction of the wind we had to sail quite a ways north of it, and then turn around to come back in.

Our ship has a good radio and Max called the Northport Harbor and reserved a slip. We were lucky to get it, and I think it was probably the last one they had.

Once we got the boat moored, Eric and I put on our bathing suits and went about two blocks to a nice public beach where we swam. The water was cold but not too cold. (On the way up Max had gotten into his suit and "swam" by dipping a bucket into the lake and then pouring it over himself. I liked our swim better.)

Having safely tied up the boat, Captain Max decreed that it would be appropriate for the cocktail hour to commence. The next couple of hours are somewhat dim, although I recall that the next morning approximately half of the gin had disappeared. Holley remarked that Bill and I "were never funnier," whatever that means.

We had a good dinner with steaks, tomatoes and coleslaw, but I didn't eat much. Instead I took a 30-minute nap, and then seemed to feel fine.

The reports for the weather were that there would be serious storms on the lake that night. In addition to its ship to shore radio, the boat has a regular radio and tapedeck player and Holley put on a tape that sounded like a thunderstorm. The Chapmans and the Halls went off to use the permanent facilities at the end of the dock, and then came back to prepare for bed. Everyone made a pact to run some drinking water before going to bed, so as to avoid running the water pump during the night. I was grateful.

The boats next to us were noisy, and we debated whether or not to take another pill, but decided not. In fact, we all got to sleep rather easily, only to be awakened by the most violent thunder storm I have ever seen. We were sleeping with all of the hatches, portholes and companionways wide open, so there was quite a scramble by all of us to close up the ship, because rain was coming in hard and fast. With all the lightning, I felt a little uneasy about sleeping with my feet about six inches from the main mast, but Max assured us that a harbor was the "safest place to be" in a thunderstorm.

The Crisis

Sunday morning we were up early, had breakfast of cereal and fruit, and made ready to sail. By the time I finished eating, Max was already pulling the boat out of the harbor. (I had been delayed because I went up to the marina to take a shower. They have pretty good facilities, including three private shower stalls with attached "dressing rooms.")

Eric and Debbie had left us the evening before, so the "crew" was on its own to get the sails up, which we did with no problem. We sailed due North out of Grand Traverse Bay and as soon as we entered the open water of Lake Michigan the wind picked up, and the waves were four to six feet. The sky began to get darker, the wind stiffer, the waves bigger, and we began to feel the aftermath of the storms that had gone through last night.

During the entire run we met only one other boat, a sailboat apparently coming from Beaver Island, close hauled into the wind and heeling. For us, the wind was again behind us, and we began to make really good time.

As the weather appeared to get more ominous I worried a little, but Max seemed unperturbed. Waves reached the eight to ten foot level but since we were sailing with the wind behind us, the waves did not break over us very often. Still, there was enough water over the decks that we closed the companionways and put on our "foul weather gear." The boat was making better than 8 knots all of the time and at one point we clocked it at 9.2 knots. Bill, unfortunately, was suffering from seasickness and stayed at the stern of the boat.

The visibility was not too good this day. Lake Michigan is a big lake, and for a while we were out of sight of all land. Max was busy navigating and kept us on a course where we soon saw Fox Island, letting us know we were heading the right way; however, by now the wind was really strong and Max decided that we would have to reef the sails in order to keep the boat under control. That made sense to me because we were pitching like crazy and the boat was really moving around a lot.

We had no trouble reefing the jib, because our boat was equipped with a "roller-furler" device which allows the jib to be wound around the forestay by using lines that run back to the cockpit. Accordingly, nobody had to go up on the foredeck in order to get the jib reefed in.

The mainsail was another matter. It is equipped with two reefing lines, the first to be used if you want to take in only a few feet of sail, the second to be used if you want to take in approximately twice as much sail. Unhappily, one of those lines had not been properly fixed to the boom and was hanging out over Lake Michigan, and we thought (erroneously as it turned out) that this was the line we would have to somehow gather in.

Max decided that the reefing would be a three-person job. He assigned me to station myself at the bottom of the mast and to lower the halyard to the proper length. This would allow the mainsail to be pulled down by a second person who would then hook one part of the sail at the mast. The third person would have the job of getting hold of the reefing line, pulling it in tight, and tying it down.

Bill made a valiant effort to help with the reefing but because of the seasickness, he and all the rest of us decided it was best he not make the effort. Instead, Betsy and Suzanne came up on deck with me to do it.

The deck was pitched at approximately a 45-degree angle and was wet and slippery, and the boat was moving a lot. In addition, when we began to lower the mainsail it flapped and fluttered and made a lot of noise, which added to the confusion and made the whole thing seem pretty scary (the noise also made it harder for us to hear the instructions that Max was giving us from the cockpit).

At the helm of the Cindy Lee.

During the time we were trying to reef the sail, Max thought we were not able to pull the reefing line, and suggested we try to use the winch that is on the boom. The winch handle lies in a bucket at the foot of the mast and I put it into the winch to be ready for use. The handle on the rear winches is a locking handle which stays secure in the winch, but it turns out that this handle does not lock and when I let go of it the boat shifted and it fell down on the deck. Fortunately, I scrambled for it and got it before it went overboard. Otherwise, Max said, I would have had to go into the water after it. This, he says, is a "law of the sea."

Needless to say, this exceptional crew performed with notable success, got the sail reefed, and all returned safely to the cockpit. With this accomplished, Max said that he had much better control over the ship and, indeed, it seemed that the ship was sailing better, with a lot less lurching and bouncing.

Within a short time after getting the sails reefed we got our first glimpse of Beaver Island. It is about 13 miles long and about 7 miles across. We were bound for St. James Harbor which is in the northeast corner of the island, so we headed up the east side of the island. Once we got within the "lee" of the island, the water smoothed out very noticeably, and Bill's spirits and condition both picked up immediately, he nibbled a little food, and even took over the helm for awhile. (During the sail up the coast, the rest of us had eaten sandwiches, juice, crackers, and some candy.)

When we finally arrived at Beaver Island we caused something of a commotion at the dock. Apparently, most of the boats there considered themselves "weathered in" because of the heavy seas, and they were quite astonished to learn that we had not only sailed in, but had come all the way from Northport. We all congratulated Max because he did, in fact, a fine job of seamanship in bringing us there.

After the boat was moored I discovered that the compartment in which I stored all of my clothes had leaked and that everything was soaked. The water had apparently come in through a partly opened porthole during the rainstorm the night before, and not during the sail north (when all of the ports were tightly fastened shut). We got out all of the hangers and clothespins we could find and my clothes were draped all over the ship for the next 24 hours, getting dry. It is an odd feeling to sit and drink a cup of coffee amid racks of one's own soggy underwear. It may have been even odder for the others who were, after all, sitting among someone else's soggy underwear.

Betsy, Suzanne and I decided to take a walk and went south on the "paved road" to a place called "Marge's Stoney Acre Cafe" which was about twenty minutes from the town. The woods are pretty and the country scenery is magnificent. On the way back, Suzanne picked some wildflowers and made us a center piece for dinner.

Snapshots

Beaver Island

The history of Beaver Island is very interesting. At one time it was settled by Mormons who came here under the leadership of James Strang after Joseph Smith was assassinated at Nauvoo, Illinois. The Mormons constituted a majority of the people on the island and Strang declared himself "king." He was later assassinated by some of his followers, after which a mob from the mainland stormed the island and ran the Mormons out. After they were gone, Irish fishermen and their families settled on the island, and the Irish tradition is quite prevalent.

I introduced myself to a gentleman on the dock and asked his name and he said "I am Tim the Harbormaster." Despite the fact that Tim has no discernable last name, he seems pleasant enough, and gave us some sweet corn which we shucked and cooked for dinner. The marina at Beaver Island has an unpleasant custom of charging $1.25 to use its shower facilities, but I understand that this is happening more and more at other marinas.

Dinner Sunday night included some excellent lasagna, fresh tomatoes and zucchini, and pecan pie. During dinner Holley played a tape for us consisting of Flamenco music. I chose not to inquire as to why she had selected Flamenco music for this occasion.

Everyone was tired after the long day. It was getting colder, so I broke out the heavy pajamas for the evening. (Translate: longjohns.) All of us turned in early. I read William Buckley's *"Airborne: A Sentimental Journey"* for a while and then went to sleep easily, and slept well all night.

Monday morning we slept late and when we got up we found a gray lead colored sky, and it was <u>cold</u>. Betsy was complaining of a sore throat, but otherwise everyone seemed to be in good condition. Max and Holley breakfasted on the boat and the rest of us went to the Shamrock Tavern where we had a splendid breakfast. The Shamrock Tavern reminds me of the setting for "Anatomy of a Murder," but the people are pleasant and the food is good.

On returning to the boat we found that Max had devised a job for everyone, including the one assigned to me for washing down the deck, which I proceeded to do. It was getting warmer all the time and with the exercise I soon decided to change into shorts and a tee shirt.

Holley cooked up sloppy joe sandwiches for lunch and we also ate Pepperidge Farms cookies, and opened some prunes (Suzanne and I are two sensible people who like prunes). I was asked to watch the coffee pot and to let someone know when it was ready to drink. I found that this coffee pot does not know when it is supposed to stop perking. Coffee pots in my life have always known when they should quit, but this one just sits on the stove and perks until you take it off.

By 2:00 o'clock my clothes finally seemed to be getting dry and I could put some of them away. Bill and Max inflated the dinghy, put the outboard on it, got it into the water, and set off to fish in the harbor. Betsy, Suzanne and I went for a hike and found the Beaver Island Lodge, which has a good restaurant with an incredible view north from Beaver Island across Lake Michigan to the mainland, and we made reservations for dinner that night. We then proceeded to walk west through the woods until we came to Font Lake, a good sized inland lake with very little development around it and reputedly excellent fishing. We were sitting on a sand dune looking over this view, thinking ourselves absolutely alone, when a woman and two small children came around a bend carrying fishing tackle. One little boy said "Mom, can we go to our favorite spot where we never catch any fish?"

Inflating the dinghy at Beaver Island.

It was getting colder and beginning to drizzle, but we were prepared for it. All of us were carrying our foul weather gear so we walked back and stayed dry without any trouble.

On the way back to the boat we passed a shop that was closing that day for the "season." Suzanne bought some postcards. After all, this would be our last chance to buy anything from that particular shop.

Passing through town we found the Island Sports Rental and learned that we could rent bicycles or mopeds, and decided that we would rent bicycles and try to ride around part of the island on Tuesday.

We stopped at the post office to buy some stamps for Suzanne and learned that Beaver Island has about 300 to 350 permanent residents. Most have a post office box or get mail at the post office through General Delivery.

When we got back to the ship, Bill and Max had already returned and we learned (much to my relief) that they had no luck at all with fishing. I had been troubled with visions of us cleaning and eating whatever they caught. Meanwhile, Holley had been shopping in town and had bought a new bracelet. Even though we had worn our rain jackets, our trousers had gotten damp, so we had a whole new generation of clothes to hang up to dry.

The rain stopped and, even though the hatches were wide open, the cabin stayed pleasantly warm and very cozy. We put some music on the tape player and opened the bar for cocktails. All of us were very mellow.

At 6:30 we left by foot for Beaver Island Lodge, about a ten-minute walk. From the restaurant we could see Garden Island to the east, and Squaw Island and Whiskey Island directly to the north. The mainland was dimly visible to the north beyond. There was a heavy cold sky and lots of wind, and yet we saw someone way out in the lake on a wind surfboard. Also, a couple of big freighters crossed to the west, the first we had seen.

The Beaver Island Lodge has a good restaurant and I would recommend it to anybody. I had beef, Holley had whitefish and everyone else had salmon. The portions were enormous but all of us have such good manners that we ate all of it. When we finished it was 9:00 o'clock but still light enough for us to go down to the beach and look at the lake. I am not used to seeing miles and miles of undeveloped shoreline.

We walked back to the boat and got ready for bed, including making our now traditional trek to use the marina facilities.

Living on Board

The Cindy Lee has a rather ingenious design whereby the foreward cabin (inhabited by the Halls) and the middle cabin (inhabited by us) is separated by a passageway that is four feet long and about one and a half feet wide. Storage space is on the port side and the foreward head is on the starboard side. The head has two doors, one that swings from the right side and closes off the fore cabin, and the other swings to the left and closes off the mid cabin. This all works pretty well except when all four of us were using all of our cabins at once. I would find myself in the head and try to open the right-hand door to get out, but could not because Bill would be standing there, whereupon, I would open the left-hand door and step out into the passageway. The door only opens

90 degrees so that I cannot push it around into our cabin and Bill and I stand there looking at each other. (Bill had nowhere to go unless he crawled up into his bunk.) I then would go back into the head, close the door behind me, Bill would exit into our cabin, I would then leave the head and go back into our cabin also, after which Bill could then go back into his own place.

How close we all became! I continued to be amazed at the good humor and congeniality that held up among everybody despite living in such close quarters.

Bedtime entailed putting down the table to make my bunk, figuring out where to put all the stuff that was formerly on the table, deciding whether or not to risk putting anything in the compartment that leaks, coping with the towels that are hanging around to dry, deciding where on earth to go in order to change into pajamas, getting the sleeping bags from the aft cabin and unrolling them, lifting some of the seat panels to get the pillows from beneath Betsy's bunk, finding my extra blanket, and all of us accommodating all of the others at the same time. Great fun.

Max told us that the forecast for the night was 44 degrees with a stiff wind. Nonetheless, we found it very comfortable sleeping with the hatches open, and we all slept well.

On Tuesday morning I got up at 8:30 and decided to take a shower. Although there are showers in each of the two heads on the ship, I have found it to be much preferable and easier to use the harbor facilities (even at the expense of $1.25). To prepare myself to walk from the ship to the marina shower I put on an undershirt, a long-sleeved pullover shirt, a sweatshirt, and my Woolrich winter coat, gloves, a knit cap, jeans and boat shoes. Walking up there it looks like we will have cold and rain all day.

Having heard all our comments about the good breakfast yesterday at the Shamrock Tavern, Max decided to make breakfast for everyone "in style" which he proceeded to do, including bacon, eggs, bread, fresh fruit, prunes and coffee. Just great. After breakfast we were all content and lolled about the cabin, sipping our coffee and just generally feeling good.

Despite the cold beginning, the weather seemed to be improving. The women went into town to shop and Max arrived with Tim the Harbormaster and his device for pumping out the boat's holding tanks. It is a wagon with a hose, a nozzle and a pump. Max and I handled the hose on the ship, and Tim worked the machine on the dock, until both holding tanks were pumped out. (We had filled the water tanks on Monday. I had the sensation that, with fresh water and the holding tanks pumped out, our boat was "ready for anything.")

Max and Holley decided to see a realtor in order to look at some possible land purchases on Beaver Island. The rest of us headed to the Island Sports

Snapshots

Rental and rented four bicycles for $1.25 per hour per bike. These are old fashioned bikes with fat tires, foot brakes, and baskets on the front. I felt a little disappointed at the fat tires, since I thought we could all do much better with the thin tires like we use at home. It was getting warm enough that we all took off our jackets and put them in the baskets of the bicycles. We first rode around the harbor to the lighthouse at the point facing onto Lake Michigan, which used to be a coast guard station, and then back into town.

The Chapmans and the Halls had decided to buy a gift for Max and Holley as appreciation for all their work and skill in connection with our trip. Betsy went into the shop and bought the gift while the rest kept a lookout to be sure that Max and Holley did not spot us, and then we hid the gift on the boat. This done, the four of us set off with our bicycles, heading west across Beaver Island.

It wasn't long before we discovered that only a very small portion of the roads on Beaver Island are paved, and the rest are a sandy gravel, and it became quite obvious why they rent bicycles with fat tires, which are much easier to ride and control on that kind of a road. We kept going in a westerly direction, stopping to look again at beautiful Font Lake, and then onward to the western shore of the island, which is called "Donegal Bay." Riding south along Donegal Bay is a lovely experience. The road winds in and out of the woods, and each time it comes out you have another view of Lake Michigan, which by now had turned bright blue under a benevolent sun. At one point Betsy's front wheel caught in some sand and got twisted, throwing her off the bike. She executed a pirouette and landed adroitly, and we agreed that she had been able to do this because of our occasional practicing of our "leaps," fashioned after ballet dancing. Bill and Suzanne have become so impressed that they, too, are taking up the art of "leaping."

After riding to the south end of Donegal Bay our road petered out but our map showed a "trail" which we found and which carried us through very dense woods until we exited on another gravel road named "Darkeytown Road," which we used to head back to the eastern shore. The fields on either side of Darkeytown Road are full of flowers, and it is beautiful, wild country. When we finally came back to the paved road it was only a short ride to Marge's Stoney Acre Cafe.

Bill and I were proud of Betsy and Suzanne. We had been going nearly two hours over difficult roads and it was, all in all, pretty tough riding, but they were holding up well and were still going strong. (They did not protest, however, when I suggested that we stop for lunch.)

We had a fine lunch (I was surprised that practically every place on Beaver Island seems to have good food). Marge's has a very civilized rule which is that you must have ice cream with any dessert that you order. Bill and I ate strawberry shortcake, Betsy and Suzanne had lemon meringue pie.

After lunch it took very little time to get back into town, return the bikes, and walk down to the boat. By now we had hot sun and decided to use the opportunity to take some pictures. Max had bought some smoked fish which he offered around, and we broke out cheese and crackers. We invited a couple from another boat to come over and join us, which they did, bringing some good snacks of their own. I changed into my bathing suit and went swimming off the end of the boat. The water was clean and felt good. Within thirty minutes after I came out, however, the clouds had rolled in and the temperature dropped precipitously. We reversed our procedure from earlier in the day and began putting back all of the layers of clothing that we had started out with. Bill got out his fishing tackle and did a little fishing off the dock, catching some small perch which, after exhibiting them, he restored to the bay.

Our captain, Max Hobbs, and his wife Holley.

This was an easy and pleasant evening. About 8:00 o'clock Betsy cooked some soup and she and Suzanne made grilled cheese sandwiches. Holley came up with some "stir and bake" cakes, a spice cake and a chocolate cake (two cakes!) After dinner we put some music on the tape machine and talked in the cabin until everybody began to get sleepy. Max had brought his game of Trivial Pursuit, but he wasn't able to generate much interest in it.

At 10:00 o'clock Betsy and I, Bill and Suzanne made our nightly pilgrimage to the marina head. I used the facilities on the boat to brush my teeth since I had learned that the sinks drain into the lake, not into the holding tanks. Only the heads on the boat drain into the holding tanks. After participating in the pumping out exercise I now have a new awareness of holding tanks, their uses and limitations.

Tomorrow we would sail for Sutton's Bay. The weather report sounded good.

The Long Trek Back

Wednesday morning breakfast was back to cereal and juice. After eating, Betsy made sandwiches to have them available during the day. Mostly they were peanut butter and jelly, and also some with cheese.

The weather was cold but calm and the reports were good from the standpoint that we would have "pleasant" weather and, once south of Beaver Island, the wind should be good. We would set a course south to Sutton's Bay and plan to make Traverse City the next day.

I had now moved nearly everything from my clothes compartment, except for laundry which I kept there in a plastic bag. I have this advice for anyone who plans to go sailing: Get a lot of kitchen size plastic bags and keep your clothes in them, using one bag for socks, another for underwear, another for shirts, etc.

We seemed to be getting better organized, and by 9:00 o'clock we pulled out of the harbor with everyone having eaten breakfast, washed, dressed, stowed their gear, and gotten the boat ready to sail.

As soon as we cleared St. James Harbor we cut the power and hoisted the sail, and went on our "watches," with Betsy on first, then me. (The person "on watch" was at the helm.) There was very little wind, and the boat inched along at about 2 knots. In fact, it was going so slowly, that I could not discern much progress from one time to the next. Finally, after more than 2 hours, we made it past the lee of Beaver Island and caught the westward wind over Lake Michigan. Not only did the wind pick up but the clouds left and the sun came out, and for the next 7 hours we had glorious sailing, with waves 2 feet and gentle, a pleasant cool wind, and bright sun.

With weather like this I was amazed that we did not see more boats. Only one freighter crossed our path, and we saw another in the distance, but no other sails except for small ones along the shore near Charlevoix. For most of the day we had this enormous beautiful lake to ourselves.

Everyone sailed (except Holley, who says she will only drive the boat under power), and we took pictures with all three of the cameras on board.

Max and Holley told us that we have had unusually good sailing weather on this trip. We, of course, assume that it is always like this. Since leaving Traverse City we have already traveled more than 120 miles under sail!

We had planned to sail to Sutton's Bay but because it was late we decided to go back to Northport, which is closer. When we entered the harbor we found one last slip, along the seawall, and got the boat moored with no difficulty. Max said that we seemed to be learning.

Another pleasant evening with cocktails and then dinner. Canned corned beef tasted good and Max cooked an excellent goulash of vegetables with mushrooms. I opened my can of Macadamia Nut Brittle that I had brought from Hawaii for a special occasion. My portable T.V. was able to pick up Traverse City and I watched the evening news.

Some of us had acquired a few aches and pains by now. Sue bumped her head on the boom, Betsy had a sore knee from bicycling, I cut my hand while closing a hatch in a hurry, Holley was wearing a knee band because of the strain of going up and down stairs, and Max had been stung on the hand by a wasp. All things considered, we were in top-notch condition.

Thursday morning we slept in (except Max) and got up at 8:30. I made a mental note that I really don't like the breakfast cereal called Grapenuts. The morning was warmer than the last few had been and the forecast was seventy degrees with light winds. Max said that, if there isn't enough wind, we may have to give in and cruise under power.

After breakfast we all took a walk around Northport. Bill and I stopped at the I.G.A. to acquire some essentials for lunch: cookies, grapes, melon, gumdrops and peanuts.

There is a big power boat race in Northport every August and this was the weekend. Some of the boats had already arrived including a huge (50-foot) boat with "Popeye Chicken" painted on the side. There is a raffle underway and for $50 we could have a lottery ticket on a big power boat. We mulled the proposition and decided we should not chip in and buy a ticket. We are sailors. What would we do with a power boat?

Back on the Cindy Lee, Betsy and Suzanne began making sandwiches, Max checked us out of the harbor, and by 11:30 we were on our way, but under power. The bay was absolutely calm and flat, and very little wind. Being under power, Holley took the helm for the first time.

Even though we didn't have "sailing wind" we had a beautiful day cruising on Lake Michigan. We reached a small island called Marion Island at about 1:30 in the afternoon, found a spot close by and dropped anchor. I went swimming off the boat and it was some of the most marvelous water I have ever been in. During lunch we ate the sandwiches plus all of the "essentials"

Snapshots

that Bill and I had purchased. Then Max and Bill fished, Betsy and I swam again, and everybody became very lazy. (While lying on deck a boat went by not too far away and we heard a small child say "Is that a pirate ship?")

After 5:00 o'clock we hoisted the sails. Still not much wind but we were able to make 3 knots. At that rate it took us nearly four hours, but we finally tied up at our slip in Traverse City at 9:00 o'clock. Bill and I drove to McDonald's, partly for a sandwich and partly to see how the van would go. It was not going very well. The transmission was slipping badly.

Back at the boat we broke out the champagne and toasted the captain and first mate (not to mention the crew) and the close of a successful, pleasant trip.

I got up early on Friday morning and took the van to a Chevy dealer who found that there was no transmission fluid in it. The simple act of adding fluid completely cured the problem and the van behaved fine.

After lunch with Von Johnson at the Pinestead Reef (in a room with a gorgeous view looking north over Traverse Bay) we headed back to Fort Wayne. We rendezvoused at Schuler's Restaurant in Marshall, Michigan, for one last meal together, then on to Fort Wayne.

How could anybody have a better time than we did?

Chapter 3

ON BOARD THE PHOENIX

One year after "The Great Sail" the same group of hardy sailors undertook another voyage, this time on board the "Phoenix[1]," a 46-foot Morgan sailing vessel chartered out of Traverse City, Michigan, by Bay Breeze Charters[2]. We arrived at the dock after dinner on August 15, 1986, and began loading the boat. Since we had not yet decided who would have which cabin, we piled everything on deck and there was a veritable mountain of clothes, bedding, groceries, and assorted gear.

After a lot of hemming and hawing, it was finally decided that everybody would have the same cabins that they had the year earlier, the Halls in the bow, the Hobbs aft, and the Chapmans in the middle, or "saloon" of the boat. The Phoenix is big enough to have a fourth cabin with two bunks in it, which we called the "companionway," and we decided that the upper bunk could be used for storage and the lower bunk for sleeping by anybody who was having trouble sleeping in his own quarters.

The initial problem of storing all of our things on the boat was rather formidable. During the ensuing confusion, Betsy reminded us that, "Marcia Adams says we're all nuts for doing this." Possibly.

When we were finally ready to turn in I remembered from last year that if anyone runs any water on the boat during the night it activates the water pump, which in turn sounds like someone is tearing up pavement right

---

1 Other helpful suggestions for the title included "Phlight of the Phoenix," "Phun on the Phoenix" and "The Madness."
2 The sailors were Max and Holley Hobbs, Bill and Suzanne Hall and Howard and Betsy Chapman.

next to my head when I'm trying to sleep. Accordingly, I urged everybody to remember to run their glass of water before retiring.

Most of us slept okay on Friday night, but not me. I was sleeping on the dining room table, converted into a bunk by lowering it and putting two cushions on it. Unfortunately, the cushions tended to separate each time I moved, and I found myself "resting" on the hard surface of the table beneath. Besides that, the ducks in the harbor made their usual outrageous clamor and I remembered that it takes a night or two to get used to it.

It is a little embarrassing to use the heads on the boat during the night. First, you have to open a valve and vigorously pump a handle two or three times in order to run a little water into the bowl. Each pump makes a loud "oogah-oogah" sound, so you can be sure that everyone on the boat is awake. After using the head it is necessary to pump the handle several more times. Your concerns are heightened by the knowledge that others are "sleeping" a few inches away from the head, separated only by a narrow piece of wood.

I got up soon after dawn on Saturday morning and decided to wash up at the facilities at the Marina, which are approximately equivalent to a third-rate gas station, only with a shower. Afterwards, since everyone else was still asleep, I thought I would drive our van into town and have breakfast, but discovered, to my chagrin, that I had left the lights on all night and that the van was as dead as a doornail. I went back to the boat and quietly sat in my bunk, took out my log and wrote, "I want to go home."

I sat there quietly until everybody finally got up and we got something to eat. Bill carries jumper cables in his car, and we found that we could easily start the van by jumping it. I was much relieved because I now knew that it would not be any problem to get the van going when we returned from our sail, but I was still sore at missing a chance for a good hot breakfast. (Hot breakfasts are not routine on a sailboat.)

Before leaving the harbor with a charter boat, you have to be "checked out," and the Bay Breeze employee named Skip again came by to perform that task. He told us that the boat's oven had no door because the last occupants of the boat had "run into some heavy weather" on Gray's Reef, and had broken the door off. Not a very cheerful thought. We also complained that the refrigerator didn't seem to be working, but Skip assured us that it was, and that it would be fine once we got underway.

Holley's sister-in-law, Von Johnson, came by and deposited her son Eric, his wife Debbie, and their son Brett who would sail with us during the day to Charlevoix, Michigan, and be met there by Debbie's sister.

Howard L. Chapman

Under Way

At last everything was ready, Max started the motor and we began our way out of the harbor and headed North up Grand Traverse Bay. Whether or not it was a good day depends on your point of view. It was sunny, clear and mild, but there was very little wind. We raised the sails and tried to sail for a while, but got nowhere, and gave up. Still, raising the sails, setting them, and then lowering them gave us a chance to get ourselves back into the workings of a sailboat.

We noted that the ship's gauges for measuring the speed and the distance of travel were not working, and we decided that it would be necessary to start making a list of complaints for Skip. The most critical gauge, the one that measures the depth of the water, seemed to be working only sporadically, and this one was particularly worrisome. The Phoenix draws 5 ½ feet, and there are lots of places in Lake Michigan that are more shallow than that.

For lunch we served corned beef sandwiches, potato chips and Lowenbrau Beer. I hoisted the Lowenbrau to Max, gave him my most sincere expression, and said, "Max, it just doesn't get any better than this." Max had the gall to tell me that it was some other beer brand, not Lowenbrau, that uses that ad.

Since we were proceeding under very calm conditions, we took time for some safety instruction. Every boat should be equipped with fire extinguishers, and we all went through the Phoenix learning where they were located and reviewing how they are used. A fire on a boat can be a real crisis, because you don't have any place to go, and it is important for everybody to know how to deal with it as quickly as possible.

In addition, every boat should have a good quality marine radio. Ours was located immediately next to the companionway and behind the chart table and had our name and call letters clearly displayed on it, "The Phoenix, WD3119." Marine radio channel number 16 is reserved for emergencies and "initial contact" calls. Our radio had a button to push which automatically put the radio on channel 16. If you disengage that button, then you can use a knob to locate other channels on which to talk, much like using a CB Radio. The correct procedure when routinely calling the harbor or another boat is to make the contact on channel 16, and then agree with the other party to transfer to a different channel on which to continue the conversation.

Bill and Max inflated the dinghy on the foredeck. The dinghy and the outboard motor for it belong to Max. It is essentially a rubber boat, with inflatable sides. Any large boat needs a dinghy so people can go back and forth when the boat is at anchor offshore, and also as a safety precaution in the event of emergency.

Snapshots

When we got close to Charlevoix we heard people on the radio calling the Charlevoix Marina and having trouble getting a place to berth. We began to suspect that we would have a problem getting a slip there ourselves. It was Saturday night and Charlevoix is a popular place.

The marina is located on Lake Charlevoix, and to get to it you have to go through a channel between Lake Charlevoix and Lake Michigan. This requires the raising of a drawbridge which goes up every thirty minutes on the hour and the half hour, so we tried to "hit it" at just the right time. We found a lot of other boats doing the same thing, but everyone got through easily into beautiful Lake Charlevoix, one of the prettiest lakes I have ever seen.

As we suspected, the public marina had no room for us, but recommended two private marinas that we might try. As a fallback, we always had the option of dropping anchor off shore and simply spending the night at anchor.

We first tried a nice looking place called Northwest Marina. Skip had assured us that Bay Breeze was well known there and kept a permanent slip that would be available for us if the public marina was full. I called in on the radio and the girl advised that, yes, they had a slip for us, but they also had a "two night minimum." I tried to reason with her, explained that our ship was a charter from Bay Breeze, and that Bay Breeze was supposed to have a permanent slip reserved, so that we should not have to pay for two nights, since we were only going to stay one night. This girl, however, only knew three words: "Two Night Minimum."

We decided to try Irish Marina and, indeed, found a slip. Maneuvering the Phoenix in the small harbor was very, very tight, and we admired Max's ability in getting us docked without any problem. (Of course, he had a magnificent crew.)

Once docked, several people went swimming, and cocktails, cheese and crackers were served on board. We noted that all of the docks at the Irish Marina are of the floating variety, and that each swell caused a squeak or a squawk. Taken together, they made a regular symphony.

The Irish Marina found it necessary to lock its marina "facilities" but did not bother to give us a key. By the time we realized this situation everyone at the Irish Marina office had gone home so we were left to the device of borrowing keys from other people in the marina. At bedtime I took a sleeping pill, one of Bill Hall's magic elixirs, slept wonderfully, and did not even notice the groaning symphony of the docks.

We were awakened at dawn by rain, feeling it as well as hearing it. We slept with all the ports and hatches wide open and, despite the cool nights, were always comfortable. When the rain came, everybody had to scurry around and close the hatches, but then we went back to sleep until 8 o'clock. Betsy and

I and the Halls walked to a nearby motel for a big breakfast. While we were there, someone from the Irish Marina came by to collect the night's rent from Max, but made no apologies for never having given us a key to the facilities.

Navigating

Careful planning allowed us to make the 10:30 a.m. drawbridge out of Lake Charlevoix. We had a gray sky and Lake Michigan had swells of one to three feet, but there was not much wind. We put up the dodger, turned on the motor, and set a course to Beaver Island. (The dodger is a canvas supported on metal stays that is shaped kind of like a cabana and is pulled up in front of the cockpit to divert wind and weather.)

On the lake, it was quite cool but calm, with occasional light rain. We got out our foul weather gear and served a light lunch. Max had set a course of 350°, but then we saw the Beaver Island Ferry crossing below us and decided we were heading too far North, and adjusted our course accordingly. We made the South half of Beaver Island easily and then spent nearly an hour traveling up the East side to the St. James harbor.

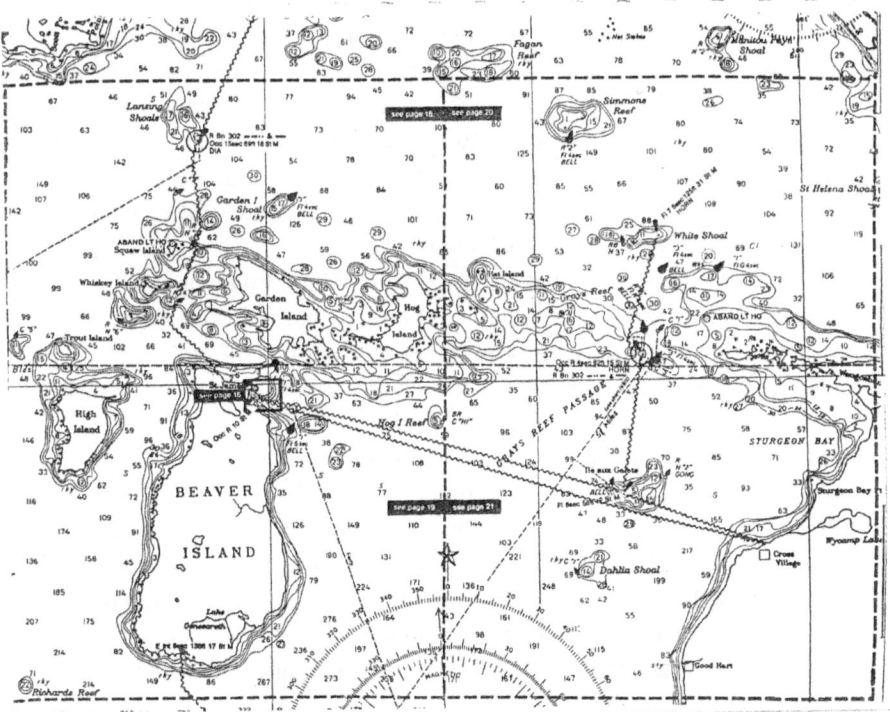

Snapshots

On this trip, I became much more aware of the importance of navigational aids, primarily buoys, but also light houses and, of course, charts.

A map is a drawing that shows conditions on land. A chart is a drawing that shows conditions on water. Among other things, a chart will show you the depth of the water at various places and the location of buoys. Buoys come in two colors, red and green, and you should always pass on the correct side of them to avoid dangerous conditions, usually shallow water or rocks. The general rule of thumb is that you pass a red buoy on your right "when returning from the sea," and a green buoy on your right when going out to sea.

Using charts, a compass, and navigational tools, it is possible to plot a course and follow it at sea. A careful skipper will regularly determine the boat's position in terms of longitude and latitude. Apart from satisfying normal curiosity about where you are, this also allows you to broadcast your position on the radio if you get in trouble and have to call for help. When the Coast Guard gets a "Mayday" call, the first question is "Where are you?" It does not help much if the answer is "Lake Michigan."

The channel into Beaver Island, as with most channels traversed regularly by boats on the Great Lakes, is well marked with buoys that allow you to safely enter the harbor. St. James harbor continues to be one of the most quaint and lovely that I have seen, and it was great to be back here after a one-year absence. We noticed that the flag in front of the marina was at half mast, commemorating the death of two local fishermen whose boat had been run over by a large freighter the day before. We saw several of these freighters on the lake during our voyage, and were very much aware of the fact that they are notorious for their disregard of smaller boats.

Betsy, Suzanne and I walked to the Beaver Island Lodge and made dinner reservations. There used to be a public phone at the marina on Beaver Island, but it has disappeared leaving only the empty booth. The only other public telephone on the island is at the Shamrock Tavern. We would have used that phone to call the Beaver Island Lodge except for the fact that there were two women crowded into the phone booth and from all appearances it looked as if they had grown there and would be there indefinitely.

At 6:30 we all walked back to the Beaver Island Lodge and, although it was still hot, we took the precaution of carrying coats, knowing how quickly the weather on Beaver Island can change, particularly at night. The Lodge was even more beautiful than last year, having been renovated during the past twelve months, but the food was still pleasantly the same and the incomparable view was still there.

In the evening, as we expected, it became very cool and we were glad to have our coats walking back to the boat. We spent the rest of the evening sitting on deck, looking at the full moon, the bright stars, and the harbor.

Gray's Reef

Monday morning we were awakened by a man in a power boat in the next slip who felt it necessary to rev his motor for 20 minutes before pulling out into the lake. It was time to get up anyway, and Max went to get the legendary Tim the Harbormaster to pump the boat's holding tanks. Tim has a fascinating contraption that he uses for this procedure, being a brown box on wheels with lots of valves, spigots, and connections that might have been designed by Rube Goldberg. He wheeled the box onto the dock opposite our boat, and ran a hose that connected from our holding tanks into the box, and then turned it on and the motor-driven pump emptied the holding tanks. I reflected that, while cars need "filling stations," boats need "emptying stations."

The Shamrock Tavern was too tempting to resist for breakfast. Straight out of "Anatomy of a Murder," it continues to be a truly great place and I think everybody should eat breakfast there at least once. Remarkably, the telephone was available and I used it to call our son Steve to let him know where we were and what our plans were. Back on board we got underway at about 10 a.m.

At last we had a good wind and while sailing with it, the boat made remarkable progress which we estimated to be at least 10 knots. Unfortunately, it soon became apparent that the wind was coming from the wrong direction so that our choices were to either take a long, long time to get where we were going, or else to put on the motor. Finally, when we were South of Gray's Reef, we dropped the sails, turned on the motor and headed North to go through the channel.

The Gray's Reef channel provides a safe passage for ships from the southern part of Lake Michigan into the Straits of Mackinac. The reef itself is a part of a chain of islands started by Beaver Island and stretching eastward across Lake Michigan to the mainland. The entire area of the reef is littered with dangerous shoals and many ships have come to grief trying to traverse this passage, particularly before the present channel was dredged and marked.

We were able to sight the Gray's Reef lighthouse through our binoculars (a necessity on any boat) and headed North toward it. With the help of the charts, we found the buoys that showed us the channel, and headed toward the next lighthouse at White's Shoals. This required some backtracking, but that was far preferable to risking the danger of the rocks outside the passage. After we got to the last buoy marking the passage, we were able to swing back to the East and could see the first signs of the outline of the Mackinac Bridge.

Snapshots

Again, the wind was steady, but directly out of the East, and in order to make way we left the motor on and proceeded toward the bridge. The weather was cold out on the water, but warm on shore where we could see people wearing short-sleeved shirts.

Two large freighters had come through the Gray's Reef channel at about the same time we did, but they were both much faster than we were, and there was no danger of any collision. The freighters do, however, make a prodigious wake, and we were a little bit concerned about how our boat would react to them, but the Phoenix handled them easily - much to our relief.

Betsy and Holley fixed lunch on board, consisting of goulash, crackers and cheese, fruit and coca cola. Even though there was no door on the oven, the stove was working fine, and the food tasted marvelous.

Mackinac Island

It was a big thrill for all of us to sail under the Mackinac Bridge. Once under, you leave Lake Michigan and enter Lake Huron. Mackinac Island is a beautiful sight and as we approached it we could make out the familiar landmark of the Grand Hotel. In the bright sunlight, the harbor and buildings looked very picturesque and we were excited to get ashore. I called into the harbor on the radio and we were assigned a berth directly in front of the Island House Hotel. We learned later that it is very difficult to get a slip at Mackinac Island because of its popularity. Apparently we were fortunate because we arrived on a Monday, which is not a very busy day.

The Mackinac Island Marina has excellent facilities but no showers. They have an arrangement with the Yacht Club, across the street, whereby patrons of the marina can use the Yacht Club showers for a fee of $2.00. I chose to take a swim off the back of the boat and found the water bracing but delightful.

Cocktails were served on board, after which we hailed a "taxi" to go to the Grand Hotel for dinner. There are no automobiles on Mackinac Island, so the "taxi" consisted of a horse-drawn carriage. Great fun. Riding up the hill to dinner it occurred to me that Bill Hall is becoming very knowledgeable in the art of navigation, and that our crew worked easily and smoothly in getting the sails up and down. We were all getting into the "boating life."

The Grand Hotel requires men to wear jackets and ties and women to wear skirts after 6 p.m. and, having been forewarned, all of us were properly attired. The hotel has been renovated from top to bottom in anticipation of its 100th anniversary next year, and looks almost like new. The grounds are gorgeous with acres of flowers, fountains and flags, and we had an excellent meal in the main dining room which seats 600 people.

The Grand Hotel boasts that it has the "world's longest porch" and it is traditional for visitors to spend a little time in the rocking chairs on the porch. This has become such a popular pastime that the thousands of daily visitors to the island had begun to make it a regular stop on their itinerary, so that the hotel now charges a $3.00 admission fee to anyone coming on the grounds (other than guests or people like us who are coming there for dinner). The porch offers a beautiful view of Mackinac Harbor and the Mackinac Bridge in the background and, behind that, a large sign made up of electric lights spelling out the number "150" which commemorates the fact that 1987 is the 150th birthday of the State of Michigan.

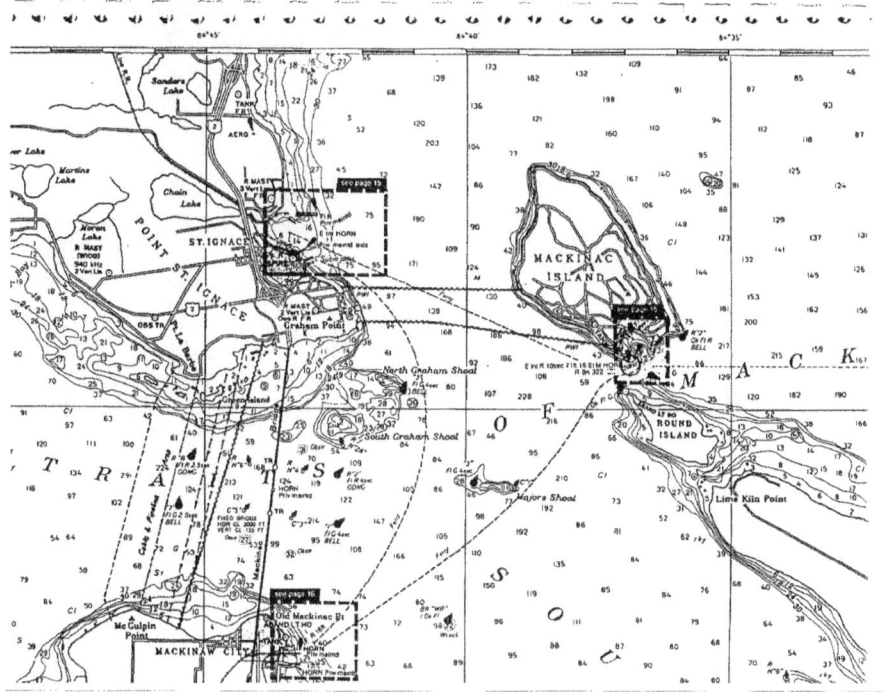

It was an easy walk back to the boat (mostly downhill) and Max announced that we would spend an additional night on the island so that the crew can have a "deserved rest." The night was eventful in part because of a wild party on the power boat moored next to us, which was inhabited by three girls whom we had discreetly observed wearing bikinis during the day. Later, about 4 o'clock in the morning, several of us heard someone walking on our boat, but no one investigated, because we all thought it was one of us. In the morning we discovered one of our docking lines had been loosened, but nothing was missing and we didn't find any damage. Max reported the incident to the marina, nonetheless.

Snapshots

On board the Phoenix at Mackinac Island. Rear, Max and Holley Hobbs. Middle, Bill Hall, Suzanne Hall, Betsy Chapman. Seated front, Howard Chapman.

The Island House Hotel turned out to be a good spot for a hot breakfast and Betsy and I went, while the others ate on the boat. I was able to pick up a copy of the Wall Street Journal and read the news that both Houses of Congress had agreed on a new tax reform bill. My suspicion was that they must have approved this bill because things had been going too well, and they just couldn't let well enough alone. Beware of any law that has the word "reform" in it.

After breakfast the Hobbses and the Halls went to see Fort Mackinac while Betsy and I took our laundry to the island's laundromat. Holley's guidebook says that there is no laundry facility on the island but we found the laundromat full of people who apparently had not read the book. While the clothes were washing, Betsy and I went to the Lakeview Hotel across the street and read our newspaper. On the way back we noted the location of a small grocery because we knew we would have to pick up a few things later for the boat. (Holley's guidebook also says there is no grocery store on the island.)

It was a wonderful sunny, cool day and after lunch Bill, Suzanne, Betsy and I rented bicycles and set off to ride around the island. Betsy and I rented

Howard L. Chapman

a tandem, which we had never ridden before, and found that the riding was easy, but the balancing wasn't so easy. Eventually, we got the hang of it. Half the roads around Mackinac Island had been washed out by winter storms and were not passable, so we followed a bicycle route up the hill past Fort Mackinac and then across the middle of the island down to the lake on the North side.

When we came out of the center of the island back to the edge of the lake we were at a place called "British Landing." The fort at Mackinac Island has a somewhat ignominious history relating to the time when it was attacked in 1812 by the British and a party of Indians who besieged the fort. The Americans had not yet been informed that there was a war on and accordingly had taken no precautions against attack and were totally surprised when they were told by the British Commander that they were surrounded by gun emplacements, troops and hostile Indians. According to the story, the American Commander was afraid of an Indian massacre if the Americans fought and lost, and so surrendered the fort without a fight. Later, American troops tried to recapture the fort but failed.

The road from British Landing back to town along the edge of the lake had survived the winter, and the ride was a pleasant experience with some of the world's best scenery. The water on the lake was calm and as clear as glass, and we stopped several times just to admire it. Returning to town, we passed several beautiful old restored homes that have been placed on the Register of Historic Places. After returning the bicycles, we stopped at the Iroquois Hotel, a beautiful old landmark with extensive flower gardens, for coffee and hot fudge sundaes (I had not eaten lunch, after all). It had become the kind of day that required jackets for those sitting in the shade, while people in bathing suits sat in the sun.

By 4 p.m. we watched the hordes of people lining up for the ferries back to the mainland. There is no bridge to Mackinac Island, but a steady stream of ferry boats brings thousands of people there every day. One of the main products sold on the island is fudge and locals refer to the tourists as "fudgies." The tourists don't seem to mind and several of them were wearing tee-shirts with the word "Fudgie" on them.

We had commented that it seemed rather extravagant and unnecessary to have a bathtub on board the Phoenix, but that night we found that it made the task of taking a shower on the boat much easier, and everybody took turns (thus cheating the Yacht Club out of a total of $12).

On Wednesday morning we prepared to sail for Les Cheneaux Islands. First, we filled the boat's water tanks, and then moved the boat to the end of a nearby dock to pump out. This operation was much less elaborate than Tim

Snapshots

the Harbormaster uses at Beaver Island. At Mackinac we simply connected a hose to a small box on the pier, put two quarters into the box, and the pumping was done. (Tim had charged us $8!)

Les Cheneaux Islands

Out of the harbor we headed northeast to Hessel, Michigan. The night before, Bill and Max had studied the charts to see where the buoys were and had plotted a course to carry us past Goose Island and then through the opening of Marquette Bay. Once in the bay we again appreciated the marker buoys, which led us into a series of channels winding through Les Cheneaux Islands. This is French for "The Channel" Islands, and they consist of a number of islands separated by relatively narrow, but navigable channels. Without the buoys to mark the channels, it would be extremely risky trying to navigate them. It is beautiful, wooded country, and even though people were swimming on shore, we were wearing heavy clothes on the water. It is not practical to sail through the channels, and we struck the sails and went by motor. Shortly after lunch we passed the small town of Cedarville, Michigan, went around Government Island, and entered Government Bay, a large sheltered anchorage with a good sand bottom.

I learned that setting an anchor involves more than just dropping it off the

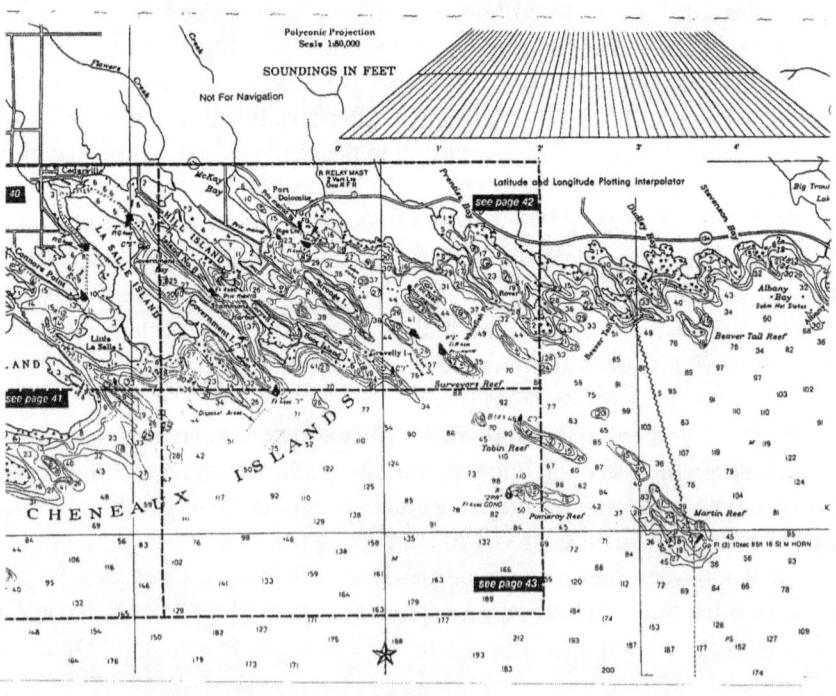

bow of the boat. First we motored in to a place that seemed to be protected from the wind, in water that was shallow enough to take our anchor, but deep enough to protect us from going aground and with enough room so that if the wind shifts and the boat swings about, it can go in any direction without running into trouble. Bill and I dropped the anchor on Max's instruction, and then paid out the line as Max slowly backed the boat away from the shore until we could feel the anchor bite. Afterwards, Max went up and tested it to be sure that it was set.

Bill and Max decided to explore and got the dinghy into the water. To attach the outboard motor, we first fastened it with one of the docking lines and then lowered it gradually onto the dinghy and Max secured it. After they went ashore and came back, Suzanne and Betsy ventured out in it and did some exploring on their own while I took a swim and bathed in the lake. I had picked up a copy of USA Today at Mackinac Island, and everybody now found time to read it.

Anchored there in that secluded bay, with the sun shining and a pleasant breeze, we all relaxed and Bill and Max decided to fish. To everyone's surprise they began to catch some lake perch. They were small and we realized that they would have to catch a lot more the next day in order to have enough for a meal.

Holley had agreed to make dinner and we had another sumptuous meal. During dinner we were joined in the bay by a sailboat from the Great Lakes Sailing Academy, skippered by a man named Joe Smith whom I had met at Mackinac Island. Although his boat is smaller than the Phoenix, he had a total of nine people on board, and they all dinghied into shore, built a bonfire, and had a party well into the darkness. We had been invited but decided to stay on the Phoenix where we could occasionally hear their camp songs.

We put out our anchor light which is an old-fashioned lantern that burns lamp oil and hangs by a rope from the end of the mizzen boom. There were a couple of other boats in the bay anchored with us, and both of them had anchor lights, and it was a lovely scene. We sat on deck under the moon and stars and did a little singing of our own, Stephen Foster, Sigmund Romberg, Cole Porter, Irving Berlin, and a few other old favorites.

This was a night that we had agreed that we would try different cabins, and Betsy and I slept in the bow, the Halls in the aft cabin, and Max and Holley in the saloon (except that Max wound up sleeping in the companionway because he didn't like the bunk in the saloon).

Sleeping in the bow is a different kind of experience. The cabin is shaped like a triangle, and the two people sleep with their feet at the pointed end toward the bow. Once in our bunks we placed a cushion into the narrow opening by the door, in order to make one broad flat bunk out of the place. Unfortunately, we discovered that when that cushion is in place it is impossible to open the door into the head. (Incredibly, after several nights sleeping there, the Halls had not discovered that fact.) Also, we discovered that our feet were higher than our heads, and I, in particular, began having a problem trying to sleep in that fashion, so I decided to turn around and put my head at the other end. This solved the altitude problem but left virtually no room to roll over. In other words, it was pretty damned uncomfortable. Later I discussed this with Bill who acknowledged that they slept with their feet higher than their heads, but for some reason it didn't bother them. Amazing.

At 3 a.m. I felt rain drops and got up to start closing the hatches above us. No one else on the boat was awake so I began going through the saloon, closing those hatches and ports also. None of this disturbed Max until I was standing directly over him, noisily turning the bolts to close a port. He grumbled, "What's going on up there," and I said, "Closing your hatches, mate." (Later, Max remembered nothing of this.)

The Dinghy

By Thursday morning the rain was over, but the wind had shifted and the other boats had moved to the other end of the bay. We contemplated heading out into the lake just to try some sailing, but decided against it. The marine forecast said winds up to 25 knots, with 3 to 5 foot waves. Betsy made breakfast and then we took stock of our grocery situation. The refrigerator had not functioned since we left Traverse City, and we were relying on ice to keep everything cold. We now found that we needed another 40 pounds of ice as well as provisions. It was decided that the best way to accomplish this was to send someone in the dinghy back to Cedarville, and Betsy and I volunteered.

We got on our foul weather gear and lowered ourselves into the dinghy. Once in we also loaded an air pump (in case the dinghy started to deflate) and a can of gasoline. The wind was coming straight at us out of Cedarville, which was out of sight about 2 ½ to 3 miles away, across the bay and across the main channel. Max gave us a lesson in operating the outboard motor, and we reconciled ourselves to the fact that there would be some water in the boat. As a last gesture, Max lowered a large bag of trash down to us with instructions to deposit it in Cedarville.

We started off for the shore of Government Island with the intent of following the shoreline around the bay in order to avoid the roughest water. Even so, the wind and waves were in our teeth and the spray continued to get us wet. Fortunately, we were wearing heavy clothes as well as foul weather gear, and, of course, life jackets.

Howard L. Chapman

The five of us (Betsy, the air pump, the gas can, the trash, and I) continued to fight our way against the elements. The gallant little craft battled valiantly against wind and sea, and eventually we made our way across the bay, around the Island, and across the main ship channel to the East end of Cedarville, where we got instructions from a fisherman as to the location of the local marina. It took us a total of one hour and 20 minutes to make the voyage from the Phoenix to the marina in the dinghy. The bottom of the dinghy is nothing more than a sheet of rubber and the water in the bay is, as you might imagine, quite cold, so that riding in the dinghy is something like sitting on a cold waterbed. We were glad to get to shore.

Once at Cedarville we discovered that it was very warm on shore, but having no place to put them, we were obliged to wear our heavy clothes as we walked in the sun about a mile to the nearest grocery store. Our usual inclination to load up on groceries was tempered by the knowledge that we would have to carry them all the way back to the marina and then on the dinghy back to the boat, so we bought sparingly, buying mainly necessities (such as Snickers candy bars). We had the foresight to bring a plastic trash bag with us in order to carry the groceries so that they would not get wet in the dinghy.

Back at the Cedarville marina, I bought nearly 50 pounds of ice consisting of three large blocks and one bag of ice cubes. Betsy was convinced that it would be impossible to put the groceries and all this ice into the dinghy, but we did it anyway. Before leaving the marina I filled the outboard motor with gas, and we struck out again.

As we headed back, the dinghy was really full, carrying Betsy, me, the gas can, the air pump, the groceries, and 50 pounds of ice; however, with the ice in the bow, and the wind at our backs, we rode better and made better time, and got back to the boat in only 45 minutes.

As we came around the corner of Government Island and entered Government Bay, the Phoenix was still a small speck at the other end of the bay, but apparently the people on board were watching for us with the binoculars and, as we got closer, we could see Suzanne waving a mop at us in welcome. Betsy drove the dinghy the last half of the trip home. She is a good sea person. We were proud of ourselves for staying dry on the trip back to the boat, but then got wet anyway in the unloading and tying up of the dinghy.

After lunch Max, Suzanne, and Betsy went to shore to explore while Bill fished, Holley napped, and I read the newspaper and Time Magazine that I had acquired in Cedarville. Since the refrigerator was not working and we were keeping things cold with ice, we periodically had to pump out the icebox. Whoever built the Phoenix apparently anticipated that his refrigerator would not work properly and installed a hand pump, and Bill and I spent about 20 minutes pumping the water out.

During the day Bill and Max had caught some more perch and there were plenty of them for dinner. The table looked so beautiful that we took pictures of it. Fresh flowers from shore had been put into a vase in the center, Bill opened a bottle of Chablis, and Holley got out her long-stemmed glasses. Max cooked up all of the perch and we had a delicious repast. After dinner Max decided to move the boat to the other end of the bay and re-anchor it. Getting the boat loose from its existing anchorage required some skill. Bill and I brought in the anchor rope and wrapped it around a winch and hauled it in until it was tight, and then Max moved the boat forward across the anchor under power until the anchor was dislodged so that we could haul it in. At the other end of the bay we re-set the anchor. The wind was still strong, but not as strong as it had been.

Back to Beaver Island

This was the night that Betsy and I got to sleep in the aft cabin, and it was great luxury. We were sound asleep at 7 o'clock A.M. when Holley stuck her head through the door and said, "We're aground." *Panic City*!

I leapt out of bed and started throwing on clothes, reviewing in my mind all of the advice I had read in the Chapman Book of Piloting on how to get a sailboat off the ground. (First, take an anchor in a dinghy off shore and drop it, bring the rope back and winch it and try to haul against the anchor, and so forth.) Meanwhile I heard Max operating the motor and by the time I got my head out of the companionway I could see that the boat was moving. Bill was already on deck hauling on the anchor and that plus the action of the motor had gotten us free. Apparently the wind had shifted during the night and the anchor had dragged. This is always a danger, particularly when you don't have a good bottom for anchorage, and we had been lucky not to get seriously stuck.

After this experience we were anxious to get going and Max headed the boat out of the channel back toward Lake Huron. There was lots of wind and the water was rough, even in the channel. Once in sight of the lake, we decided to go back into the channel to set sail because Max felt it would be easier to get the sails up before heading into the rougher water on the lake.

With the sails up the Phoenix shot into Lake Huron like an arrow fired from a bow. It was a beautiful sight, with all the sails set, as we churned through the waves back toward Mackinac Island. A sailboat handles much better under sail than it does under motor and we had no problems with the Phoenix. Max had decided that we would head back to Beaver Island, about

50 miles, which meant that we would have to use the motor if the wind didn't hold up. (If the wind had stayed the way it was, I think we could have sailed 100 miles that day.)

It is my theory that, if possible, you should eat something before heading out to sea on a boat, particularly in rough weather. I made a point of getting some cold cereal and milk as soon as the sails were up. Bill, Sue and Holley all had some temporary problems and decided to defer breakfast; however, by the time we reached Mackinac Island their stomachs had settled down enough for them to eat and after that everyone was fine. The weather had reached 40 degrees the night before, so all of us were wearing heavy clothes.

We sailed under the Mackinac Bridge, and found Lake Michigan much calmer, but with the wind still good. Several of us took turns at the helm, and I became aware of the fact that there was much less anxiety sailing back through waters with which we were now familiar. It seemed easier to spot the buoys and the lighthouses, and we had a sense of how much time it would take us to go from one place to another. Sailing pleasantly, Max went into the fore cabin to read and I went below to jot a few notes for my log. Lunch *en route* consisted of hot dogs, beans, bread, nuts, bananas, and the ubiquitous Snickers Bars. We sailed past the abandoned lighthouse on Gray's Reef and thought about anchoring and going onto it to explore, but decided not to. The wind had died down and we knew we would have to drop the sails and motor in if we wanted to make it to Beaver Island.

We had no problem getting a slip at Beaver Island and Tim the Harbormaster came out to greet us personally. We were old friends by now, and I suspect that he sensed the possibility that we might be good for another "pump out" fee of $8. Betsy and I went onto the island and took a 30-minute walk and when we returned the cocktail hour was underway. It was decided that we would dine that evening at the Shamrock Tavern, where the special of the evening was Steamed Shrimp (you peel them), a full meal for $8.50.

It turned out that somebody was having a wedding on Beaver Island the next day, and the marina filled up with sailboats from Charlevoix, people coming to the wedding. We were lucky that we got there ahead of the crowd. By evening a light rain began, and we noted that it was "Beaver Island weather."

During a conversation with another boat owner we learned that the speedboat race called the "Northport 500" was to run that weekend. Cause for concern. We had planned to dock the next night at Northport, but probably would not be able to get in there.

The forecast was for rain and possible thunderstorms and Max got busy adjusting the docking lines. Bill and I decided to try the $1.25 showers offered by Tim the Harbormaster. Unfortunately, by 8 o'clock Tim had gone for the evening so everyone used the showers on the boat once again. By then it was raining hard and the boat was rocking. When the wind goes through the rigging of a sailboat it makes a moaning and groaning sound, kind of eerie, but we were all snug, safely in port and below decks.

At 4 a.m. I was awakened when the water pump fired off mysteriously and ran for about 30 seconds. We decided later that the water in the tanks had gotten so low that the pump began to run even though there was no call on it. Too many showers, apparently.

Weathered In

When we got up on Saturday morning we found a leaden sky and a stiff, steady wind. We turned on the marine radio and found that there were "small craft advisory" warnings in effect. Any boat under 60 feet is usually considered a "small craft," and the decision of whether or not to sail when a "small craft advisory" is in effect is generally up to the skipper. Max decided that he did not want to risk it and, although I was getting concerned about getting home, all of us were relieved at the decision. During the morning a couple of other sailboats did venture out of the harbor, but they soon returned and decided, like us, to spend the day.

It was surprising how fast the day on Beaver Island passed. Betsy and I had breakfast at the Shamrock Tavern while the rest ate on the boat. After breakfast I got out the hose and filled the water tanks on the boat and then washed down the cockpit. Filling the water tanks requires attaching the hose provided by the marina to a spigot at the end of the dock, which is connected to the city water supply. The water tanks on the boat are closed by fittings that require a special key to unscrew them. After that, it is simply a matter of putting the hose into the opening and letting the water run, and in our case the water ran for nearly 30 minutes! We were really dry.

Next, Tim the Harbormaster appeared once again with his amazing contraption and, with Max's help, they pumped out the holding tanks. I went for a walk about the harbor and back, took a little nap, and drank a little coffee, while Betsy, Holley and Suzanne did grocery shopping and stopped at the "Boat-Tique," which is a well outfitted dress shop right next to the marina.

Bill and Max resumed their fishing off the pier and began catching very good sized lake perch, big enough in fact that six of them made an ample meal for all of us. At 6 o'clock the Carillon at St. Anne's Catholic Church began playing "When Irish Eyes Are Smiling," Max was fixing fresh perch, Holley was preparing pasta, beets and fresh potatoes were already fixed, and it seemed like a very nice place to be.

Howard L. Chapman

About 8 o'clock I wandered over to the Shamrock Tavern because I had been told that the Chicago Bears would be playing a football game that night. The good natured proprietor offered to turn on his big screen television so I could watch the Bears, and I ordered a beer and settled in. It turned out, however, that the people are very provincial in that part of the country and they were showing the Detroit Lions game instead of the Bears game. Thus disappointed, I used the public phone to call our son Steve in Fort Wayne to give him an update on our status, and all were aboard and in bed by 10:30.

The Return Journey

Sunday morning broke calm and sunny and we were on our way out of the harbor by 9 o'clock, with the sails up 30 minutes later. The wind was out of the Northeast and thus favorable, but not very strong. With our gauges not working we had a problem figuring out how much speed we were making, but Max estimated five knots. I figured three.

By 11 o'clock the boat seemed to be barely moving and I began to suggest we drop the sails and start the motor. I described the experience as "sitting on a boat with the sails up." We passed the time taking a couple of pictures, looking at Beaver Island through the binoculars and reading, until the boat seemed to be absolutely dead in the water and Max, at last, agreed to drop the sails. Motoring South, the day was pleasant, and the trip was uneventful. When we got to Northport the marina would not answer our radio call so we went in, only to discover that the entire harbor was like a zoo, with thousands of people crowded around, apparently involved in some proceedings involving the speedboat race. We tried to call the marina at Sutton's Bay, to the South, but found that they would not answer either, and decided that they were probably full up too. There was still no wind and we decided to head back to Traverse City. This meant running a little later than usual, but it would get us back on the schedule that we had disrupted with the extra day at Beaver Island, and we had the boat tied up in its home berth by 8:30 in the evening.

This was the 29th wedding anniversary for Max and Holley, and Bill Hall had saved a bottle of champagne to celebrate. Bill and I went into town and brought back sandwiches from Arby's and from Burger King, and we used up some of the paper plates and plastic utensils that we had acquired for the trip. After this festive meal we all retired.

Monday morning we "took advantage" of the showers at the marina, had breakfast on the boat (Holley said we "have to eat up the eggs"), packed and loaded the van. The van started easily with the help of the jumper cables from Bill's car, and we were ready to go.

The proprietor of Bay Breeze Charters came down to "check us out,"

Snapshots

which involved going over the boat to be sure that it had not suffered any damage. Since we had given him a $750 damage deposit, we wanted to be sure that he cleared everything before we left.

This done, and the sail complete, we headed back to Fort Wayne, facing the glum prospect of returning to the lives of landlubbers.

Chapter 4

DOWN UNDER

This journey begins on January 7, 1993, the 58th birthday of my wife, Betsy Chapman, and (almost) of Elvis Presley. Betsy celebrated by playing tennis in the morning, and received several cards from her friends. My gifts to her included a user-friendly luggage strap and an inflatable "snooze pillow" for the long Los Angeles - Auckland portion of our upcoming flight to New Zealand.

We left Fort Wayne, Indiana, at 2:15 P.M. and had a three hour layover at O'Hare Airport in Chicago. Thank you, United Airlines, for the Red Carpet Room! I had time to call my mother, have a cappuccino, and get through the Fort Wayne papers I had brought along. Betsy noted that this is the first day of issue of the new Elvis stamp, although his birthday is actually January 8. If so, we will miss it entirely, since we will cross the International Date Line, and January 8 will not occur for us.

Our flight to Auckland, New Zealand, left L.A. in a heavy rain, 45 minutes late. In the seat pocket on the plane is a card that says, "If you are sitting in an exit row and you cannot read this card, or cannot see well enough to follow these instructions, please tell a crew member."

We had dinner about two hours out of Los Angeles. We were flying on United because we could use Frequent Flyer miles to upgrade to Business Class, and the bigger seats really do make a difference on a flight that long. We each took a pill, and I think I actually slept a couple of hours - resting in a state somewhat better than agony the rest of the time. The total flight time to Auckland was about eleven and one half hours.

Betsy wore some wrist bands that Carolyn Ewing, of Covington Travel, gave her to ward off travel sickness. For whatever reason, Betsy felt o.k. throughout the flight.

Auckland

When we landed at Auckland, men came through the plane spraying pesticides throughout the cabin and we all had to sit there in the fog for five minutes before we could get off the plane. The Kiwi version of "ethnic cleansing." What a welcome!

On the plane I had started a book called "The Great White Lie" by Bogdanich. It purports to be an expose on hospitals, but does not impress me much. (I carried this book around for the next couple of weeks and finally pitched it after about 150 pages.)

Our bags appeared in good order. Unfortunately, I picked up one that looked like one of ours, but wasn't, and did not realize the mistake until we got to our hotel in downtown Auckland. The bag belonged to a man named Mark Haggarty of Mill Valley, Cal., and if I ever get there I'll call Mr. Haggarty and apologize. I phoned United Airlines, then called a cab and drove all the way back to the airport and exchanged bags. They said they knew where to find Mr. Haggarty. This was not the kind of experience you want at the beginning of a trip when it is a hot day and you have been traveling for about 24 hours! Note that, because we had crossed the International Date Line, it was now Saturday, January 9.

The New Zealand Dollar was worth a little more than 50¢ US. For US$100 I got: NZ$186 at the airport and NZ$172 at the hotel.

We had checked in at the Regent Hotel and, despite the poor currency exchange rate that they gave me, I must say that the Regent is very nice. We bathed and rested, then went to the waterfront for lunch at a place called "Cin Cin on the Quay." (They say "Kay.") Very good. Then we browsed around downtown. Very quiet, it seemed to us, for a Saturday.

We came back to the room and wrote some postcards, then walked to Albert Park, a pleasant and colorful park on a hilltop with fountains and flowers. It's already obvious why New Zealand is famous for its flowers. We stopped at the Hyatt Hotel (next to the University) to get out of the heat and have a coke on the way home.

The Auckland International Tennis Tournament is in town and a lot of the players are staying at the Park Royal Hotel. We stopped in there on our walk and saw some of them. This tournament doesn't seem to attract any of the big name stars.

We called the local office of Abercrombie & Kent, our tour company. We are to join their tour on Tuesday afternoon. The lady in charge was Rachel

Fox who told us that there would be eleven folks on our tour, counting our guide, an Australian woman named Diana Stock.

Since our tour will not include the "glow worm caves," we decided to book a tour to Waitomo to see them on Monday, and a "Bush and Beach" tour for Tuesday morning. Suzanne and Bill Hall had told us that the glow worm caves are a "must see."

Peter and Noela Gibbons

On Sunday morning we reminded ourselves that it was now January 10, not 9. The concierge at the Regent helped us locate the St. Andrews Presbyterian Church, and we went to the 11:00 service. Like our church at home, it has two ethnic congregations, one is Anglo and (in their case) the other is Indonesian. Once a month they have a combined service, in English, and this was that Sunday. The minister was an Indonesian named Jusak Susabda who spoke well. We could sense that he would be exceptional when preaching in his native language.

Before church we had called the Gibbons family, Peter, Noela and son Rainer. They are native New Zealanders who were a part of our group that traveled in Spain last summer. Fort Wayne friend Mac Parker (who had been with us in Spain) had put us in touch with them.

Peter and Noela picked us up at our hotel at 1:30 and we spent several hours with them seeing Auckland. We went to Cornwall Park and drove to the top of One Tree Hill, site of a Maori Memorial, and got a good overview of the city. Weather was perfect. On the descent we stopped at Langton's Restaurant, Ltd., a tea room, and had Devonshire Tea - tea with scones, whipped cream and strawberry jam. We also visited several beaches and took a pleasant walk on one of them.

I'm finding two problems: 1) I can't find out for sure how Noela spells her name; and 2) I can't remember any of the obtuse and convoluted Maori names for everything in Auckland. (I later learned from Pat Parker that it's "Noela.")

We went to the Gibbons' home at about 7 PM and met their son, Rainer. He is 13 and interested in music. They have a lovely home with an extensive garden and a swimming pool. Peter cooked steaks and sausages on the "barbie" and Noela served two delightful salads, with fresh fruit for dessert.

Even though it was nearly 9 PM, dusk was just settling in. There was a strange glow over downtown Auckland, with the sun behind the hills and behind our backs as Peter took us over the bridge and back into the city. The original bridge has been widened from 4 lanes to 8 lanes by a Japanese company that did the job by prefabricating the additional lanes and then attaching two lanes on each side of the original. Locals refer to these as "The Nippon Clip-Ons."

It was a wonderful day, a great way to begin our journey. We knew that we had made some good friends in Peter and Noela, and were sure that we would be seeing them again.

The Caves

We got up at 6 AM, had room service bring us breakfast, and were collected at 7:10 by Vanways Ltd. for a day trip to the glow-worm caves at Waitomo. Our driver was David Wright, a Kiwi, and there were three other tour members, all in New Zealand on business for The Boston Company, an American financial services company. They were James G. (Jim) Stephen, Karen Combs and Jill Pletcher. All of them work in personal money management. They were a lot of fun and we were glad that they were along.

The drive to Waitomo took nearly three hours (with a tea break). Much of the drive is along the Waikoto River, through good agricultural country. New Zealand is famous for its sheep and Kiwi (fruit and birds). People who are natives here are also called "Kiwis." Kind of like "Hoosiers." The country has a population (of humans) of about 3 million, of whom nearly a million live in Auckland. The weather was a little gloomy, but the scenery was still pretty.

At the caves we dropped off the "Boston Company 3" at the "tubing caves." They were to don wet suits, get in inner tubes and walk-paddle-float through some narrow caves, also with glow worms, using flashlights and a guide to find their way.

Betsy and I went on to the main caves and joined another group with a guide to take us through. He explained all about the evolution of caves in general, and these in particular, and took us through a labyrinth of tunnels, caverns, stairways and bridges. The high point came at the end when we got into small boats and floated in the dark down the underground river, watching the spectacle of the glow-worm colonies overhead. It was very reminiscent of looking at the Milky Way on a dark night.

The glow-worms are insects that, in their larvae stage, cling to the roof of the cave and drop a lot of string-like webs below them to trap tiny insects for food. The larvae with the strings hanging down look a little bit like a jellyfish in the water. When they mature they become winged, but have no mouths, and survive only long enough to mate and reproduce.

At the end of the cave the boat floated into the open air and we got out. We went to the Waitomo Resort Hotel for a buffet lunch. There were a whole lot of Asian tourists there. As we learned, both New Zealand and Australia have very large numbers of Asian tourists now, including Japanese, Korean and

Chinese. We shared a dining room with a group from Taiwan, while another room had a Korean tour.

After lunch our driver took us to the so-so Museum of Caves, where we killed some time, and then went to "Angorra Rabbit World," where we killed some more time. At the rabbit place they showed us how they shear the rabbits and use the fur, and offered to sell us sweaters for about US$225. We passed. Both of these attractions are of only moderate interest, but offered by the tour at no extra charge.

Eventually we found out that the reason we were killing time was that the Boston Company 3 took that long to do their cave tubing. We picked them up at 1 PM and came back to Auckland, stopping to see the rose garden at Te Awamutu, and also stopping for the obligatory tea break.

After bathing and resting we walked down to the waterfront and had dinner at the Harbourside Restaurant. Grade-C. When we returned we sent out our first batch of laundry. For some reason, I had not shaved since Wednesday, January 6. Betsy said that I was "very grubby."

Flora and Fauna

We were up at 6:30 (jet lag not a problem going west). We had booked a half day tour with Bush & Beach, Ltd., to visit Muriwai Beach and to see the Gannet colony there. The beach has black "iron sand" and the Gannets will be breeding. Gannets are white sea birds, similar to gulls, that are prolific on the North Island of New Zealand.

At 9 AM we were met by our guide, Raimund Platzer. Raimund is a native German who married a Kiwi girl and has lived in New Zealand for about 15 years. We were his only customers on this morning.

En route to the beach we stopped in the forest and got a nature lesson. This also afforded Raimund an opportunity to have a cigarette, since he did not smoke in the van. The New Zealand "national emblem" is the Silver Fern. The leaves are silver on the bottom and the Maoris once used them to leave a trail in the forest so they could find their way back. The Silver Fern is also the symbol used by the New Zealand national soccer team, the "All Blacks." It comes as no surprise that their uniforms are all black.

We also examined a black fern, which looks more like a small tree, and, on the end of each new shoot, has a kind of curly-cue ball which is the emblem used by Air New Zealand. You see it painted on their airplanes. The black ferns are endangered by the Australian possums, introduced to New Zealand with the idea of using its fur, but now not harvested because of the drop in the fur trade (animal rights, general economic decline). Raimund says that they

Snapshots

now are estimated to number 80 million (?!) and the Kiwis are trying to figure out how to get rid of them.

We also learned about the "cabbage tree," (which is really a lily, but is called a Palm in Florida), the Nikan Palm, and the Pohutukawa - thought of as a Christmas tree because it blossoms in red flowers in December.

We drove on to Muriwai Beach and saw the Gannet colony. Actually, several colonies. They are located on the Tasman Sea, on the west side of the island, which is much rougher than the Pacific on the other side. The beaches are endless and gorgeous, but very dangerous to swimmers. They are popular with surfers who are ok so long as they stay with their boards, but tend to drown if they lose them. Betsy and I walked down the hill to the beach and Raimund drove around and met us. He opened the back of the van and served instant coffee and cookies. (The brochure had said there would be a "morning tea" before returning.)

After the bird colony, I snapped a photo of a bunch of cute little kids. I will try to send a copy to Kindercare Learning Centre, the organization that was in charge of them.

Joining Abercrombie and Kent

After a quick bite of lunch at the Regent Hotel we linked up with our Abercrombie & Kent travel group, met our guide, had an orientation meeting, and set off on their version of a tour of Auckland. One man on the trip was Steve Feagler, an orthopedic surgeon from Albuquerque who is originally from Auburn, Ind. He knows many of our friends in Fort Wayne, in fact, he interned there. He and his wife, Lynn, know our friends Gene and Marcia Laker very well. The Feaglers were traveling with their son Stan, and his friend, Susan Gary. Stan and Susan live in Chicago. Small world.

We drove by bus to the Auckland War Memorial museum, where we saw a production of Maori music, posturing and tongue out-sticking, followed by a private guided lecture by Leo Rothschild, an old Kiwi who is very knowledgeable about the Maori.

After the museum, the bus drove around the city, with a stop at the home of the US Consulate. While we were out of the bus, two cars came by and stopped. It was the Boston Company 3, with some Kiwi friends! We had old home week.

Another stop in the suburb of Parnell to see the rose garden, then home. Betsy and I went to the Shakespeare Tavern where they are reputed to make and serve their own beer. Steve Feagler and his son Stan were also there.

Our travel group gathered at 7:30 for dinner in a private room at the Regent. It was an elegant affair hosted by Abercrombie & Kent, and our tour escort and guide, Diana Stock. All of our traveling companions are pleasant folks. A compatible bunch. Diana would turn out to be a treasure, a gem, assigned to us by serendipity.

Betsy and I retired at 10:30, about an hour later than the first three nights. It appeared that we were making progress on jet lag.

Rotorua

We awakened on Wednesday morning to RAIN. Went to the hotel shop and bought Betsy an umbrella (NZ$22). Then closed out the lock box with the hotel and checked out. Everyone boarded the bus at 9:30 and we set off for Rotorua, best known (only known?) for its geothermal springs and geysers, and strong odor of sulfur. We had a full size bus with our group of eleven, so everyone had a window seat if they chose, and there was ample room to spread out.

About an hour south of Auckland the rain stopped and it began to clear up. It was the same road we had traveled to Waitomo on Monday, along the Waikoto River, and we had a "morning tea" at a place we had visited on that day. Our bus driver/local guide was a sturdy Kiwi woman named Aline, who discoursed on the scenery and history as we travelled along. The bus was equipped with a microphone and loudspeaker system so that she could be heard in all parts of the bus.

For lunch we headed to Matamata, where Kerry and Sylvia Simpson run a dairy farm and restaurant called "Longland's Farm & Restaurant." They farm approximately 190 acres and have 240 cows, each with a numbered tag in its ear. There is a year round growing season, with temperatures no lower than 40 or higher than 80, and lots of rain. They must do all right, since they have a swimming pool and two Mercedes Benz sedans in the garage.

Kerry demonstrated a milking machine and told us a little bit about his farming operations, and then we had lunch in what seemed to be a converted barn close to their house. The restaurant is cozy and rustic - quite pleasant.

Before lunch, Kerry persuaded me to try a bottle of Waikoto Bitters, made with water from the nearby Waikoto River, and described by him as the "best beer in the world." It isn't.

Lunch included "barbecued" steaks, scalloped potatoes, a squash/cheese casserole, a couple of salads, and bread & butter - all served buffet style. Dessert was a homemade pastry "mit schlag," homemade ice cream, tea and coffee. Both the Kiwis and the Aussies think something is "barbecued" if it is cooked on an open grill. They do not use or understand barbecue sauce.

We drove completely around Lake Rotorua, with Aline expounding all the way, and by now the weather was fine. We stopped at a marvelous redwood forest called Whakarewarewa Forest (or something like that).

Locals just say "Waka." Betsy and I, along with Stan Feagler and Susan Gary, plunged into it and started up a big hill, but finally turned back for fear we'd hold up the bus.

We checked in to a very nice Sheraton Rotorua, where our room overlooked the hotel pool and adjacent golf course. It is a nice pool with nearby private "grotto spas," which are enclosed hot tubs with water that pours in from one side like a small waterfall.

Betsy and I had dinner at a restaurant called "Poppy's Villa," which is a short walk from the hotel. The food was good, but service was slow. In New Zealand they do not practice the custom of tipping in restaurants, and accordingly service is often quite casual - but always <u>friendly</u>. I give "Poppy's Villa" only a high "B" because of the uncomfortable chairs. If service is going to be slow, they should at least provide comfortable chairs.

I put in ear plugs at bed time because of the noise from the pool below our room. A daytime asset, a nighttime nuisance. We slept fine.

Queenstown

We were up early on Thursday, but when we got to the hotel dining room for breakfast we found it jam packed with Asian tourists. Only after some discussion were we able to persuade the hostess to let us have a table.

The big news in the local papers is about the fact that Prince Charles had a juicy telephone conversation with his girlfriend, Camilla Parker-Bowles. He was stupid enough to do it using a cellular phone, the conversation was taped, and now a transcription of it is making the rounds, although the English papers have been trying to suppress publication there. They refer to it, though, as "Camillagate."

We left the hotel at 9:00 and drove to the nearby geothermal springs and geyser area. We were conducted by a Maori woman who took us through some craft buildings and a meeting house, past a war canoe, and then to the thermal area. The Maori stuff appears to have been added as an afterthought to have something for the tourists to look at when they come to see the hot springs. The latter are worth seeing - hot, bubbling mud, boiling water, hot rocks and geysers (we didn't get to see a geyser go off, but we were assured that it happens).

We exited through a Maori village (again, kept for the tourists) where we saw people using the hot water pools for cooking, curing flax, and other things.

The bus took us to the Rotorua airport with a stop on the way to see an exhibition of sheep shearing and to watch how sheep dogs work.

Aline said goodbye to us and we flew on Ansett Airlines to Queenstown, with a stop to change planes at Christchurch. Ansett gives its passengers a meal on *each leg* of a flight, no matter how short.

Queenstown is located at the southern part of the South Island of New Zealand, amid the Southern Alps, and the scenery hit us as soon as we got off the airplane. There are high mountain ranges in all directions, fjords and lakes, and lots of flowers. It has about 6,000 year round residents and is a year-round resort, with skiing in the winter (our summer).

From appearances, every one of the 6,000 permanent residents works in the tourist industry in some way. There are blocks of shops, hotels and restaurants. All in all, though, it's still quaint and pleasant, and everything seems to be done quite well.

Our new bus driver, Jeff, has been a driver in Queenstown since 1979. When he took us on our trip to Milford, it would be his 766th trip there.

Our hotel was the Park Royal. It has a heated pool, guest laundry facilities, and a fine view across the bay. It also has street noise, but the double glazed glass seals it out pretty well.

The Feagler family went to dinner at a resort outside of town called "Nuggett Point." They were picked up and returned by the resort's van. They reported a good view, good food, and slow service.

The rest of us went to try a new place called "Pot au Feu." We sat down at 8:00 and at 9:15 still did not have any food (no tipping in New Zealand). After "mentioning" the matter, we finally ate at about 9:30 and got out by 10:00, skipping dessert and coffee. The food, anyway, was excellent.

Betsy and I joined the others (seven of us counting our guide Diana Stock) to have dessert at a place called "Death by Chocolate." Skip it! Overpriced, poor food. They must find that they can survive on one time customers. It took an hour, and we were glad to leave.

The headline the next day tells us that US forces have again attacked Iraq. Saddam Hussein has proclaimed another "jihad." This is certainly *deja vu*. Future President Bill Clinton says he supports current President Bush in the action. Five days until the Clinton inauguration.

The hotel has a nice breakfast buffet. We notice that all of the tourist hotels include dishes that cater to asian tastes. Soy soup, noodles, whatever. Ugh.

It is raining and we cannot go on the "Shotover Jet" boat ride as planned. The water level in the Shotover River is too high. The river was named by an Englishman after a place in England, but we can't find out much more about how it got its odd name. The jet boat has no propellers, which allows it to travel on as little as 4 inches of water, and can go when the river is low; but today we cannot go because it is too high (?). (This made sense later when we found out that the dock was under water.)

Snapshots

Our driver, Jeff, trundled us up and down a mountain but the rain spoiled the view. We headed for Arrowtown and the weather began to clear. By the time we got there it was fine. Arrowtown is an innocuous little tourist trap that was once the site of gold mining activity.

Next we went to a place where a high bridge crosses a steep gorge over heavy rapids. From the center of the bridge, people were "Bungee Jumping." For a price, they would tie a rope around your feet and let you dive off. You (are supposed to) stop short of the water and a special boat goes out and plucks you out of the air. Lots of young Japanese men were lining up to do this, and Stan Feagler, from our group, jumped. It's a long way down and looks very dangerous, but apparently thousands of people have paid for the opportunity, including elderly ladies. In addition to the experience, each jumper got a T-Shirt.

On the way back the group split up. The Feaglers went white water rafting. The rest of us took a gondola up a mountain called "Bob's Peak." (I don't know who made up names for things around here, but he certainly was no philosopher.) At the top is the Skyline Restaurant, a lookout deck, and a wide screen movie theater. Also, naturally, a shop full of Kiwi relics and sheep products. We got a marvelous view of Queenstown and its surroundings - including a mountain range called the "Remarkable Mountains." Another zinger of a name - although we had to admit that they are indeed remarkable.

The theater shows a half hour movie called "Kiwi Magic" starring Ned Beatty as an American tourist. No real plot but lots of great New Zealand scenery. The photography is excellent and the wide screen does, in fact, draw the audience in.

We went back down Bob's Peak in a gondola and found a hamburger place in town for lunch. Then we walked to the park and gardens on the side of the bay opposite the Park Royal Hotel. The flowers are magnificent and Betsy was baffled as to how roses can get so big in this supposedly cold climate. The park is quite tranquil with quiet ponds, lily pads, ducks, a few sunbathers, and rampant flowers. It was one of those days when you carry a sweater and continually put it on and take it off.

The park is also the home of the Queenstown Lawn Bowling Club and we spent about 30 minutes on a bench watching the bowlers.

On the walk back to town we stopped for coffee at the THC Resort Hotel (THC = Tourist Hotel Corporation). It is very nice. We did not get into any of the rooms, but from what I've seen I would not hesitate to stay here. It, too, has several stands of amazing roses.

We stopped to shop at a "chemist" and then returned to the hotel to do laundry. Of course, all of the machines were in use, so we sat in the room and watched the news on television, then went to dinner. We decided to try the Promenade Restaurant that we had seen in the THC Hotel. Roast leg of lamb, and the whole meal was great. Even the service was excellent. Grade-A.

After we returned, the laundry machines at our hotel were available, so we did a load. We figured we must have saved about $250 by not sending it out.

A 6 AM wakeup call tomorrow to go to Milford Sound. We kept our fingers crossed for good weather.

Milford Sound

Finger crossing works again. Saturday is a fine day, and the locals say it is the first in quite a while. We had a different driver. Jeff's daughter had been in a serious car accident and was in a hospital in Christchurch. Jeff went there to be with her. The new driver is Alister.

The Queenstown-Milford route is very circuitous. On the map, it almost makes a square. The road runs along the side of Lake Wakitupu for a while, then through mountains, then along Lake Te Anau, and eventually into Fjordland National Park. The large valleys were often full of herds of sheep, cattle and domestic deer. Incredible beauty on all sides, at every turn. It impresses me as the most spectacular scenery that I have ever seen.

We stopped at the Kingsgate Hotel in the town of Te Anau for morning tea. A delightful place overlooking Lake Te Anau, serving Devonshire tea and a homemade "bran bread" (already buttered), and surrounded by flower gardens.

Fjordland National Park is on the register of World National Parks. All of us were taken by the grandeur of the place, a combination of Colorado and Norway. In the park, we had another stop (a "comfort stop") at Otaparu Lodge - a nice place.

We finally got to Milford at about 12:30. We had left Queenstown at 7:15. There is really nothing in Milford except a THC hotel and a terminal for the tourist boats that cruise on Milford Sound.

Our boat was the "Lady Bowen." Abercrombie & Kent had reserved a private room on the top deck where an excellent lunch was set out for us. We spent about the first hour of the cruise dining, but didn't miss anything because we all had big picture windows next to us. After lunch we went on deck to gawk, take pictures, look at seals sunning themselves on rocks, take more pictures, and generally try to absorb what we were seeing. Majestic beauty. Our "private lounge" adjoined the bridge so, from time to time, we could go in and discuss things with the captain.

The cruise lasted about 2 1/2 hours, and the weather held up throughout.

Snapshots

There were vast mountains, waterfalls, dense foliage, wildlife – spectacular scenery of many kinds.

When we got back to Milford we went to the "airport" and got on a 14 passenger plane operated by Fjordland Travel Service. Steve Feagler rode in the co-pilot's seat. The plane was a twin engine (DASH, I think).

We flew back to Queenstown at low altitudes through the mountain passes, and it looked to me like we were pretty darned close to the mountains. The ride was very bumpy, but wonderful, and the pilot later said that this was as good as their flying conditions get.

Back in Queenstown, Betsy and I had some film developed, then shopped and lazed around. We joined the rest of the A&K group for dinner in the Park Royal hotel restaurant, the "Brasserie." It was o.k., a "B" with slow service. Why do so many otherwise good restaurants take forever to bring the customers their bills?

This was our last night in Queenstown and the last evening we would be with the Feagler family. Betsy and I had re-prints made of a family photo I had taken of them with Diana Stock, and gave them copies. They were to fly to Christchurch tomorrow with us, then leave our group and go on to Melbourne, Australia.

Christchurch

We got up early on Sunday morning and were taken by coach to the jet boat launch on the Shotover River. Everyone was issued a life jacket, although it seemed to me that there was more risk of being smashed on the rocks than of drowning. They should have given us hard hats. The boat was big enough to hold all of us plus the driver-cowboy-astronaut.

The jetboat can turn on a dime and the driver would run right at rocks and cliffs and somehow miss them at the last second. He also drove at high speeds over shallow places where it seemed that the gravel should scratch the bottom of the boat. It was the White Knuckle Special, and lasted about 25 - 30 minutes.

Diana had warned that some of us might get "a bit damp." I sat in the back on the outside and got completely drenched. Fortunately (it was cold) we went right to the hotel after the ride, where we could shower and change before packing.

At the airport we got a cup of coffee and bought Betsy a New Zealand sweatshirt with a neat design, then flew on Ansett Air to Christchurch. We have noticed that there is no airport security at all at New Zealand airports on domestic flights.

At Christchurch, we were met by a new driver, Ken, and a full size bus.

Howard L. Chapman

The Feaglers rode into town with us to take advantage of Ken's narrative and to see a little of the city, then returned with him to the airport and left for Melbourne.

Diana took our now depleted group on a walking tour of the area of Christchurch near our hotel. Being Sunday, many stores were closed but there were a lot of other things going on, and the weather was balmy. We visited the historical museum, which includes an interesting exhibit on Antarctica. Explorers Amundsen and Scott both launched their expeditions to the South Pole from Christchurch, and many Antarctic operations start from there even today.

Betsy and I struck off on our own, left the museum, and went to the adjacent botanical gardens, which are huge and beautiful and, like all of Christchurch, full of flowers. There were lots of Sunday strollers and bench-sitters, and we did some of both. After about an hour we found a stand selling ice cream cones dipped in chocolate, bought two, and took them to a shady bench to watch the world go by.

Walking back to our hotel (the Park Royal) we crossed the River Avon and saw some punts going up and down river. We made inquiry and decided to book a punt ourselves. This kind of punting is far superior to what we did in Oxford, England, a few years back in that, here, the punt comes with a young man who does all the work. Our punter, Bruce, was decked out in shirt and tie, striped pants and vest, and a boater; however, he would not be available for an hour, so we walked up to Cathedral Square and went through Christchurch Cathedral. It's a fine cathedral, but I question just how religious the Kiwis are, given the fact that there is a souvenir stand operating in the sanctuary.

After a little wandering through a few tourist shops that were open, we returned to the punt departure station and enjoyed a relaxing trip on the river, then back to the hotel. At 7 PM a van picked us up and took us (all six of us) to the home of local residents Jim and Robin Melville for a "home hosted dinner."

The New Zealand home hosts sign up with a local group that arranges these dinners, and A & K had it set up for us in advance. The Melvilles are a delightful, gregarious couple, and Robin served a delicious meal. The *piece d' resistance* was a Pavlova topped with sliced Kiwi fruit and sprinkles of chocolate. A&K had given each couple a bottle of wine to take as a "bread and butter" gift, which the Melvilles served at dinner. New Zealand has a growing wine industry and some of it is very good.

We stayed until about 10:30 when the van picked us up and returned us to the Park Royal. The Park Royal, by the way, is a very nice hotel and can be recommended.

Snapshots

Sydney - Australia

After breakfast the next day, our driver, Ken, took us on a tour of Christchurch. Everywhere we were impressed by neat, well-kept homes with lovely gardens. The city prides itself on its gardens and has an annual competition among homeowners. We saw the homes of some of the contestants and their gardens were unbelievable.

We stopped at a former private estate called "Mona Vale," walked through it, and met driver Ken on the other side. It's a pretty place with a small restaurant and a departure point for punts. The main attraction, of course, is the gardens. We also visited "Riccarton House," nice but not in the same class as Mona Vale.

Heading out of town and over the mountains we stopped at a place that looks like a medieval castle but is, in fact, a restaurant built about 70 years ago. It is called "The Sign of the Takahe," the Takahe being the name of a local bird. The restaurant is very nice but a little pricey. Betsy, Diana and I had coffee, and then spent some time viewing Christchurch from the nearby "lookout."

On the other side of the mountain we came to Lyttleton Harbor, a deep water port serving Christchurch. Lots of older homes. This is where then Governor Gray watched for the English "Four Ships" that brought the first settlers. The English beat the French by about a week. When the French arrived, the English allowed them to establish a settlement, but it was soon assimilated and disappeared. At the dockside we went through a full size replica of the New Zealand yacht "Endeavor," which competes in some sort of competition (America's Cup?).

There are some serious mountains between Christchurch and the harbor, and for many years all traffic had to be routed over them. A few years ago, however, a tunnel was completed through the mountains, and we used it to return to town.

Our driver took us to see some "factory gardens" at a company called "Sanitarium" (they make and sell food products). American factory owners would be embarrassed at a comparison between their factory grounds and this place, which has landscaped and gardened the land in back of the factory to make a lovely park complete with a pond and fountain. We were told that factory gardens are rather common in Christchurch.

We had some free time in the afternoon. Betsy and I walked to Cashel Street, which is a big pedestrian mall, and looked for a lunch spot. We chose a place called Bardelli's. A "C plus."

After lunch we stopped in at a very nice department store called

Howard L. Chapman

Ballantyne's and got some stationery and a couple of souvenir gifts, including a pen for my mother. She will be 87 on January 19th - tomorrow. Except that, because of the dateline, it's the day after tomorrow. So when is her birthday?

We had time after shopping to bathe and change clothes and pack. It was hot: 31 degrees Centigrade (about 90 Fahrenheit). Our bags were getting to be hard to close - a mystery, since they closed easily when we left home.

We were booked on a Qantas flight to Sydney, Australia, leaving at 6 PM. The traveler gains two hours (2 time zones) between New Zealand and Australia, a three hour trip! We calculated that the Christchurch - Sydney flight was the eighth airplane flight for us so far on this trip.

On the plane we were given current copies of the *Sydney Morning Herald*, which said that yet another Iraqi plane has been shot down by a US F-16, and everyone expects another major confrontation. Meanwhile, Washington is gearing up for the inauguration of "Billary" Clinton on the 20th of January. Qantas also had copies of the Aussie magazine *New Ideas*, with the full transcript of the absurd telephone conversation between Prince Charles and Ms. Parker-Bowles. Apparently, people in Australia have been copying it and sending it by fax to friends in England, where publication is still prohibited.

On arrival in Sydney we had to clear customs. They demanded to know whether we had any food, and I had written (truthfully) on the form that I was carrying "a can of prunes." The customs agent looked a little perplexed and muttered, "A can of prunes?", but then he waved us through.

We were met at the airport by a small and uncomfortable van with a driver named Ted. The seats in the back are bumpy and so high that passengers can't see out the windows. Also it is cramped and offers no leg room. Unhappily, we were to have this van throughout our stay in Sydney. This turned out to be the only serious complaint we had with Abercrombie & Kent - not too bad in retrospect. On the bright side, Diana Stock advised us that she had secured tickets for all of us to attend the opera tomorrow night at the Sydney Opera House. They are presenting *Lucia D'Lammermoor*.

We transferred to the Regent Hotel, which is very elegant, first class in every way. As we entered the hotel we saw a large, handwritten sign with recent results from the NFL playoffs. Buffalo had beaten Miami, and Dallas had upset San Francisco. The two winners will meet in the Super Bowl. We had eaten on the airplane and, having gained two hours, were ready for bed.

On Tuesday morning, Betsy and I ate breakfast in the restaurant off the Regent Hotel lobby. Since breakfast was included in the price of the A & K tour, we seemed to always have breakfast in the hotel. Today, the U.S. Dollar brings 1.47 Australian Dollars. The concierge at this hotel sells the Asian Wall

Street Journal, The *International Herald Tribune*, and *USA Today*. All of them are at least one day old, but we hadn't seen any "American" news since we arrived in Auckland.

At 9 AM we were collected by the same dismal van and proceeded around Sydney. Fortunately, there were a lot of scheduled stops.

First, we went to the famous Opera House where we were met by a private guide and given a tour through all of the theatre and backstage. Next came the Botanical Gardens, Mrs. Macquarie's walk (and perch), Bondi Beach, and a fantastic lunch at Doyle's on the beach. Send anyone there. An A plus. Doyle's has a water taxi that will come get people at the dock at Circular Quay (here they say "key") and return them after dinner.

We got back to the hotel at about 3 PM. Betsy and I took a walk through the Rocks and under the huge Harbor Bridge. We passed a nice looking Hyatt hotel with a great location.

At about 6:00 we walked to the Opera House. We had eaten late and lots at Doyle's, so we skipped dinner and got some juice and rolls when we got to the Opera. We saw an excellent performance of *Lucia d' Lammermoor* by Donizetti, sung in Italian, but with English translation projected above the proscenium. It was three acts with 2 twenty minute intermissions, a total of 3 hours. We loved it. A high point of the trip.

It was a pleasant and interesting walk back along Circular Quay, which is the departure point for most of Sydney's ferry boat fleet. It's very active at night.

A Free Day in Sydney

Wednesday is Inauguration Day, except that in Sydney it's tomorrow, meaning that the inaugural is still a day off.I hope that Mr. Clinton will be a better President than I think he will be.

This is also a "free day" on our tour. Our guide, Diana Stock, has given us lots of good ideas. She has been a real delight and we appreciate her more every day.

After breakfast at the Regent Buffet, Betsy and I set off walking. A warm but pleasant day. We went first to see John Cadman Cottage, in the area known as "The Rocks," built in 1816. Next door is a visitor center where we watched a 10 minute film about the history of The Rocks. The Regent Hotel is considered to be located in The Rocks, and there are a lot of nice shops and restaurants here.

We walked to the Botanical Gardens and strolled through them to Hyde Park, then through the Sydney Hospital grounds. There we saw a cafe with a dining room where people sit in a line looking out the window while they eat.

I think it's a good idea for lone diners because it makes it easy to read while you eat.

Next we found the Monorail station and took it around for a one loop trip. The fare was A$2.50. It was jammed and not something you do twice. It was getting close to 1:00 and Betsy was getting peaked, so we took a cab to the Waterfront Restaurant back at The Rocks. We ate outdoors at a table overlooking the harbor. Very good. An "A."

After lunch Betsy crashed in the hotel room. Her old suitcase had finally given out, so I went to Grace's Department Store on George Street, and got her a new one. It was hot, really hot, and George Street was very crowded. I was reminded of Oxford Circus on a July day. When I finally got back with her new suitcase, Betsy pronounced it to be "too big," and I returned to Grace's and exchanged it for a smaller one, and schlepped it back to the hotel.

At 6 PM we went to Merrony's Restaurant. It's a short walk from the Regent and very convenient to the Opera House. They served rack of lamb "Irish Stew Style," and it was great. A Fort Wayne friend, Jim Vann, had

Howard and Betsy Chapman at Sydney Harbor,
with Opera House in the background.

lived in Australia for a while, and had contacted a local friend in Sydney, Bob Slagle, to get some restaurant recommendations for us. Merrony's was one of them. Bob had sent his list of recommendations to Jim in Fort Wayne, and Jim faxed them to us at our hotel in Queenstown!

Snapshots

After dinner we returned to the hotel, then went to the Theatre Royal to see Andrew Lloyd Webber's *Aspects of Love*. We were half way up in the balcony and there is not nearly enough leg room. Worst of all, the show is a turkey. Still, it was very nice of Diana to have arranged tickets for all of us.

After the show we went to a beautiful and very British lounge at the Regent Hotel for a beer before turning in.

Canberra

On Thursday, all of the papers are full of the Clinton inaugural. Also, there were more hostilities with Iraq.

We had an easy morning, leaving the hotel at 11 for a cruise of Sydney Harbor on a Catamaran called the Aussie One. It was another hot and sunny day and the harbor is truly beautiful.

After the cruise we were taken to the airport and caught a flight to Canberra on Australian Air Lines. On arrival we checked in at the Hyatt Hotel Canberra, a very nice hotel with lavish marble bathrooms. It boasts what is touted as Canberra's "best restaurant," the Oak Room; however, it seems that the Oak Room is temporarily closed for renovation.

Canberra was built from scratch to serve as Australia's capital city, a compromise between Melbourne and Sydney. It began to grow after World War II and now has a population of about 250,000.

The weather had been overcast ever since we arrived, and had been raining most of the time. Worse, I am coming down with a cold. By Friday morning, my cold is going full bore. YUK! Nonetheless, up at 7:30 and off at 9 for a tour of Canberra. Sky is gray and weather is cool.

We drove to a lookout outside of town to view the city. Diana and our driver told us that there are lots of kangaroos living in the bush around (and even in) the town, and that we would probably see some - but we didn't.

Our second stop of the morning was the Australian War Memorial. They have a museum inside with exhibits about Australian involvement in various wars in the past. It's well done.

Next was Parliament House. Today, Australia is a parliamentary system similar to that of the U.K. How will they handle it if Australia becomes a Republic? We are told that about one-half of the Aussies are in favor of it (maybe more after the Prince Charles nonsense). Australia has six states, and each state has 12 senators. Guides at Parliament House took us through both the House and the Senate. The Parliament Building is impressive and worth a visit.

We stopped at the High Court (Supreme Court), a modernistic building, 12 years old. There are seven judges. They are appointed to their jobs by (for all practical purposes) the Prime Minister, although, technically, the Queen's Representative has to approve. They must retire at age 70.

The final stop was the Art Museum, which is quite good.

Betsy has been taken with a bout of sneezing, and my cold has gotten me down. We would have liked to stay at the museum but, by 1 PM, neither of us felt up to it. We returned to the Hyatt and burrowed in for the rest of the day, with room service for dinner.

ROTTEN COLD!

Melbourne

It was raining in Canberra on Saturday morning; however, Betsy and I both felt better. Happily, Betsy does not seem to have caught my cold. We left for the airport to catch a 9:55 flight to Melbourne.

The weather was fine in Melbourne and our new driver, Jack, met us with a comfortable bus. We registered at the very nice Regent Hotel, and Betsy and I got lunch at the adjacent food court.

After lunch our group gathered for the City Tour. We went to the Botanical Gardens and had a walk through. Many, many families, picnics, outings. One part of the park is an artificial rain forest (rain piped in). Lots of folks enjoying a pleasant Saturday in the park.

We drove through an affluent residential suburb called "Toorak," and stopped for ice cream at a place Diana Stock knows about called "Brunetti." (Melbourne is Diana's home town.) Brunetti has marvelous ice cream, baked goods and sandwiches.

We were taken next to the Victorian Arts Center, a huge complex on the Yarra River, with theaters and a concert hall. A guide met us and escorted us through. There is a ticket agency in the lobby and we bought tickets to see *Joseph and His Amazing Technicolor Dreamcoat* for tonight and, best of all, tickets to the Australian Open tennis tournament for the Monday daytime session.

After returning to the hotel to rest, we came back to the theater area and ate at an open air cafe called the "Treble Clef," overlooking the river. I had been feeling pretty good, but would have been better off to go to bed early. Instead we went to see *Joseph*. It was a fantastic production, doing everything possible to make a big deal out of what began as a one act play. As always, the Pharaoh's Song was the big hit of the night and stopped the show. At the end of the play, they put on a 15 minute revue that concluded with Joseph flying out over the audience with a gigantic "cloak" trailing behind him.

I had begun going downhill after about an hour, sniffing and blowing, with a relapse of my head cold. By the time we got to bed I was really sick and didn't sleep until 3 AM.

Snapshots

I woke up Sunday morning feeling terrible. Betsy went off with Abercrombie and Kent to an animal reserve and a winery. I spent the morning resting and reading. About 12:30 I mustered the energy to walk to the National Gallery (near the Victorian Art Center) and spent an hour there. There was some very nice Australian art. I liked the paintings by Rupert Bunny, E. Phillips Fox, Bernard Hall and Longstaff. There was also an exhibit of works by Hugh Ramsey, who studied there. (We later learned that Diana Stock, who has a degree in art appreciation, is a docent at the National Gallery and very fond of it.)

On the walk back to the Regent I stopped at McDonald's and had a cheeseburger and a cup of coffee. Wonderful! No "English Language" (*i.e.*, American) newspapers (*WSJ*, *Herald Tribune* or *USA*) are available on Sunday. A current events drought.

After a nap I still felt lousy.

It had been raining since 2 PM so I didn't mind being inside so much. There was a local golf tournament being played in conjunction with the Australian Open tennis tournament, and it was washed out. (It was finally won by an Aussie named Robert Allenby, who locals think will become a big star.) All of the tennis at the Open was also rained out except for Center Court, where they could close the roof and keep playing. It provided something to watch on TV.

President Clinton had announced Zoe Baird to be his Attorney General, but she has withdrawn her name because of the flack over the fact that she failed to properly report and pay tax for child care, and hired illegal aliens besides. Clinton insists, however, that her replacement will be a woman, in keeping with his determination to have a "Quota Cabinet." Other news: more attacks on Iraq; bitter fighting in Yugoslavia; religious warfare in India; some of the U.S. Marines have returned from Somalia; some Aussie troops have arrived there.

I have been growing a beard, but I'm starting to regard it a nuisance. I always feel unkempt, and Betsy said I remind her of our Fort Wayne friend Jim Miller.

The Australian Open

We had another "Free Day" on Monday, which meant a leisurely morning. I tried to get the Super Bowl on the TV but couldn't find it – and was content to relax with the newspaper. My cold seems to have "broken" and I feel much improved – in fact, pretty much back to normal. Betsy went off with our friends to shop for opals. Australia is supposed to be a good place to buy them – if you are interested in opals.

At 11 o'clock, Betsy and I took a cab to the Flinders National Tennis Center, where the Australian Open is held. We had seats in Center Court that we were able to purchase because a corporate sponsor had decided they would not use them this day and had turned them in. We saw lots of terrific tennis and some "names," including Jennifer Capriati, Pete Sampras and Stefan Edberg. We were also able to go to other courts and watch matches, including some doubles.

Center Court is an excellent facility with comfortable seats and a retractable roof that allows it to be open in good weather and closed if it rains. It was sunny but not too hot, and the crowd was interesting. We got some souvenirs and some of the fast food that was offered. The souvenirs were fine but the food was awful.

We watched one match involving a Swede named Bergstrom who was playing Wayne Ferreira. There was a large group of young Swedes in the audience who were loud and rude to the point of being obnoxious. They had painted their faces blue and yellow and chanted, yelled and whistled, always calculated to harass and distract the Swede's opponent. We were told that these people, and other Swedes, regularly attend tournaments and carry on this way. It was the first time in my life that I ever had any negative feelings about Swedes.

We spent about five hours at the Open, and then walked back along the Yarra River to our hotel. On the walk back, we stopped to explore the Grand Hyatt Hotel, where many of the tennis players were staying. Elegant. The following Sunday, American Jim Courier won the tournament by beating Stefan Edberg, and celebrated by diving into the river!

It was warm, so when we got back we went to the lobby lounge and had a beer. Toohey's Red - Good Stuff.

A nice waitress suggested we go to dinner at a restaurant named John-Jacques. We booked, but then cancelled when Diana invited us to join the rest of our group at Marchetti's, a good Italian place. We began packing at 10:30 for the early departure and long day coming up.

Cairns

January 26 is "Australia Day." It has been 205 years since the first convicts arrived in Sydney Harbor from England. The English started sending them here because the American Revolution made it impractical to continue sending them to America. Some Australian states celebrate today as a holiday, but others (including Tasmania) will celebrate on Monday, Feb. 1, in order to have a 3 day weekend.

We had a very uncivilized 5:45 wakeup call and had breakfast sent to the room. At 8:15 we caught an Australian Air flight to Cairns, with a stop in Brisbane. I continued to look for the Super Bowl results, but couldn't find anything in the Aussie papers. I complained about it for awhile, until I discovered that the Super Bowl isn't until <u>next</u> week!

I have given up reading *The Great White Lie* and left the book in Canberra. I keep finding other books, newspapers, and magazines to read, and doing crossword puzzles. Betsy says that I am "pencil sharpening" to avoid reading my next book, *Iron John*. She is probably right.

We landed in Cairns and were met by a new driver and coach. The drive North from Cairns to Port Douglas takes a good hour and it rained most of the way. The road follows the coast and there are a lot of beautiful beaches; however, we were warned not to swim because of the danger of jellyfish that are common this time of year. The danger is only near the shore and the jellyfish are not found as far out to sea as the Great Barrier Reef.

We were in the Northern part of Australia and this was the wet season. It was so soggy that we thought the whole place might drown. Their "good" weather is April - September, their winter. Nonetheless, they get tourists this time of year, who come to see the Reef. Cairns now has two flights a day from the US and 7 a day from Japan.

We checked in at the Sheraton Mirage Resort located outside Port Douglas. It's a huge place with lots of pools, lagoons, gardens, waterfalls, beaches, foliage, a marble lobby, and shops. Rooms are very fancy, but the humidity is so heavy in this season that they have to treat the rooms with a chemical to keep everything from becoming mildewed. The chemical smells funny, but not as bad as the mildew in the elevator. I believe that this resort would be very nice "in season." In January, it only makes the gloomy, brooding climate more bearable.

We were tired and took a nap, then went exploring. It was easy to get lost on the resort grounds. The hot weather persuaded me to shave off my beard. Betsy took a photo for posterity, and off it came.

We took the hotel shuttle bus into the little town of Port Douglas. Most shops in town were closed for the holiday, so we went instead to the Mirage Marina. This is the departure point for our boat tomorrow to the Reef, and has a nice shopping mall with about 40 shops, all of which were open and full of tourists. We tried to buy a tape of Aussie songs called "Up the Down Under Track," but were told it is out of date and no longer available. The clerk persuaded us to buy a substitute called "The Big Aussie Album," which turns out to be no good. Betsy also found a cord to put around her neck to hold her glasses when she sleeps on airplanes.

When we got back to the Sheraton, Betsy and I headed for the "Plantation Bar," where we each had a "pot," being a mug that holds about 10 oz. of Toohey's Red Beer. The manager let me take home a "Toohey's" sign as a souvenir.

After a nap we joined our group in the hotel restaurant for an elaborate buffet dinner. Because of the gloom and rain, and especially because we want more time in Tasmania, we have decided to leave the A&K tour group a day early and go down there on Thursday instead of Friday. We will miss an A & K "free day," when our companions plan to travel to see some of the rain forest.

Diana Stock was great. She got the plane reservations switched for Betsy and me, arranged a taxi for us to Cairns airport, and reserved a hotel room for us a night early in Hobart, Tasmania.

The Great Barrier Reef

After breakfast on Wednesday, we gathered at the front door of the hotel, where each of us was issued a large towel, and then we boarded a bus for the Mirage Marina.

The boat that took us to the Great Barrier Reef is a huge catamaran called the "Quicksilver," owned by a company of the same name. It holds busloads of people. There are no changing rooms, but one can change in the toilets, which are surprisingly clean. I carried my flight bag with bathing suit, camera, cap, sunglasses, and sweater. I also brought my prescription glass swim mask, carried on this whole journey just for this day.

When we got off the bus at the Marina, it was pouring down rain, and everyone got soaked getting onto the boat. Diana charged ahead of the pack

The catamaran "Quicksilver" at the dock in Port Douglas.

Snapshots

and secured seats for all seven of us on the top deck. The seating is reminiscent of an airplane, with seats configured 3-4-3. Beverages are available on board, but no hot beverages are served while the boat is in motion.

It takes about one and one half hours to get from Port Douglas to the Reef, heading straight out to sea at 55 kph. En route we had two lectures, the first about ship board safety from a crew member, and the second by a marine biologist who showed slides and lectured about the Reef, and how we should behave when we get there.

For A$24 we could join a small group to go off with the marine biologist to snorkel over the Reef and have the benefit of his explanation of it. It required being in the water for 45 minutes, and I was a little apprehensive and decided not to do it. In retrospect, I wish I had. The water is warm and buoyant, and 45 minutes was very easy to handle.

The floating platform located over the Great Barrier Reef, offshore from Port Douglas. The Quicksilver took about one and one-half hours to reach it.

We got to the Reef at 10:30 and the Quicksilver tied up to a huge, floating, aluminum pontoon that is anchored out there permanently. It has a roof over much of it, and lots of picnic style tables, so passengers can bring their lunches onto it to eat if they choose. There are a couple of small pontoon-type boats that go out with the biologists, two "submarines" for underwater viewing (like glass bottom boats), and several tenders and other craft for safety purposes. The platform itself has two underwater viewing galleries.

Lunch was put out on ship, buffet style, almost as soon as we tied up, and was available until about 2:00.

Betsy decided not to snorkel, so I asked Diana to be my "buddy." I also bought a T-shirt against the sun. Once we cleared landfall, the weather had broken and it was a pleasant, sunny day. I put sun block on my face, arms, and backs of my legs, but forgot the top of my head, which got slightly sunburned during the times in the water. The ship was well equipped with swim fins, snorkels and masks. It also offered (at a price) scuba gear and lessons.

There is no way to do justice to the beauty of the Great Barrier Reef. It is abundant with fish, who show no concern at all for the swimmers and divers. I could not count all of the varieties of sea life, and the colors were magnificent. Diana and I swam over a shelf that was several blocks in diameter, and where the water is not more than 4 feet deep. The coral was right below us and the water so buoyant that, in snorkel gear, we could just float and watch what was going on. Unforgettable.

After 30-40 minutes in the water we got out and joined everyone for lunch, which we ate out on the platform. Betsy also had a swim, and the two of us went into the platform's "undersea observatory" and watched the scene for a while.

Some of our group did not return to the water; however, at about 1:30 Marilyn, Anne, Diana and I went back to snorkel as a "team" and spent 30 - 40 minutes over various parts of the Reef. Betsy snapped a couple of underwater pictures of me from the platform's underwater observatory.

We emerged from the ocean, dried off, and then all of us went for a trip in one of the "submarines," which really are an excellent way to see the coral and the fish. The ride lasted about 30 minutes.

Once back on board, we changed to street clothes, and, at 3:15, the boat headed back to Port Douglas. Once there, Diana guided us to an ice cream shop, and then we returned to the Sheraton. Back on shore, the gloom and rain returned, and Betsy and I reinforced our opinion that we had made the right decision about going to Tasmania a day early.

That night the group gathered for our "farewell dinner" in the hotel restaurant. Diana Stock sat down with Betsy and me and went through our schedule for tomorrow, gave us departure data, and the name of a guide to call in Hobart. She has been great and we gave her a "love letter" with a check in it.

Tasmania

"The Australian" is a national newspaper, and the Thursday edition says that IBM has cut its dividend by more than fifty percent, and CEO Akers has said he will quit. Bill Clinton is putting Hillary in charge of "fixing" America's health care system, and the Aussie private insurers have offered to give her advice on the perils of national health schemes. Australia already has national health care, and it is common for a person to wait 18-24 months for "elective" surgery or "routine" care. Based on conversations with Aussies, I conclude that the terms "elective" and "routine" mean that you are miserable and want it taken care of now, but won't die from waiting. Accordingly, many Aussies have private pay insurance, in which case they can be treated at once - as one can in the US today.

We said our goodbyes at breakfast and Diana saw us off. We took a taxi (a fancy new Mercedes sedan) to Cairns for A$95. The driver told us that the Cairns area is glorious from April to September, but this is the wet season. On the way, he took us to see Paradise Palms golf course, owned by a Japanese company named Daikyo, who has apparently bought up huge tracts of land in and around Cairns. The course operates on a public fees basis. We went into the clubhouse and had a look, and it really is pretty. There is no "accommodation" there, but several Japanese have built private vacation homes around the course.

Our Ansett flight left on time and we were glad to see the sun again. I have finally been reading *Iron John*, but my instincts about it were right. Pop psychology and bad writing. We changed planes in Brisbane, where I got a copy of the *Herald Tribune*. Changed again in Melbourne, and finally arrived in the City of Hobart, on the island of Tasmania, at 6:30 PM (we lost an hour between Brisbane and Melbourne). We figured we had now completed 15 separate airplane flights on this trip.

The Hobart airport was fun because it was reminiscent of airports at home in the fifties. All of our bags were there and, unlike Fort Wayne, there were lots of taxis. The town is spread out on each side of the Derwent River, and the houses are neat, in good repair, and have well-tended gardens. The population is approximately 175,000. It's very British and very attractive.

The climate in Tasmania is temperate. Snow is rare, except in the mountains, and summer never gets much warmer than 75 degrees.

The physical beauty of the place is apparent, too. Most of Tasmania is uninhabited. Even around Hobart, the capital, you quickly find wide open spaces. Also, being an island about the size of Scotland, it has lots of shoreline and beaches. Finally, much of it is covered with hills and forests.

Our hotel was the Sheraton Hobart. Once settled in the room, I promptly called Jill Bennett, who also worked for Abercrombie & Kent. Diana Stock had given us her name, and recommended her as a guide. Jill was not available to "hire out" for us, but gave us some names and ideas which turned out to be very helpful.

We weren't hungry because of all the airplane meals (3 flights, 3 meals), so we took a walk through some of the downtown and around the docks. Back at the hotel we had some soup and sampled the local beer, Cascade Premium, which has two Tasmanian tigers on the label. The waitress was enthusiastic about it. She said, "It's the Tazzie beer."

Port Arthur Penal Colony

After breakfast the next morning, I called Budget Chauffer Drive. This was a recommendation from Jill Bennett. We arranged for a car and driver at a cost of A$45 per hour, the car to be a Mercedes Benz sedan. After leaving some film with the concierge to be developed, we met Brian Nicholson, our driver and guide for the day.

The drive through farmland and bush country was pleasant. Our first stop was Bonorong Devil Park, where we saw most of the native wildlife and fed kangaroos and wallabees. After telling us that the Tasmanian Devil has an incredibly strong bite, Brian asked us if we'd like to hold one, and have our picture taken with it! We declined.

The koalas were all asleep, although we could see them. They sleep all day and most of the night, when they awake for a few hours to eat eucalyptus

Betsy Chapman and a friendly Tasmanian Wallabee.

leaves. Diana had instructed us that they are not koala <u>bears</u>, they are marsupials, and are properly referred to simply as "koalas."

We went next to the village of Richmond, an old and still unspoiled town, where we saw Australia's oldest bridge, and explored the "Old Gaol." Virtually all old buildings in Australia were built with convict labor. At the Old Gaol we went into the solitary confinement cells and entered one and closed the door. It was pitch dark, and the prospect of spending any time in there was frightening. Some prisoners were put there for weeks. The old hotel on the main street looked charming and is reported to serve good food.

After leaving Richmond we drove for about an hour and ten minutes to the outskirts of Port Arthur, on the bottom of the Tasman Peninsula, and had lunch at a restaurant named Kelley's. Our decision to employ a local driver was a good one, because I don't think we'd have been able to find anything on our own. Kelley's served us a sumptuous, delicious and inexpensive meal. The main course was Trevalla, a local fish. This was another good steer from Jill Bennett.

We were running behind and did not get to the Port Arthur Historical Site until nearly 3 PM, too late for the escorted tour. Instead, we rented individual audio cassette players with self-guided tours on them, picked up maps, and saw it on our own.

The Port Arthur penal colony is said (by those in Port Arthur) to have more tourist visitors than any other place in Australia, even though Tasmania is off the beaten track. Much of the site is now ruined buildings, and the setting is beautiful, but you still get a chill as you walk through and realize the conditions that existed here for many years. In the Separate Prison men and women were kept in solitary confinement, and the "chapel" was built so that they could be kept isolated even during religious services. It seems to me that the people running the prison were the ones who needed religion.

There is too much history, too many impressions, to be recorded here, but Betsy and I agreed that it was a highlight of our trip.

On the return we stopped along the shore to look at some "tessalated rock." Great, flat areas of rock look like a pan of fudge, all sliced up into uniform squares. The interest arises because it is done by nature, not by man. Besides, anywhere you get out and walk here is beautiful.

Back in Hobart, we tried to arrange for dinner at "Prosser's on the Beach," because it is run by the Target family, friends of our Fort Wayne friend, Joey Christoff. None of them, including Joey's friend Adrian, were at home, and the restaurant was closed for "the regatta." For some reason, none of the other restaurants were closed. We did manage to call Mr. Earnest Target at his place in St. Helen's and gave him Joey's regards.

Port Arthur Penal Colony on the Island of Tasmania.

With Prosser's closed, we went to a restaurant called "Dear Friends." It was recommended both by Fodor and by the hotel concierge. It's a nice place with good food, and Betsy and I would both recommend it.

Tasmania is wonderful! Every once in a while we felt as though we had fallen back in time about forty years.

Farewell to Hobart - Or Is It?

The Saturday morning headline jolted us with the news that *a strike has shut down the Sydney airport, and it is expected to continue indefinitely*! We are supposed to fly there tomorrow, and out to the USA the next day! We called Ansett Air, and they said that only the international terminal is affected, and domestic flights are going in. If that holds, we can go there tomorrow, but getting out on Monday will be another matter.

We spent the morning at the Salamanca Market, a huge market held in Hobart every Saturday morning all up and down Salamanca Place. It was only a short walk from our hotel. It stretches for blocks and was packed with people on this pleasant, sunny morning. All kinds of things are for sale, from tourist items to household needs, also toys, crafts, and all kinds of food to eat there or carry home.

While at the market we found our driver, Brian Nicholson, manning a stall with his son, selling craft items made by his wife. He told us he does this every week. Nearly all of the merchants there seemed to be non-commercial, once a week types. We shopped and looked, but the only thing we bought was a little framed array of pressed flowers made by Brian's wife.

About 12:30 we returned to the Sheraton and took a cab to the top of Mount Nelson. It was used during the old days as a semaphore station, where flags were run up and down to send signals cross country. Today it has a delightful teahouse and restaurant that looks over a marvelous view of the harbor. Its "official" name is "Mt. Nelson Signal Station Tea House." The owner, Rob Farrington, was intrigued with visiting Yanks and talked with us for quite a while. He told us that he came to Hobart from England 27 years ago, and "has no desire to go back."

Lunch was excellent and very reasonable–more good advice from Jill Bennett. We even enjoyed the music they played.

Our taxi driver, Angela, was waiting for us as scheduled and took us back to town, dropping us at the Franklin Wharf, from whence left the tub "Emmalisa" at 3:15. We paid A$10 each for a 1 1/4 hour "coffee cruise" of Derwent Harbor. The sunshine held out strong all day long.

We tried to get a dinner reservation at Wrest's Hotel Rooftop Restaurant, but it was full, so we decided on Mure's, a seafood place on the dock right across the street from the Sheraton. A lucky break, as it was very good. Mure's had excellent seafood and fast service. Be sure to go to the *upstairs* dining room. For dessert, we got ice cream cones at the little shop below. It had gotten quite cool and we took a walk through town, down Salamanca Place, and then back along the docks.

We watched the TV news for a little while and learned: President Clinton has declared that the US military will no longer bar homosexuals; and, Monica Seles has defeated Steffi Graf to win the women's Australian Open tennis tournament.

Return to Sydney

Ansett Air confirmed that domestic flights are still getting into Sydney, and that we will go as scheduled. (Whew! So far, so good.)

After breakfast we took a cab (uphill) to "Arthur Circus," a lovely circle of small homes built around a little park, each with lots of blooming flowers. We walked back (downhill) and stopped on Runnymede Street to look at Lenna's, a hotel and home to Alexander's Restaurant. The lobby and restaurant areas looked Victorian and pleasant, if perhaps a little bit gloomy. Rooms there ran from A$125 – 145.20, and suites were available.

Betsy purchased an Australian book at the local book store, and then we returned to the Sheraton, packed, and got a taxi to the airport. The flight to Sydney went fine and upon arrival there we checked in once again at the Regent Hotel, after a tiresome ride with a garrulous Greek cab driver.

We have been favorably impressed with both Ansett Air Lines and Australian Air Lines.

The Regent's premier restaurant, Kable's, is closed on Sunday, so we went to Bilson's. It's located on the upper floors of the International (Boat) Terminal at Circular Quay. Bilson's has a fantastic setting, looking over the harbor at the Opera House, and very good food, but service was <u>slow</u>, and it's expensive.

There is no word on the airport strike except that, as we go to bed, nobody is flying international flights in or out. Sydney hopes to host the Olympic Games in 2000, but this strike will be a black eye for the city. Two Olympic officials have been stranded at the airport!

Homeward

The Monday Morning News: The Strike is Settled!

Jim Courier has won the Australian Open.

I called United Air Lines and they said we are "go." Our plane was scheduled for 3:15 that afternoon.

Betsy and I took a walk along the Quay and to the Opera House for a last look, and then went to the Ken Done shop in The Rocks. Ken Done is a well-known Australian Artist who also markets clothes and other items with his designs on them. It was a marvelous, sunny morning to be on and around Sydney Harbor.

As we packed, the Super Bowl was live on local TV and I got to watch the first half, which was enough because the Dallas Cowboys routed the Buffalo Bills.

Sydney to Los Angeles was non – stop, about 13 hours, and all of our connections went well. We calculate that the total number of airplane flights on the trip was twenty (20!). Our son Steve, bless him, met us at Baer Field, and we got to 7014 Woodcroft Lane at about 10:30 PM, Fort Wayne time. Since we left the Regent Hotel in Sydney, we had been traveling about 25 hours, and, because we again crossed the International Date Line, it was still Monday, February 1st.

Jet lag - here we come!

Chapter 5

ENGLAND, WEST COUNTRY AND LONDON

Betsy and I left Fort Wayne for Chicago on Sunday, June 6, 1993, at 10:50 A.M., and for once United Express was on time. We were traveling all the way with United Air Lines because we had been able to use frequent flyer miles to upgrade from "Cheapflite" to Business Class. We made our flight connection in Chicago and flew to Washington Dulles, and from there connected to London Heathrow. On the flight over we saw the Australian movie "Strictly Ballroom," but the sound system on the plane was so bad that we really only picked up about half of it. From that we could see that it's a good movie and we decided we would make an effort to see it again in a theater.

We got to Heathrow Airport in London the next day at 6:30 A.M. local time and went straight to the British Rail desk, where we bought two 1st class tickets to Exeter for a total of £95. The fare included a bus from Heathrow to the rail station in Reading, which took about 45 minutes. There we were lucky to catch a train that was arriving a little late. We grabbed our bags and ran through the station and jumped on it just before the doors were about to close. Luckily it turned out to be, in fact, the right train. This saved us a wait of 1½ to 2 hours, and we were grateful because we were tired. (The railroad station at Reading was pretty nice, so, under normal circumstances, it wouldn't have been too bad to have had a wait there.)

Howard L. Chapman

Exeter

The weather was fine and we had a pleasant train ride to Exeter. Once there we took a cab to the Royal Clarence Hotel where we had fortunately reserved a room. I say "fortunately" because it was full. It appeared to be popular with tour groups. The hotel has a good location in the center of Exeter, directly opposite the famous Cathedral. Our room was small and noisy, but did have a good view over the Cathedral Green.

After a nap we walked across the Green to the Cathedral and went through it. It's well worth seeing. Although Exeter was badly bombed in World War II, the Cathedral was spared. A volunteer there told us that it has the "longest continued vaulted ceiling in the world." Outside the Cathedral we encountered a lady in a red blazer who told us about walking tours that are available throughout the day. They go in and around the town for various lengths of time, leaving from in front of the Cathedral. Easy to find and join. We decided on one for tomorrow morning.

We walked down the hill to an area on the river known as the "Quay," and found a pub called the Prospect Inn where we each ordered "a half" and relaxed by a window looking out over the River Exe. It was only about 4:30 but for some reason we both got really sleepy, but because of jet lag we thought we shouldn't sleep any more until bed time. We straggled back up the hill to the Royal Clarence and sat in the lobby, trying to keep awake until 6:30. That was when the pub next door, the Sir Francis Drake, began to serve dinner.

The restaurant is a really old and historic place but, as my mother once said, "it's not old enough to be worth it." I ordered plaice and Betsy had lamb cutlets (chops). It was o.k., but not a bellringer. Of course, we were tired. On the other hand, we were also hungry and "hunger is the best sauce."

After dinner we walked for about an hour through this lovely Devonshire town. It has lots of parks, historic buildings, and huge roses. It was a beautiful summer night.

Like most English hotels, the Royal Clarence has no air conditioning, so we needed to keep the window open for circulation. There were some loud, scruffy kids outside on the Cathedral Green, but before long, we went to sleep anyway.

Gidleigh Park

I woke up at 5:30 and didn't feel well. Finally, about 7:30, Betsy had some toast and coffee sent up, but I couldn't eat. Jet lag had me. We both slept some more and finally, about 10:30, I began to come around. Betsy left for the walking tour of the Cathedral Close, and I stayed in bed. At 11:30, I went downstairs for a cup of coffee, and the desk clerk told me that check out time is 11:00, *and they need our room*! Our stuff was scattered all over the tiny room, but I tried to pack up as best I could and told the maid to go ahead and start cleaning the room.

Meanwhile, I called Auto-Europe about our car. They said they have it but it is in the shop! And they have no other cars with automatic transmissions. (It was going to be bad enough, driving on the left side of the road, without having to use a manual gearshift on the wrong side of the car.) I told the lady we were going to the Gidleigh Park Hotel near Dartmoor, and she offered to drive us there and said they would deliver the car to us there tomorrow (Wednesday morning).

We had read about Gidleigh Park in some literature we got from our Fort Wayne neighbor, Marcia Adams. £340 a night includes tax, service and dinner for two. I hoped we'd be hungry! Auto-Europe showed up in the person of "Roy" at 1:00, packed us into his car, and drove us to the Gidleigh Park. This was serendipity. On our own, we'd have spent all day finding it. After about an hour of driving from Exeter we came to a little narrow lane that said the hotel was up there, one and a half miles away. After winding and twisting on the one lane road for what seemed like ten miles, we saw another sign that said "Keep heart - Gidleigh Park only 1/2 mile ahead."

From the first glimpse, it truly is magnificent. New and newly decorated, but in traditional English style. Modern plumbing. Fabulous grounds, gardens and flowers. Owned by Mr. and Mrs. Paul Henderson (Americans). Chef - Shaun Hill.

Roy left promising to return tomorrow morning with our car. Our room was big, gorgeous and quiet. 180 degrees from the night before. We went out on the terrace and had lunch - welsh rarebit and coffee. What a spot. Down below runs a branch of the River Teighn, just fast enough to make a pleasant murmur. Perfect for sleeping.

After lunch we asked the lady at the desk about suggestions for a walk. She said, "Well, you could go up over the hill and walk out onto the moor." The Moor! Heathcliff! The Hound of the Baskervilles! She had ordinance maps with directions on them already made up for hotel guests. Nonetheless, we nearly needed an Indian Guide just to get "up over the hill." It was very steep, heavily wooded, virtually unmarked and with a very narrow path, where there was a path.

When we finally got out onto the Moor, Betsy and I were immediately struck by the wild beauty of the place. No path or trail, sheep roaming freely. No fences or boundaries. Soggy marshland here and there in unexpected places. Rugged outcroppings of rock and not much vegetation that grows above knee level.

Even with the map we weren't sure we were following directions. In fact, after walking a while, we began to fear that we were lost. Fortunately, we met a British couple out for a stroll and found that they had a compass. *Good idea*! They reassured us that our proposed heading was correct and would lead us back to familiar terrain, from whence we could get back to our hotel. By the time we returned to the Gidleigh Park we were both exhausted and exhilarated. All in all, we had walked about three hours, but it was not like any other walk in our experience.

Dinner was a fancy deal. First we went into the bar, ordered a drink, and looked at menus, then gave the hostess our dinner selections. While we were doing this, the father of the owner, Paul Henderson, Sr., introduced himself. He's a Purdue graduate who once worked in the steel business in Gary.

It took about two and one half hours to "dine," and by the time we went to bed, I was wide awake. Jet lag again. Halcion was my friend, and I woke up the next morning when Betsy said, "My Lord, it's 10 o'clock!"

Lewtrenchard Manor

A beautiful day. We have been fortunate - three in a row. Amazing, for England.

We made it downstairs for breakfast, but I wasn't up to eating much. For me, jet lag seems to be a problem going east, but not going west. It took a couple of phone calls to Auto Europe, but "Roy" finally showed up with our car at 1 PM. Not a lot of day left, but not so bad for us since we had gotten a late start anyway.

The car was a four door Ford, somewhat like a Taurus wagon. An automatic, but with a right hand drive. I was forever getting into it on the wrong side. I decided that maybe some of my stomach ailments of the last couple of days had to do with anxiety about driving on the left side of the road.

We left Gidleigh Park via the hamlet of Chagford, then went straight across Dartmoor to Tavistock. There were sheep all over the road. You just have to accommodate them, because they have absolutely no fear of automobiles.

After Tavistock we followed our directions down narrow roads with hedges (made of stone) on each side, and eventually found our country inn for the night, the Lewtrenchard Manor. It is owned by Jim and Susan Murray, who have owned it for about 5 years. It's a true "country inn," stately, elegant, peaceful, beautiful gardens, and full of history.

We unloaded our bags, checked on the dinner hour, and then drove back to Tavistock to explore. It's a pleasant West Country town with a lovely church. In the church we sought and received directions to a tea shop named "Kemble's," where we found tea and some good pastry (if we had known how big dinner would be we would have skipped the pastry). We wandered through some shops and I bought some maps. The good road maps in this area are called "Ordinance Maps." They aren't cheap.

Finding Lewtrenchard Manor was a lot easier this time. We "dressed for dinner" (coat and tie) and came downstairs to the sitting room where we were offered drinks (they were carefully logged and added to the tab). Susan Murray gave us a rundown of the history of the place and introduced their huge dog, Duma, which means "thunder" in Zulu. It turns out they had lived previously in South Africa and brought Duma back with them. Duma is a Lab, and thus has a nice disposition.

There were four other guests, two of them Americans. The other couple was English and was on holiday, traveling with their two small dogs, which they left in their car all night! Dinner was superb, but I ate too much and got indigestion. Betsy and I took a walk after dinner, but I still felt miserable. Having trouble getting to sleep, I took another pill at 1:30 AM. At precisely 4:21 AM the alarm clock went off! Lesson - in a hotel that furnishes an alarm clock, always check it before you turn in to be sure that the maid or the last guest hasn't left it set to roust you out at 4:21 in the morning. Anyway, no more sleep, and up at 8:00.

Intrepid Travelers

The next morning, I was still fighting jet lag, especially after eating too much last night, and then being awake since 4:21! The breakfast was served in a different room, and was lovely, except that I didn't feel much like having any. Betsy, fortunately, was fine.

The weather had turned gray and wet - no big surprise for England, and especially the West Country. We planned to head to Truro in Cornwall and had booked a room at the Alverton Manor there, but had no definite plans after that. At the urging of Jim Murray, we made reservations at a country inn named "Buckland Tout Saints" for Saturday and Sunday. It has been newly reopened and is reported to have a fine chef.

We left Lewtrenchard Manor and drove north to Boscastle (pronounced as written - Boss cas sel). It is on the coast, and to get there you drive up over surrounding hills, then down to the shore. In the high country the fog was really dense, this made it all the more harrowing to be driving on one lane roads. We had a book called "Best of Britain," about the West Country, and it outlined a walking tour along the seaside; but it was pretty scary with a lot of wind and rain, up on a cliff where a lot of the footing was slippery, over wet rocks or mud. Still, a lot of Brits were out in their foul weather gear, tromping around and enjoying the day.

We walked out on the path along the edge of the harbor to the "head," looked at a blowhole, started to venture out on some precarious places, and then headed back to town. An English couple on the trail recommended the "Carpenter's Kitchen" tea room, and it turned out to be good advice. I ordered a grilled ham and cheese sandwich, and Betsy tried grilled cheese and apple. Then we split a huge bowl of fresh strawberries and cream. Fantastic!

We left Boscastle and drove down the coast to Tintagel (Tin- TADGE-el), supposedly where King Arthur lived and built his castle. The town itself is too touristy, but the trip out to the castle is well worth it. Pay £1 to take the Land Rover each way if you can, because it's a long walk over a poor path and no fun in bad weather, especially coming back, which is all uphill.

Once we got to the castle, we found we had to pay an entry fee and then climb up some really steep steps to get to the top. The steps go along the side of a cliff, are made of stone, are rather narrow, and were wet. With the rain and the waves crashing below, it was an interesting but daunting climb. A young family of three was trudging up the steps ahead of us, with mother in front and father trailing, with their infant child on his shoulders, and a back pack underneath. Half way up, we heard him say, "Another one of your brilliant ideas, Sylvia!" There is a good railing, and it's not really as dangerous as it seems, just dramatic.

The castle was built in the 13th century and was used by Cornish Kings as a defensive retreat. It couldn't have really been King Arthur's since it was built about 500-600 years after his time. But who knows, he could have been at Tintagel before that.

Because of the bad weather we decided to cancel our visit to Port Isaac, which we'd hoped to see, and drove to Truro, where we checked in at the Alverton Manor. They had nothing but a suite available at £120 per night, which included breakfast, but not dinner. The Manor was built in the 20's, and was a convent for a while. It's pleasant enough, but not as much fun as the places we'd been. We went into the town and did a little exploring. It's probably nice when the weather is good, or when you've done some planning, or know someone. Not so great for strangers in the rain.

Lots of people had told us to eat at pubs, but whenever we asked an Englishman to recommend a pub to eat at, he always wrinkled up his nose. We seemed to have a hard time finding one with good food. This time I asked the young man at the hotel desk, and after a lot of thought he sent us to a pub called "The Heron Inn." You would really have to have a car to get there. We

Snapshots

drove along the river about 1 1/4 miles to a place called "Malpas" before we found it, but decided that, for once, it was worth it. We both ordered "Cottage Pie," which was a huge plate of ground beef and tomatoes, mashed potatoes, plus lots of peas and green beans - all served with a very good local beer.

The weather continued to be wet, cold, gloomy and very windy. A big storm had come through Cornwall the night before, and some Cornish towns had suffered severe flooding. We began to talk about changing our plans for the rest of our trip if this kind of weather "settles in."

Weathered In (or Maybe it was "Weathered Out")

We got our wakeup call on Friday at 8 AM. I was still not feeling right! A combination of ingredients, I think. Breakfast at the Alverton Manor was served in their main dining room, a pleasant place, with the ubiquitous buffet and loud, canned music. There were no other guests in the room so, when the waitress went to the kitchen, I found the controls and turned down the music. Nobody seemed to notice or care.

The weather was truly grim. It had all the symptoms of "socking in," and local weather reports confirmed that it was likely to continue for several days in the West Country area. Betsy and I decided to cut and run for London tomorrow (Saturday). This needed about 45 minutes of telephone calls. We had to:

- Call Europe Car and arrange to return the car early.
- Cancel our reservations at Buckland Tout Saints.
- Find a room in London.
- Cancel our reservation for a room next Tuesday at the Sheraton Heathrow.

We accomplished all of this by 11 AM. For a hotel in London we decided to try the "Howard" (where else?). It had been recommended to me by my law school classmate, Con Callahan, about a year ago, and for some reason the name had stuck with me. Next, we arranged with the Alverton Manor to switch to a twin bedded room for tonight (Friday). It turned out to be a much nicer room for less money (£105)! We were finally ready to start what was left of our day in Cornwall.

The hotel desk offered us a few tourist promotion maps and some advice, part of which was worth having. We had been told by some English ladies in Exeter to be sure to go to St. Just in Roseland and to St. Mawes, to skip "Land's End," and to go to "The Lizard" only as Plan B. (Steve Norrish, our British country club manager, was from Devon, and had also suggested we skip "Land's End.")

We drove first to Trellisick Gardens, to the South of Truro. They are very nice, with extensive grounds, and we spent nearly an hour walking through them. The rain had slowed to a light mist, so it wasn't too bad. Their dining room was "fully booked I'm afraid" for lunch, but there was another place on the grounds that proved adequate. It is sort of a cross between a buffet and a coffee shop. Our lunch consisted of carrot soup, "filled rolls" and tea (the filled rolls were filled with ham).

To go from Trellisick Gardens to St. Just in Roseland, one takes the King Harry Ferry across the Fal River. When we got to St. Just in Roseland, we went to see the old church. There are, indeed, palm trees here, though God only knows how they survive in this climate. Betsy and I were each wearing all of the layers of clothes that we had brought to England, and we were still shivering. The guide book calls this area "sub-tropical," a fallacy that is perpetuated by many Brits. This was mid-June. What must it be like in January?

We did a little more sight-seeing from the car and then drove on to St. Mawes. It's a lovely and quaint fishing village that is giving way grudgingly to the tourists, but is still delightful. It was too cold to see much on foot, but we did wander about for a while. The locals seemed oblivious to the weather. We stopped in a shop that sold candy and ice cream, and noticed that the door was propped open. The clerk was wearing a tee shirt. I asked her if it was often this cold here, and she said, "Most of the time, about 75% of the time."

It was "close enough" to tea time, so we found a tea room for tea and "pudding." To the English, most desserts are "puddings." In my case, it was a fudge cake.

After we left St. Mawes, we continued along the coast, via very narrow roads, to the village of Veryan, where there are some round houses with crosses on the top. They were reportedly made round so that there would be "no corner for the Devil to hide in." We followed more one lane roads to the lovely coastal village of Portloe (Port-loo). The main industries seem to be fishing and tourism, with not too much of either. We didn't go in, but the Hotel Lugger looked o.k., and there were many attractive Bed and Breakfast spots. Parking is at a premium here, but we finally found a lot with an "honor box" advising us to deposit 20p as the parking charge. We spent 30-40 minutes walking about, visiting the tea room, and shivering. It was cold.

When we returned to Truro, the weather was still dismal. We stopped at a Shell station and filled the car with gas, and then went back to Alverton Manor to rest. Because of the crummy weather we decided to stay there for dinner. The food rated a grade of "C." We ate it and survived.

News of the day: The English are agog over a man named Norman

Lamont. Prime Minister John Major fired him and he then made a speech in Parliament that was highly critical of Major. Now the Tories are all mad at him, but the Laborites are enjoying it. (Major later survived a vote of confidence.) Other news: War in Bosnia; Brits calling for withdrawal of English troops from the area.

Escape to London

When I got up on Saturday morning I was hungry for the first time since we got to England. I actually felt like eating breakfast! Maybe it was because I was soon to return the car and be relieved of driving on the left. For whatever reason, though, Betsy was a little "off her feed."

When we got packed and ready to leave there was an absolute downpour outside. I put on a raincoat and backed the car up as close to the hotel as I could, and we simply got wet loading it. We plunged (almost literally) ahead through the weather and drove back to Exeter. I was able to find the place at the railroad station where Roy had said to return the car, parked it, and called Europe Car to come and get it. It was Saturday, so their office closed at noon, and I was glad we made it in time so that I could be sure that they were aware of it and would come and collect it.

We caught the 11:03 train from Exeter to Paddington Station in London. I had forgotten how big the place is! We found a taxi and went to the Howard Hotel located on the Victoria Embankment at Temple Place. The weather was a little gloomy but immensely improved over what we had left behind in the West Country. Besides, London is the world's greatest city and we were thrilled to be there again.

Because it was a weekend the hotel was not crowded and we had no trouble getting a lot of attention from the Concierge (in England they call them "Bell Porters"). He recommended The Ivy Restaurant for dinner. We had been there twenty years earlier and found it to still be excellent. Grade-A. While there, a man came up to the table and said hello. It was Paul Henderson, the owner of Gidleigh Park. He, his wife and parents were dining a couple of tables away! When we left, we saw an actor there named Hugh Lorry, who plays Bertie Wooster in the PBS "Jeeves" series that Betsy and I enjoy. In person, his mannerisms were very much like Bertie's.

After dinner we saw an American musical called "Five Guys Named Moe." It was disappointing. We had been warned away from it once before, but had forgotten! For some reason, it's been running in London for three years.

Howard L. Chapman

The Campions

The next day The Howard Hotel was quiet – "Sunday morning coming down." Weather was gray and cool, but dry. We took a walk to Covent Garden after breakfast. It's now a large pedestrian mall with shops, indoor and outdoor restaurants, street entertainers, fast food, etc. It's a good place for children and young people, and it was full of them. We wondered what the crowds would be like on a Saturday night.

Next we strolled along the Strand, looking in at the Savoy Hotel, and exploring the Charing Cross tube station. At the station I found out you can get those convenient maps of the Underground from the ticket sellers at no charge. Betsy and I got one for each of us.

At 1:00 we met John and Jean Campion at the Howard. They are friends from our visit in 1985 when we attended the American Bar Association annual meeting, held that year in London. Each couple had signed up for a weekend visit, they as hosts and we as guests. They're easy to know and we felt as though we had only just seen them last week. We drove in their car to "Rule's," located in Maiden Lane. Rule's is another restaurant that is an old time favorite, and is still wonderful. Was I ever happy that John was the one who was driving! We enjoyed a fine English lunch with New Zealand white wine, and then walked back over to Covent Garden to see the scene at a different time of day. Among other things, we heard some people performing opera in one of the squares, and they were really good. There was a big crowd, and we listened for quite a while.

We left Covent Garden and drove over to the Albert Embankment to find the place where the Globe Theater is being reconstructed. We went first to the National Theater, thinking someone there would know where the Globe is, but everything was closed up. By now we had a nice, sunny day - cool but pleasant. As a last resort, we pried out our map and found where we wanted to go and drove there. The "new" Globe was just being framed in, and would be an interesting place to someday see Shakespeare performed. Then we walked along the Thames, stopping in to see the Southwark Cathedral. It's a very nice, active church that most tourists don't seem to know about, but worth a trip to see, especially if you could manage to attend services.

It was late afternoon, and we wanted to find a pub, but learned (from some plainclothes policemen that were sitting in a parked car) that the pubs are not allowed to open on Sundays until 7:00PM. Eventually, we drove back to the Howard and had a beverage in the lounge. Hotels, it seems, are not restricted to pub hours if they are serving guests.

We said goodbye to John and Jean and they headed home. Betsy and I moved to a hotel room with an operating air conditioner (the windows at the Howard cannot be opened). It was a cool evening, so we donned warm clothes and walked over to the McDonald's on the Strand. Betsy was originally aghast at the idea of going to McDonald's, but was a good sport about it. McDonald's was fine, with "no surprises," other than the fact that the menu featured "Trifle." (We didn't try it.)

The Strand, sadly, is a congregating spot for homeless people, especially in the evening. Most of them seemed to be young and in good health. It's unfortunate for them and somewhat daunting for passers-by, who have some feeling of running the gauntlet.

Just Plain Tourists

Monday in London. A gray, rainy day. I kept thinking of that song, "*Rainy Days and Mondays Always Get Me Down.*" But in London, you can't stay down for long. To start with, London is the world's best theater town.

We had no luck trying to order opera tickets. First, there aren't any, but if there were, they cost £88 (poor seats) to £129, published price. Next we tried to get to see "*Separate Tables*" with Patricia Hodge and Peter Bowles, but found it wasn't opening until next week. "*Inadmissible Evidence*" was at the National Theater, but was in "previews," and no tickets were available to the public. We asked the Porter to try for: a) *Phantom of the Opera*; or, b) *The Gift of the Gorgon*.

We got out our umbrellas and walked to a place called "The Breadline." It is sort of on the order of a diner, where two full English breakfasts came to less than £6. It was only a short walk from there to Trafalgar Square where Lord Nelson stands majestically atop his column, which he shares with a number of pigeons.

The National Gallery fronts on Trafalgar Square, and was a perfect refuge on a rainy morning. We spent about an hour and a half going through various parts but, as usual, enjoyed the French impressionists the most. There is a pleasant cafeteria in the museum, and we stopped for coffee.

When we left the National Gallery, Betsy decided to go see Whitehall, while I sloshed back to The Howard. On the way I stopped at several spots making key purchases to better pass an hour or two, being: 1) a *Herald Tribune*; 2) some fresh fruit; 3) some "cheese crisps;" and 4) a bow tie. Actually, the bow tie was for the next day.

Betsy returned to the hotel at about three o'clock and we set off to take the tube to Oxford Circus. You get tickets at the station before you get on, and there are machines to sell them to you if you know where you are going and can figure out how to use the machines. Fortunately, there is also someone in a teller cage to sell them. Inflation has struck the Underground! At least it seemed a lot more expensive than I remembered.

When we got to Oxford Circus, the rain had become an occasional drizzle. We walked down Regent Street, browsing in various shops along the way, including Liberty, Waterford, Burberry, Scotch House, and China Craft. We timed our walk so as to end up at the Prince Edward Theater in Soho at about 5:15. We had tickets to see "Crazy for You," which is a make-over of Gershwin's "Girl Crazy." (A "make-down" would be more descriptive.)

We logged about thirty minutes at a nearby pub over a "half" while we waited for our restaurant, Wheeler's of St. James, to open. It's a seafood place across the street from the theater on Old Compton Road. Even though Wheeler's is a part of a chain, dinner was good, and we were lucky to get in without a reservation.

The show was another "o.k." - light, colorful, energetic, and corny.

For the second night in a row, we actually found a taxi amid the after theater mob.

Legal London

We decided to splurge by having breakfast on Tuesday at the Savoy Hotel, which is only a couple of blocks from the Howard. It was a gorgeous day, a complete reversal from Monday. John of Gaunt once lived on the site where the Savoy stands. The present building was built by D'Oyley Carte about 1880-1890. We were shown to a window table looking over the Thames and had the usual stellar English breakfast in what must be one of the world's best settings.

After breakfast we walked to the Royal Courts of Justice. We had to go through security to get in, similar to boarding an airplane. There were lots of cases in session. Only civil cases are tried here, with criminal matters being over at the Old Bailey. We went into one of the courtrooms and listened for a while. It was a tax appeal, a very dull case, but still fun to watch the English procedure and all the barristers and judges in their wigs and gowns.

When we left I bought a *Herald Tribune* and went back to the hotel to rest a little. Betsy went off by prearrangement to meet Jean Campion at Harrod's handbag department at one o'clock. They planned to combine some shopping with lunch at Harrod's. She went there on the number nine bus. Fare was 80p, and the driver made change.

I read the newspaper for a while. The Phoenix Suns had won the third game of the NBA championship playoff series against the Chicago Bulls, and the Bulls now led by 2-1. Michael Jordan is the star of the Bulls and Charles Barkley is the Suns' hero. President Clinton has appointed a woman, Ruth

Snapshots

Bader Ginsburg, to the U.S. Supreme Court. American airships have attacked strongholds of "warlord" Aideed in Somalia.

I left The Howard and walked to the chambers of John Campion in Lincoln's Inn, and met him there at 1:00PM. There are thirteen (I think) barristers in his chambers, and he is "head of chambers." This is the equivalent of "Ballard" on the "Rumpole" series. It turned out that he, too, watches "Rumpole." His initials: D.J.M. Campion. The address of his chambers is Eleven Stone Buildings. Even though his chambers are at Lincoln's Inn, he is a member of Gray's Inn, and we walked to the dining hall there for lunch. It has a "High Table" where the "Benchers" sit. They are a self-perpetuating governing body for Gray's Inn. The "Benchers" sit in chairs with arms, while everybody else sits on benches. Go figure!

We had a choice of going through cafeteria style, or ordering from a menu, and chose the latter. We enjoyed a good lunch with a bottle of Muscadet wine, chosen by John. Most of the Hall was destroyed during World War II, but the wooden "screen" was saved, and (maybe) also the windows. The rest of the Hall has now been restored. There are plaques on the walls commemorating all of the past Treasurers of the Inn. Each Treasurer is appointed for one year. John showed me the plaque for his grandfather, who was treasurer in 1920.

After lunch John took me to see the Inn's library. It is used by law students as a study hall. It, too, was destroyed in the war, and has been restored.

Next we took a taxi to the Old Bailey. Security again. Once in, we had our choice of 16 trials in progress, and the guard ticked off the various offenses being heard in each. We chose murder and spent an hour watching. At 3:30 we cabbed back to Gray's Inn and met Betsy and Jean. We grudgingly said goodbye to the Campions. They have been delightful.

Betsy and I walked back through the Temple, with its pleasant gardens (but Lincoln's Inn has the best gardens), then to our hotel. At six we went to the lobby and had toasted cheese, ham and tomato sandwiches and hot chocolate. It was plenty for dinner since we'd been eating a lot all day long.

The weather was still beautiful at 7:15 when we walked to Her Majesty's Theater to see "The Phantom of the Opera." It's on Haymarket Street, and "Phantom" has been playing there since 1986. Our Porter had located two tickets in the first row of the balcony. They were "good" seats, but this is a show that definitely should be seen from the orchestra (or, as they say in England, "The Stalls"), not the balcony.

After the performance it was a pleasant evening and we walked back along the Strand, street people and all. We passed the Adelphi Theater, where workmen were putting finishing touches on the marquee for "Sunset Boulevard," the new Andrew Lloyd Webber play. We wondered whether or not it will be any good. Being by Lloyd-Webber, we know it will, at least, make money.

And Home

Wednesday was our day of departure, and we thought we would be smart and have breakfast sent to the room to save time. Unfortunately, the order got "lost" and our breakfast never showed up. Too bad, because it was the only problem we had with The Howard Hotel in the four days we were there. It was, in most respects, excellent, which is to say, it lived up to its name. Besides, we enjoyed staying in a different part of London, being able to walk to theaters, and looking out over the Thames and Big Ben.

The hotel had arranged for a car to take us to Heathrow Airport. The fare, £40, was about the same as the cost of a taxi (they told us). At the airport we shopped a little, had a coffee at the Red Carpet Room, and left on time. United Airlines took us all the way home with the same stopover at Dulles, and *sans* glitches. Our son Steve, bless his heart, met us at the airport in Fort Wayne. The trip hadn't gone as planned, but was a good one.

Chapter 6

BERMUDA SHORTS

I

This is a chronicle of a visit to Bermuda during March, 1994, with a group sponsored by the Art Institute of Chicago. There were a total of nineteen travelers, including Betsy and me, and our Fort Wayne friends, Ron and Patti Gettel. We were accompanied by Nancy Ganiard from the Art Institute, and Meg MacDonald, representing Passages, Unlimited, the Boston-based travel agency that put the trip together.

Most of the group gathered at O'Hare Field in Chicago on the morning of March 22, 1994, while the Chapmans and Gettels left from Fort Wayne. We joined ranks in Atlanta for a non-stop flight on Delta Airlines to Bermuda.

The airport in Bermuda is presently a U.S. Navy base, acquired by gift in 1970. It began life as a joint U.S. Army Air Force and Royal Air Force base during the Second World War. Congress has now decided to close the base (in September of 1995) and it will be turned over to the government of Bermuda.

Bermuda is a member of the British Commonwealth, self-governing since 1684, with a locally elected cabinet, but with a governor appointed by the Crown. There are about 59,000 permanent residents on the island which is, in fact, several islands that have been linked with bridges, and contain about twenty-one square miles of land surface. It is twenty-one miles long, and never more than a couple of miles wide. It is located about 600 miles due East of Cape Hatteras, N.C., and describes its climate as "semi-tropical."

Visitors from the U.S. require passports, and we went through a perfunctory customs check before going out to our taxi-vans for the ride to our hotel. The temperature was mild, but sweaters felt good, and it was obvious that a rain storm was on its way. The drivers were capable, friendly, and (at least in our case) talkative. Ours, Mr. Rahman, advised that we would have a ride of about 40 minutes to our hotel, the Lantana Colony Club, located at the other end of Bermuda. We needed all of the 40 minutes because the speed limit in Bermuda is 25 mph, the roads are narrow and congested, and there was rush hour traffic.

The racial makeup of the population is about 60% black and 40% white, and race relations appear to be cordial. Slavery was abolished in the British Commonwealth in 1834, and both races have coexisted and prospered ever since. There is little evidence of poverty, and 95% of the people are literate. Tourism is the main industry, with about 600,000 visitors per year, most from the U.S. and Canada. There is no income tax, and its second "industry" is off-shore investment companies (tax-avoiders).

The emphasis of the visit for our group can be summarized as follows: Art; History; Historic Preservation; and Architecture. The Art Institute and Passages did a wonderful job of arranging private entrees, behind the scenes tours, and meetings and lectures with local Bermudians in such a way as to enhance the experiences we had in each of these areas. We had virtually no time for the typical pursuits of a tourist in Bermuda, *i.e.,* swimming, boating, and golf; however, we were about 4 weeks early for the "season," and didn't really come for those things.

"Our pool" at the Lantana Colony Club.

Snapshots

We got to the hotel at about 5:30 p.m. and learned that most of its accommodations are in private cottages. We shared a cottage with two units, with Ron and Patti Gettel in the other unit. Each unit had a sitting room, bedroom, bath and patio, and our two units shared a kitchenette area. By this time it was raining pretty hard, and one of the hotel staff, "Tony," was kept busy following people with his umbrella and helping us get moved in. We had a little over an hour, and then gathered at the hotel's waterfront restaurant, "La Plage," for cocktails and a slide presentation on Bermuda history by Ann Smith Gordon of the Bermuda National Trust. Because of the rain, hotel vans transported people back and forth.

After the lecture, the group was invited to the home of Mr. and Mrs. John H. Young, II, the owners of Lantana Colony Club, and located right next door to the hotel grounds. The Youngs are one of the founding families of Bermuda. We were greeted by their son-in-law, Paul Leseur, who is the general manager of the hotel, his wife Penny, and by John and Nelga Young. There were also a number of Bermudians there, including some of the painters, sculptors, and others that we would see and talk with over the next few days. The Youngs are art collectors, and they allowed us to wander through their home and see their extensive collection. I admired four works by Jean Dufy, and two large works by Simbari. There are additional Simbari paintings in the hotel lounge, and they seem to be very appropriate for the climate and atmosphere of Bermuda. A sculptor, Desmond Fountain, was there and told us that some of his pieces are displayed around the hotel grounds.

We had our first meeting with two representatives of the Bermuda National Trust, who would be our local escorts and guides for many of our activities. One, William Zuill, is a past director of the National Trust. The other, Connie Dey, is a present employee. Both turned out to be charming and multifaceted people.

By the time the reception was over, the rain had stopped, and the group made its way to the hotel main dining room for dinner. It is a first class restaurant that serves from a "prix-fixe" menu. We dined in the atrium area, which has a lot of plants and a few of the local tree frogs. They are not much bigger than the end of your thumb, but they make a distinct chirping noise as a part of their mating ritual. The sounds were only occasional and added to the atmosphere. In fact, Ron Gettel thought that they were the result of piped-in sound effects, but a waiter was able to find one and show us that they were real.

It had been a long day, but the trip was starting out with real promise.

II

Wednesday began with breakfast in the hotel's "Atrium Dining Room." Most of our meals were included in the price of the trip, including all meals at the Lantana Colony Club. We noticed that it seemed to take a long time to get breakfast served, and eventually figured out that the *modus operandi* for service was to make everyone at the group table wait for their "next course" until all the people at the table had finished the course before. Good manners generally, but not so good for a travel group breakfast. Once we learned to ask the waiters and waitresses not to do that, the service problem disappeared.

Betsy Chapman, Howard Chapman, Ron Gettel and Patti Gettel.

Activities started with a trip by taxi-van to Woodside, the home of Henry D.W. Laing. The house was once the home of Hereward Watlington, a successful painter and collector, whose collection of European art is now the core of the Bermuda National Gallery. Mr. Laing met us and escorted us through his historic house, a museum, really, full of paintings, sculpture, antiques and history. Much of the furniture was made in Bermuda from cedar, which was native to the island and used to grow in profusion. Recently, it has been blighted and most of it has been lost, and Bermudians are trying to find a way to bring it back again.

Mr. Laing is a genteel and interesting man who has inherited the home and cannot quite decide if it is a blessing or a burden. In any event he has decided, fortunately, that it is his duty to "share it with the public." We learned from Connie Dey that our visit was arranged by the Bermuda National Trust, and that Mr. Laing neither asked nor was paid any compensation for opening Woodside to our group. In fact, this was true of all of the private homes and galleries that we would visit on this trip. The Trust itself did receive remuneration from the operators of our trip; however, Mr. Laing, and others to follow, were "contributing" their portion of our tour in order to help support the Trust.

William Zuill and Connie Dey joined us at Woodside, each resplendent in a "Bermuda National Trust" sweatshirt. It was a clear sunny day, but mild, and a sweater or sweatshirt felt just right.

The group proceeded to Orange Valley, the home of the Cox family. The information furnished us in advance said that Mrs. Cox is the widow of the former Michael Cox, and that her son's name is John. John is a likeable person who, I would guess, is in his mid to late thirties, and was dressed conservatively in dark slacks, navy sweater and tie. John's great, great, great grandfather built the house in 1802, and the family has been there ever since. Like Woodside, it is filled with art, and I was especially impressed with two seascapes by Montague Dawson that were hanging in the den. There was another one upstairs that John Cox recalled only after prodding from Ron Gettel. (Ron is himself an accomplished painter who once studied in the art school at the Art Institute of Chicago.) We took a photo of one of the seascapes for the benefit of our Fort Wayne friend, Max Hobbs.

We proceeded to Garden Gallery, the studio of local artist Otto Trott. We recognized Mr. Trott as one of the customs officers who had cleared us the day before at the airport. His studio contains a number of excellent Bermuda scenes, and especially pictures depicting black families and workers. We then stopped for lunch at a place called The Plantation Restaurant. Not to be recommended.

After lunch we met William Zuill (pronounced "Zoo-el") in the delightful town of St. Georges, the original town in Bermuda. We began with a lecture at Tucker House Museum, open to the public. The Tuckers have always been prominent in Bermuda, but a lot of them were named "Henry," so each is identified in some other way (*i.e.* "President Henry Tucker"). Mr. Zuill seemed to know everything one could think to ask about the house, its furniture and its art; but what astonished me was his incredible knowledge of *American History*. He certainly has a better grasp of it than I do.

We had planned to next visit the Historical Museum, but learned that it was indefinitely closed. It seems that a clerk was discovered fudging the books, and a substantial sum had gone missing. The place was shut down while they tried to decide what to do about it. Accordingly, our next stop was

Howard L. Chapman

St. Peter's Church (Anglican), Bermuda's oldest church, and well worth a visit. An American sailor is buried in the churchyard, the first American to be buried in Bermuda. There are cedar beams in the restored ceiling, memorials on the walls have been restored, and I even enjoyed seeing the Church Silver. It looks ordinary enough, but William Zuill can *talk* about it!

One cannot write for long about Bermuda without mentioning the roofs. Since there is very little fresh water available on the island, the law requires that roofs be designed and built to catch rainwater, which is then stored in basins beneath the building. Each roof is coated once a year with a white, lime-like substance, that helps to treat the water and kill bacteria. Accordingly, the landscape often resembles a sea of bright white rooftops, each distinctive and eye-catching, and this gives Bermuda a special charm that I have not found in any of the islands in the Caribbean.

St. George's has several art galleries, and we were allowed a little time to browse and shop. There must be thousands of original watercolor landscape scenes for sale, and many can be had for less than $100.00. How good they are is, of course, a matter of taste. Before leaving St. George's, we visited the town square, and Ron Gettel and I took the opportunity to have our picture taken in the stocks in front of the town hall. I am told reliably that we are the first tourists to ever do that.

With the day now heading toward 4:00 P.M., we traveled to the fortification known as Fort St. Catherine, where we were met by the amiable

Howard Chapman and Ron Gettel "in the stocks."

and knowledgeable curator, Lance Furbert, for a private, conducted tour. The Fort is well preserved and interesting *if* you have a competent guide. We learned about George, the Fort ghost, and then actually saw him! We also went through the "Light Passage," and learned how ammunition was stored and then brought up-top for use when needed, without blowing up the whole place. There is, curiously, a room that displays replicas of the Crown Jewels. It really is irrelevant to the Fort; but, according to Mr. Furbert, there are local supporters of the Fort who simply would not permit it to be removed. Like most forts, it never saw any real action. Its guns were fired twice in anger, once at a ship that turned out to be Bermudian, and the other time at someone who might have been an enemy, but who sailed away without anyone ever knowing for sure.

After this exceptional, but long day, we were quite content to return to the Lantana Colony Club for cocktails and dinner at La Plage. It was a lovely night, and the sky was crystal clear.

Ron Gettel had been negotiating with our friend Tony to have a television set in his room on Friday night so that we could all watch the Indiana University vs. Boston College basketball game. The NCAA tournament was down to the Sweet Sixteen, Ron is an avid I.U. fan, and he told Tony that it was a matter of life and death.

III

The first thing that has to be said about Thursday is that it was absolutely some of the most perfect weather that anyone could describe, and that it lasted all day. Try to imagine an ideal day to play golf, and this was it.

After breakfast we walked to the ferry boat station at Somerset Bridge, which took about five minutes. Somerset Bridge is billed as "The World's Smallest Drawbridge" because it has a small opening covered by a board which, when lifted, will allow the mast of a sailboat to pass through. One needs a token to ride the ferry, but these are distributed at no charge by Lantana Colony Club to its guests. If you have to buy your own, they cost $3.00 one way. The ferry to Hamilton runs on the hour, but you have to be careful to look at the schedule. On some trips it's a 30 minute passage, on others it takes an hour and a half. Our 10:00 a.m. departure was of the 30 minute variety.

The ferry ride was gorgeous, and entry to the harbor at Hamilton was spectacular on a morning like this. Hamilton is the capitol of Bermuda and is a noticeably clean and attractive little town, with several good restaurants, stores and shops. Everything is geared to the tourist. As our boat pulled in, we saw William Zuill and Connie Dey standing on the dock, all smiles, waving to us. Old friends by now!

Howard L. Chapman

Our first stop was at Par-La-Ville Park, where William Zuill found us a shady spot and gave us a brief history lesson on Hamilton, including the nearby Perot Post Office. (The Perot family has been in Bermuda a long time, and Bermudians pronounce it, emphatically, "Pe-rott," which seems wonderful to me. I shall pronounce it thus for evermore.) We were told that the American Perot, H. Ross Perot, owns a big estate on the island and endeared himself (**NOT**) to the populace when he blew up a coral reef to make a boat mooring for his personal use.

We walked to the Cabinet Building and went upstairs, where Mr. Zuill discussed a number of large oil paintings, including a rather whimsical portrait of Queen Victoria "on one of her better days." While there, we saw the present Premier, the Hon. Sir John Swan, as he was leaving, and Mr. Zuill introduced us to him.

When we left the Cabinet Building, we divided into two groups, one of which went off with Mr. Zuill to the archives. Betsy and I, and the Gettels, joined Connie Dey and the "fast walkers" and made a bee-line for The Cathedral of the Most Holy Trinity (another Anglican church). It's a very fine cathedral, and it is a little surprising to find it in a place the size of Hamilton. It is as if a classic European church were set down in Bermuda. (The pews, by the way, are made from *Indiana* oak.) Understandably, they are very proud of it.

Inside the church, we learned the reason for our haste. Awaiting us was Andrew Trimingham, a member of one of Bermuda's oldest families, owner of Bermuda's largest department store, benefactor of the Bermuda National Trust, and God knows what else. He is also the model for St. Andrew, one of the excellent life size statues of the Saints lined across the front of the church. We arrived with about 20 seconds to spare, and I told him that it was a pleasure to find him there ahead of us. He said that his slavish punctuality was a burden that he has always carried. Connie Dey, of course, knew this, which explained her insistence that we be on time for our appointment with him.

Mr. Trimingham has extensive information on the creation of the works of sculpture in the church. He had known the sculptress as a good friend, had, of course, posed for the statue of St. Andrew, and still had many plans and drawings that were prepared at the time. He had a few with him, and shared them with us. I hope that he takes the time to write his notes and memoirs on the church and the sculpture.

Leaving the Cathedral, the "fast walkers" visited the Bermuda Archives, where we were met by a pleasant lady who had taken a great deal of trouble to select, and lay out for us, a large number of watercolor paintings acquired over the years, showing the history and development of Bermuda from its earliest days until the present. After giving us some background explanation, she allowed us to browse and answered our questions. We continued to be impressed at the variety of activities that were being offered to us.

The rest of the day was on our own in Hamilton, and Betsy, Ron, Patti and I decided to have lunch at a pub called the "Hog Penny." The reverse side of the Bermuda Penny depicts a hog, which is a salute to the wild hogs that populated the island in 1609. At that time a ship, the Sea Venture, was wrecked here, and the hogs were important in providing food to the survivors, and to subsequent settlers. Anyway, the food at The Hog Penny was acceptable and the beer was good, and before we knew it, a lot of the afternoon was gone.

We used what was left of the afternoon for shopping up and down Front Street. I found a belt (festooned with tropical fish), and Betsy bought two bottles of Outerbridges Original Sherry Peppers Sauce, made in Bermuda and, so far as we know, only available there. (I later mentioned the Sherry Pepper Sauce to the van driver, Mr. Rahman, and he said "Ah yes, spice up your soup.") The extra bottle was for Fort Wayne friends and neighbors, Marcia and Dick Adams. Dick was collecting our mail while we were gone, but Marcia got the present. We reasoned that Dick would benefit indirectly.

The 4:00 ferry took us back to Somerset Bridge, and the short walk back to the Lantana Colony Club. We went in to the main building so that I could pick up the copy of the Wall Street Journal that I had ordered, and found that tea was being served in the Lounge. Best of all, *there was no charge for guests*. The news of the day included a story that additional charges have been made involving the Clintons in the Whitewater scandal; and, the fact that the prime rate of interest had gone up to 6.25%, the first increase in five years.

Later, we went as a group to a small Italian restaurant called "Il Palio," located on the second floor of a building on the main highway, not far from our hotel. It was a set menu, but with choices of entrée, and very good.

IV

Our familiar taxi-vans and drivers picked us up and drove us to the Royal Naval Dockyard, located at the West End of Bermuda. The British built it after they "lost the colonies" during the Revolutionary War (or War of Independence, as they prefer to call it). During the War of 1812, the British fleet sailed from here to sack Washington, D.C. Today, the entire dockyard has been transformed into a sort of multi-use theme park and is, I think, a legitimate tourist attraction.

We went first to the heart of the Dockyard, to the Bermuda Maritime Museum, which is operated as a separate entity, with its own Board of Trustees.

Howard L. Chapman

We were met at Commissioner's House by our friend Paul Leseur (manager of Lantana Colony Club), who is presently President of that board (he is also a former Member of Parliament). Paul was wearing a conservative blue business suit which included Bermuda Shorts. In downtown Hamilton, this is a very common sight. Some of the men wearing shorts look almost formal in every other aspect of their attire. Paul was accompanied by Sandy Brown, a member of the museum Board of Trustees, and an architect and engineer.

Commissioner's House is atop a hill in the center of what was once "The Keep," that is, the most highly fortified part of the Dockyard. It's an enormous building that originally housed the Commissioner, but is now in the midst of total restoration for offices, displays and shops. Paul advised us that we were the first group to be taken through the house since the visit by Queen Elizabeth just over two weeks earlier. As we went through, Paul gave us the history of the place, and Sandy Brown explained the engineering and architectural aspects of what was being done to it.

We next went to the museum laboratory where marine archeological recoveries are monitored, including wrecked ships recovered from the ocean, and also relics and booty that were on them. When these items are brought up, they have to be carefully handled and stored in water tanks until sea chemicals can be leached out, and replaced with other substances that will allow them to be brought out into the air again. We were shown an example of a cannonball that had gone untreated and after a time had simply crumbled. An identical ball, that *had* been treated, could be handled safely.

We were introduced to Ivor Grant, the Warden of the Museum, and he conducted us on a tour of several large museum buildings full of historical items, and also explained the fortifications and design of the entire Keep area. Mr. Grant proved to be extremely well versed on everything we saw. As an interesting aside, they keep a herd of sheep on the premises as lawnmowers; however, they have had to plant cactus along the edges of the walls because they were losing sheep over the side.

On leaving the Keep we were met by Mr. Brian Darby, a Bermudian who is something of an institution at the Dockyard. I'm not sure what his official title is, or if he has one, but he is a wonderful storyteller, who advised us right off that there were at least two, and often more, historical versions of events involving the Dockyard, one of which was his. He took us through the Dockyard, including the Bermuda Arts Center and Craft Market, showed us where there are restaurants and a large mall of attractive shops, showed us a sculpture of three huge anchors left by the U.S. Army (the Navy would not have left its anchors), and took us up on the ramparts for a look out to sea. With all of this, it is still a functioning dockyard.

V

After lunch we launched into a very full afternoon of visits to the homes of artists living in Bermuda. First was Tranquility Hill, the home of artist John Kaufmann, who is both a painter and an architect, as well as an inventor and designer. Their home, which is approximately 300 years old, sits on a hill looking over a pleasant yard, then over a harbor and out to sea. The house has a large number of excellent pieces including, of course, many by John Kaufmann himself. John showed me a little of the way he uses the Auto-CAD program on his computer for his architectural work, and I learned that he is on the Compu-Serve network.

The next stop was the home of Sheilagh Head, a painter who does excellent landscapes (and serves lemonade). She had a variety of her work set out for us and was happy to talk about it and answer our questions. Her husband, Pete, is a pilot with TWA, and commutes to New York and Boston! They have lived in Bermuda for 25 years, and their home has a view of the major lighthouse on the island. Only a few doors away, but up the hill, we visited the home and studio of artist Diana Tetlow, who specializes in portraits. She recently spent a year in Kenya living with the Masai, and this resulted in an exhibition in the U.S. I was very impressed with one of her paintings of a Masai warrior. The view from her porch is spectacular, as her house is quite high on the hill, and looks across harbors, bays and islands, and finally, the sea.

We proceeded to the monstrous Southampton Princess Hotel with 1200 guest rooms and a golf course, and also the location of The Sculpture Garden, a salesroom for sculptor Desmond Fountain. Desmond and his wife were there and talked about his work. He makes a mold and casts nine pieces from it before destroying it. If it is a "major work," (a big piece), the prices start at $19,500 for the first six pieces cast, and then go up. The last piece, if it is a very successful work, may cost as much as $65,000.

The last stop was at the home of Dennis Sherwin, an avid collector of various kinds of art that might be called an "eclectic" collection. He has some very nice paintings, prints and drawings, some by "names" like Picasso, but my favorite was a John Kaufmann seascape hanging above his fireplace. Mr. Sherwin was a congenial host, serving drinks and *hors'd'oeuvres*, and took us out on his patio to see his newly constructed bathroom. It was installed for people coming up from the beach below, and to Mr. Sherwin, this was essential. Most stunning of all was the view, with the ocean directly below, and the house designed and built to make the most of it.

We got back to the hotel at about 8:00, and confirmed that there now was, indeed, a television set in our room, and also a case of beer and four tuna sandwiches. Shortly thereafter, Tony appeared with four desserts, so we were well prepared to watch THE BIG GAME (Indiana University vs. Boston College). It was on CBS, and our TV picked up CBS; however, when the game began, the Bermuda CBS affiliate was showing a rerun of "Lovejoy!" Finally, at 9:00, they switched to basketball, but started showing the Arkansas vs. Tulsa game, instead of Indiana vs. Boston College. That game turned out to be a rout, however, and they soon switched to the Indiana game, which was a close one that, sadly, had a bad ending.

VI

Our first destination on Saturday morning was Verdmont, a historic house restored and maintained by the Bermuda National Trust. We were met by Mr. Hugh Davidson, a Vice President of the Trust, who spoke to us about the house, its grounds and its history. It is estimated that it was built around 1710, and was inhabited as a residence until 1950. The last occupant was a "maiden lady" who was born before the turn of the century, lived there all of her life, and never saw the need to install electricity or modern plumbing. Thus, the house is a valuable replica of houses used before those things were available. It has many interesting paintings and furnishings, including some imported items. It used to be more fashionable for Bermudians to have imported furniture, rather than locally made cedar items; however, now that cedar is very scarce, the reverse has come to pass.

The next visit was Camden House, the official residence of the Premier, located within an area that includes the Botanical Gardens. It is not really where the Premier lives, but rather serves as a place for him to receive and entertain prominent visitors "in an appropriate style." Built in the 1700's, it was acquired and restored in 1979 so that even a poor person could serve as Premier and not feel embarrassed about entertaining such guests. The house has a great deal of cedar furniture, but they found that the cedar does not do well with air conditioning. Apparently, cedar likes the usually humid climate of Bermuda, so the air conditioning is used sparingly. In addition to its historic interest, the house contains a number of interesting artworks, especially watercolors. Connie Dey met us here, and gave us a private tour.

For one of the few times since we arrived in Bermuda, it was beginning to rain. Naturally, this coincided with our plans to go through the Botanical Gardens with a private guide. Umbrellas came out, but the rain was too stiff. It was already noon anyway and we decided to begin our afternoon activities. Our vans took us to Hamilton, and we were "released" for the rest of the day. The Chapmans and Gettels made our way to the Harbor Front Restaurant, directly opposite the Ferry Terminal. The food and service were very good and, on a nicer day, it would be pleasant to eat outside on the balcony.

We caught the 2 P.M. ferry back to Somerset Bridge and returned to Lantana Colony Club for a nap, then tea (free!) in the main building, followed by a walk. The rain was past and there was some weak sunshine which gave everything a pastel hue, but it was still a little bit cool.

At 6:30 we left to return to Hamilton by van, for a "gala farewell dinner" at the Bermuda National Gallery. Well, it lived up to its billing. The gallery has only been open since 1992. It was formerly an unused space in the City Hall, but John Kaufmann designed a gallery for it, and it is well done and should be on everyone's "to see" list.

The core exhibit was donated by Hereward T. Watlington, who provided in his will that Bermuda would have it if a proper gallery, with appropriate climate control were built; otherwise, it was to go to the Metropolitan in New York. It is a fine collection of 15th to 19th Century European art, including a large Gainsborough, two paintings by Joshua Reynolds, a Romney, a Murillo, and many other masterpieces. Laura Gorham, the Director of the Gallery, and Connie Dey, met us and escorted us on a tour of all of the wings, and lectured on several works, and their history.

One gallery contains the "Green Door" exhibit, a large number of very good Bermuda watercolors by two sisters who, for many years, operated a series of tea rooms, each called the "Green Door." They supplemented their income by selling their watercolors. Another gallery contains works by a black Bermuda artist named Charles Lloyd Tucker, who painted in a variety of styles.

Several tables had been set for our dinner in the main part of the gallery, and a very good meal was catered for us. We were surrounded by works of a current black artist named Bill "Mussey" Ming, and some of them are very strong.

Bill Ming is a descendant of slaves once owned by the Trimingham family. When slavery was abolished in 1834, all of the blacks in Bermuda assumed the last names of their former owners. The Trimingham family was not in favor of this, and paid their former slaves not to use their family name. The former slaves accepted the money, and then divided into two groups with two different last names – "Trimm," and "Ming."

VII

Sunday, March 27, 1994, was our scheduled day to depart Bermuda and to return home. But neither the Art Institute nor the Bermuda National Trust were about to send us off without squeezing the most out of the morning time we had before our flight took off.

Howard L. Chapman

We finished breakfast, loaded everyone's baggage into the vans, checked out of Lantana Colony Club, and drove to Waterville, a 17th Century building that is the home of the Bermuda National Trust. The property was once part of an estate owned by the Trimingham family, and donated to the Trust by them. The National Trust offices are there, and part of it is a museum, and, of course, it has a shop. Connie Dey met us, and saw to it that the shop was opened in our honor! Wanting to be good guests, most of us bought things. I purchased a small replica of Waterville itself, simply because I thought it was interesting, and then learned that it is one of a numbered set. The lady required my full name, address and telephone number as a condition of purchase because, as she put it, the Trust "wants to keep track of where these go."

We took time outside to admire the view that Waterville has across a small harbor toward a building called Pembroke Hall. There are two or three varieties of ducks, lots of boats and, at least this day, plenty of sunshine. It was quite a pretty spot. Before re-boarding the vans we said farewell to Connie Dey, who had been a most thoughtful hostess and guide for the last six days.

We drove to Orange Grove, the home of William and Joyce Zuill, for a final sendoff from our other guide, William Zuill. The estate consists of 20 acres and has been in the Zuill family since the 1700's. William and Joyce now live in the main house, but earlier (before his parents died) lived in the former servants' quarters which they call "Calabash Cottage," in honor of a giant Calabash tree that grows nearby. I had never seen a Calabash tree, and found it to be very unusual. The fruit is green and the size of large grapefruit, and seem to just "pop out" on the tree wherever they please, high or low, including on the trunk. William said that they smell bad and his family has never eaten them, although he has heard of people who do and say that they are O.K.

The estate grows a variety of fruits and vegetables, and we were served lemonade from lemons grown at Orange Grove. The gardens were full of flowers, especially salvia at this time of year, and Joyce Zuill's gardening touch was evident.

I had been constantly amazed at William Zuill's grounding in history, and was even more impressed by his depth of historical knowledge about Orange Grove. It is no small matter. The house is crammed with art, antiques and artifacts, including works by most of the artists we had met on our visit. There are excellent portraits of William and Joyce Zuill by Diana Tetlow on the inside, and the entire wheel of a wrecked ship, mounted as a swiveling gate, on the outside. Betsy was impressed that the house had two large

Snapshots

dining rooms, one of which was surveyed by a stuffed deer's head brought, obviously, from beyond Bermuda. If I return to Bermuda, high on my list will be to try to revisit Orange Grove and to hear from William Zuill the many stories he didn't have time to tell us.

Joyce and William Zuill at Orange Grove.

At noon, we had to leave to meet our Delta flight, scheduled to leave at 1:30. At Atlanta, the group disbanded as we went in different directions, but we were all complimentary to Nancy Ganiard and Meg MacDonald, and to The Art Institute of Chicago, for their work, planning, and success in making Bermuda memorable.

Chapter 7

KENYA - THE AFRICAN SURPRISE

Out of Indianapolis

The idea for this trip began with our friend and next door neighbor, Marcia Adams, who suggested that six of us travel together in order to have a ready-made group for the vans that are used by all of the safari operators. Each van holds nine passengers, but if there is a group of six traveling together, they usually don't put any more people in that vehicle. Bill and Suzanne Hall were to be the third couple, and all of us signed up and were looking forward to going until, a few weeks before departure, Marcia and her husband Dick had to cancel. The Chapmans and the Halls decided to plunge ahead and, on November 20, 1994, we flew out of Indianapolis with the Ambassadair Travel Club on their L-1011 airplane.

The first leg of the trip went to Nice, France, a 7 1/2 hour flight which crosses six time zones. There were two movies offered, "The Client" and "Casablanca." I didn't watch either because first, the sound was terrible or, second, I was engrossed in *Wind Fall*, the latest William F. Buckley, Jr., sailing book (I was doing research for a Quest Club paper on Mr. Buckley). The flight was uneventful and comfortable except that both Bill Hall and Betsy were on the end of colds, and also the fact that the people who configured the seating in the plane assumed that all of the passengers would be five feet two inches tall. All of us who are taller were folded into our seats like stick insects.

Before one goes to equatorial Africa there are a lot of health precautions to consider. The Ambassadair material had recommended only an anti-malaria regime, but our own research indicated (and we all got): vaccinations against typhoid, tetanus, meningitis, yellow fever, polio (booster); an injection of gamma globulin (against hepatitis); and the malaria stuff. There are some strains of malaria that are now resistant to the available medicine, so everyone also took a supply of insect repellant. We intended to drink only bottled water, but I took a supply of water treatment tablets (Aqua Potable) as a backstop.

We got to Nice at about 5:30AM local time and checked in at Le Meridien, a very nice, four star, French hotel. To my surprise and delight, the hotel had rooms ready and available for all of us at that hour, and I gave Ambassadair a gold star on that account. All of our luggage remained on the airplane overnight, so we had packed our carry-on bags as "overnighters."

I brought one sweater on the trip, a maroon cashmere that I bought in England about 20 years earlier, and have loved ever since. It has been a lot of miles, including our trip to China a few years back. A few miles too many, it appears, because in Nice I discovered a large hole in the elbow. Well, I decided that there was no way that I was going to buy another sweater while abroad (especially at French prices), but I made a mental note to jettison the old one before leaving for home.

Nice is a delight. Even in November it is mild (a few people on the beach), there is a marvelous pedestrian mall area, and lots of good restaurants. We napped, then snacked at a "salon de the," bought 3 bottles of Vittel water (one for Nice and two to carry to Nairobi), napped again, then had dinner *outdoors*. The waitress coaxed us to choose the place by stopping us as we walked by and telling us that: 1) there was a menu in English; and 2) we could eat *then* (about 6:30 PM), instead of waiting for the other places to open at 7:00 or later. The place had no visible name, but the bill said it was the "Aux Thes Nice, Brasserie and Bar." (Note: you can get the house wine in France by asking for "Vin Maison.")

Out of France

Off to the airport with only the usual chaos and one hour departure delay, then a 7 1/2 hour flight to Nairobi, Kenya. We crossed two more time zones, and arrived in the dark. The Nairobi airport is disorganized and unpleasant, but we were met by representatives of our tour operator, Micato Tours, who herded us into vans and drove us and (we hoped) our luggage to the Nairobi Hilton in the downtown part of the city. The lobby of the Hilton was a zoo. There were about 100 arriving Ambassadair people, two flight crews, a contingent of soldiers who were U.N. peacekeepers en route to (or from) Rwanda, plus a mob of people there to celebrate the Hilton Hotel chain's 25th anniversary.

Ambassadair arranged an "orientation" on the deck by the pool, and we had our first bottle of Tusker Beer (one acceptable feature of Kenya). Although there were about 100 people with Ambassadair, it turned out that only fourteen were in our "Kenya Explorer Safari," which was definitely a positive.

Every once in a while, Ambassadair and Micato Tours subjected us to what I came to call a **"schedule joke."** The joke was always on us. The first one occurred the night we arrived in Nairobi. By the time we got to bed it was after midnight and everyone was exhausted; nonetheless, we were told to "have all the bags out at 6:15," meaning get up at approximately 5:30. Just what one needs to hear after two long days of flying and 8 hour jet lag!

As it turned out, it didn't make a lot of difference to me since I could not sleep anyway. The body clock has a way of deciding whether or not one will sleep, and when. The Nairobi Hilton is listed as a "five star hotel," but probably could not stay in business more than six months if it had to compete in an American or European city. "Not to worry," we thought, "because it is going to be a lot better from now on." The only concern was that our schedule called for us to return for a night at the Hilton during the middle of the tour, and again at the end.

Wednesday morning everyone gathered in the hotel lobby, all luggage was identified and loaded into Micato vans, and we met the Micato guides and drivers who would accompany us. Andrew was to be the guide for our fourteen person group, and Kennedy was to be the driver of the van for the Chapmans and the Halls. We got a couple of good breaks here: first, both Andrew and Kennedy are amiable, bright and capable people; and, second, there being three vans assigned to the total group of fourteen, Betsy, Suzanne, Bill and I had an entire van to ourselves.

Out of Nairobi

Our three van caravan set out for Amboseli National Park, after a detour to the airport to try to find the missing suitcase of Anne Lear. (Anne was a member of our fourteen person Micato touring group. Her suitcase was not found.) Amboseli is pretty much due South from Nairobi, and is about a 5-6 hour drive. The first couple of hours were on the "main road" which is paved, but otherwise terrible. Narrow, potholed, and full of vehicles, it also serves as the main artery for pedestrian traffic, and is jammed with domestic animals, donkeys loaded with cans of water or pulling carts, and assorted other obstacles. Games of "chicken" are common and expected. Todd Black, the Ambassadair representative assigned to accompany us, was in our van on this leg, and told us that, "the most dangerous thing you can do in Kenya is to get into a moving vehicle."

After a couple of hours we made a stop at a place set up to provide toilet facilities for tourists, which also gives local Kenyans a chance to set up stores and try to sell things to those who stop. There was a myriad of carved animals, jewelry, batiks, native artifacts, and other craft items. (A batik is an art form that is somewhat like a silk screen. Many of the designs were very attractive.) The vendors set upon the tourists with a vengeance, and, in our case, the hard sell got so bad that we retreated to the vans in self-defense.

After the stop, we left the main road and started down a dirt road for another 2 1/2 hours to Amboseli. It can be called a road, because other vehicles have used it before, but in reality it is just a path over the hard ground, and is like riding on the proverbial washboard. We had to hold on with both hands and, after about an hour, everyone was tired and unhappy, and some were getting headaches and sore backs. A *very* unpleasant ride.

"Amboseli" is a Swahili word that means "Bowl of Dust." Most of the time, I suppose, it lives up to its name, but this was the season of "the short rains," and the dust was not too bad. On the other hand, there was a lot of mud, and an ever present concern about getting stuck.

Not long after turning onto the dirt road we began to see game animals. The first were ostriches, then giraffes, and then gazelles. It became rather commonplace and it really is a wonderful experience to see these animals in their natural habitat. Kennedy was very accommodating (and patient!) and stopped whenever any of us wanted to take a picture. We passed a number of Masai villages and saw hundreds of Masai people (more on that later).

We had to stop for clearance at the entrance of Amboseli State Park and, when we stepped out of the van, there were several more "tradesmen" selling things, especially things made by the Masai. One man tried to persuade me to trade my socks for a Masai necklace. Another wanted to trade for a roll of film or a T-shirt (film is very expensive in Kenya).

After another 45 minutes to an hour we arrived at Amboseli Lodge, where we would spend two nights. How to be charitable? On the exterior, it is reasonably attractive – rustic and scenic. Certainly better than living in a Masai village. It is near the border of Tanzania, and when the weather is right, has a view of Mount Kilimanjaro. We were served a buffet lunch, bought some bottled water (at about $5 per liter!), and got settled in our quarters. These are duplex cabins, and we shared ours with Percy and Beth Clark. Percy is a former NBD Bank executive who is now retired, and he and Beth live in Blackshear, Georgia.

It was a warm afternoon. Amboseli is at 3,500 feet elevation, but is also close to the Equator. The cottage was very hot, but we were advised not to open any windows. During the day the monkeys (black faced varmint monkeys and baboons) will come into the room and carry off things. We heard lots of stories about people who lost their medicine, cameras, and other items. The monkeys, we were told, have even learned to unzip bags that are left closed up in the room. At night, they said, we should not leave the windows open because of mosquitoes. The rooms were furnished with mosquito netting over the beds, but one does not want to take any chances. There is a lot of marshy ground in the area, and plenty of places for mosquitoes to breed.

Amboseli Lodge.

At 4:00 we all assembled for our first Game Run. A long parade of vans filed out of the Lodge, down the road, and onto the Amboseli game preserve. All of the vans are equipped with pop-up tops so that the tourists can stand up and look out, use their binoculars, and take photographs. Bill Hall had the only camera really suitable for that purpose, a Nikon with long lens. Betsy and I each had a point and shoot camera and had decided that she would shoot prints and I would shoot slides. Bill and I also agreed that once home, we would pool our slides on a temporary basis to put together a program on the trip.

Kenya does, absolutely, deliver animals! Baboons, elephants, hippopotami, hyenas, wart hogs, gazelles, water buffalo, zebras, and a huge variety of (to us) exotic birds. Bill and Suzanne are great bird watchers and enthusiasts, and even managed to get *me* excited at seeing blacksmith birds, crowned cranes, secretary birds, flamingoes, and karibu storks. Every van was equipped with a set of binoculars for each passenger and a cooler of soft drinks in case anyone got thirsty.

I had purchased a new Olympus camera for the trip, but began to have misgivings about it because the automatic exposure did not seem to be operating properly. It was taking flash pictures even in bright sunlight. I began to have visions of a lot of wasted film, and was glad that there were a lot of cameras in the van besides mine.

After the game run, we returned to the Lodge and took a bath - which was not such a great experience since there was no hot water. There was some kind of device in the bathroom that was supposed to heat the water, but never did. The rest of our folks reported the same thing.

Dinner was - what to say - edible. A poached fish, boiled potatoes and boiled vegetables. Anyway, there *was* Tusker Beer. Each label has a picture of an elephant with its trunk in the air.

Andrew taught us a Kenyan toast, "TRUNKS UP, ITS TUSKER TIME!"

At a place like Amboseli, everyone goes to bed early. For one thing, they shut off the electricity at 10 PM. Our room was, by now, more or less like an oven, or so it seemed. The temperature had to be in the high eighties, at least. Despite keeping the windows shut, some mosquitoes and other bugs had gotten in. We unraveled and lowered the mosquito netting, slapped on a lot of "Muskol" insect repellant ("100% Deet"), and laid down on top of the sheets to see if we could sleep.

There was a game run planned for 6:30 in the morning, but we were exhausted, and decided that if we ever got to sleep we would sleep through it.

The next day, Thursday, was Thanksgiving Day back home, and we did, indeed, celebrate by sleeping through the game run. The room began to cool down a little bit around 3 AM, and I must have gone to sleep sometime after that. Breakfast was o.k. In fact, breakfast turned out to be the one meal we could usually count on. Of course, it meant eating eggs and sausages, since we weren't sure the milk was pasteurized (for cereal), but it kept me going. When I returned from Kenya I had lost eight pounds, but imagine that my cholesterol count went up about 30 points.

After breakfast, all of the tourists at the Lodge were taken to visit a Masai village. The Masai are a friendly, engaging, attractive, but very primitive people, who live pretty much as they did 1,000 years ago. They are nomads who tend cattle and live off of them. They build villages of huts made with sticks, dung and mud, always in a circle, with the cattle kept in the middle at night. They strew dried branches of thorn trees all around the perimeter to keep out other animals, and it is a very effective barrier. I certainly would not want to try to get through it. The cattle are tended by boys who have not yet reached manhood, and virtually all other work is done by the women. When an area becomes overgrazed, they simply move on and build a new village. The Masai does not consider himself to be a "citizen" of any country, nor does he recognize any national borders.

Somehow, the Masai have always been able to coexist with the wild animals. Several times on the trip we looked over vast expanses of totally desolate terrain and would see, out in the distance, a spot of red. A Masai, walking - to where? Who knows? These areas are full of dangerous animals and yet, as Andrew told us, a lion will not attack a Masai. The same lion that would stalk and kill you or me will run in the other direction at the approach of a single Masai. Is this true? Or folklore? I wonder. At any rate, I can attest that they go forth, alone, and seem to be completely at home in the wildest bush country, armed with nothing more than a long stick.

At the Masai Village. Howard Chapman, Masai Chief and Betsy Chapman.

The Masai, we have been told, object vigorously to being photographed. There is, in fact, a sign posted at the Lodge that says "It is illegal to photograph Masai - Fine KSH1,000." Andrew informs us that, nonetheless, for a fee of KSH700 per tourist, to be paid to the Masai village chief, we will be allowed to take all of the pictures we want, of anything we choose. (The Kenya Shilling is currently quoted at 44 to the US Dollar. It is a controlled economy and the shilling is, of course, worth virtually nothing outside Kenya. KSH1,000 is about $23.00).

There was a tall wooden flagpole in the center of the village flying a white flag which meant, Andrew said, "Peace." The Chief, wearing sunglasses, met us in front of the entrance, and Andrew negotiated the financial arrangements. Then we went in and watched a ceremonial song and dance performed by women - the men have a much different dance that they do as warriors. After the dancing we talked to people, went into a couple of the huts, and browsed around. Most of the women and adolescent children were selling craft items that the people in the village had made, and some of us bought things. The children were poorly dressed, ragged really, but the adults wore beautiful and very colorful robes. Red is the predominant color, which is why it is so easy to see the Masai when they are out in the bush.

Masai man and his children in front of their home.

This particular town has a permanent well and a couple of permanent buildings located outside the barrier of thorn tree branches. It is my guess that the tourist trade has proved to be good enough that this tribe has decided it is worthwhile to stay here for a while. As for the homes, they are as primitive as one would imagine. There is a fire kept going, a pile of papers and cloth to sleep on and, in one, a bicycle. The men and children live in huts that are separate from the women, and each hut has a segregated area to be used when a wife "visits her husband."

Kenya, like all of Africa, is very poor. All of us had brought donations for the Kenya schools in the form of pens, pencils, paper, books, and art supplies. When the Ambassadair plane landed in Nairobi, about a truckload was taken off. Here, we saw a school where the Masai children attempt to learn English (English is the official language of Kenya), and we were asked to help again. The school consists of a place under a tree where a circle has been marked off by rocks on the ground, and there are a few benches inside the circle. Most of the village children gathered and the teacher took them through the alphabet, numbers, and songs in English. Like all children, they were beautiful and wonderful.

The rest of the Kenyans have an interesting relationship with the Masai. On the one hand, there seems to be great admiration for their pride and dignity, and respect for their independence and resourcefulness in the wilderness. On the other hand, there is a history of shunting them around, depriving them of prime grazing areas, and neglect of their education and other needs.

Back to the Lodge for a buffet. The varmint monkeys are all over the place and just look mischievous. Bill and I drank a Tusker Beer with lunch, and then found the idea of a nap very inviting. Tusker is a little more potent than our beers, which may be why the small size bottle is so popular.

When we got up, it was raining, and everyone got on their rain gear. Last August our family had a Chapman reunion at Disney World, and I still had my yellow poncho with Mickey Mouse on the back. Rain at Amboseli means muddy roads and a concern that the vans will get stuck. If that happens, it is a real problem because the presence of the animals makes it dangerous to get out of the vehicles. It is more of a problem on the evening runs than in the morning. If you get stuck and nobody else happens to see you, you won't be missed until after dark, when there is no way to find you in the preserve or to get you out. We heard tales of people being stranded until midnight, or even all night. If the rain is bad enough, the game runs can be cancelled.

Anyway, Andrew finally announced that "We will go." And so, off we went, slipping and sliding. The rain let up and we saw a lot of birds, including karibu storks, a big bird with legs that bend backwards at the knees, and whose head seems to disappear into its body when it is resting. The elephants had headed for higher ground, but we saw hippos, water buffalo, antelope, gazelles and hyenas. Also, an absolutely gorgeous sunset topped off when the clouds parted to reveal, in great majesty, Mount Kilimanjaro.

The Lodge was absolutely packed for dinner. It was Thanksgiving and

Todd Black served everyone Papaya Wine to toast the occasion. We were at the same table as the Two Annes, Anne Mallot and Anne Lear, traveling together. The former is about 20 years older than the latter, but looks much younger than her age, so it was understandable but still the cause of great hilarity when Betsy inquired if they were sisters. Anne Lear could be a stand up comedienne if she chose, and she made the most of it. Suzanne Hall laughed and had so much fun that she pretty much forgot to eat dinner!

If you go to Kenya, be sure to bring a flashlight and extra batteries. When we returned to our room to pack for the early morning departure, there was no electricity *or* hot water. We lit a candle and I went to the Lodge office and found a security guard who accompanied me back to the cabin. He tried several light switches and walked around the building with his flashlight and then pronounced, "There is a problem," and disappeared. The lights went on again in about 30 minutes and we put out the candle, brushed our teeth and packed. The room, again, was at a temperature of about 90 degrees, and there were mosquitoes around. We plastered on the Muskol, dropped the netting, and settled in for yet another short night. The Nairobi Hilton was beginning to look mighty good!

Out of Amboseli

At 5:30 AM a man pounded on the door of our neighbors, the Clarks, and hollered "Jambo," which caused everyone at the Lodge to wake up. I had *been* awake until 3 AM, which made me unhappy about the newest Micato/ Ambassadair **schedule joke**: bags out at six!

After breakfast our three Micato vans headed north in a caravan. The roads were muddy but not as bad as Andrew had feared. (A couple of years ago heavy rains had closed all roads and tourists were stranded for several days and finally had to be flown out.) For some reason, Andrew seemed to be in a big hurry, and Kennedy drove like hell over the muddy, rutted "road," rattling our bones and jarring our teeth, for two hours, until we reached the same pit stop we had visited on the trip to Amboseli. Once there, we learned that we would have to wait for 30 - 45 minutes while the other vans caught up. It was bright and sunny, so Betsy, Bill, Sue and I found a shady place and drank a bottle of pop. One of the local salesmen found me and I succumbed to the extent that I bought a batik - price $40 (he had started at $200). "You are very sharp," he told me.

Eventually the other vans arrived and in due course we drove on to Nairobi, stopping at the Hilton at 12:30. We assumed we would have lunch, but Andrew told us that another **schedule joke** was planned: there would be no lunch until we get to Mountain Lodge, near Nyeri, another 3 hour drive.

Howard L. Chapman

We said we would pay for our lunch twice if we could eat then, but it was no dice, and off we went, headed north out of Nairobi. Fortunately, I had packed some Kellogg granola bars which the four of us ate, and which we were glad to have, and we were able to grab a sandwich on the run at the hotel. One bit of good news - the lost suitcase of Anne Lear had been found and was retrieved at the Hilton (it had gone to Germany).

Driving through Nairobi was an interesting experience because it was a very busy time of day, the streets were full of people and the roads were gridlocked with vehicles. The population of Kenya is overwhelmingly black. When we entered the South side of the city I began to observe how many white people I saw and, when we left the North side, I had seen six (not counting the tourists at the Hilton Hotel). Outside Nairobi, there were no whites at all. There are several tribes represented in Kenya, including Masai and Kikuyu (Kennedy is Kikuyu), and a group called "Bantu," which I think is a sort of mixture of two or more tribes. The tribes have their own languages, but most people also speak Swahili, and English is commonly used by many.

On the way North from Nairobi, Andrew pointed out the town of Thika. It was immortalized by Elspeth Huxley in her book, "The Flame Trees of Thika," which was later made into a successful television program shown on the PBS television series *Masterpiece Theater*. To make the experience complete, we even saw some of the Flame Trees in blossom, showing in real life where they get their name.

Finally, at about 3:30, we arrived at Mountain Lodge, located well up the side of a mountain, and rather isolated. It overlooks a water hole-salt lick that is used by a lot of animals, and is designed with a deck for spectators. Every guest room has a small balcony with chairs so that one can sit there in privacy, if one chooses, with binoculars and camera and watch the constantly changing panorama of wild life below. When we alit from the vans, we walked through a narrow passageway with a high fence on either side, and a shed labeled "Man Hide Hut" every 50 yards. These are for people to duck into if attacked by a wild animal. Such attacks have occurred, from time to time, I was told, by elephants, lions, water buffalo, leopards, and others. There were signs around telling guests to stay within the Lodge, but I doubt that many tourists needed to be told!

Mountain Lodge has an excellent dining room where the food was a pleasant change from Amboseli; the staff is friendly; the rooms are small and rustic, but clean and comfortable; and, because of the altitude, we were refreshingly cool. The best part was watching the animals, and we saw elephants, water buffalo, bush bucks, water bucks, and (during the night) rhinos. There is also a platform on a stick where fresh meat is put to attract cats and we saw one, called a Genet. At night they turn on floodlights, which the animals seem to tolerate. We had just gone to bed when someone came down the hall knocking on all the doors to alert guests to go out on their balconies and see the rhinos. The animals seem to pay no attention at all to the people in the Lodge who are watching them.

We had spent a pleasant evening, explored the shop and bought some nice souvenirs to bring home, and went to bed about 10:00. Hot water bottles were available, and Betsy had hers filled and took it to bed. She said it kept her feet warm all night.

We were up at seven on Saturday morning and found the water hole full of a large herd of water buffalo. I got dressed, took my camera, and went downstairs to the underground tunnel that comes out in a bunker just a few yards from the animals. They saw me at once and began to move away, but I managed a couple of photos.

After breakfast several of the porters came up and asked me to exchange money. Guests had been giving them dollar bills, and they wanted Kenyan shillings. The catch: at the hotel desk they gave me 38 shillings to the dollar; but these guys wanted an exchange rate of 45 to a dollar. They must have found that most tourists wouldn't catch on. Anyway, the amounts involved were small, so I bought all their dollars until I ran out of shillings. They seemed so pleased that I figured it was worth it.

Out of Mountain Lodge

The luggage was loaded onto the Micato vans and we set off for the Mount Kenya Safari Club. En route we crossed the Equator and stopped for a photo opportunity and to serve as fodder for a band of waiting local merchants. Unfortunately, these people are so high pressure in their selling tactics that most Americans are turned off, and some even got angry. Betsy wanted to buy some carved animals, but was reluctant to open the door by even talking about it. Eventually, we went into a shop together and managed to buy a wooden giraffe and a water buffalo, at about the same price as they cost at the Bookstore in First Presbyterian Church in Fort Wayne. Even then, one of the other shop owners berated me as we walked back to the van. Why hadn't I bought those things from *him*!

Bill Hall had a pretty good approach. The salesman would say, "Give me your best price," and Bill would say, "$5." This would generate a lot of moaning and groaning from the salesman, who would insist that the article was a steal at $100. Finally, he would again say, "Give me your best price," and Bill would say "$5." It turned out that he could buy about anything for $5.

The Mount Kenya Safari Club is fabulous. It was started by movie actor William Holden in the fifties and is still luxurious, with beautiful grounds, excellent food and accommodations, and a view (when the clouds part) of Mount Kenya. We were all given a welcome drink and then taken to our rooms, each of which had a fireplace and a view of the mountain. We bought some postcards, and spent a little time exploring the grounds. At lunch, the Halls and Chapmans shared a table with Percy and Beth Clark, the Two Annes, and the Two Janes. (Jane Bloom and Jane Hitchcock were traveling companions.) The food was elegant, and the dessert buffet included an option I have never before seen on a buffet - Bananas Foster.

There is a golf course and clubs can be rented (extra charge for a putter). We visited an art gallery on the grounds and admired a lot of items that were nice but pricey, and stopped to watch a big tree in the middle of a pond that was serving as a nesting place for what must have been hundreds of large birds. There were several varieties of tame birds strolling the grounds, including peacocks and storks.

At 5:00 we joined Bill and Suzanne in the Zebra Bar for a Tusker Beer. Trunks Up!

A little nap, then change for dinner. While changing, a maid came to the room and started a fire in the fireplace. The Club requires that men wear jackets and ties at dinner and, we were advised, "There are no exceptions." We had been warned of this, so all of the men had packed a jacket for this one occasion. The dining room looked like a spawning ground for blue blazers.

The night was cool but the fire kept the room cozy. We went to bed early, wishing we were going to spend another night. With the early bedtime and jet lag, we were up at 5:30 and at 6:00 I went for a walk through the grounds. It was a sunny Sunday morning, and I was delighted to come upon a small, splendid chapel with a cross over the entrance. After breakfast and some last minute shopping, we were off again, heading back to Nairobi.

Out of Mount Kenya Safari Club

Andrew was, again, unexplainably in a big hurry, and Kennedy drove like a man possessed into Nairobi. Kennedy told us that he had attended Kenyatta University in Nairobi and had studied to be a tourist guide. He had proven to be a very capable, knowledgeable and courteous driver, and we resolved to tip him when we got to the Hilton (this would be the last time we would be seeing him). It later appeared that the reason for the hurry was the (unsuccessful) desire to avoid another **schedule joke**. Our itinerary promised we would get to Nairobi "in time to have lunch on your own at one of Nairobi's fine restaurants." Instead, we arrived at the Hotel and were told that the planned

Snapshots

City Tour would begin in an hour. Time only to check in, change some money (to give to Kennedy), eat a granola bar, and leave again!

Every trip seems to have a Canned City Tour, and they are nearly always duds. This was no exception. Too many people jammed into a bus designed to accommodate pygmies, with air conditioning that does not function, listening to a "guide" up front who cannot be heard and, if heard, cannot be understood. For two hours we passed a blur of assorted buildings and landmarks. Fortunately, the tour included a trip outside of town to visit the Karen Blixen Estate, and let us spend 45 minutes there. Karen Blixen wrote the book "Out of Africa," which was made into the movie starring Meryl Streep and Robert Redford. Betsy, Bill and Suzanne had read the book, and enjoyed exploring the estate grounds and museum.

When we got back to the hotel in Nairobi it was nearly 4:00 and everyone was hot and tired, hoping for a bath and maybe a little time to rest. **Schedule joke**. We were to be in the lobby ready to go to dinner at the Pinto home at 5:30. The Pintos are the people who own the Micato Tour Company. They used to have a taxi business called MIni CAbs and TOurs, and when they went into the safari business, they put the first two letters of each word together to make "Micato."

The drive to the Pinto home confirmed that Nairobi, for all its big buildings, is very much a third world city. Dirty streets, litter, broken windows, high heavy fences with broken glass on top around properties, a number of people begging, and lots of things obviously broken and unrepaired. Many people seem to do heavy physical labor, and it was not uncommon to see women with large containers or sacks on their heads, others carrying huge bundles of sticks, or men working with shovels in ditches up to their waists.

The Pintos live in a high rent district and their house is pleasant and airy, stuffed with so many artifacts, *objets d'art*, and African crafts that it almost seems like a store or a museum. Mr. Pinto did not show up (I doubt that he ever shows up) and Mrs. Pinto joined us for dinner, but did not eat. She told us that she entertains tour groups like ours 2 or 3 times a week, and I imagine that she waits and eats with her husband later. The meal consisted of African foods, many of which were identifiable, prepared and served by a servant. We admired some fine ebony carvings that Mrs. Pinto showed us, and everyone signed her guest book (does Kenya have an IRS?).

Mrs. Pinto also told us that all three of their children are grown, married and living in the United States (the Pintos are originally from India).

We returned to the Hilton at 7:30 faced with the task of totally unpacking and re-packing. Tomorrow we would fly on a small plane to the Masai Mara, and each passenger is allowed no more than 33 lbs. in luggage. Betsy and

I boiled everything down to our carry-on bags, plus a lightweight duffle. Everything else was to be left behind and stored at the Hilton until we came back, three days later. We also divided the dirty laundry into three parts, one to leave with the Hilton so we would have clean clothes for the trip home, the second to pack away in the bags we would leave behind, and the rest to take with us to be done at the Mara Sopa Lodge at Masai Mara. Meanwhile, we had discovered that a pharmacy off the hotel lobby sells bottled water for KSH80, whereas the hotel has been charging us 200 for a smaller bottle!

Earlier, Bill Hall and I had talked about the daunting prospect of flying on a small, propeller driven plane, into the African Bush. I was a little concerned, but Bill explained to me that this was simply one of the risks one assumes when one travels. I felt better.

Here are some Swahili words: Jambo (Hello); Asante Sana (Thank you very much); Hakuna Matata (No problem); Karibu (Welcome, you're welcome); Mara (open plain); Uhuru (Freedom).

Out of Nairobi (Again)

The bags had to be outside the room at 6:00, but at least we had gotten a little sleep. The Hilton breakfast buffet was good, and Betsy and I were the first people there when it opened. At breakfast, we were joined by Percy and Beth Clark. Percy gave me his three rules for making life easier: 1) Do not open third class mail; 2) Do not be the one who does the pushing on the revolving door; and 3) Do not expect anything from the government.

After breakfast we had a little time in the room which gave me a rare chance to read my Buckley book. I reexamined my red sweater with the hole in the elbow and decided, what the heck, I'll take it along. At 9:00 we were off to the airport, but to a different terminal serving private carriers. It is much nicer than the international terminal, including toilets with seats.

We boarded Air Kenya, a 16 passenger plane that Andrew described as a "twin Otter." It was the last time we would be with Andrew, so we gave him a tip. (Micato had recommended tips of $4-$6 a day per person for the drivers, and $2-$4 a day for the guides). It was raining when we took off, but we soon flew into better weather, and had a pleasant and interesting 45 minutes flight to the landing strip at Keekorok Lodge. Micato vans drove out to meet us, and we met our new group guide, Osman, and Charles, the driver of our new van. The vistas here are incredible. There had been a lot of rain, the vegetation was lush, and we were reminded of "The Green Hills of Africa." Todd Black told Suzanne Hall that she looked like she belonged in Africa, and that she could pass for one of the British settlers. (From what I could see, none of them seem to be around anymore.)

Snapshots

It was about a 45 minute ride from Keekorok Lodge to the Mara Sopa Lodge, which is located just outside the limits of the Masai Mara National Park. "Sopa," it turns out, is the name of a chain that has a number of lodges in game areas. Each couple was assigned to a separate hut with a thatched roof, and with an "appropriate" African name. The Halls were assigned to a hut called "Crocodile," ours was "Baboon."

The huts were sparsely furnished, with only two beds and a luggage rack for furniture, plus a wall mirror with a shelf. The walls of the bathroom were made of flagstone, without mortar, as was the fireplace (only used, we were told, in July). The molding along the ceiling and around the doors was pulled away from the wall by a good half inch to an inch and this, coupled with the flagstone construction, seemed to offer a perfect place for all kinds of critters to live/hide. Sure enough, on the shelf next to the mirror was a can of insecticide. The label said it *"Kills All Dudus Dead!"*

Our first meal, lunch, was such that I was satisfied that we would not starve; however, I was also sure that we would finish eating up the granola bars and cheese and crackers we had brought. There was a sign in the dining room that told us that we were 206 kilometers south of the Equator, and at an altitude of 2104 meters (more than 6,000 feet). At least it ought to be cool at night.

After lunch, we strolled around the Lodge to the extent that we could. There are signs all around the perimeter warning guests to stay within the

Elephants crossing our path in the Masai Mara.

marked areas, because of danger of wild animals. How, I wondered, do the animals know to stay on *their* side? There is an attractive (though seldom used) swimming pool, and wonderful vistas from the main Lodge and from most of the huts. There was time for a nap and then off at 4:00 for a game run.

The difference in foliage, as compared with Amboseli, was striking. Here, there was an abundance of vegetation, trees, streams, and lots of bush area. We came across Topi, Gazelles, Hartebeests, Wildebeests, Impala and Lions. Most interesting was an enormous herd of water buffalo. One concern, the reserve has so many vehicles running all over it that the terrain is being torn up and rutted by tires. Before long, there may not be any habitat left for the animals.

While we were out a van got stuck and some German tourists waved us down. The drivers talked, and ours said he would ask a 4-wheel drive vehicle to come and pull them out. The roads in the park are really just paths and full of ruts and chuckholes. At one point we hit a hole and I bounced up and cracked the top of my head on the roof of the van – ouch$*&$@%. That night, Bill Hall gave me some ibuprofen to help ease my sore neck and head.

By dinner time it was starting to rain, and we all walked to the dining lodge in our ponchos and carrying umbrellas. During the meal, the rain came down in buckets, some of it coming through the thatched roof and making puddles on the floor. A buffet was served, and a grill had been set up from which a cook offered several different kinds of meat. We bought more bottled water (captive customers), and watched some dancers, the last of which were Masai men. They wore bright orange sarongs and carried sticks, and did a kind of chant and grunt, finished by a series of remarkable jumps. They seem to stand flat footed and, hardly bending their knees, go straight up in the air by as much as three feet.

It was still raining after dinner, but lighter, and we walked with umbrellas to the building where they feed the hyenas at night. A large area between the building and the bush is lighted, and there is a deck for the tourists to stand and observe. An employee of the Lodge walked out to the center of the lighted area (brave man) and threw raw meat in all directions, then hustled back onto the deck. Almost immediately the hyenas came charging out of the underbrush, perhaps as many as a dozen, and carted the meat off into the darkness. Our guide, Osman, told us that hyenas will occasionally attack a man or another animal, but usually not until they are reasonably sure that the victim is dead or too sick or wounded to retaliate. Even a wounded lion would not be immune.

As we walked back to our huts along the dark path I commented that those hyenas were probably not far away from us. Bill Hall agreed and pointed out that Africa is also known for an abundance of poisonous snakes. I took out my flashlight and began illuminating the path ahead of us.

It is easy to be in bed by 10:00 since there is nothing else whatsoever to do here. Still, we were a little apprehensive about "who else might be sharing our room." A direct quote from my traveler's log that night says, "I do not want to turn out the lights in this place!"

The next morning, Tuesday, November 29, offered the opportunity for a balloon ride at dawn; however, it cost $390 per person, and most of our group decided that, at that price, we could stay on the ground and sleep a little longer. Still, at 5:25 AM a man banged on our door and yelled "Jambo - Good Morning," and everybody started getting up to go on the 6:30 game run. There was no hot water, so I simply got dressed and went to the Lodge, where coffee was available.

Our driver, Charles, told us that, because of the heavy rain last night, we will not risk driving off the roads in the game park; however, 5 minutes later he blithely took off across a field to go see some lions, digging huge ruts and demolishing the terrain. When we got there, 7 or eight other vans were doing the same thing - but the lion, a grown male, seemed unconcerned. A moment later a female weaved her way through the collection of vehicles to the male and, to the delight of the crowd, they mated. Charles told us that these two lions are "on their honeymoon," during which a pair of lions will separate from the pride for about ten days for mating. Soon, the male ambled off, still showing no acknowledgement at all of his audience.

A lone lion (if you can spot him) surrounded by a plethora of safari vans.

Howard L. Chapman

We drove to another spot (off the road) and saw a cheetah, again with lots of other vans for company. The cheetah had made a kill earlier in the day and was resting. We could see a hyena, 50-75 yards away, finishing off the carcass, and two vultures sat in a tree above, waiting their turn. Nature's disposal crew. Later that day Betsy counted 27 vehicles surrounding a lion!

On the way back to the Lodge, we saw one of the other Micato vans stuck, and some of the folks were out trying to push it. Not too comfortable a feeling, since, as Charles pointed out, "there are usually a lot of lions around there." The pushers got the van going and then ran like crazy to catch up, which was easy because it got stuck again. Finally, someone dispatched a 4 wheel drive Jeep to pull them out and, when we returned for breakfast, the van driver and Osman, who was in the van, were both pretty embarrassed. Breakfast, at 8:30, was the usual (and relatively safe) sausage and eggs.

We hurried back to "Baboon" after breakfast because electricity would go off at 10:00 and hot water would go off at 10:15; but, the houseman had been in the room and taken all of the towels, without leaving replacements. A frantic search turned up both him and some towels, and we managed to get showers while the water was still hot. How was the trip going at this point? My traveler's log says, "Only 3 more nights in Kenya!" Percy Clark was sharing my thoughts. He said that "When I get home, what I took for granted is going to seem like luxury."

There was a lot of time to kill until the next scheduled game run. Several people gathered on the Clarks' porch to socialize, and I tried to catch up on my reading. It started to rain again, and got cold, which for some reason seemed to bring out the mosquitoes. I put on my sweater (thank goodness I brought that sweater!) and jacket, and applied Muskol to every place that was still exposed. Someone should have warned us that this was the "season of the short rains," which seems to mean that there are a lot of short rains, one after another. At the Mount Kenya Safari Club I had met a man who, discussing tourism, said that "this is the low season." Small wonder. When it rains, you can't put up the tops on the vans, the animals seem to disappear, the vans have to (or *ought* to) stay on the roads, and it is cold and depressing to be at Mara Sopa Lodge.

The discomfort was aggravated because no one had forewarned us, and people had left most of their warm clothes back at the Hilton in Nairobi. My traveler's log at 3:40 PM says; "I am sitting on the porch of 'Baboon.' Betsy is reading inside because it is too cold out here. I am wearing a shirt, a sweater, a safari vest, and a lined jacket. I would put on more clothes if I had them. It has been raining, the air is damp and clammy, and I can see more rain coming.

Snapshots

People are heading for the Lodge for the 4 PM game run, but I am going to pass."

I did pass and so did Percy Clark. The two of us sat in the Lodge and shivered (he had even fewer warm clothes than I did) and commiserated over coffee. I met two women from Spain who spoke no English, and they were glad to find someone to chat with. Virtually no one here, they said, spoke Spanish.

At 5:45 two of the vans returned, but the van with Betsy, Bill and Suzanne did not. I talked to Osman who said that at least 4 and possibly as many as six vans from the Lodge were stuck out in the park. I was worried, but our van showed up about an hour later. It had been stuck, but within view of the Lodge, and had required eight men pushing it to free it. Osman told us that if the other vans can't get out of the mud, "Helicopters will be sent to rescue them." (Frankly, I was dubious about this, but said nothing.)

Dinner was only partly buffet, with the rest served at the table by our waiter, "Bob," who had been very friendly, attentive and efficient ever since we arrived. It was just occurring to me that he would be assigned to our table throughout our stay. After dinner, some sort of video was being offered somewhere, and a few people went to see the hyena feeding. It rained again all through dinner, and I began to get leery of tomorrow's program – a long drive to the Mara River and the border of Tanzania. I might, I thought, go if it is a nice, sunny day.

Well, the next day, Wednesday, *was* a nice, sunny day, clear cool air, green hills and birds singing. Unhappily, Mother Nature was advising me that it would not be wise for me to venture off into the bush to spend five hours in a van. I saw everyone off and retired for a shower and a rest, then applied more insect repellant and went outside to read. About 11:00, the temperature began to drop again, and the rain returned, bringing mosquitoes with it. A mosquito sets off a whole different set of alarm bells when you know that it may be carrying malaria. Malaria has an incubation period of 2 to 3 weeks, so we won't be sure we're all right until New Year's. Something extra to celebrate.

At 1:15 the vans returned, and reported seeing hippos and crocodiles, and having "set foot in Tanzania." I had anticipated lunch with cheese and crackers from my suitcase larder, and Betsy and I skipped the dessert in favor of "Kudo" bars, also brought from home. Tusker beer at lunch made us all eager for a nap. My traveler's log says: "Mañana salimos. Gracias a Diós!"

The evening game run set off at 4:00, but Charles said that, this time, he really would not get off the roads. We all emphatically reinforced his decision. He said that, the week before, his van was stuck in the park at night and they did not get back until 11:00 PM. We did not want to repeat that experience!

Besides, said Charles, the tires on his van were "not very good." Bill Hall confirmed this. The tires were in fact, he said, "smooth."

By 5:00 it was raining hard and we had to put down the top on the van and headed back to the Lodge, which was o.k. with us. The rain continued through the dinner hour, and we needed umbrellas and our ponchos to walk from the huts to the dining area. I decided to list some of the positive things in favor of Micato on this trip, and here they are:

1. They gave everyone a safari hat. We *needed* these, and lots of other tourists did not have them.
2. They flew us in and out of the Mara. Other guests at the Mara Sopa Lodge had driven for six or seven hours over bad roads to get there.
3. It was interesting to visit the Pinto home.
4. The guides and drivers have been excellent.

I had a little time to read William Buckley during the day. I've now read six of his books, plus a biography by John Judis, and I'm beginning to feel as if I know him. I hope I'll get the chance to meet him, I think I'd like him.

Out of Masai Mara

Thursday was another gorgeous morning, and Betsy and I were up early and walked around the grounds of the Lodge before breakfast. (We had hidden our towels from the houseman so that we would be able to use them when we returned to Baboon after breakfast.) After eating, we packed up and assembled in the lobby of the Mara Sopa. The vans left at 9:00 AM and drove for 35-40 minutes to Keekorok Lodge, where we waited for our airplane. There was a lot of time to wander about, to go into a guest room, and we discovered that Keekorok Lodge is much nicer than Mara Sopa Lodge. Why, I wondered, didn't we stay *here*?

Eventually, we drove out to the airstrip, took some pictures, said goodbyes and gave tips, and got on Air Kenya for the flight back to Nairobi. During the drive over, Charles had commented about a certain man whom he described as "a good man, a Christian." When I said goodbye to him, I asked him if he was a Christian, and he said yes. I said, "So am I. I wish you peace." Big smiles and we shook hands. "Yes," he said, "peace is the best thing." It was a nice moment.

After a smooth flight we returned once again to the Nairobi Hilton, where we retrieved our luggage and checked into our rooms. We had some time, so Betsy, Bill, Sue and I took a cab to the Norfolk Hotel for a drink. It is lovely and charming, and far superior to the Hilton. Why, I wondered, didn't we stay *here*? Among other pleasant things, Bill and I were able to buy copies of the *Herald Tribune* (yesterday's), and to get caught up on the news. Here is some of it:

The U.N. is threatening to pull out of Bosnia. (The Serbs are worried about this?)

Congress is about to vote on the GATT agreement. It is expected to win easily in the house, but be close in the Senate. President Clinton is for it, and there are people pro and con in each party.

The Dow Jones Industrial Average is at 3738. The Prime Rate is 8.5%. The British Pound is at $1.56, and the Japanese yen is at 99 to the dollar.

The Bears have a record of 8 - 4 and lead the Central Division.

Norway has voted (once again) to stay out of the European Union.

We returned to the Nairobi Hilton by cab at a cost of KSH200. The cabs have the windows fixed so that they are always open. Whenever our cab stopped in traffic, small boys would run up and thrust their hands in, asking for money, pens, or sweets. We had been warned that, whenever this happened, to hang on tight to purses, cameras or other loose articles. Betsy gave the first boy a pen from her purse, which promptly produced a swarm of additional boys.

Once back at the hotel, we browsed through some nearby shops and bought a few souvenirs. We had been warned not to stray very far from the hotel (where there were lots of policemen) because of street crime. Even where we did go, we were stopped several times by men with a broad variety of excuses and lead-in lines. Andrew had said that virtually all such persons are thieves.

We returned to our rooms to totally re-pack one last time. We were going to the "Carnivore" restaurant for dinner, and Micato gave everyone traditional African clothing for the event. (They also gave each person a rather nice Batik.) Once again, we would pack enough clothes for 2 days in our carry-on bags, since our luggage would stay on the airplane while we spent the next night in Lisbon, Portugal.

When we assembled in the hotel lobby, there was a bulletin board set up by Ambassadair with the latest **schedule joke**. Bags were to be placed outside the hotel rooms at 4:15 AM! Breakfast would be at 5, and then we would go to Nairobi airport for a 9 AM departure.

The Carnivore specializes in meat. It is an open air place located at the end of a dirt road, about 30 minutes from the Hilton (when there is no traffic). Waiters come around to the tables with big hunks of cooked meat, and slice it onto your plate. The "game meats" offered this night were Eland (a large antelope), Crocodile and Zebra. The customers are exclusively tourists. Bill Hall sampled all the game meats and pronounced them "good." I took his word for it. By 9 PM they had not yet served dessert, but we were all zonked after a long, tough day (after 10 long, tough days), and oppressed by the knowledge that we would have to get up so early the next morning. The Ambassadair people began to file out, and we joined them.

Howard Chapman, Betsy Chapman, Suzanne Hall
and Bill Hall at the Carnivore Restaurant.

Out of Africa! ☺ !

Breakfast at the Hilton was identical to the prior experiences, but a great relief after the Mara Sopa Lodge. (In fairness, Betsy had *liked* the food at the Mara Sopa Lodge. Go Figure!) The lobby was a sea of bags and commotion. Todd Black presented each of his brood with a gift, necklaces for the ladies and key chains for the men. Very nice.

The process of getting through customs at the Nairobi airport was endless and agonizing - and pointless. It seems that the more despotic the government of a nation, the more red tape and rigmarole at customs. Once we got into the area of the duty free shops, I approached one of the women behind a food counter and offered her the maroon sweater. I explained that it had a hole in the elbow, but she seemed genuinely pleased to have it.

Snapshots

Our plane finally lifted off, and Percy Clark and I exchanged high fives. We were happy. Five and 1/2 hours later we landed at Cairo and spent two hours on the ground (without leaving the plane) for refueling, then flew another 5 1/2 hours to Lisbon. We transferred to the Sheraton Lisboa, which proved to be an excellent hotel (impeccable plumbing, instant hot water, *potable* water) and got in the rooms at about 8 PM (10 PM Kenya time).

A quick bite in the coffee shop for us, and then to bed, but for a lot of the Ambassadair people, it was time for another **schedule joke**. They had signed up for a night tour of Lisbon, and set off at 9 PM (having been up for 18 hours after a short night) for an evening of night clubs and Fado music!

Out of Lisbon

We were up early and had breakfast, and then Betsy and the Halls left for a city tour of Lisbon. I cancelled and instead walked to the harbor (about a 40 minute walk) and the heart of the old city of Lisbon. The pedestrian mall in the old city has tiled pavement, shops, balloon vendors, street theater, and lots of outdoor cafes. Even though it was December 3rd, people were having their morning coffee outdoors. It was great to be in Europe!

The flight back provided the last opportunity for a **schedule joke**. Because we were on a chartered plane, we could have left Lisbon much earlier, but did not do so until after 3 PM. With a 2 hour stop for fuel in Gander, we did not reach Indianapolis until about 8:30 PM (6:30 AM in Nairobi), after which we had to clear customs, go get our car, and drive back to Fort Wayne. It was a long, tough drive home but, as always, worth it.

SAFARI CHECKLIST:

The following is a checklist of items recommended by Micato tours for your Safari:
- Adaptor, 3-hole type, for electric items. Kenya and Tanzania use 220 volt electricity
- Any special medicine or prescription you will need while on safari
- Ann-malaria pills
- Ballpoint pen and paper for notes (Inexpensive ball point pens are much appreciated by village school children)
- Binoculars (each client receives complimentary use of Binoculars)
- Camera/equipment/film (film is considerably less expensive in the U.S.)
- Chapstick/moisturizing cream

- Correspondence/postcard address list
- Cotton bush jacket/windbreaker
- Electrical/battery operated items: razors, hair dryers, rollers, etc.
- Extra batteries
- Extra pair of prescription glasses if you wear them (copy of prescription)
- Extra set of luggage keys (if available)
- Hat, visor or scarf
- Insect repellant
- Laundry soap
- One sports coat and slacks/One dress and shoes
- Passport, health card for Tanzania, travellers checks, credit cards,
- Driver's licenses
- Pocket-size calculator
- Reading material
- Several pairs of shorts/slacks/shirts/blouses/skirts
- Small lightweight flashlight
- Small travel alarm clock
- Snack food while on Safari in Tanzania
- Suntan lotion and sun screen
- Sweater/light jacket
- Swimsuit/bathrobe
- Toiletries/personal cosmetics
- Two pairs of sunglasses (in case one is misplaced)
- Walking shoes/tennis shoes/casual shoes/sandals (2 pairs)
- Wash-N-Dry towelettes, Kleenex packets

Chapter 8

TURKEY

I

This journal begins in Chicago, on September 27, 1995. The plane connections between Fort Wayne, Indiana, and Chicago, have become so unreliable that Betsy and I decided to fly up a day early in order to be sure that we didn't miss our flight the next day to Istanbul.

September is always pleasant in Chicago and we booked a room at the Park Hyatt, across the street from the Water Tower. There was an added incentive to go a day early: the Art Institute was hosting its Monet Exhibit, which was a huge success. It had been written up in TIME, and was drawing enormous crowds. Dinner at old favorite, Avanzare, and breakfast at the Drake, and time left over for some shopping. (Why do they call it "Filene's Basement" when you have to go up three floors to get to it?)

We were booked on Lufthansa to go to Turkey and join a tour with Abercrombie and Kent, who had given us two guidelines: a) do not drink the water; and b) do not send out laundry. In view of (b), I decided to buy two more pair of socks for the trip.

Lufthansa flies out of the United Airlines terminal under some kind of reciprocal agreement with them, and we were able to use UAL frequent flyer miles to upgrade to business class. At the terminal, we found Bill and Suzanne Hall, our traveling companions, and spent a couple of hours before flight time in the Red Carpet Room. Bill and Suzanne were both fighting colds, but seemed to be about out of the woods with them.

The flight left on time (German punctuality) and we settled in for the first leg. I had brought two books, *Hitler's Diplomat* (a biography of Von Ribbentrop), and David Brinkley's *Washington Goes to War*. All four of us were carrying an assortment of Turkey books, including the Fodor and Frommer guides. To help us procrastinate with our reading, there was a little TV at each seat on the airplane, showing movies. Today they were offering a choice of *Don Juan de Marco, Blue Sky, Casper,* and *Outback*. We had seen *Don Juan de Marco*, so Betsy chose to read, and I switched back and forth between *Blue Sky* and *Casper*.

II

We landed at the Lufthansa hub in Frankfurt, a huge, crowded airport, and between planes I was able to buy a copy of the *International Herald Tribune* (one cannot travel properly without occasionally reading the *International Herald Tribune*). We learned that the O.J. Simpson murder trial is finally over, after more than a year, and the parties are preparing for final arguments. Also, President Clinton and the Republican Congress have been unable to agree on a budget, and have signed an "interim funding bill" in order to avoid a default by the government. Would a government shutdown really be so bad? Other news items: "NATO may use force in Bosnia;" "Japan may have to bail out its ailing banking system;" and, "The Chicago Bears are 2 and 2."

Here are a few statistics for posterity: the Dow Jones Industrial Average is at 4,770; the prime lending rate is 8.75%; a cab from downtown Chicago to O'Hare Airport costs $30; and the Turkish Lira (written "TRL") is at the rate of 48,000 to the dollar (yes, one dollar).

The flight from Frankfurt to Istanbul was another three hours and we were surprised that it took that long. On arrival, we were all just about shot, but still excited about being in this exotic city. Istanbul sits on both sides of the Bosporus, a body of water that is the dividing line between the continents of Europe and Asia. The Prime Minister of Turkey is a woman named Tansu Ciller, or at least she was until a few days before we arrived. She had just resigned amid public unrest, and a massive general strike, with some disturbances, and we hoped that none of this would affect us while we were there.

Abercrombie & Kent had arranged for us to be met at the airport by a nice young man named Aton, who took us to a van with a driver to bring us to our hotel. He said that we would meet our A&K guide tomorrow, a woman named Olcay Bergman, pronounced, he said, "Ole-jigh Bahg-mann."

Here are some first impressions recorded on the way into the city from the airport:

Snapshots

> Even though it's late September, it still seems to be very much summer here;
> Traffic is out of control. I'm glad *I'm* not driving;
> No evidence of extreme poverty;
> Istanbul is a really big city (12,000,000);
> Cars drive on the right-hand side of the road;
> Turkish sounds like gibberish to me. I have no sense at all of what is being said.

After a long drive we arrived at the Ciragan Palace, a Kempinski hotel that once really was a palace, at least part of it was. A friend had told us that, if we came to Istanbul, we should be sure to stay there, and he was right. It is a magnificent place, fully restored and modern, with beautiful grounds and a spectacular view across the Bosporus. ("Ciragan" is pronounced "Sha- ran.")

We knew we were going to need some bottled water, and had noticed that there was absolutely no place close to the hotel that might sell it, which left only room service. Four large bottles cost TRL840,000 (840,000 Turkish Lira), and it took some courage to sign the tab. I told Betsy that I was sure that James Bond did not have to run around Istanbul worrying about whether or not he should use bottled water to rinse out his toothbrush.

The hotel had furnished us with a beautiful basket of fresh fruit, which we took out onto the balcony to eat while we looked across the Bosporus to Asia, and then took a nap. By the time it began to get dark the temperature started to drop, and we turned off the air conditioning in the room.

We had arranged to meet Bill and Suzanne for dinner at the Ciragan Restaurant, just off the hotel lobby. Dinner with wine was excellent, but it was hard to get used to the inflated exchange rate. Our dinner came to TRL 2,745,000 (plus 15% for a tip!). Still, this amounted to less than $65.00.

After dinner we strolled through the fabulous "Palace" portions of the hotel, and around the grounds. We came upon a rather lavish gambling casino that is a part of the Palace, but found that one could not enter unless he first registered at a window at the entrance and presented a passport and a photo I.D. This apparently is because the casino is only supposed to be open to tourists, and Muslims are prohibited from gambling. There were lots of "bodyguard" types standing around in gray pants and blue blazers, looking sinister, for the apparent purpose of enforcing this rule. Nevertheless, we watched several luxury cars pull up in front of the Palace, driven by chauffeurs, and the occupants, obviously affluent Turks, got out and went into the casino.

The only crisis of the day occurred when Betsy discovered that she had forgotten to pack two pair of daytime slacks. From what we had seen so far, it would not be easy to replace them in Turkey.

By 10:00 o'clock, we decided to head for bed, after one more stroll out on the balcony to look at the phenomenal vista across the water. By 11:30 I was still awake (jet lag) and got up to seek out a sleeping tablet. I didn't know it then, but I was in for the worst bout with jet lag that I have ever experienced.

III

The weather on Friday morning was cool and gray, but the Ciragan Palace continued to please with a very good breakfast. After eating, we met our guide Olcay, and also a lady named Yelda Okan who works for a local travel company called Iliada. Iliada acts as an agent in Turkey for Abercrombie & Kent.

The typical A&K tour is usually 15 people or less, but ours was 19, 20 counting Olcay. Happily, we had been furnished with a large bus that would hold 100 people, so there was plenty of room for everyone to spread out comfortably as we set out for a day of sightseeing in Istanbul.

Our first stop was the Hippodrome, which once was the Emperor's stadium and racetrack, and is the site of an Egyptian obelisk which dates from the 15th century B.C. (Pity Egypt. Her treasures and artifacts have been plundered to all parts of the world.) From the Hippodrome, we went to the famous Blue Mosque with its six minarets. When the Blue Mosque was built, between 1609 and 1617, some Moslem clerics complained because the Mosque in Mecca also had six minarets, and it was not deemed appropriate for Turkey to have a Mosque with the same number. Since Mecca was then under Turkish rule, however, the Sultan simply told the Arabs to add another minaret to the Mosque in Mecca, because the Sultan was not going to change the Blue Mosque.

The Mosque is carpeted, immaculate and generally fabulous. According to the usual custom, visitors must remove their shoes before they enter. Olcay gave us all little cloth bags for carrying our shoes into the Mosque so that they would not "get lost" while we were in there. She advised that the Turks are very honest, but that Istanbul is a big city and there are a lot of non-Turks around.

When we left the Blue Mosque we walked to the nearby Museum of Turkish and Islamic Arts, originally the residence and palace of Ibrahim Pasa, built about 1524 as a grandiose home. It is interesting enough to see, but its major importance to us seemed to be the fact that it had reasonably clean and modern restrooms for tourists. (Western style, rather than a hole in the ground.) These are fairly rare in Turkey, and the tour company had been

Snapshots

careful to schedule our itinerary to hit them, like reverse oases, at critical intervals. We learned that, at virtually all of these "public" toilets, there will be a man or woman sitting at the door collecting a small amount of money as a fee. This particular man wanted TRL10,000 ($.20), but I had no small Turkish money. I borrowed TRL5,000 from fellow traveler Ed Eigner, and handed it to the man with a smile, and he let me go (pun intended).

The next stop was the Hagia Sofia (pronounced A-Ya So-Fee-A), which is not very far from the Blue Mosque. It is a huge place, first built in the year 537 as a Christian cathedral. It has lots of beautiful mosaics around the walls, but many of the tiles are missing because people have been stealing them for souvenirs. The dome is huge, 55.6 meters in diameter, and Olcay told us that it was the largest in existence at the time that it was built. The Hagia Sofia has been razed twice, and the present version required 10,000 men and six years to build. In 1453, when the Moslems took over Istanbul, it became a mosque, and was used as a mosque for centuries. When Ataturk came to power, he declared that it should become a museum, which it is at this time.

Olcay asked if there were any Scandinavians in the group and, when I raised my hand, she took me to a stone railing where a Viking prince had carved his name in runic letters in the 9th Century. (My maternal grandfather was born in Copenhagen, Denmark.)

The place was **full** of school children, all in blue outfits, paired off in columns, and holding hands as they marched through with their teachers. They all seemed to be somewhere in a range of ages of about 10-12, and there were busloads and busloads of them. They were a delight to watch.

We proceeded on the bus to the "Basilica Cistern," which is an underground reservoir built by the Romans, and used by them to store water. It is an incredibly vast, cavernous place, dimly lit by electric lights, with only a few feet of water in it today. When it was built, the Romans needed stone columns to hold up the roof, and in many places they used statues, or parts of statues, from ancient cities and shrines. The water that is in the Basilica now comes from seepage, through the roof. There are raised wooden walkways so that tourists can wander through the place, and the walkways, of course, get wet too, so you have to watch your step. The water is very clear and there are fish in it, and one can see coins lying on the bottom. The coins are collected periodically and used to buy food to feed the fish.

The Basilica was "lost" for centuries after the Romans left, but was rediscovered when someone noticed that people living above it would lower buckets through holes in their floors, and bring up excellent water - sometimes with fish in it. The Turks have installed a sound system which constantly plays soft (and pretty weird sounding) music, which adds to the effect. It doesn't cost very much to go in, and apparently a lot of Turks like to go there to relax. In one area, there is even a small cafe with tables and chairs where people bring their newspapers and sip coffee.

We were gradually adjusting to the fact that we always needed to be on the watch for an opportunity to get bottled water. **Nobody** drinks the water in Turkey. The tour company had provided a cooler on the bus, with a large number of small, individual bottles of water, and we had our first chance to use the "tall straws" that we had brought from home. This was a tip learned from Suzanne Hall when we were in Kenya. Straws are a good idea because you can't always be sure the bottles are exactly clean, but if you have regular sized straws, they tend to disappear down into the bottle.

It was well into the lunch hour, and we were running late, when we arrived at the "Spice Bazaar," a large covered bazaar area also sometimes called the "Egyptian Bazaar." Olcay led us in and up a long, narrow flight of stairs to a restaurant named *Pandeli*, and it was obvious that no tourist would ever find this place without a guide. It was loud and crowded, with the ambience of a diner, but the food was pretty good. Here is a tip for travelers to Turkey: learn to ask in advance how many courses there will be in the meal, and what they are. We all supposed that the first course was the meal, when in fact, there were several more courses to come, including a magnificent sea bass *en papillote*, which we were all too full to eat.

The Spice Bazaar in Istanbul.

Snapshots

There was time after lunch for a walk through the bazaar and it was fascinating. Real culture shock. We were, of course, set upon by numerous people wanting to sell us things, but no one was intimidating or unpleasant. Some of the most interesting shops were the food shops, each of which seemed to have a considerable variety of foods that none of us could identify. Bill Hall began inquiring, from time to time, as to what this or that was, and the shopkeeper's answer was always the same: "An aphrodisiac."

We left the Bazaar on foot and walked through some traffic and busy intersections, then through some empty lots until we reached the Golden Horn. It is a bay that opens into the Bosporus. There we got on a boat for our promised "Cruise on the Bosporus." The boat was a real tub, old and rusted out, with tables and benches set up on the lower level, and chairs and benches sitting on top, which also had a railing around it. "There is a good possibility," I thought, "that this boat will not sink."

We were the only people on the boat, although it would have held five times as many, and we all went up top in order to observe the panorama, a fascinating parade of expensive houses, ancient palaces, modern office buildings, and hotels, as we motored east until the point where the Bosporus opens into the Black Sea. Soon after we set out it began to rain and everyone went below for the rest of the trip. We observed several commercial fishing boats using large nets, so the fish must be edible, despite the pollution in the water. Olcay told us that the Soviet Union was (and still is) a terrible polluter, and that they polluted the Black Sea so badly that the pollution spread throughout the whole area and has even contaminated the Bosporus, the Golden Horn, and the Sea of Marmara.

Since even the locals do not drink the water, everyone carries the small, half liter bottles, such as we had on the bus. When the bottles are empty, people apparently cap up the bottle and throw it into the Bosporus, and the surface is dotted with them. Because the water is so full of oil and other pollution, the bottles soon turn gray and get to looking really scuzzy.

After about an hour or so of "cruising," the combination of cool weather, steady rain and jet lag caused me to put my head down and nap. The boat eventually docked near the eastern end of the Bosporus, rather than returning to its point of origin, and our bus was waiting for us with the driver sound asleep in the baggage compartment. It was late, we were scheduled to go out for dinner, and all of us were exhausted, but Olcay said there was *yet another* museum to visit. Howls of protest went up from the group, so a vote was taken (with Betsy and Suzanne opting for the museum). Sanity prevailed, and Olcay agreed that we could go directly back to the hotel (which we did). The bus ride back along the edge of the Bosporus was interesting, even though it was raining and most of us were nodding off. Even having skipped the "last museum," we did not get back to our hotel until 5:30. Lord knows when we would have gotten back if we had tried to see that museum!

Once in the room, we called room service and had a pot of coffee sent to the room. (That turned out to be a big mistake!) We also sent out laundry, even though the guidebooks had told us it was not a good idea to have laundry done in Turkey. Yesterday's laundry had come back and the total cost was only $13.00, and it all looked fine. We cleaned up and I went down to the lobby to pick up the latest issue of the *Herald-Tribune* from the hotel newsstand. The current edition usually arrives there at about 4:00 o'clock in the afternoon.

We had been told to gather in the lobby at 7:30 in order to meet with Yelda Ocan, who loaded us onto the bus and took us to dinner at a restaurant called *Park Samdan* (pronounced "Sha-mahn"). We were joined by another Iliada person, a woman named "Tony." This turned out to be the best restaurant that we visited all the time that we were in Turkey. Dinner consisted of white wine, an eggplant and onion appetizer, a veal kabob (cooked with yogurt and pita bread), and a gorgeous mixed salad which we and the Halls did not touch. There was a dessert of vanilla ice cream on "bread" (like pound cake), with a sour cherry sauce, followed by Turkish coffee.

After dinner, it was dark and still raining, and we had to walk up a rather precarious hill and along a path of about one block to where the bus was waiting. Turkey provides endless opportunities for pedestrians to fall down, especially at night. Lots of the walkways are paved with big round stones, or flagstones, and every few steps one of the stones is likely to be missing or, there may simply be a hole or, perhaps a tree planted in the center of the walk with a small trench around it. Nonetheless, everyone safely navigated back to the bus.

Back in the hotel I sat down to write postcards and wondered why I was so sleepy on the bus, but wide awake *now*. Totally unable to sleep, I took a sleeping pill at 2:30, and dozed until 7:00 o'clock.

IV

Saturday was scheduled for another full day in Istanbul, and we were happy to see the sun shining, even though it was still cool. The fact is, a properly guided tourist could probably spend days, maybe weeks, sightseeing in this fascinating city.

Our bus took us to Topkapi Palace, a vast, rambling palace set on beautiful grounds, overlooking the Bosporus and the city. It is so big and has so much history, that it was obvious that we would only be able to scratch the surface. Still, we had our guidebooks, and we had Olcay, and in we went, first through

Snapshots

the grounds, then through some of the living quarters and work areas, then the Treasury, and finally (and best) the Harem. In the old days, when Topkapi was used as a palace by the Sultans, all of the Sultans' wives and concubines (usually more than 200) lived in the Harem, and no men were allowed to enter except for the Sultan, and the eunuchs who lived there and tended the women. It is full of ornate carvings, mosaics and other tile displays, marble floors, and magnificent vistas.

The Harem at the Topkapi Palace.

There is an outdoor restaurant located along the hillside on the palace grounds, and it is very big, but was mobbed at lunch time. When we arrived, there was considerable confusion about where our tables were (or whether we had tables), but eventually we all got seated. The food was passable, and we enjoyed the marvelous view across the Bosporus, feeling that this compensated for the plethora of bees and cats that seemed intent on sharing our meal.

After lunch, Olcay intended that we all use the public facilities at the restaurant; however, there were long lines, probably 15 minutes for men and 40 minutes for women, so everyone decided to try to get by until the next stop.

The bus took us to a little town on the outskirts of Istanbul, by the name of Chora, to see an ancient Christian church that is now a museum, with murals and mosaics that are centuries old on the walls and ceilings. Olcay has proved to be the most informed tourist guide that I have ever seen, and she could give the history of everything in the museum. After a while, I began to feel "museumed out," and wandered across the street to a little outdoor cafe to buy a cup of coffee. I got totally confused about the money and tried to give the man $20.00 for the cup of coffee, but he refused to accept it and explained my error, and insisted on giving me correct change. Once again, the Turks appear to be extremely honest people (at least when they are not trying to sell you a rug).

We joined the Halls for dinner at the famous Tugra restaurant, located in the restored palace part of the Ciragan Palace Hotel. It is expensive, but good enough that it can be recommended.

V

Our schedule called for us to be up early on Sunday morning to catch a plane from Istanbul to Ankara. The terminal for domestic flights reminded us of the proverbial Chinese fire drill, and we were happy that Olcay was responsible for weaving us through the maze and getting us on our plane. Unhappily, my suspicions were confirmed that I was coming down with a cold. Otherwise, we had a good flight to Ankara on Turkish Airlines.

The city of Ankara is in the central part of Turkey, not a port city, but once the home of Mustafa Kemal Ataturk, who made it the nation's capital when he came to power as the first President of the Republic of Turkey. At that time, Ankara was a rather sleepy and rustic village, but today is a cosmopolitan city, albeit one with terrible weather.

We were met at the airport by another large bus that took us directly to the Ataturk Memorial, a large and impressive array of monuments, statues and buildings, the focus of which is the tomb and perpetual flame honoring Ataturk. Olcay told us that she starts all tours of Ankara here because Ataturk was so important in preserving the independence of Turkey and "westernizing" its customs. "He deserves it," she said, "and more." There were several armed guards around the premises, and they are not strictly ceremonial. Modern-day fundamentalist Turks, and various Kurdish groups, are opposed to the present western ways of Turkey, and might conceivably choose to stage some sort of attack upon this memorial, as a means of protest.

According to Olcay, 99% of Turks are Moslems, but only 20% are Fundamentalists. She said that some of the people we see on the streets wearing traditional garb (chadors, turbans, and robes) are paid to do so by clerical groups in Iran and in Iraq.

After touring the memorial, we went to the nearby *Zenger Pasa* restaurant, high up among the walls of the Citadel, where we had good food, including a beautiful salad, which Olcay insisted was all right. Betsy ate the salad, I did not. During the meal, one course that was served was a kind of pizza on a huge flat wooden board, and sliced by a man in a traditional Turkish outfit, wearing a turban, and wielding an enormous knife that looked almost like a sword. Lots of us had our pictures taken with him.

There was a lot of activity out in front of the restaurant after lunch, primarily, I suppose, because of the fact that we had been inside. Numerous children came up to us and wanted to shake hands and say a few words in English. There was a little bit of begging, but none of it was offensive. In general, the Turks do not approve of begging; however, Olcay regrets that this may be weakening to some extent because of the influx of "foreigners" into Turkey.

The bus proceeded to the Museum of Anatolian Civilizations, which Olcay described as "Turkey's best museum." The Museum was large, well designed, well displayed, and generally interesting - but, unfortunately, of no interest to me, because by this time my cold had me totally subdued. I found a soft chair near the front of the Museum, ordered some hot apple tea, and crashed while the rest of the group went through the Museum with Olcay.

Olcay Bergman and Howard Chapman at the Kapadokya Lodge.

At 4:00 o'clock the group left the Museum and began the long drive into Cappadocia. We arrived at the Kapadokya Lodge, outside the town of Nevsehir, at about 8:00 o'clock p.m. Cappadocia is a region in the central part of the country, and our route took us generally Southeast from Ankara. Occasionally we saw large fires burning, and were told that these were set by farmers who were burning off their fields. It is a practice that persists, even though it is now technically illegal. It was a long and tiring ride, and everyone was happy about the fact that this bus was equipped with its own biffy.

We were able to see a little bit of the countryside before it got dark, and it seemed to me to very much resemble the southern part of South Dakota. Olcay told us that this is a very dry part of Turkey - but it certainly was raining on us.

The Kapadokya Lodge was okay, meeting the needs for comfort, but obviously built exclusively for foreign tourists. It was warm in our room, but cool outside, so we opened the windows to get the fresh air. All of us were pretty tired from the long day and my cold was getting worse.

Dinner consisted of a "big buffet" in the main dining room, where most other Lodge guests had finished by the time our group arrived. Some of the food was local, but most of it was generic tourist fare. It would sustain life.

Back in our room, we noticed a sign that says that the water here is all drawn from local springs, and perfectly safe to drink. We observed the Turks drinking bottled water, however, and so did we. It was another sleepless night, but I felt so crummy with the cold, that I was able to rest quietly, even though I couldn't sleep.

VI

We got up at 7:15 on Monday, October 2, 1995, and I realized several things: the weather was gray and chilly with heavy rain; my cold was progressing, currently producing a sore throat and stuffy head; and, it was my birthday.

Breakfast in the large dining room again was buffet style. Betsy and I joined fellow travelers Marvin Kagan and Diane Austin at their table. They live in Chicago and Diane had admired my cap from Border's Book Store on Michigan Avenue. At Marvin's suggestion, I tried the French toast and the strong coffee, which seemed to fit the weather just right.

Before heading out for the day, I layered on as many clothes as I could, including a turtleneck shirt, a sweatshirt, my khaki "safari" vest, a windbreaker, and a waterproof poncho. The safari vest came from our trip to Kenya. The poncho came from DisneyWorld, is bright yellow, and has a picture of Mickey Mouse on the back. For Turkey, it was unique.

The bus began to wander through the landscape of Cappadocia, which is really more like the surface of the moon, with lots of odd formations of rock with ancient houses carved into them. These formations are sometimes referred to as "Fairy Chimneys." It is a rather unusual kind of rock that is hard enough to resist the elements, yet soft enough to be (relatively) easily hollowed out for human habitation. Lots of the villages that we went through are built in and around these archeological sites, and many of them still appear to be occupied. Because of the rain, nobody was eager to get out of the bus to go wandering through the many interesting places, and Olcay decided to take us to a pottery factory.

The pottery factory really did have a lot of great things to buy, and Betsy and I selected a beautiful bowl which had, as its only drawback, the fact that we would now have to lug it home. The owners of the pottery factory offered all of us some hot apple tea, which felt good on my sore throat. The roof leaked in several places, and there were some gorgeous pots and buckets placed to catch the drops. Someone remarked that the roof must have been designed by Frank Lloyd Wright. We also spent some time at a place right next door, which (I think) sold crafts made of onyx - but I'm not too sure, since I didn't spend any time there.

Betsy Chapman "negotiating" the purchase of a Turkish rug.

The rain was still drumming down, so we went to a town called "Avanos," where there is a rug factory which, of course, sells rugs. Because of the weather, there wasn't much business, and when our tourist bus pulled in, all of the employees ran out in the rain to greet it. They were happy to see us!

Everybody went into the rug factory/store except for the bus driver, his "assistant," and me. I felt too rotten to get off the bus, so I sat there and worked on a crossword puzzle and wrote some postcards. The driver and his assistant sat up front and watched a portable TV with American programs dubbed in Turkish.

After about half an hour, I looked out the bus window and saw Betsy standing just under the roof of the factory, waving at me and gesturing for me to come in, so I did. It turned out that everyone else had gone through a show and tell area downstairs, watching Turkish women make rugs by hand, and then come upstairs where they have a very nice store stocked with zillions of Turkish rugs. Some of the others in our group had bought rugs, and after a great deal of discussion, Betsy and I wound up buying one too, at a price that shall be unnamed, but which included having the rug shipped to us at home.

Bill and Suzanne Hall had also bought a rug, but did not want to entrust it to the international mail; so, they had it wrapped up and arranged in some sort of a carrying bag, and took it with them.

We proceeded to a restaurant called Ataman Hotel and Restaurant, built right into the side of one of the large rock formations. There was a daunting climb up the wet stone steps outside, without the benefit of handrails, and I observed that there must not be anything comparable to the Americans With Disabilities Act or OSHA in Turkey.

Once inside, however, the place turned out to be very nice, and served good food. The first course was a marvelous looking salad which I pondered for some time. Finally, I looked across the table at Bill Hall and said, "I am going to eat this salad as soon as I see Bill Hall eat his." To which he replied, "You will wait a long time." After further reflection, I decided that I might eventually eat a salad in Turkey, but not until the incubation period for dysentery was longer than the length of time before I would arrive back in the USA. There was, fortunately, a very good melon served with the meal, which all of us enjoyed.

Olcay announced that we would next go to visit another store (it was still pouring) and then proceed to the *Goreme Open Air Museum* which, she said, we "must see, even if we all get soaked to the bone." I felt really rotten because of my cold, didn't want to spend any more time in any stores, and was determined not to go walking in the rain and getting soaked to the bone. I persuaded Olcay to find me a taxi that would take me back to Kapadokya Lodge, at a fare of TRL 250,000 (about $5.00).

When I got back to the Lodge, it was deserted. All of the tourists were off on their sightseeing buses, and all of the employees had gone home until the tourists would return later in the evening. The hotel shops were closed, and all of the lights were turned off except for one small light at the reception area. There was one person in the reception area, who appeared to be in charge of the entire establishment, and she helped me get our postcards mailed, and then helped me call the rug store to give them my passport number, which they claimed they needed in order to mail us our rug. (Incidentally, about two months after we got home, the rug appeared, in fine shape, and without any request for payment of customs duty.)

I was happy to fall into bed and to sleep for nearly two hours. For some reason, I was suffering from persistent jet lag, and found it easy to sleep in the *daytime*, even though I still couldn't sleep at night.

When the group came back (at about 6 p.m.), I got up and went down to dinner. It was, once again, buffet style; but Olcay, bless her heart, had arranged to have a "birthday cake" in honor of my birthday! Everybody from our group gathered round and sang "Happy Birthday," while I blew out the candles. The birthday cake was really very good, and covered with a glaze of fresh cherries, which had not been pitted. As soon as someone discovered this, the rest of us were able to chew carefully, and thus avoid the pits.

VII

The following morning we boarded our tour bus and traveled to the underground village of Kaymackli. Considering that it had been another sleepless, jet lag night, I was reasonably awake, but still encumbered by a cold. Kaymackli was hollowed out of the rocks, totally underground, by ancient Christians who needed a place to hide and, if necessary, to defend themselves if they should be set upon by their enemies.

It is worth the trip to Turkey just to see this place.

We entered through a hole in the rock that resembles the opening of a cave, and then began a descent through narrow, low tunnels, that took us through a series of rooms that had been used for various purposes, including ordinary living, and maintaining animals. The entire underground city goes down as many as eight stories and was big enough to house a population of 20,000 people, and their livestock, and enough food to survive for as long as two months. At one point, we walked past a vertical shaft that goes both up and down, up for fresh air, and down for water. We could lean over a railing and look in both directions, but Olcay warned us ahead of time, "don't lose your glasses."

The passageways are narrow and we could only proceed from one area to the next in single file. At many places these passages are so low and small that we had to bend almost double in order to go through. This is no place for people with claustrophobia! There were electric lights placed along the way to guide us, but it is amazing to contemplate that Kaymackli was originally inhabited by people without electricity, and who could only use torches to provide light in order to get around. We were told that torches were considered to be precious objects, and that, for most of the time, the inhabitants moved around in total blackness. All of us marveled at the fortitude of one of our travelers, Margaret Steed, the oldest member of our group, who cheerfully scrambled all through the place with us, keeping up without any trouble.

As one might expect there are a number of bazaars and shopping areas in the vicinity of a tourist site like this, and on the way out we bought various kinds of "evil eyes" for souvenirs and some of us bought shawls and caps against the ever present cold weather of this area. The ceramic "evil eye" seems to be ubiquitous in Turkey, often worn on the clothing or hung in doorways, and it can be found in objects that are hundreds of years old. The superstitious believe that it does, in fact, ward off evil. I bought several.

We traveled on about 30 minutes to the edge of a cliff looking down over the immense Ihlara Valley, which cuts a huge gorge through what appears to be generally flat terrain. It is not easy to go down into the valley, requiring about 400 steps down, and it is even harder coming up. Nonetheless, most of us buttoned up our coats and started the descent because, at various places along the lower reaches of the valley, there are early Christian churches that were carved out of the rock walls during the 10th and 11th centuries.

Once we got to the bottom of the several flights of stairs, we set off across a series of narrow dirt pathways, sometimes walking along a space no more than two or three feet wide between the edge of the river and the side of the canyon wall, over some rather crude bridges, and sometimes using stepping-stones. Olcay seemed indefatigable, and charged ahead, occasionally stopping and looking back, waiting to gather her flock. We could see the entrances to several churches at various places, and went up and into three of them, and were amazed to find that you can still see religious icons and paintings on some of the ceilings and walls. It must have been enormously difficult to build these churches. I tried to imagine those early builders thinking, not "Where shall we build the church," but rather, "Where shall we carve the church out of the side of the rock."

When we got ready to start the ascent, Olcay told us she knew a "shortcut" that would be a little bit scarier for a while, but would save us going down to the river, and then climbing back up part of the way. We all agreed and set off, like mountain climbers, going hand over hand across big boulders, through narrow crevices, over fallen trees, always upward, until we reached a landing on the staircase. I looked back and got a couple of photographs of Tim and

Snapshots

Betsy Chapman and Suzanne Timken climbing out of the Ihlara Valley.

Suzanne Timken helping Margaret Steed over some of the tougher places, and it looks like we are all a bunch of mountaineers. (Margaret, once again, was amazing, and got a big hand from everyone when we got back on the bus.)

We rode for nearly two hours on the bus to the lunch stop, with the wild and weird Cappadocia landscape on all sides. By now we had learned that the traveler does best in Turkey if he likes rice and eggplant, and can do without ice. The salads again looked pretty good, but we, and the Halls, continued to pass them up. Anyway, with my cold and lack of sleep, I didn't have much of an appetite.

This restaurant was another place where the main attraction seemed to be that it has clean, western-style toilets. Olcay referred to these restroom stops as "daisy picking." A man was stationed at the doorway, seated at a small table between the entrances for men, on one side, and women on the other, collecting TRL5,000 from people going in. This fellow was one of the few that we encountered who was able to make change. (As with most third world countries, there is hardly ever any toilet paper in public restrooms, and the experienced traveler learns to carry his own supply.) Before re-boarding the bus, we bought two oversized plastic bottles of drinking water for TRL60,000 ($1.20) in order to avoid the hassle of dealing with room service that night at the hotel.

It was another long day, made longer by the fact that the bus broke down twice. We arrived late (well after dark) in Ankara at the Ankara Hilton, got into our rooms, and ordered room service. While eating, we tuned in to CNN and learned that the jury had acquitted O.J. Simpson of charges that he murdered his ex-wife, Nicole, and a friend, Ronald Goldman. The evidence against Simpson had been overwhelming and the reaction among Americans in Turkey was a mixture of anger and revulsion. The news also reported that an Arab, Sheik Omar, and a group of Moslems, had been convicted in New York of terrorism involving the bombing of the World Trade Center. Despite feeling exhausted all day, I was confounded with another "jet lag night" without sleep.

VIII

Our schedule called for us to be up at 5:00 a.m., with breakfast in the room, followed by a departure to the Ankara Airport for a 7:45 a.m. flight to Izmir. Izmir is one of Turkey's three largest cities, the others being Istanbul and Ankara. Again, the local airport proved to be a beehive of activity. All signs were in Turkish, and all the employees spoke only Turkish, and I was convinced that, without Olcay, we never would have figured out where to go or what to do in order to get on our plane.

What a relief to arrive in warm, sunny, Izmir, on the Aegean coast! We arrived at the Hilton Hotel in mid-morning, but our rooms were not ready. So, I found a soft chair in the lobby and ordered coffee while Olcay took Bill Hall, Suzanne Hall, and Betsy for a walk to see the Citadel and the Agora (market). The Agora in Izmir was built by the Romans and is thus considered "new" by Turkish standards.

It was reported that major league baseball was in the middle of the playoffs, but I ignored the news. I have been irritated ever since the major league players went on strike and killed the season in 1994, including the World Series, and no longer seem to care about the sport at the professional level.

Olcay offered to take the Halls, and Betsy and me, for a walk to show us where there is a good bookstore. Bill and Sue's travel agent had sent Olcay some money with instructions to buy a book for Bill and Sue, and Olcay decided to let them pick it out. (Incidentally, of the 19 passengers on the A&K tour, there were three "Suzannes" and two couples of "Bill and Suzanne.") At the bookstore, the rest of them looked at books, while I grabbed the last copy of the *International Herald Tribune* (only one-day old!) and began to devour it.

When we left the bookstore, Olcay steered us to a delightful waterfront restaurant called "Deniz Seafood." "Deniz" means "sea." When you go in, there are large glass cases with a variety of fresh fish displayed, and you select your meal right there. The price of the meal depends on how many kilograms of fish you order. We tried the fish soup and grilled shrimp, which was plenty, and then let the waiter talk us into ordering an "assortment of desserts" for the table. It was huge, and we could not do it justice. After lunch, we headed back to the hotel to check out the news on CNN and take a nap, and found that our laundry sent out that morning on arrival, was already back.

The main event for the evening was a "dress up" dinner that A&K hosted for the whole group on the 31st floor of the Izmir Hilton. We sat in a private room with glass on three sides looking out over a fantastic view of the city and the waterfront, lit up like a Christmas tree, and quite resplendent. Jerry Olin regaled us with a couple of stories, and Joan Goldsmith presented Olcay with a pin with an American flag on it, which she dutifully wore for the rest of the trip. The dinner was fine, and there was a consensus that our group of twenty (counting Olcay), all strangers a few days ago, enjoyed an amazing congeniality. After hearing all of the mutual compliments, Ed Eigner said, "I guess we're having a better time than we thought."

I had been griping about not being able to sleep for several nights, and David Goldsmith gave me a tablet to try, which, he said, was not really a sleeping pill. It was called (he thought) "ambient." I took it and, whatever it was, it must be good, because I slept well. Finally!

IX

The next morning, Betsy awoke to find that she was coming down with a cold too, as well as suffering a modest case of "tourist's lament." Now we would *both* be taking pills.

Our schedule for the day began with a trip to Pergamon, which also shows up as Bergama on some maps. It was a pleasant, clear blue sunny morning, and the ruins of the ancient city are marvelous. We started by going to the *Acropolis*, and stopped at the huge, ancient theater, with steep steps (which also served as seats) making a horseshoe around the stage. The Turks have figured out that the *Acropolis* is a place with a tremendous number of excellent photo opportunities, and accordingly there are several small stands scattered about where it is possible to buy film, and even batteries for your cameras.

Another stop was the large, red stone ruin originally known as the *Serapsis*, now sometimes called the *Red Courtyard*. We saw several school boys in uniform, and as soon as they saw my camera, several of them wanted their pictures taken. They then insisted on writing down the address of one of them, and I promised to send enough copies for all of them (which I eventually did after we got home).

Lunch was a debacle. It was at a place in Pergamon called *Kardeslar*, that was open air, and very much in need of a bath. It had bad food, was overrun with tourists, and invited you to ask the question, "Are we going to get sick from eating here?" Olcay apologized, but said it was the only place that was available in the area, and I imagine that this was true. It's too bad we hadn't known to bring box lunches from the hotel in Izmir.

In the afternoon we visited another vast ruin, this one called the *Asklepion*. It was used by the Romans as a hospital and features an enormous auditorium with incredible acoustics. We seated ourselves as a group near the stage and Olcay gave us a lecture on the history of the place. It was thought that the water from the spring here has therapeutic value, and the spring is still used. Tim Timken drank from the spring, and later showed no ill effects. (Also, no therapeutic effects.)

The Theater at the Asklepion.

Back at Pergamon, some of the group went to (yet another) archaeological museum, while others shopped. Successful shoppers included Marvin Kagan, who bought a rug, and Bill Hall, who bought a sack of almonds. I have a wonderful picture of Jerry Olin sitting sound asleep in a store selling copperware, while his wife, Suzanne, dickers with the shopkeeper.

It had been a full day, and we were all pretty quiet on the 1-1/2 hour bus ride back to Izmir, for a quiet meal and evening.

Snapshots

X

On Friday morning I got a copy of a British newspaper to read at breakfast, and found a lot of extremely candid commentary about the obvious guilt of O. J. Simpson. After breakfast, we departed on our bus for the ancient city of Ephesus which is, in my opinion, one of the great wonders of the world.

Turkey has a lot of ancient ruins, some that they have not even started to excavate, but Ephesus is in a class by itself. It is very much restored, covers a vast amount of ground, and is extremely beautiful. When it was built, the ocean came right up to the edge of the city, but over the centuries the harbor area has gradually filled, and the former city docks are now more than 20 miles from the edge of the sea.

We were fortunate, again, to have a guide like Olcay, who led us from place to place, explaining the various buildings, means of construction, their uses, and history. One building, she said, was once used as a brothel, and a Latin inscription written into the stone wall translates, "Do not leave valuables unattended."

The Romans, in addition to being great builders, were also great lovers of the theater, and practically every Roman city of any size had one. I had heard that the theater at Ephesus was remarkable, but I still wasn't prepared for the reaction I had when we walked into it. I simply stopped and held my breath. I can recall reacting this way on only one other occasion, that being when I first saw the Great Pyramids in Egypt.

Ephesus was, for many years, the home of Saint Paul, and it was to its inhabitants that he wrote his "Letter to the Ephesians." It was also the last home of Mary, Mother of Jesus. A shrine and a number of other buildings are still maintained by a Catholic order of nuns, who welcome visitors. There was a large metal sign saying, in several languages, that all Christians were invited to gather at this place on August 15, 2000, in order to honor the observation of the 2,000 anniversary of the birth of Christ.

We spent the morning visiting Ephesus, along with lots of other tourists who came both by land and by sea, from a number of cruise ships. Ephesus is a favorite stop on many Mediterranean cruise itineraries, and well it should be. No one should ever pass up a chance to see it.

When we left Ephesus, we proceeded to the port city of Kusadasi, which used to be a little fishing village, but has thrived with the advent of tourism. We had a good fish lunch at a restaurant called *Kazim Usta*, and then had a little time to browse through the myriad shops at the nearby bazaar. They were completely riddled with cheap junk, and Olcay explained that this was because Kusadasi is a place "where the cruise ships come."

Howard L. Chapman

The Library of Celsus at the ruins of Ephesus.

After lunch the group had its option of visiting a museum, or a church, or shopping. Some of us did one thing, some another, but in any event, I had the feeling we were trying to cram too much into the schedule. We were supposed to drive to the city of Pamukkale this evening, and would not be able to get there until 8:00 o'clock or later.

The long drive included a "daisy picking stop," and Olcay called ahead to our hotel and asked them to hold dinner for us. At that stop, there were a few small shops nearby, and some of us bought cookies, broke out granola bars, and ate candy. A lot of the Turkish cookies that we encountered were very good, and reminded me of the kinds of cookies we often find in our own grocery stores - butter cookies, oatmeal cookies, and the like.

It was, as expected, well after dark when we arrived in Pamukkale at the hotel Thermal Collosae. It wasn't a very good night. For dinner we were squeezed into a crowded dining area below ground; the food at the buffet was poor; there was no ventilation; people were sweltering; and Betsy and I were still struggling with our colds.

One interesting point about this hotel, the room key is attached to a plastic square, and you have to drop the plastic square into a little slot when you go into your room, in order to activate the electricity. I had not encountered this anywhere else except in the Hotel New Otani in Takaoka, Japan. It's a good way to save electricity, but causes a lot of confusion until people get used to it.

Snapshots

XI

We set off the next day for the ancient city of Hieropolis. Like most of these sites from antiquity, Hieropolis is much older than the Romans; however, it is the Roman ruins, primarily, that remain. Although it is a vast area, most of it has not been excavated, and parts of stone buildings, columns, and even statuary, are lying out on the ground. At one point, two women came through the middle of the place, driving several head of cattle. We were again reminded of the fact that Turkey has so many locations full of ancient history and archaeology that there is simply not enough time or money to excavate all of them. Someone observed, and it is true, that "Turkey is one big museum."

True to form, the Romans had constructed a large and impressive theater, and I noticed that there was a sign over one of the doorways that said "Vomitarium." Olcay told us that this was the word that the Romans originally used to mean "exit." The phrase "ium" or "eum" often means "house of." Thus, the word museum - house of muses.

We came to a hole in the hillside, identified as the "Apollonium" (presumably, "House of Apollo") which, we were told, is the entrance to an underground cave. There is supposed to be a source within the cave that emits some kind of noxious gas, and if we all stood quietly, we would be able to hear

The amazing hot springs at Pammukkale.

the gas gurgling. All I heard was a motorcycle, which also emits a noxious gas, carbon monoxide.

Next we went to the famous hot springs, and these almost have to be seen to be understood. The hot water comes out of places near the tops of large cliffs, and spreads out along the edges of the cliffs for hundreds of yards, and eventually spills over and down the side of the cliffs. The water is blue and crystal clear, but as it evaporates, it leaves mineral deposits, so that the bottoms of these "pools" are bright white, and shimmer in the sunshine. Although the water is hot, it is cool enough for wading, and the tourists take off their shoes and socks and wander across these unusual cliff side pools, with the water rarely getting above the knees.

The next scheduled "daisy picking" occurred at a large store for tourists called Kayalar. It had all kinds of cheap cotton goods for sale, and interestingly enough, most are no longer made in Turkey. Still, some of them were fun, and I bought a few items, including some colorful ties to bring home.

Proceeding to lunch, the bus was stopped twice. The first time was to allow a herd of goats to get across the highway and the second time was because the police were stopping all vehicles in order (according to Olcay) to check the driver's "speed log." As near as I can tell, the drivers are supposed to somehow register the time when they leave somewhere, and if they arrive at this checkpoint too soon, it means they have been going too fast. (?) In addition to having predominately two-lane roads, driving is also made difficult by a large number of tractors, pedestrians, and carts pulled by animals, all competing with huge trucks and buses that seem to drive much too fast for conditions. The accident rate in Turkey is terrible.

The road wound along the side of a mountain for several miles, through some beautiful scenery, until we came upon a large lake, Lake Salda. We stopped for lunch at an outdoor restaurant called *Sultan's Fountain*, overlooking the lake, near the town of Yesilova. The terrain all around was rugged and scenic, and would make a perfect set for a western movie.

Much of the afternoon was consumed in driving on to the seaside city of Antalya. There was one "daisy picking" stop *en route*, and, as always, there were lots of little shops, merchants and assorted vendors around the area. At one place, a man had big piles of oranges, grapefruit, and pomegranates, and a mechanical "squeezer." For a small charge, he would squeeze a glass of fresh juice, and he was doing a good business. Betsy bought a glass of fresh squeezed pomegranate juice, but made the mistake of standing a little too close to the squeezer, and was liberally sprayed with pomegranate juice. I bought some fruit, some cookies, and some gum, and again encountered the common problem that vendors do not seem to have any change. Instead, they would happily give me my change in fruit, or whatever else they happened to be selling. The amounts involved are small, and everybody just shrugs.

The *Sheraton Voyager Antalya Hotel* in Antalya was to be our last hotel before returning to Istanbul. It is very big, very American, and was very full. We were sharing it with the "First Annual Convention of the Peripheral Nerve Society." They had commandeered all of the hotel restaurants except for one outdoors which promised a "Turkish feast." Bill and Suzanne and Betsy and I didn't really want to go to the "Turkish feast," but couldn't get in anyplace else, until we went to the hotel manager who arranged to get us served *a la carte* at another restaurant. This turned out to be a very good decision, because the food was wonderful and the prices quite reasonable, with a dinner consisting of rack of lamb for two people at $24.00.

After dinner, I bought the most recent copy of the *Herald Tribune*, and we retired to our hotel room. It had a nice balcony and a spectacular view, looking east along the shoreline of the Mediterranean Sea, over the city, with high mountains as a backdrop.

XII

Sunday, October 8, 1995, dawned as an absolutely perfect, Mediterranean day. We ordered breakfast from room service in order to sit on the balcony and enjoy the weather and the view.

We were going to spend the entire day sightseeing before returning to the same hotel, so I packed my flight bag for the day, including the following essential items: a cap, a jacket, the newspaper, several crossword puzzles, a pencil, camera, extra film, granola bars, two bottles of water, tall straws, a poncho, a map, a compass, an apple, an inflatable pillow, a package of Kleenex, a half roll of toilet paper wrapped in cellophane, a box of Tylenol Cold tablets, sunglasses, and a flashlight. Fortunately, when we got off the bus to go look at things, we were able to leave anything that we chose on the bus, secure in the knowledge that the driver or his assistant would stay with it, and look after it.

As the bus left the hotel, we realized that we were missing the Goldsmiths and the Eigners, who had chosen to remain behind. We had had several very long and arduous travel days, and this may have been taking its toll. (We later lost the Chamberlains at Perge.)

The first stop was the nearby *Antalya Archaeological Museum*, which is a really good one, especially the rooms filled with Greek statues excavated from Perge. The Greeks occupied much of Turkey for centuries before the Romans came. I was finally getting over my cold, and was surprised at how much more interesting this museum seemed than the one we had visited in Ankara, where I had felt lousy.

It is amazing that so many of these beautiful statues have survived since Hellenic times, and that they are in such good condition. At one point I came around a corner of the museum into a hallway full of them and simply stopped and stood in awe. I decided that I could not do them justice by trying to photograph them myself, but rather would buy postcards at the shop in the lobby. Another interesting exhibit showed artifacts taken from an archaeological dig, including a large metal spoon, centuries old, three or four feet long, and ornamented with jewels. Significantly, there were also a number of ceramic evil eyes dotted among the jewels, showing how far back this tradition extends.

From the museum we traveled to the ancient city of Perge, passing many other ruined cities that are still unexcavated along the way. Perge is an exceptionally good ruin, full of history, and in most countries would be **the** major archaeological attraction for tourists and scientists. In Turkey, it is one of many. The vast Roman theater was being reconstructed and was not open, but we were able to visit the huge stadium, the baths, and several other buildings, many with beautiful mosaic tiles (that, unfortunately, do not seem to be getting any protection from the elements).

It is hard to believe that we were doing all of these things in one morning, but we still managed to visit Aspendos. Only the theater was presently open to visitors; however, seeing the theater was well worth the visit. It is in exceptionally good condition and is still used on a fairly regular basis. Only a few days before, the Turkish television companies had held their *Golden Ball Awards* in the theater, and there were still two large statues that had been brought into the theater for the event. It is also used for plays and concerts, and holds nearly 20,000 people.

The walls of the theater look like stepping-stones, and the audience sits on these. They are entirely made of stone, are very steep, and offer no handrails or guardrails. I asked Olcay if this wouldn't be a source of frequent liability claims, and she said, "If you fall down in Turkey, it's your own fault."

We arrived for a late and leisurely lunch at the town of Manavgat, at the *Delevi Restaurant*, located outdoors along the shady banks of the Manavgat River. The weather was fine, the scene was picturesque, and the food was very good.

We used what was left of the afternoon to drive back to our hotel at Antalya, arriving at 4:00 p.m., and relaxed in our room until it was time to prepare to go to dinner - the Abercrombie & Kent "farewell dinner."

Tomorrow, some of us would be coming back to the U.S.A., while others would be getting on a cruise ship to spend a few more days cruising among Turkish ports.

We went into the center of Antalya, a charming, walled city on the Mediterranean, and descended a flight of stairs to a restaurant called *Club 29*, where tables were set for us outdoors, along the harbor. It was another gorgeous setting at a good restaurant with good food and service.

We had all gotten dressed up for the occasion, and were kept busy saying farewells, taking pictures, exchanging addresses, and discussing how compatible the group had been. There was also a lot of praise for Olcay, who had been a patient leader, guide and friend.

XIII

The next morning was, again, perfect, and again we decided to have breakfast on our balcony. Betsy and I were finally close to sleeping normally, were getting over our colds, and could enjoy the spectacular view. To my surprise, I think I may even have picked up a couple of words in Turkish. Here are a few key words that a potential traveler can try to plug in to his or her vocabulary:

Thank you - Te-shay-kuhr ed-er-im

Hello- Mehr-ha-ba

Please- Lewt-fehn

Toilet- Tu-va-let

Beer- Beer

Eight of us, the Halls, Eigners, Olins, and Chapmans, were returning to Istanbul, while the rest of the group was proceeding to a cruise ship. Olcay accompanied us to the airport and, in her usual efficient fashion, got us checked in and boarded, at which time we said goodbye to her. This would be our last day with Olcay, so we put together an envelope with a gratuity for her. A&K had recommended the amount of $10.00 per person per day.

At the airport in Istanbul we were met, once again, by Aton, to take us back to the Ciragan Palace. We learned that Aton is a university student who has been to school in the United States.

We got to the Ciragan Palace at about 2:30 in the afternoon and learned that all of us had been "upgraded" to big, fancy rooms, close to the water. Opposite, anchored in the Bosporus, was the yacht that once belonged to Ataturk, and is now used as a museum. The Halls and Betsy decided to take a taxi to see the *Suleiman Mosque*, while I stayed at the hotel to tie up some loose ends, and relax.

I called Yelda at Iliada Travel Agency to verify that they would be picking us up the next morning to take us to the airport, and then called Lufthansa to reconfirm our morning flight. After that, I went for a long walk outside the hotel and established, once again, that there do not seem to be any stores of any kind within walking distance of the Ciragan Palace. Back at the hotel, however, I was able to get a copy of the *Herald Tribune*, which helped to pass away the rest of the afternoon.

Betsy and I joined the Halls once again in the Ciragan Restaurant for a nice evening, and then, keeping in mind our early departure, went to bed at 9:30 p.m.

XIV

Our Tuesday morning wake-up call came, as instructed, at 3:30 a.m. As Betsy and I stumbled around in the pre-dawn darkness, getting ready to leave, we made a solemn pledge that *we will never do this again*. At 4:14 a.m. we checked out of the Ciragan Palace and, upon payment of our bill, I was given a "departure ticket" which, when exhibited at the door, would allow not only us, but also our luggage, to leave the hotel.

Aton was there with a van and driver and, even in the middle of the night, it took a long time to drive from the hotel to the airport. The flight back was uneventful except for the fact that, in Frankfurt, we were once again shocked at the low value of the dollar.

It is always nice to get home; but, this time, we brought with us a new knowledge and increased awareness of ancient civilizations and, especially, the "one big museum" that is Turkey.

Chapter 9

YORKSHIRE PUDDING

I

The idea for the Yorkshire trip started with a brochure from Northwestern University, advertising an "Alumni Campus Abroad" in Harrogate, England, in July, 1996. Betsy and I signed up, along with Bill and Suzanne Hall, Cliff and Elaine Shultz, and Dick and Marcia Adams. The Adams went to England early, and the rest of us left from Fort Wayne on July 6, 1996. Our British Air flight left from Chicago, and we learned that there were additional Fort Wayne travelers on board for the seminar: Max and Elsie Fetters; Dick and Adie Baach; and Greg Fryzel. British Air is a very civilized operation with a two-three-two seating configuration in coach class. This was quite an improvement over the sardine cans provided by most other airlines.

Harrogate is a small town located about 17 miles west of the city of York in the heart of Yorkshire, and we would spend a week there, staying at the St. George Swallow Hotel with daily lectures and trips to the surrounding area. (Swallow is the name of a hotel chain.) Northwestern structured the trip with a tour company called Alumni Holidays, who had done all of the detail work and would be in charge of us once in England.

Chicago to London was only 7-1/2 hours and, after clearing customs, we had a lot of time until our connecting flight to Manchester. I did what I usually do in this situation: bought a copy of the *International Herald-Tribune* to see what is going on in the world. The Wimbledon tennis tournament was finishing up, and Stefi Graf had just beaten Aranxta Sanchez Vicario. American Mal Washington would play Richard Krajicek later this day for the men's title, the first time in history that two unseeded players have met for the championship. American money could be exchanged at $1.60 to the British Pound. Cliff Shultz, on the other hand, tried to spend some of the British Pounds he had brought from home (from a prior trip) and was told that the money "was no longer any good." He was unable to exchange it for "new pounds," but did eventually find a shop that would let him spend it.

The layover in London was nearly four hours, but the 35-minute flight to Manchester was pleasant. When we got off the plane we were met by Claire Bostel, our Alumni Holidays guide, and went by bus to Harrogate (about one hour and fifteen minutes). In retrospect, it seems to me that it would have been a lot simpler and a lot quicker to have taken the train from Heathrow Airport to Harrogate.

As soon as we got off the bus in Harrogate we knew that we had not brought enough warm clothes, and that some of us (I, at least) would have to buy a raincoat. Yorkshire is well to the North of London, and can have cool, wet weather at any time.

When we registered at our hotel, there was a letter waiting for Betsy and me from our friends John and Jean Campion, who live near London. We were planning to visit them at the end of the trip, and they were confirming the details.

Late in the afternoon we were served an English tea, which included sandwiches and scones with heavy cream and strawberry jam. Betsy and I have finally learned that, on arriving after a long trip, and hoping to minimize jet lag, we should avoid alcohol and coffee.

After tea the rain let up outside so we went for a stroll through the quaint and pleasant town of Harrogate. We learned that our hotel is located directly across the street from the Royal Baths, about which we would learn much later. We also walked past, and looked in on, the renowned Betty's Tea Room, with hours of operation being 9 to 9, seven days a week.

Back in the hotel while waiting for dinner, I turned on the television and we watched the end of the Wimbledon match, with Krajicek beating Washington in straight sets. The most interesting part of the match occurred when an attractive blond woman ran across the court without any clothes on, and was escorted away by two policemen. Watching the match on BBC was a real treat as compared to watching American sports programs. There were no commercials, and there were reasonably long periods of time when the announcers just shut up, and let us watch the play.

Our tour package included most of our meals, and we gathered in the dining room a little after 7 o'clock. "Our group" of eight (Adams, Chapman, Hall, and Shultz) were able to get a table together. At 9:30 p.m., there was still plenty of daylight, and it didn't really get dark until after 10 o'clock.

II

We were joined at breakfast by Dick and Adie Baach, and their friend Greg Fryzel. Everyone was talking about the pending British Air strike, scheduled to begin on July 16th. Betsy and I were scheduled to fly home on British Air on July 18th. I thought, "Why me, Lord?" Kurt Vonnegut responds, "Why anybody?" Anyway, there was nothing we could do about it at the moment. The dining room was pleasant and the food was good.

At 9 a.m. we adjourned to a nearby room for a lecture by Malcolm Neesam, a Yorkshire native and scholar, who has lived in Harrogate and written about it, including a good history, entitled "Exclusively Harrogate." After the lecture, he led us on a walking tour through the town, and lectured some more as we went.

Harrogate has been a "town" since 1332. The Royal Baths were a typical 19th century spa, opened in 1897 to exploit the waters that are prevalent there. The word "spa" comes from the name of a town in Belgium, famous for its spring water. Harrogate's springs were not thought to be commercially useful for a long time and, in fact, were called "the stinking wells."

King George III gave an enormous area called "The Stray" to the town, along with all of the wells and mineral springs on it, a total of 228 acres. Today, The Stray makes a marvelous green belt of park land, trees and flowers that forms a horseshoe around the town.

The place thrived as a spa from 1897 until 1914, but began to decline after World War II. In order to keep the tourists coming, the town built an international conference and exhibit center, which appears to have been quite successful.

As we walked, we passed numerous shops and pubs, and learned that the whole place is full of history. When we stopped at the Royal Baths, Malcolm Neesam took a shot glass of the mineral water, claimed to be therapeutic, and asked if anyone would care to drink it. **It smelled awful!** None of us would touch it, let alone drink it, so Malcolm pinched his nose and swallowed it down, to the acclaim of all. He told us that when he was conducting a group for our guide (Claire Bostel) a few weeks earlier, she had managed to substitute gin for the mineral spring water. He was rather surprised when he drank it but, on the whole, thought that the gin was far preferable to the water. Before we left, Betsy did manage to screw up her courage and drink a shot of the stuff, and she confirmed that it was terrible.

We were finished with our walking tour at noon, and I went to a bank to cash a traveler's check, then off to the local McDonald's for some real American coffee. McDonald's was thriving, and there was such a long line that I decided to skip it. Our walk had passed the railroad station, and I doubled back and bought us two tickets by train from York to London for the following Sunday. British Rail has a special on Sunday that allows you to "upgrade" to first class for an additional six pounds. The usual "coach" fare is 47 pounds, so we were able to go "first class" for 53 pounds ($94.40) each. I also bought the Monday issue of the *Herald-Tribune*, which confirmed the glum news that it now seemed probable that British Air would, in fact, be going on strike, in time to strand us in London. Well, there are worse places to be stranded.

Several of us had decided that we wanted to be sure to visit Hadrian's Wall while we were in Yorkshire. Claire said she would hire a van to take us there on our "free afternoon" on Wednesday.

At two o'clock our bus set out from Harrogate for Harewood House, a fabulous but not untypical English landed estate where Lord Harewood and his family now live in upstairs apartments. The rest of the place is essentially a museum, 200 years old, and well maintained with beautiful intricate ceilings, gardens designed by Capability Brown, and a bird garden. We rented headsets with a taped tour, dictated by Lord Harewood himself. That led us through the house and described the rooms and their contents, including the huge art collection with works by such artists as El Greco, Tintoretto, Picasso, and Turner. The English are great on refreshments, and one can usually find a place for tea. Harewood House was no exception. Betsy and I stopped for a cup of hot chocolate before returning to Harrogate.

Our evening lecture was given by Ann London, a native Scot, and the Director of History at Harrogate University. She talked in her delightful brogue for an hour on British government and politics, had everyone in stitches, and made us all sorry when her lecture ended.

A brief review: Magna Carta was signed in 1225. In 1701, Parliament passed a law that required that there be a Protestant succession of the crown. Today, the Queen is symbolic, without any real power, all of which resides in the House of Parliament. The House of Lords is unelected, and is the highest court in the country, led by a Speaker, Lord McKay (a Scot).

There are 651 Members of Parliament, and the Prime Minister is chosen from them by the party in power. The PM has a lot of patronage, with 120 Ministers to appoint, and gets to choose the "Whip." "Whip" is a hunting term. The "Whipper In" sees to it that all of the dogs do what they are supposed to do. Very little real work is done on the floor, where people mainly insult each other, and leave the actual work to be done in committees. The earlier political parties were the Whigs and the Tories, who became the Liberals and the Conservatives. Later, James Keir Hardie began what is today's Labor Party. Women were given the vote in 1918, and in 1928 Britain granted full suffrage to everyone.

Talking as fast as a machine gun, but maintaining total clarity, and the complete attention of her audience, Ann London also managed to discuss Margaret Thatcher, Milton Friedman, Adam Smith, John Major, Tony Blair, the Maastricht Treaty, the European Economic Union, and Mad Cow Disease!

There was still time for questions and answers, and by then, we were ready to turn in.

III

Jet lag got us up early, so I walked into town to the train station to buy the Tuesday *Herald-Tribune* for myself and also one for Dick Adams (Dick is as addicted to them as I am). It was cold and wet, so I bundled up, but the walk felt good, and I got back easily in time for breakfast.

At 9 o'clock we left by bus for an all-day trip to the Yorkshire Dales. A "dale" is a valley. The first stop was the town of Grassington, a picturesque village, where I was able to buy a lightweight rain jacket, and Betsy a scarf.

From Grassington we went to Hawes, where we would have a chance to walk through some open countryside. Half of us were walkers and the other half stayed in Hawes to shop, drink tea or coffee, and otherwise pass the time. The walkers, led by Claire, set off through the meadows amid lots of sheep and cows, whose "calling cards" were everywhere. Accordingly, we watched our step during the 45-minute trek to Wensleydale, a little hamlet down the road. On a couple of occasions we had to pass, single file, through a "squeeze style." It is a device that, as its name implies, allows one person at a time to squeeze through, but cannot be navigated by a sheep.

Once in Wensleydale, we crossed the road, walked through a small pub, and then along a path in order to have a look at Hardraw Falls, a very nice waterfall. After that, we returned to the pub (The Green Dragon). Some stayed there, while others went across the street to a little shop advertising coffee. Betsy and I joined Jack and Shirley Geary, of Jackson, Mississippi, where we could sit at a table out front. Even though still cool and damp, the weather did not seem unpleasant and, after a while, Cliff Shultz joined us.

Within a half hour, our bus showed up from Hawes with the non-walkers aboard, and we all drove on to the town of Richmond, a pleasant Yorkshire town, and the locale for the television program, *All Creatures, Great and Small*. In Richmond, we visited the theater designed by Samuel Butler and built in 1788. Closed for 100 years, it has since been renovated and now is back in use.

Howard L. Chapman

Our bus was equipped with a television monitor, and on the way back to Harrogate, Claire played an episode of "All Creatures," with lots of scenes of Richmond to keep us entertained. Once in a while the bus would have to slow up, or even stop, because of sheep on the road. We were told that in an emergency sheep can be scattered by shouting "Mint Jelly!"

IV

Everyone cheered a beautiful, sunny Wednesday morning, as we set out for the day with a first stop being at a little place called Ripley, just on the edge of Harrogate. Then we were on to Ripon, where Claire led us through the marvelous cathedral. It is in excellent condition, with a magnificent wooden ceiling, ornate wood carvings, and the kind of peace that emanates from these great, heavy stone churches of Europe.

Cliff Shultz and guide Claire Bostel at Fountains Abbey.

We spent a little over an hour at Ripon, and then motored on to Fountains Abbey. I had never heard about it and was only mildly interested in the fact that it was on our itinerary. But later I listed it as my "highlight" of the trip. It began as a small abbey run by a group of monks, but grew in size as wealthy nobles donated tracts of land to it. Eventually, Fountains Abbey owned an enormous estate that covered a large part of northern England, and was incredibly rich. The abbey itself had two kinds of monks, including about 96 "lay monks," who handled the business of the abbey, and approximately 46 upper crust monks who prayed and chanted all day. This went on for about 400 years.

When Henry VIII confiscated all of the property of the Catholic Church, the monasteries and the abbeys closed down, and Fountains Abbey was looted. Today, it is a ruin, but a wonderful ruin. The grounds and buildings are under the care of the National Trust, which has built a large, modern, and very comfortable Visitor Center, with a shop, restaurant and other facilities, and which provides the visitor with a short movie about the history of the place.

We saw several groups of school children who were visiting with their teachers. Each group, children and teachers, was given robes similar to those once worn by the monks, and spent a few hours living as the monks did, which included, among other things, not talking. We watched one group sit on the ground in a "room" (the roof is now gone) which had been actually used as a dining area. Each child had been given a lunch similar to the food that the monks had eaten, and while they sat in rows, silently eating, their robed teacher appeared in a balcony above them and read passages aloud from the Bible.

Most of our Northwestern group returned to Harrogate for a free afternoon and an evening lecture. But the Shultzes, Halls, and Chapmans bundled into a private van along with three other members of our group, Orrin Richards, Bernice Williams, and Shirley Dupuis, for a trip North to visit Hadrian's Wall. Both the driver of the van and the guide for the trip were named "Dave," which at least made it easy to remember. It was meal time, but Claire had provisioned each of us with a box lunch prepared by the hotel, so that we could eat as we traveled. There were 14 seats in the van, so one would think that we would have had plenty of room; however, the designers of European vans seem to have given little thought to legroom, so the nine of us felt pretty much like sardines during the two-hour drive to the Wall.

The Emperor Hadrian had the wall built across all of northern England, from coast to coast, in order to defend the land to the South against the wild tribes of the North. It was originally 15 to 20 feet high, but much of it is gone. In most places, it is no more than five feet high, sometimes less. For years, no one paid much attention to it and local farmers cannibalized it in order to use the stones to build their enclosures.

We started at an area known as "Housestead's Fort," where the Romans kept a large contingent of soldiers. There was a very long walk from the parking lot up a steep hill to the fort, and the weather had turned very cold and very windy. (This, we were told, was a nice day!) The foundations of the old fort and much of the wall are still there to explore, and it was fun to imagine the Roman legions there. It was the northern-most part of the Roman Empire and, to the Roman soldiers, it must have seemed the equivalent of Siberia.

Walking along the wall, and reviewing the fort, seeing the topography, and the ingenuity that the Romans used in placing the wall, one could certainly see why it would have been easy to defend this place.

The Romans were in England for approximately 400 years, and when they left they took with them their knowledge of central heating and brick making, as well as other skills, many of which were not re-discovered for centuries.

We made brief stops at other places along the wall, and then headed back to Harrogate. About 30 minutes after we started, our guide cheerily told us that, since we had "extra time" we would take "the long way home," three hours instead of two!

We arrived home at 8 p.m., exhausted, and I had already made up my mind that the next day was going to be my day "out of the bus."

V

Betsy arose dutifully at an early hour in order to leave at 8:30 with the rest of the group for a day in the North York Moors, traveling all the way to the town of Whitby, on the North Sea. I slept in.

Since the hotel only serves breakfast until 9:30, I made sure that I only slept in until 9 o'clock, and made it downstairs to the restaurant in time to eat. Having the day to myself, I started by reading the *Daily Telegraph*, an English newspaper, and spent a little time updating the notes for my journal. I also reflected on the state of modern plumbing, evident in the St. George Hotel, which includes "mini-flush" toilets, designed to conserve water; with the problem, of course, that it takes five or six flushes to thoroughly flush. I wonder how much extra water these devices actually use, as compared to the old ones?

It was a pleasant day, and the five-minute stroll to the railroad station to buy a *Herald-Tribune* stretched into one and a half hours. I found myself detoured by shops, including the local Marks & Spencers. Browsing through it, I found that they sell both wine and mixed drinks in cans (two glasses to a can). The prices throughout the store would be approximately the same as the prices in the U.S., **if** you assumed that the pound and the dollar were equal. The clothes would be expensive even if the prices quoted were in dollars!

Harrogate really is chock full of excellent shops and stores and I had a great time. After buying two copies of the *Herald-Tribune* (one for Dick Adams), I walked to Betty's Tea Room, an institution in Harrogate. There was a line for lunch, but I only had to wait seven or eight minutes, and wound up with a table right next to the window overlooking The Stray and a large flower garden. I accepted the suggestions of the waitress and ordered "Betty's

Rarebit," followed by a strawberry tart with vanilla ice cream, and coffee. We ate no beef, by the way, during our entire time in England. There is a *chance* that the Mad Cow Disease may be contracted by eating tainted beef, and although beef was often on the menu, nobody, even the English, ever seemed to order it.

After lunch (getting past 2 p.m. now) I wandered back to the hotel and found that all of the public areas had become construction zones. I learned that a convention was coming to town and would start on Sunday afternoon, filling up all the hotels within a 50-mile radius. Each hotel was taken over by various exhibitors, and people were building their display cases and exhibit areas - a clamor of banging, grinding, saws, and yelling.

I had contemplated spending a leisurely time with my newspaper and crossword puzzle, but there was no way to hear myself think at the St. George Hotel, so I wandered up the hill to the Old Swan Hotel, found a quiet room called "The Library," and spent a delightful time reading, writing cards, and working the daily crossword puzzle. The Old Swan, which is a four-star hotel, is superior to the St. George and, frankly, I would recommend it for the next visit.

Next, I took a walk to the Valley Gardens, a part of The Stray, with huge beds of roses of all colors. The whole town of Harrogate is crammed with flowers. If it were possible for a place to have too many flowers, Harrogate would have too many. But, of course, such a thing is not possible.

The walk took about 40 minutes and I got back at 6 p.m., and learned that our group had returned, with glowing tales of the visit to the North York Moors and to Whitby.

After dinner, Alumni Campus provided a seminar which was, really, a panel discussion including all of our prior speakers plus another local scholar, Peter Barnwell. Most of the session was given over to questions and answers, give and take with the audience. Everyone was very frank and the discussion was quite interesting, and covered a wide range of topics including the "troubles" in Northern Ireland, the way that England is dealing with immigration, the British national health care system, an evaluation of Prime Minister John Major, and the Royal Divorce.

VI

Friday was a warm, sunny day, although the evening had been cool, and we had slept with the windows open. The main news from the *Herald-Tribune* was that the Dow Jones Industrial Average had dropped more than 100 points the day before.

After breakfast, we left for the city of York, and began with our guide,

Claire, giving a tour of the famous York Minster, a wonderful cathedral. It is an enormous place, but it had lots of people and lots of groups in it. Claire led us through and told us about its history, and about the architecture and the beautiful stained-glass windows. Amazingly, Cliff and Elaine Shultz ran into one of Cliff's patients from home as we were going through.

When we left the Minster, Claire gave us directions so that we could find our restaurant, and we all wandered off with about 45 minutes to explore the "old city" before lunch. It had been 22 years since Betsy and I last were in York, and it has changed some. The change we noticed the most was the fact that it seemed to have so many more people on the streets than we remembered. Still, York continues to be a fascinating and diverting place, where one could spend several days without boredom.

Betsy and Howard Chapman on the wall surrounding the City of York.

The old city is very popular with tourists, which means it is also full of people trying to solicit money for various causes. We were approached by people asking for money to fight kidney disease, help the homeless, or support street musicians. There was no outright begging, however, and none of the behavior was aggressive or offensive.

We gathered at Noon at "Harker's Restaurant" on St. Helen's Square, and I can recommend it. Visitors should also note that there is a "Betty's Tea Room" across the street. Claire had taken orders from everyone on the bus as we drove to York, and then phoned ahead from the bus to the restaurant, so that the meals were served immediately after we sat down. What a good

Snapshots

idea! I wonder if we couldn't use the same procedure when we are traveling at home, and are planning to stop at a particular restaurant.

After lunch, we had more time to wander the city. Bill and Suzanne Hall joined Betsy and me for a walk on the ancient city wall which still goes all the way around the City of York. Betsy and I had done this on our last visit and it lived up to our memories as a wonderful experience, tranquil, uncrowded, and affording excellent views of beautiful lawns and well-tended gardens.

In mid-afternoon we gathered again to travel to Castle Howard, the huge estate that was used as the setting for the public TV series, *"Brideshead Revisited."* The house and grounds are still owned by the Howard Family, who try to keep up with the enormous cost of maintenance by admission fees, concessions, shops, and (I suspect) private donations. The British tax system imposes outrageous death taxes (as in the United States), so it becomes increasingly difficult for a family to maintain ownership of such a place. Many such properties have been given over to the British National Trust as the only means to keep them intact.

Castle Howard. Bill Hall, Suzanne Hall, Howard Chapman, Betsy Chapman, Marcia Adams, Dick Adams, Elaine Shultz, Cliff Shultz.

Both the house and grounds at Castle Howard are amazing. The art that is located in the house is incredible, with many readily recognizable works, including the original Holbein painting of Henry VIII that is so famous.

We visited the beautiful family chapel, that was important in many parts of *Brideshead Revisited*, and a guide there confirmed that the property is *definitely* not part of the National Trust. "That is what you do," she said "when you've given up."

Some members of the Howard Family still live on the premises in private apartments, and each year they close the place to tourists during the Christmas season so that the entire extended family can use it.

There were terrific photo opportunities here, and we drafted some passing Brits as photographers so that "our Fort Wayne group" could all be in the picture at once. They were very kind, with only the small problem that, while one man was taking our picture, his five-year old son disappeared down some steps into the basement of Castle Howard. After some anxiety, the boy was later retrieved without any mishap.

Walking from the mansion to the parking area we walked through the fabulous gardens, which seem to extend forever. They are dominated by all kinds of flowers, including huge roses. Many of the flowers had nametags giving their Latin names. I was able to give the Latin names for all of the others, provided no one else in the group already knew them.

We returned to Harrogate in time for a cocktail party hosted by Dick and Marcia Adams in their "Royal Baths Suite," which easily accommodated all of the Fort Wayne travelers, including the Fetters, the Baachs, and Greg Fryzsel.

After dinner, the lingering daylight left time for an evening walk. Betsy and I ran into the Shultzes, and the four of us came upon a place called the "Delaine Hotel." It is a very small inn with a stunning garden that, given its size, may be the best of all the gardens that we saw.

VII

On our last day with the Northwestern group we proceeded to Haworth, a small village to the southwest, that is now famous as the home of the Bronte Sisters. The father, Patrick Bronte, was the curate at the village church and his job entitled him to a life tenancy in the parsonage, now a museum. Close by the parsonage is the village church where he preached and, between the church and the parsonage, lies the village churchyard, or cemetery.

He had six children altogether, but the literary sisters, Charlotte, Emily and Anne, were the most famous. Charlotte is best known for "Jane Eyre," Emily for "Wuthering Heights," and Anne for "The Tenant of Wildfell Hall." Patrick's wife, and all of his six children, died before he did, and he lived out the rest of his life in the parsonage where he died in 1861.

Snapshots

Charlotte was the last child to die, and her father resisted her marriage plans for the very reason that she would probably get pregnant and die in childbirth which, in fact, is about what transpired. She died shortly before her 39th birthday, in the latter stages of pregnancy.

The parsonage is not very big, and visitors are only allowed into it in small groups. Those who are waiting cue up in a line from the front door and, if it is raining, they simply get wet. We were fortunate in that, although it was a gray day, it was not raining and, besides, Claire had arranged for us to go around most of the line. The museum is very well maintained, very well exhibited, and very much worth the visit.

A lot of the furnishings that are now on display are nicer than I expected to see; however, we learned that most of them had been purchased by Charlotte after she had begun to earn substantial sums of money for her writing. The sisters had to write their books on very small pieces of paper, not much bigger than a modern post card, and their handwriting is so small as to be almost illegible. Several examples are on display. Some of the clothes worn by the family were mounted on models, and we were struck by the small stature of the people of those times, less than 150 years ago.

During the 1800's, a lot of people died young. Patrick Bronte was a crusader against open sewers, contaminated water, and "overcrowding" in the cemetery (all of which appear to have contributed to a general lack of sanitation and a short life expectancy in the village). In the cemetery, for instance, it was common that persons be buried as many as ten people in one plot, one on top of the other, with only a few inches in between.

The parsonage itself faces east, looking across the churchyard toward the church, and the west faces out across the moors. It is not hard to imagine Emily Bronte writing "Wuthering Heights" in such a place.

Bill Hall and I set off for a walk across the moor, but found that the path led us only to a highway, and that most of the areas that we could see have now been enclosed by local farmers. A sign directed walkers to stay on the path, which we did, except for the times that we had to step around sheep or their calling cards. Had we been able to venture further we probably could have found the "open, unenclosed, and very wild moors" that have become so famous in English literature.

Walking back through the churchyard, we stopped to examine some of the tall, vertical tombstones which listed, in chronological order, all of those laid to rest beneath them. At the base of one, I noticed what appeared to be a furry ball, about the size of an oversized softball, and Bill told me that it was a hedgehog, rolled up in a ball in defense against a possible enemy (us). We got down close enough that we could see the slight movement caused by breathing, but otherwise decided to leave it alone.

The church is small but quite pleasant. Perhaps nicer, in fact, than it was when the Brontes were there, and undoubtedly helped by contributions from the constant procession of tourists. There is a bronze plaque in the floor in memory of Charlotte Bronte and Emily Bronte, and a sign on a pillar says that they are interred beneath.

There was a little time before lunch to browse through the town, which is very quaint and cheery, and doubtless reflects the fact that it is a substantial tourist attraction.

Haworth Parsonage, home of the Brontes.

Lunch had been arranged at a tavern/restaurant called "The Black Bull," which can be recommended, especially the Yorkshire pudding or the chicken pie. Out in front of "The Black Bull" was a sign advertising the day's menu, and another sign above it that said, *"Well behaved children are welcome until 8:30 p.m."*

As in York, our guide, Claire, had called ahead to The Black Bull and given our lunch orders, so that the food was served almost as soon as we sat down. (How did tour guides manage before the invention of mobile phones?) The Bronte sisters had a brother, Branwell Bronte, who may have had some talent as a painter, possibly a modest talent as a poet, but mainly seemed to have been frustrated by his sisters' success, and his comparative lack of it. He was

Snapshots

a "regular" at The Black Bull, to the extent that he had his own chair reserved, together with a "pull for service" cord, which he used when his tankard ran dry. Not surprisingly, Branwell died at an even younger age than his sisters.

For the first and last time on this trip, the price of the tour included beer or wine at a meal, so we all took advantage of the opportunity. The barmaid asked me what I wanted and I said that I wanted a pint of her best beer, after which she brought me a pint of Stella Artois, which was, indeed, very good. She being a barmaid, I asked her if she enjoyed reading the comic strip called "Andy Capp;" however, she advised that she had never heard of "Andy Capp."

With the weather cool and a slight drizzle, we began our trip back to Harrogate at 3:30 p.m. When we got on the bus, we found that Claire had festooned it with red, white and blue streamers, and British and American flags. She handed out copies of the words to several British patriotic songs, and then played the music over the loudspeaker. Whenever it was time to sing, she led us all in boisterous songs including "Land Of Hope And Glory," and "Rule Britannia." Even after a week, we were all impressed with the enormous level of energy and enthusiasm that she brings to this job!

Once back at the hotel Betsy, Bill and Sue Hall, and I hired a taxi to take us to Harlow Carr Gardens on the outskirts of Harrogate. These are considered to be "experimental" gardens and, although they are very extensive, they are also "different."

We encountered Dick and Adie Baach, and Gregory Fryzel, who told us that they had walked from town, so we decided we would walk back. It was a nice walk, only about two miles, and all either level or downhill. On the way, we went through still more gardens, the "Valley Gardens," and then strolled on back to the Hotel St. George.

Alumni Campus Abroad had arranged for a ceremony at 6:00 p.m. in one of the hotel's meeting rooms, where champagne was served, and everyone received a "Northwestern University Certificate of Achievement," and a Northwestern University lapel pin. I told Cliff Shultz, Bill Hall and Dick Adams that they may now all proudly consider themselves "Northwestern Alums," and insisted that they put their lapel pins on their jackets. I explained that their achievements will entitle them to receive future mailings soliciting funds for the school, and that they, as alums, should feel proud to participate.

The "final" dinner included entertainment: a performance by four singers who sang, *a cappella*, English madrigals, and then some more modern pieces. Then it was time to pack and get to bed early for a travel day tomorrow.

VIII

It was Sunday morning, July 14, 1996. Amidst a flurry of goodbyes, the group scattered. Half were going home, and the rest were "extending." Thankfully, the dispute between British Airlines and its employees had been resolved, and the threat of a strike was over. We would all be able to get home!

Claire had arranged for a car to pick up Betsy and me at our hotel and to drive us to the railroad station in York. At 10:30 a.m., our train rolled in and, at 10:36 a.m., exactly on schedule, it left. Our coach only had about six passengers in it (because, I suspect, it was a Sunday), and we "spread out" for the trip to London.

What a joy to travel by train in England! It is clean and comfortable, has a buffet car, and even has pay telephones onboard. It was a pleasant summer day, perfect for traveling and for watching the countryside go by until our arrival at Kings Cross Station.

We were staying at Claridge's, a lovely, if pricey, and very comfortable hotel. Claridge's has a special arrangement with the American Bar Association, whereby American members of the ABA can obtain a very favorable rate, and I recommend the hotel highly.

It was Sunday night, so all of the theaters were dark and a lot of the restaurants were closed. After several calls, we wound up at a restaurant called "LeCriterion" on Piccadilly Circus. It turned out to be very French, very expensive, and very unsatisfying. First of all, Piccadilly Circus has become a little bit like Times Square in New York was ten or twenty years ago: hordes of people, most of whom seemed to be trying to make themselves look as unsavory as possible. Tattoos, skinheads, drunks, pierced parts, pink hair, black lipstick, on and on. Brits in rebellion, I guess. We had walked over, but decided to take a taxi back.

IX

Claridge's is a very formal atmosphere, and the telephone operator advised that a coat and tie would be required in the dining room for breakfast. This turned out not to be true; in fact, some of the people eating breakfast looked as if they had slept in their clothes.

It was a sunny and very warm day, much hotter in London than in Yorkshire. In London the subway is called "the tube," and for the sum of three pounds each, we were able to buy all day tickets. These allowed us to go anywhere in London, as much as we liked.

We started by taking the tube out to Little Venice, an interesting neighborhood which actually does have canals. We strolled about, considered a boat ride and then reconsidered, walked some more, and came upon the former home of Lillie Langtree, mistress of Edward VII. It is a gorgeous, serene and heavily secured house with fences, gates, dogs, surveillance cameras, and a speaker/buzzer device at the door. Who on earth lives here now? We never found out.

After walking through the neighborhood, we went to a little pub called "Warwick Castle," where we shared a "ploughman's lunch," and had a beer. It is a good place to stop if you are in the neighborhood.

Back on the tube, we headed for the Albert & Victoria Museum to see the William Morris Exhibit. Halfway there, a voice came over the loudspeaker of the train and announced "a problem with the doors," and said that everyone would have to get off at the next stop, and wait for another train. Naturally, everyone on the train thought "bomb." Anyway, there was no bomb, and I think it probably was just a "problem with the doors."

The Albert & Victoria Museum is huge, much larger than I expected. The William Morris Exhibit was also enormous. We did not have nearly enough time to take it all in, but it was certainly well worth doing.

After a nap and a change of clothes, we went to get a bite to eat at a tearoom called "LeRichoux," a short walk from Claridge's on South Audley Street. I believe that "LeRichoux" is a part of a chain but, in any event, they do very well, the service was good, and so was the food. (In London, having dinner before the theater is a little bit of a problem because the shows tend to start earlier than they do at home, as early as 7:00 or 7:30 p.m.)

After dinner, a taxi took us to the Garrick Theater to see *An Inspector Calls*. We had tried to see it the last time we were in London, but had not been able to work it in. It was written by J. B. Priestly some fifty years ago, and was intended as a "drawing room drama." The modern version has been substantially "theatricalized," but it was still fun.

X

We had arranged with Claridge's for a 4:00 p.m. check-out time so that we could spend Tuesday shopping, and then meet our friends, John and Jean Campion, who would join us at 5:00 p.m. The *Herald-Tribune* told us that the Olympic Games were about to begin in Atlanta, and that the stock market had dropped 161 points the previous day.

I had intended to replace my Burberry raincoat, which I bought in London in 1985. Burberry was, in fact, having a sale, so we walked to the original store on Haymarket Street. There were lots of raincoats like mine "on sale" but none of them in my size. The salesman said that there was "plenty of non-sale merchandise in regular stock downstairs," and that I could doubtless find my size there. Problem: "the sale price" was 245 pounds, whereas the "regular price" was 425 pounds, a difference of nearly $300! I decided to try the other store.

We walked back up Regent Street and stopped at Tower Records, where Betsy bought a CD with all the patriotic music that Claire Bostel had played for us in the bus on the way home from Haworth. The Regent Street Burberry Store had a bigger selection of "on sale" raincoats, but none that fit me. The salesman there picked out one that he insisted I put on, and told me that it fit, but it was much too big with sleeves so long that my hands disappeared. I gave up on Burberry in London and decided to try again in Chicago.

We stopped at an ATM machine, and once again marveled at modern technology which allows us to insert a plastic card into a machine, anywhere in the world, and get back local currency.

Our next stop was The Wallace Collection on Manchester Square. It is an excellent art collection housed in a large and interesting house, with free admission. Notable works include "The Laughing Cavalier," by Hals, and "Lady With A Fan," by Velasquez.

We got back to Claridge's in time to clean-up and pack, and had room service send up some soup and tea, after which we checked out of the room and read in the lobby until the Campions arrived. We had booked a table in "The Causerie," a small and somewhat informal restaurant located in Claridge's, which opens at 5:30 p.m. John Campion had arranged for us to go to the Old Vic to see Oscar Wilde's "The Ideal Husband" this evening, and it was necessary to dine early in order to make the curtain.

John and Jean appeared separately, but both on time, and it was wonderful to renew our acquaintance and bring each other up to date. Dinner was a little bit rushed, but we found a taxi to take us to the theater, and had no trouble getting there on time. The show was quite good, and the Old Vic is a wonderful theater. After the play, we got a taxi back to Claridge's where we picked up the Campion's car, loaded in our luggage, and made the 30 minute drive to their charming home. Although their address is "London," they are close to the edge of the city, and almost in the village of Richmond on Thames (not to be confused with the Richmond that we visited in Yorkshire). Jean served tea and biscuits, and we chatted until after midnight. Once again, they proved easy to be with, and stimulating company.

XI

Wednesday was a sunny, cool morning, and very pleasant. After breakfast we took our coffee in their marvelous garden. We were not sure whether John or Jean is the "real" gardener, but John insists that it is Jean.

After breakfast we drove through Richmond Park, once the King's private hunting area, unfenced, and full of deer. Large herds of them could be seen sitting around in shady spots, oblivious to people and passing cars. Once in Richmond, John and I went for a stroll along the Thames (it is still tidal here), and then through the town. John took me into the handsome theater, which houses events from opera to dance to readings to rock bands. Richmond is a pure delight. My notes include: "flowers, boats, quaint buildings, interesting shops, clean, sedate, peaceful."

We met Betsy and Jean, who had been shopping, and went to a pub called "The White Swan," where we were able to eat lunch in a garden in the back. (One has to know about these places!)

It seemed to be a lovely day to visit Kew Gardens. The village of Kew is right next door to Richmond, so we drove over there, only to find the gardens absolutely packed. There were endless lines of cars and tourist buses, one group after another, and numberless backpackers and hikers. Jean suggested that we forget Kew Gardens and go instead to Syon House. Neither Betsy nor I had ever heard of it so, of course, we were eager.

Serendipity. Syon House, house and grounds, is the estate of the Duke of Northumberland. It has a fine botanical conservatory, grounds and gardens. We all rented the audio tape tour of the house, which is a beauty, and was not crowded! The place is now operated by the British National Trust, which means a National Trust Shop, and Betsy got - yet another - tea towel.

We left at 4:00 p.m. to go back to the Campions' for tea, stopping on the way at the railroad station so that I could duck in and buy a current *Herald-Tribune*. The market had dropped 161 points on Monday, and was down as much on Tuesday, before recovering to a 9 point gain. The British Open Golf Tournament was about to begin, and John Daly would defend his title. Would the warm weather favor the Americans? (A lot of the British players had been tuning up in recent weeks at inclement places like Carnoustie.) The opening ceremony of the Olympic Games would occur on Friday night. Will Atlanta be too hot and steamy? (The BBC news showed a Welsh cyclist training for the games and trying to acclimate himself at home by riding a stationary bicycle in his kitchen, with a teakettle steaming at his feet.)

After tea, we relaxed, read and napped. Jean, living up to our recollections of her excellent cooking, served a delicious meal at the very civilized hour of 8:15 p.m., leaving plenty of time afterwards to visit, and then pack for our departure home.

Betsy Chapman and Jean Campion in the Campion's garden at Richmond on Thames.

XII

On Thursday morning we said our farewells to Jean, and John drove us to London Heathrow Airport. The drive took longer than usual because of the traffic, which may have been aggravated by the fact that there was a "one day strike" imposed by the London subway workers. John got us there, nonetheless, in good time.

After clearing customs, Betsy even had time to buy "one last plate" from the Harrod's Shop in the duty free area.

Chapter 10

TAKAOKA: 20 YEARS

A Saga That Began In 1977

I

All of the airlines seem to be crammed full of passengers these days, and Northwest Airlines seems to be overbooked every time we travel with them. Our flight from Detroit to Osaka, Japan, on May 25, 1997, was no different. There were thirty eight of us traveling from Fort Wayne, Indiana, to Takaoka, Japan, to commemorate the twentieth anniversary of the official affiliation between Fort Wayne and Takaoka as Sister Cities. Our party included Fort Wayne's Mayor, Paul Helmke (who would join us in Kyoto), the Freimann Quartet from the Fort Wayne Philharmonic Orchestra, several members of the Fort Wayne Sister Cities Committee, and others interested in the Sister Cities program.

Rain was coming down in buckets all morning and Northwest was offering a $1,000 "travel voucher" to anyone who would agree to take a different flight. Airlines seldom tell their passengers the truth. In this case, the gate attendants insisted that the plane was not overbooked, but that the airline simply had to "reduce the weight" of the cargo. We were traveling on a Boeing 747!

The flight from Detroit to Osaka is 13-1/2 hours in length, and the time in Japan is 14 hours ahead of Fort Wayne (in the summer). The Wall Street Journal indicated that the Dollar was worth ¥115, although I later found I could only get about ¥112 at the Currency Exchange. Betsy checked her notes

Howard L. Chapman

from our first trip to Takaoka in 1977 and found that, at that time, the Dollar was worth ¥275. No wonder things now seem to be expensive in Japan!

The airport in **Osaka** is built on a man-made island, and there is nothing else but the airport on the island. This seems quite an engineering feat, but the result is a very user-friendly airport. The drive from the airport to our hotel, the Hotel Nankai South Tower, took nearly an hour. It is a huge hotel, new and glitzy, and all of the Japanese were very well dressed. We, of course, appeared in blue jeans.

While driving to the hotel, we learned that this was Ginny Clark's birthday. Deb Nitka, one of the Freimann Quartet members, asked to use the bus microphone in order to make the announcement, but the bus-girl attendant did not understand English. Fortunately, Hiromi Ito was handy and explained what we wanted in Japanese, and then Deb got on the mike and led us all in singing "Happy Birthday" to Ginny. Hiromi Ito is the Concertmaster for the Fort Wayne Philharmonic and a member of the Freimann Quartet. He was born in Japan, and tells us that he is not related to the Judge in California that became famous by presiding over the O.J. Simpson case.

We arrived hot and tired, but the hotel room was very comfortable. As with many Japanese hotels, there is no electricity available in the room when you enter. There is a piece of plastic attached to the room key and, in order to turn on the electricity, you have to drop the key into a little box on the wall next to the door. As soon as you do that, the lights come on.

Inspecting the bathroom (Western style) we noticed that there was a drain in the floor that was outside the tub. Jane Keltsch explained to me that this is so that Japanese guests can bathe before they get in the tub to soak, as is the Japanese custom.

The room had a mini-bar with bottled water, canned coffee, and an assortment of soft drinks, all available at a charge of ¥350 (about $3.00) each. In addition, there was a device that would allow you to prepare hot water, and bags to make green tea, apparently at no charge.

Betsy and I were practically the only people there when we appeared in the "Wedgewood Tea Room" on the main floor of the hotel. We were served orange juice and "tea sandwiches" by high school girl waitresses dressed in black and white outfits. They had no English, but lots of giggles.

As we were about to turn in for the night, at 6:30 p.m., Will and Ginny Clark came to our room, all dressed up, and asked if we wanted to go out to dinner and sightseeing with them. Where do they get the energy? Maybe they had slept on the plane. Anyway, we begged off and were asleep by 7:00 p.m.

II

Our first full day in Japan was a pleasant, sunny day. The hotel offered continental breakfast for ¥1200 (about $11.00), or "American Healthy Style" breakfast for ¥2300. Our group had been offered a package deal to buy eight full American breakfasts for $150.00 while on the trip, but no one had taken them up on it, because everyone thought it was too high. We began to see, now, that maybe it wasn't such a bad deal after all.

After breakfast, our group assembled in the lobby and we met our guide, Mr. Kondo, an employee of Japan Travel Bureau (everywhere referred to as "JTB"). The Sister Cities Committee had retained JTB to arrange our trip for us. After everyone got on the bus, Mr. Kondo used the microphone to tell us about the schedule for the day, emphasizing the need to stay on schedule. "You will please cooperate," he said.

Going through the city of Osaka, we learned that it has a population of 2.6 million. It's a very clean, modern city, with a good network of subways, and mucho traffic. During rush hour, we were told, "walking is better than driving." A recent earthquake in nearby Kobe did terrible damage and killed an astonishing 6,000 people, but Osaka was relatively unscathed. Mr. Kondo (the Japanese would say "Kondo-san") also gave us a thumbnail history of Japan, starting with the feudal period (seven centuries of control by warlords), then the civil war period, under the Shoguns. At one point a young man in a yellow jacket and black helmet zipped through traffic and around the bus on a noisy motorcycle, and Kondo-san told us that he is referred to as "a Kamikaze."

Tourist buses in Japan often have uniformed young women attendants on board, much like airline stewardesses. I asked Kondo-san what this person is called, and he said "bus guide." "Yes," I said, "but what is she called in Japanese?" Very slowly - "Bus-guide."

Our first stop was **Osaka Castle**, a huge place, centuries old, surrounded by two large moats, with steep stone walls, and thought, in its day, to be invincible. It was built by a man named Hideyoshi, who is credited with unifying Japan. When he died, factional fighting broke out and the castle was destroyed, only to be rebuilt. This began a cycle that was repeated many times over the centuries. In recent years it has been renovated extensively to restore it to its 16th Century style.

I was again surprised at how many signs are written in English, on stores and buildings, on highways, and in public buildings and railway stations. There was a steep climb going in to the castle, and we passed our first bank of automatic beverage machines, found everyplace in Japan. There are often as many as seven or eight of them in a row, offering all kinds of things to drink, including Coca Cola, juices, hot coffee - even canned tap water. They will accept coins or paper money, and make change as appropriate.

Once inside the walls and up the hill, we entered the castle itself, which is now a museum. One takes an elevator to the top (whence a fine view of the city), and walks down a floor at a time. The museum is well done and, as with most public places we visited, was full of school children. Those of high school age travel in their school uniforms, while the younger children, even if not in uniform, can be identified by some common item of apparel, usually a distinctive cap. The children are always friendly, curious, happy and well behaved.

Japanese often practice both Buddhism and Shintoism. Buddha was originally from India, but Buddhism has been practiced in Japan since the 6th Century and one sees many Buddhist temples. Shintoism developed from nature worship and ancestor worship, and considered the Emperor to be a living God. It is unique to Japan and there is very little written record of it.

We went on to the **Shitennoji Temple**, built near the end of the 6th Century. It has been razed, burned down, and rebuilt many times, most recently after World War II. There is an impressive pagoda in the center and Kondo-san explained to us that pagodas always have an odd number of levels or floors. On the first level there was a shrine and evidence of incense and other offerings, including extraordinary fresh apples that looked too good to be real. We were told that these apples (and other varieties of fruit) are very expensive, and are only purchased for the purpose of making offerings at shrines or for a special occasion such as a gift to someone in the hospital. The temple had another bank of soft drink machines and just about any beverage was available for ¥110. Betsy bought a can of lemonade, and I bought a coke.

We left Osaka and drove for about two hours to **Kyoto**, my third visit, and Betsy's second. Kyoto was once the capital of Japan and now is its cultural and historic center. Although it is a city of 1.7 million people, it is not known for its industry. Kyoto is a glorious place, full of temples, shrines, cherry trees, and parks. It was not bombed during World War II. Mac Parker was in Japan in the U.S. Navy during the fifties and said that Kyoto was spared pursuant to express instructions from Franklin D. Roosevelt.

One of the things I noticed on this trip was that the Japanese toll roads are not cheap. The toll from Osaka to Kyoto can run as high as $32, depending on what kind of vehicle you are driving. It is possible to buy a prepaid toll card that can be presented at the toll booth and "punched" electronically to charge the tolls.

We were to stay at the New Miyako Hotel, across the street from the

Snapshots

enormous main railroad station, the same hotel where we stayed when our Sister City delegation came here in 1989. After settling in the rooms, cleaning up and resting a little, it was time for lunch. Betsy and I went across the street to the railroad station with Mac and Pat Parker, Bill and Anita Cast, and Mike and Grace Mastrangelo, and found a place that had a table big enough for all of us.

The menu was in Japanese, but had a little English, plus pictures. As with most Japanese restaurants, there was a display case in front of the restaurant with plastic replicas of various dishes, so we all went out front with the waitress and pointed out what we wanted. Some had the "daily special," mainly rice, with beef curry and gravy. Others had what turned out to be strips of beef, and I had Spaghetti Napolitan. All of it was good, and mine was *really good*. The people who waited on us were lovely, and there was beer and good cheer all around.

After lunch, our group was joined by Patty Griest, Jane Keltsch, and Will and Ginny Clark. We decided to go exploring. Mac Parker and Bill Cast had maps that they had gotten at the hotel, so we knew we would have no problem getting around. Our hotel also provided us with a shuttle bus that took us through the city for about a half hour, and then let us out at an interesting, historic part of town. Of course, we were totally lost.

We set off walking past fascinating stores of all kinds, and through several tranquil and lovely parks and shrines (Kyoto is full of them). Eventually, we came to **Chion-In** temple, and walked up a monster flight of steep steps, which led to even more steep steps, onward and upward, until we finally came to a beautiful Shinto shrine. There was also an interesting cemetery, with prayers written on slats of bamboo, and fresh flowers on many of the graves.

The site invited more climbing, but some decided to head back down the hill to the Miyako Hotel (not our hotel, but owned by the same company). The rest kept climbing. Eventually, we got to the top of the hill and started down the other side, through more gardens, exotic plants and flowers. We stopped in an antique shop and spoke to the owner, an elderly man who spoke excellent English and had a shop full of lovely things. I was especially interested in a framed Bernard Buffet print, signed and numbered, which he offered for ¥360,000 (I was not interested in buying it, but because we own one, purchased years ago, and I was amazed at the price).

We wandered along our way and eventually found our friends at the Miyako Hotel, where a round of seven beers cost ¥5,775 ($52.00!). We were able to get the shuttle bus back to our hotel, the New Miyako, and by then it was nearly 7:00 o'clock in the evening.

We headed back to the railroad station with the Parkers and Casts to find a different restaurant, followed by more pointing at things in the front window. I started by pointing at a salad, thinking I would order just the salad, but a Japanese man standing next to me explained that the salad was part of a "set" - a whole dinner. One cannot buy just the salad. If I had continued to order the way I intended, picking out a salad here, an entree there, and a vegetable somewhere else, I would have gotten several "sets," and would have had enough food to feed ten people! What I finally got, shrimp tempura, rice and a salad, was excellent, enhanced by the Japanese beer. Asahi and Kirin are both good brands.

After eating, we explored the bustling railroad station, and then walked outside past a sea of bicycles and scooters. People park them at the train station, and then take the train to wherever it is that they work. On the way back to the hotel we stopped to check out a restaurant called "Colorado Coffee House," and then went back to our rooms to be in bed by 9:30.

III

Wednesday was another beautiful day. Betsy and I were joined in the coffee shop of the New Miyako Hotel by Jane Keltsch and Patty Griest for another absurdly expensive breakfast. At 8:30 we departed by bus with Kondo-san for a day of sightseeing in the delightful city of Kyoto. This was my third visit, and I had seen some of these things before, but they are so interesting and attractive that I was quite content to visit all of them again.

We began at **Nijo Castle**, which is really a number of buildings and extensive grounds, covering several acres. Here, for the first time, we encountered the Japanese custom of leaving shoes at the door and walking in slippers that are provided. This usually occurs only at places that have wooden floors or tatami mats on the floor. Photographs were not permitted in any of the buildings because the light from the flash is considered harmful to some of the art, especially that which is quite ancient. The castle is chock full of carvings and paintings and surrounded by fine gardens.

We continued to encounter large groups of school children, and Kondo-san took the opportunity to tell us a little bit about the Japanese school system. Six years of elementary school and three years of junior high school are compulsory, after which 95% of Japanese children attend an additional three years of high school (which is not compulsory). About 40% of them go on to college, a four-year program.

The Japanese school year begins in April and ends in March, with five weeks summer vacation, two weeks winter vacation, and two weeks spring vacation. Each school year is divided into three terms. During the six years

Snapshots

of junior high school and high school, the students study English. However, in the past, emphasis has been on reading and writing, and not much on conversation. As a result, most young Japanese can readily read and write English, but are unable to speak hardly at all. We were told that this is changing, and that schools are beginning to put more stress on actually speaking the language.

The public elementary schools do not have uniforms, although the private elementary schools may have uniforms in some cases. Beginning with junior high school, and including high school, nearly all Japanese school children have uniforms. These uniforms are always worn when traveling on school excursions. This explains why we continued to see one group after another in their uniforms.

At Nijo Castle, we saw several uniformed groups, and all were delightful, as usual. At a souvenir shop, one group of girls struck up a conversation with Lenelle Morse (one of the Freimann Quartet), and had her pose for photos with their cameras. (I think that every vacationing school child in Japan carries a camera.)

Another Freimann Quartet member, Hiromi Ito, had been unable to accompany us for the sightseeing trip in Kyoto because of a problem that developed with his violin. Each member of the Freimann Quartet carried their instruments with them on the airplane, and Hiromi's violin suffered from some damage, which may have been attributable to the dryness and changes in air pressure during the long flight. Hiromi had gone back to Osaka on Tuesday to see if he could have it repaired, but found that it could not be done in time for the performance that was planned in Takaoka. This day he went again to Tokyo in order to borrow a suitable violin. I could see that Hiromi was pretty concerned about all of this, but I also reflected that it was very fortunate that he was able to speak Japanese and could easily travel to these various places and make these arrangements; it sure would have been hard for any of the rest of us.

We passed a newsstand and I managed to pick up a current copy of the *Herald-Tribune*. Here is some of the news of the day: the Supreme Court has ruled that President Clinton has to respond to the Paula Jones lawsuit, and cannot postpone it until he is out of office; the Indianapolis 500 mile race was delayed for two days in a row because of rainy weather (glad *we* were in sunny Japan!); it was eventually won by Arie Luyendyk; the Miami Heat is playing the Chicago Bulls in the NBA playoffs; the Bulls are up three games to one; and, the United States and Russia have entered into an agreement whereby several Eastern European countries will be allowed to join NATO.

Howard L. Chapman

IV

We next came to the **Gold Pavilion**, built by a Shogun in the 14th Century, and probably one of the most popular, and most familiar tourist attractions in Japan. A deranged Buddhist monk set fire to it and burned it down in 1950, but by 1955 an exact replica had been constructed. The place was loaded with tourists, tourist buses and school children, but they are long accustomed to big crowds of tourists here, and it didn't seem too congested, notwithstanding all of the people. The beautiful gardens evoked a feeling of tranquility, even though there were hoards of people all around them. When the school children saw Americans, they would say "Hello," and then break up into helpless laughter when we said "Hello" back to them.

At the entrance, Kondo-san received a stack of papers and distributed one to each of us, explaining that each paper had good luck properties. It would keep us and our families well, and otherwise bring good fortune "for a period of one year." After one year, one is expected to come back and get another one.

Traveling to the next stop gave Kondo-san a chance to tell us a little bit about Japanese writing and language. The Japanese "borrowed" Chinese characters and have used them since the 3rd Century. The characters have the same meaning as in Chinese, but are not used in the same way grammatically, nor are they pronounced the same.

In the Tenth Century, a Japanese alphabet was created by women in the Imperial Court, which used some aspects of Chinese characters. A Chinese character is like a word, whereas Japanese characters are phonetics, much like our own alphabet. The Japanese language uses both, and they are interspersed. In order to read and write Japanese, one must learn a minimum of 3,000 "basic" Chinese characters (the average person learns more), as well as the 46 Japanese characters.

We passed a subway station and were told that Kyoto has only one subway line, running North and South. There have been efforts, from time to time, to dig additional subway lines, but each time they dig they unearth so many relics that they have to stop and excavate, and the original project eventually fades away.

We arrived at a Buddhist temple with the mouthful name of **Sanjusangendo Temple**. It is famous because it has 1,000 life-size statues of Buddha in addition to a giant, center statue. The number 1,000 signifies "perfect mercy" or "perfect peace." It was originally built in the year 1164, and rebuilt in 1266. Each statue is different, with a different face, and multiple hands. A monk was busy in front of the main, central image performing a ceremony, which appeared to include offerings of fruit and sake. Each evening, we were told, the Monks are allowed to consume offerings like this that are presented during the day.

We proceeded to drive to our final sightseeing stop of the day, another enormous complex, called **Kiyomizu Temple** (Kiyomizu means "pure water"). It was originally built in the year 798, and has burned down and been rebuilt several times, but the present buildings date from 1633. To get to the temple itself, it was necessary to walk quite a long way up a very steep hill, through streets so crowded with people that the buses could not go up the hill. There were throngs of tourist groups, and each leader had some device, such as a flag or an umbrella, that they would hold over their heads to help their group stay in touch. The huge mobs of people did seem to be too much; and yet, everyone was polite, friendly and orderly.

Once at the gates to the temple, Kondo-san bought entrance tickets and we followed behind his orange flag into the garden area. There was time for photos and then several more sets of stairs and climbing. Once on top, it was possible to look down on the entire city of Kyoto, which is set in a form of basin, with mountains on three sides. There were several places where one could take a drink of the "pure water," and thus achieve health, wealth, and wisdom. Metal cups on long arms were set around at various places, and people would use these to dip the water, or reach under a waterfall, and catch the water and drink it.

Although the water may be pure, I wasn't so sure about all the people using those cups, so I decided to pass up the opportunity for assurance of health, wealth and wisdom, and just hope for the best. The enormous crowds of people made us feel like sardines in a can, and there was a tremendous amount of noise including a couple of people with radios, lots of laughing and yelling, and numerous ebullient children.

The crowds made it impossible for our group to stay together, but we had been given instructions to gather again at a prearranged time, which we did, and wandered back down the hill to our waiting bus. On the way, we passed shop after shop, and all of the world's knickknacks and kitsch appeared to be on display. By now I knew enough to look for one of the ubiquitous vending machines, and was able to buy a cold can of Coca-Cola to drink as I walked back to the bus. I was able to dispose of the can at the bus lot where, as is common throughout Japan, there were three trash cans in a row, one that would accept only cans, one for paper (such as magazines or newspapers), and the last one for "other." Each receptacle had the appropriate words written on it, both in Japanese and in English. Clearly, the Japanese are well into recycling.

V

It was past lunchtime, and it seemed impossible that we could have seen and done so much in a morning. Our bus dropped us off at 2:25 at the "Handicraft Center," an above-average souvenir and craft store that, I think, is publicly owned. I recognized it from my last visit in 1989.

There is a buffet available on the top floor, which was cold and blah, but we were hungry and decided that it would do. After lunch we did a little shopping, and then got on the free shuttle bus that got us back to our hotel by 4:00 p.m.

The New Miyako is not nearly up to the standard of our Osaka hotel, but it is ahead in one respect: our room was equipped with the new Japanese high-tech toilet. The bowl had a big, plastic attachment on it, with an arm sticking out on the right side. The arm had five buttons and a dial on it, with instructions under each one. There were still more instructions on the lid of the toilet seat and on the wall above the toilet. Nearly all of the instructions were written in Japanese, but there were a few words in English. For example, on the instructions on the wall, I could read "Important: Always follow safety instructions." A few lines down appeared the word "WARNING," and, a few lines below that, the word "CAUTION." Everything else was written in Japanese.

We had received prior warning of these devices and thus were very careful to figure out how to flush before using. Once we figured that out, we left all the buttons and dials alone. Bill Cast, on the other hand, reported that he used all of his buttons and had a satisfactory experience. This could not, however, be verified.

VI

Betsy and I met Bernard and LaDonna Huntley James at breakfast in the hotel dining room, and had a great time catching up with them, and talking about "old times" with the Sister Cities Committee. LaDonna and I have been involved in it from the beginning, and she was with us on our first trip to Takaoka, in 1977. She has retired from her job at Lincoln National Corporation and she and Bernard have bought a home in North Carolina, where she is writing saucy "romance" novels. It was Thursday morning, and we were excited because this was the day we would arrive in Takaoka.

Our delegation gathered in the lobby and was introduced to Susan Lane and Syuji Sasaki. The two of them had come yesterday afternoon from Takaoka to escort us on the train today. They distributed copies of a schedule

Snapshots

(*several pages, and bound*) of the events that were planned for our group while we would be in Takaoka.

Susan Lane is from Fort Wayne, and became interested in Japanese while a student at North Side High School. She continued studying Japanese in college, and studied and lived in Japan, and eventually took a job in Takaoka, working with the City Administration. Mr. Sasaki, one of her bosses, is "Chief of International Affairs Section, Takaoka Planning and Coordination Department."

As we walked across the street to the Kyoto railroad station, this time to catch a train, not to eat, there was a light rain falling, but not enough to get us seriously wet. There were several platforms, and a first time traveler to Japan might have had some trouble figuring out just where to catch his train; but, with Susan and Sasaki-san with us, we easily found the correct spot to wait. Our train was scheduled to leave Kyoto at 9:39. Several trains came and went, but we held our place until a train came at 9:37 (according to the station clock) and left (with us on it) at 9:39 precisely.

Traveling by train in Japan is a delight. There are things to eat that are sold on the train; however, there was no "dining car" on this particular train. Accordingly, while we were going to the platform to wait for our train, several of us stopped and bought sandwiches and other things for lunch on the trip. Later, women did come through selling beverages and snacks, and Karen Barker bought some sushi from one of them. Yuck. (Karen is my *profesora de Español*, and is known to be willing to try anything.) The coffee, however, was fine. Once again, language would be a real problem here, except that we had several capable interpreters available to help us out.

While riding on the train, we had time to review the schedules we had received for our time in Takaoka and it was clear that we were going to be busy. Our mayor, Paul Helmke, learned that he would be expected to give three speeches at three different occasions between the time that we arrived and *this evening*.

VII

TAKAOKA

Our train arrived in Takaoka exactly on time and, as we anticipated, a tremendous welcoming committee was there to meet us. Paul Helmke was the first off the train, in order to greet Takaoka Mayor Takashi Sato, and there were several members of the Takaoka City Council and the Chamber of Commerce, as well as old friends like Kimio Arai and Dr. Koichiro Kitamura, the Chairman of the Takaoka Sister City Committee. Kazunobu Nakashima, who had served as an interpreter 20 years ago, was there, as well as Kiiko Ikadai, who spent three weeks in Fort Wayne as an exchange student living with Mac and Pat Parker and their family.

Betsy and I had a big hug for Hisako Tanabe who also came to Fort Wayne in 1976 as the leader of a group of high school girls under the auspices of The Experiment in International Living (Kiiko had been one of the girls). Hisako lived with us during that time, and we became great friends and have seen each other often since then. At the entrance to the train station there was a band from one of the local high schools playing American music and, immediately outside, a crowd of several hundred people cheering and waving American and Japanese flags. We were in a constant barrage of flashbulbs, since several newspapers were there to cover the event, as well as at least four different television stations. (TV crews seemed to be omnipresent during the entire three days that our delegation was in Takaoka.)

There were a few short speeches, and our Mayor was presented with a bouquet of fresh flowers, after which a waiting bus took us off to the New Otani Hotel. On arrival at the hotel, the entire hotel staff was in the driveway to greet us, waving flags, and applauding us into the lobby. Once inside, we found two giant flags posted in front of the reception desk, one Japanese and the other American.

Fort Wayne Mayor Paul Helmke, Mary Ball Brant, LaDonna Huntley James, Howard Chapman, Betsy Chapman, Gabriel DeLobbe.

The only thing that was not going splendidly was the fact that Ginny Clark was not feeling well, and had to retire to her room for the rest of the day and, in fact, for the entire rest of the time that we were in Takaoka.

After we checked in and regrouped, we reassembled at the entrance of the hotel and went by bus to City Hall. There we went to the Mayor's Assembly Room where there were greetings from Mayor Sato, and Mayor Helmke responded. Gabe DeLobbe, the current Chairman of the Fort Wayne Sister Cities Committee, spoke and LaDonna Huntley James and I also said a few words. We began receiving what seemed to be a steady stream of gifts, beginning with lovely lacquer boxes presented to each of us by Mayor Sato, as well as local maps and information about Takaoka.

When this concluded, everyone walked next door into the City Assembly Chambers for more speeches, but shorter this time. I met Masato Kubota, a member of the Assembly, who came to Fort Wayne and visited with us in our home in 1991, and also Mitsuhiro Nakao, who had been with him.

More gifts. In addition, at each of our places was a can of authentic Takaoka tap water. I later told our mayor, Paul Helmke, that Fort Wayne has been overlooking a valuable revenue source.

After these ceremonies we went back to our hotel and found more gifts in our room, and also found that our luggage had been delivered. Betsy and I would be here for four nights, so we decided to unpack completely. We agreed to set aside one dresser drawer for gifts we had brought with us to give away, and another for gifts we received. As it turned out, drawer number two was not nearly big enough.

VIII

Our schedule permitted us a little free time before dinner, so Betsy and I decided to take a walk. Around the corner from the Hotel New Otani we found the covered shopping street with many stores and shops, and encountered Jane Keltsch who had gotten there ahead of us. She had bought a sack of pre-shelled pistachio nuts, covered with some kind of a thin coating, that were delicious, and we went to that store and bought some of our own.

We discovered that the Daiwa Department Store has been extensively restored and renovated since my last visit in 1989. It is bigger, very upscale, with beautiful merchandise, and one entire floor full of restaurants. We made a note to go back later for shopping, but never found time to do it.

We had a chance to rest a little bit before Mayor Sato's welcome dinner, held conveniently on the fourth floor of the Hotel New Otani. All seating at this event had been carefully arranged and all of us had been given a copy of the seating chart, telling us where we should sit, and who we would sit with.

Betsy and I were delighted that Hisako Tanabe was sitting at our table, which gave us a chance to catch up with her as to her daughters and grandchildren, and also gave us the benefit of her language interpretation and advice on the food. Each table had a large "Lazy Susan" in the middle, and once the courses began to be served, they seemed to go on forever. Soon after we began, the speeches started also, the first by Mayor Sato, then next by Mayor Helmke. As is traditional in Japan, there were many toasts, using the beer and sake that was on the table.

It seemed that we were served every kind of food imaginable, which meant that there was bound to be something that everybody liked. During the meal there was traditional entertainment on a stage at the front of the room. Women in kimonos and wearing traditional masks, performed a variety of dances and interpretations. Later, five other women dressed in the manner of ancient soldiers (headbands, *hopi* coats) performed by beating large drums in an unusual rhythm. The food was fine and the only problem was that, between the speeches, the toasts, and the entertainment, there wasn't much time to eat. I am told that Japanese often go home and have dinner after "banquets."

IX

The Hotel New Otani has a very nice dining room on the top floor, which affords a fine view of the city. On Friday morning, we were joined for breakfast by Mike and Grace Mastrangelo, and we all ordered the "set" breakfast, which included eggs, toast, sausage, juice, and a green "morning salad." Takaoka has a very scenic location, with the Sea of Japan on one side, mountains on another, and when the sky is clear, one can see the snowcapped mountains in the distance.

We boarded our bus shortly after breakfast and drove to **Zuiryuji Temple**, where we were met by several Takaoka hosts and an English-speaking guide. When one passes through the first gate to enter the temple complex, one encounters an enormous "lawn" made entirely of small, white stones, which have been raked meticulously so as to form a rectangular pattern. This is one place where it is okay to walk on the grass, but not on the rocks.

Our guide led us through all of the buildings and explained the history and architecture for us. Inside the rock rectangle is another rectangular building and, inside that, a grass courtyard. In the middle of the courtyard is an ancient building with a roof made entirely of lead tiles. We were told that if they were made into bullets, they could be fired one a minute into the next century. The weight of this roof must be ponderous!

Snapshots

In the grass courtyard there was an arrangement of benches and tables for the presentation of a special tea ceremony in our honor, and about 20 monks and women in traditional dress were assembled for the purpose of performing the ceremony. First, they prepared the tea (in the meticulous manner that Westerners have no hope of understanding) and served each of the Mayors, then Gabe DeLobbe, and eventually all of us.

We each got a bowl with freshly made green tea, and were told that we should bow, gaze thoughtfully into the bowl, turn it part-way, hold it just so, then tip it up and drink all the tea. Then we were to turn the bowl back in a certain way before returning it to the server, and so forth. We later learned that green tea, when served "straight" like this, contains quite a lot of caffeine, substantially more than a cup of coffee. We also learned that most of the people who participated in the tea ceremony would be coming to Fort Wayne to visit during the Three Rivers Festival in July, and that they would be presenting tea ceremonies at schools and other public occasions while there.

Fort Wayne Mayor Paul Helmke participating in tea ceremony at the Zuiryuji Temple.

We returned to the hotel in order to prepare for the **20th Anniversary Celebration**, to be held in the ballroom on the fourth floor of the New Otani. There was a large crowd and, not surprisingly, a huge battery of cameras with flashbulbs, and TV crews. A dais was set up at the front of the room with Mayor Sato, Dr. Kitamura, and three other Japanese officials on the left side of the lectern, and Mayor Helmke, Gabe DeLobbe, Mary Brant, LaDonna Huntley James, and me on the other side. All of us at the dais were recognized, and then there were speeches, first by the two Mayors, and then by the Sister City Chairmen. The representatives from the two cities exchanged a number of gifts, including plaques, artwork of various kinds, and congratulatory telegrams. One telegram pointed out that in 1996, Sister Cities International had recognized the Fort Wayne-Takaoka relationship as one of the world's outstanding Sister City programs.

The schedule said that this ceremony would end at noon and, of course, it did. Everyone went to the large ballroom next door for a "standing" reception. There were several tables covered with a buffet with all kinds of food, and bars and waiters serving beer, whiskey, juice, and other soft drinks. At one table, chefs were busy cutting excellent beef, and at another table a large display of fresh fruit, including an outstanding pineapple and melon was available. A huge birthday cake was provided for dessert, and all in all, this affair had to cost a small fortune. It was really first-rate.

During the reception, Betsy and I got to talk to lots of old friends, including Jinichi Miyazaki (who played tennis with me in Fort Wayne more than 15 years ago), Takeo Arai, Kimio's brother, who has been to Fort Wayne many times, and is always good company, and too many others to list. There was a special presentation made by the Takaoka Chamber of Commerce honoring Mac Parker, who has been active for years as a liaison between the two Chambers of Commerce, and then even more speeches. After the first of these speeches, someone decided to make a toast ("kampai"), which everyone took as a signal to start mingling, eating and drinking, even though subsequent speeches were going on.

After the reception, we were provided "free time" for awhile, and I changed into some comfortable clothes and went out to do errands. For my first chore, I needed to find a drugstore. Karen Barker had burned her hand, and I had loaned her my tube of Polysporin ointment, so I wanted to replace it with some kind of antibiotic cream. I knew I would have no luck on my own, but Nakashima-san saw me looking confused on the sidewalk and offered to help me, escorted me to the drugstore, and helped me buy what I wanted. I had to assume that it was what I wanted, since I couldn't read a word that was written on it.

My next stop was to go to a bank to find an ATM, so that I could get some cash. (Cash evaporates in Japan.) The people at the bank were very friendly, but no one spoke any English. Since most Japanese can read and write English, I wrote out my request for help on a piece of paper and handed it to a young lady who went to the ATM machine with me, and we tried to get it to cough up some money, but to no avail. It kept sending out pieces of paper written entirely in Japanese except for the word "rejection." The young lady then got on the telephone and I sat with her while she talked to someone for about 20 minutes, before explaining to me as best she could that these ATM machines would not take any international card, but that there was an ATM machine in the nearby city of Toyama that would do so.

I later learned from Susan Lane that there is, indeed, no ATM machine in the city of Takaoka that will accept an American card, and that there is such a machine in Toyama. Susan told me that she makes regular trips to Toyama for that very purpose, and said she would help me in this regard on Monday.

Walking back to the hotel, I passed a little shop, and walked in to buy a couple of cans of cold pop (it was hot). When I entered, the older lady who was tending the store took one look at me, turned on her heel, and disappeared into a back room. Momentarily, a teen-age girl wearing blue jeans, a plaid shirt, and a big smile came out and spoke perfect English. I carried lemonade and grape soda back to the hotel. During all of my adventures, Betsy was in the room napping and reading.

X

Mayor Sato had invited a group of us to have dinner with him this evening at a traditional Japanese restaurant. There were seven of us from Fort Wayne, including LaDonna and Bernard James, Gabe DeLobbe, Mary Brant, Paul Helmke, Betsy and me. We were picked up at the hotel entrance by huge black limousines that transported us to the restaurant, where we met our hosts. This was an occasion when we left our shoes at the door, and put on slippers that were provided to us. We had a small dining room to ourselves where we sat on cushions at a long table that was only a few inches above the floor, and the waitresses, in traditional dress, never stood up, but moved about and served us while on their knees. The restaurant must have been somewhat accustomed to Western guests, because each of our places had a device that slid under the pillow and provided a backrest.

In addition to Mayor Sato, we were joined by Dr. Kitamura, Nakashima-san, Susan Lane, Hisako Tanabe, and Harue Oki. The first course was beautiful but raw seafood, followed by some excellent soup, and then a meat course, "beef no-chu." Beverages included beer and sake, both warm and cold, and still more gifts were presented to us. Susan Lane helped to explain the various courses that were served, and tried to give us a short course in using chopsticks, but without much success (at least in my case). Just after I began eating an uncooked oyster, she said, "I sometimes avoid the oysters."

After dinner, we joined everyone at the **Takaoka Concert Hall** for the 7:00 o'clock performance by the Freimann Quartet. Kimio Arai was a former Vice-Mayor of Takaoka, and the concert hall had been one of his projects. It is an excellent space with good acoustics, and it was packed full for this event. Prior to the concert, we had a chance to see a display of mounted photographs of Fort Wayne, taken by Gabe DeLobbe and presented to the City of Takaoka.

The four musicians performed a variety of pieces and, of course, were splendid. Our Fort Wayne group had been given the best seats in the house, so we could really enjoy it. After playing the first selection, Hiromi Ito stood up to talk to the audience, and, before he could utter a word, everyone applauded. I believe that it made a very good impression on our Japanese hosts that our concertmaster was, himself, Japanese. Hiromi explained the music that was to follow, speaking first in English, then in Japanese. After completion of the regular program, there were three encores, so the event must be considered a great success.

When the concert was over, Betsy and I went to the hotel and went to bed, but we learned that the Freimann Quartet and several others went to a "Yakitori Bar," which is a place that serves food on sticks (chicken on a stick, fruit on a stick). It also serves beer, and has a "sing-a-long" audio system, and we were told that this event lasted longer than the concert itself.

XI

Saturday morning began what was to be the last full day that the Fort Wayne delegation would spend in Takaoka. Betsy and I met Will Clark for breakfast in the restaurant on the top floor of the hotel and commiserated about the fact that Ginny Clark was still not feeling well. Will had hopes that she would be able to join the group for some of the events today.

This was to be a day of sightseeing, on another beautiful, sunny day; however, when we got to our room, I discovered that I had a message to call to the United States "on business." Betsy went on the bus with the group, while I stayed in the hotel and tried to make the call, which turned out to be quite a formidable task.

First, I went to the lobby to ask the desk clerk how to make a call to the United States from the hotel room, but she didn't speak enough English to understand what I wanted, or to give me any answers. Fortunately, Hisako Tanabe was in the lobby and helped with the translation. We went over the instructions three times, so that I was sure how to do it, but still wasn't able to place a call because, as it developed, the hotel clerk didn't know the correct way to do it. Anyway, after spending about an hour, I finally got through to an answer machine in the United States and, figuring this was about the best I could do, left a message about where and how to reach me.

The Freimann Quartet had been out for the morning giving a concert at one of the Takaoka schools, and would have to come back to the hotel to change clothes, and then go off to join the group. I decided to connect with them in order to get transportation, and Will and Ginny Clark were doing the same thing. A van came, and all of us went out to rendezvous with the bus, but Ginny had to turn around and come back, much to the disappointment of her and all of us.

During the morning, the others had visited: a park with a fine floral display and attractions aimed at children; the Manyo Historical Museum; and, the scenic overlook from atop Mount Futagami. Betsy and Jan McNellis got to ring a great bell that is sounded by pulling back a huge log suspended from a rope, and then banging it against the bell.

After I joined them, the group continued to the coast of the **Sea of Japan**, and stopped at the Amaharashi Hotel, located on the Noto Peninsula, which forms a part of Toyama Bay. The coastline here is spectacular, reminiscent of the Monterey Peninsula in California, and, when the weather is clear, magnificent snow-covered mountains rise up in the distance. The scene has been captured in six zillion photographs.

The Amaharashi Hotel served us lunch, with raw fish, rice, unidentifiable cooked food, custard soup (with a sea urchin in it), hot, clear soup with crab legs in it, and beer. Betsy and I discussed the fact that we thought we were beginning to lose weight, and I began to fantasize about McDonald's. When lunch was over, we walked across the road and down the stairs on to the beach to get a group picture using the bay, the mountains, and an island with a famous "lonesome" tree as the background.

Takaoka is a center for the production of all kinds of objects of art, including sculptures, metal castings, paintings, wood carvings, heavy castings in bronze, fabulous vases and ceramics, wind chimes, and many more, and all of these are collected, displayed and sold at one location called the "**Craft Center**." We stopped there on the way back to the hotel and everyone had a chance to shop. Betsy and I bought a framed painting on wood, showing the "lonesome tree," painted in the Japanese style, and also a very small metal sculpture. We would have liked to have gotten a lot of other things, but there was no way to get them home. The Craft Center did not have any facilities for shipping, which surprised me, given the Japanese knack for trade and commerce. Perhaps there are just not that many foreign visitors coming through at this location.

Driving back to the hotel, our bus passed a **McDonald's** and, right next door, a Baskin & Robbins; however, we didn't stop. (Sob.) When we returned to our rooms, there was time for a quick wash and change of clothes, and then we went down to the lobby to meet Hisako Tanabe, her husband Yutaka, her daughter Yumiko, and Yumiko's son Naoki.

XII

When we visited at the Tanabe home in 1977, Yumiko had been a little girl. She had been very impressed with Betsy, and told her mother that she was going to learn English, so that she could talk to Betsy the next time they met. Sure enough, Yumiko, now a lovely young lady, speaks excellent English, and remembers what she told her mother about Betsy. We had a terrific reunion, took lots of pictures, and exchanged gifts - and, of course, all of it was captured by a TV crew! (We began to understand why Princess Di might get tired of this.)

Our reunion with the Tanabes ended, but another one began in the hotel coffee shop with our dear old friend, Masaya Hashimoto. He was the first person to visit Fort Wayne from Takaoka, in 1976, as a personal emissary from the then Mayor Kenji Hori. Since then, a number of us have kept up with him over the years.

The reunion with Masaya Hashimoto. Standing: Nakashima-san, Mrs. Hashimoto, Pat Parker, Mary Brant, Howard Chapman, Betsy Chapman, interpreter. Seated: Gabe DeLobbe, Masaya Hashimoto, LaDonna James, Mac Parker.

Snapshots

Hashimoto-san has suffered a stroke and has been very ill. He needed a wheelchair, and had very little speech, but his mind seemed good, and he recognized all of his old friends: Gabe DeLobbe, Mary Brant, Mac and Pat Parker, LaDonna Huntley James, Betsy and me. His wife had arranged, with the help of some family and friends, to bring him to the hotel to see us, and Nakashima-san, another old friend, came along to interpret.

Mrs. Hashimoto had brought some photo albums with pictures of the "old days," and several of us had pictures as well. We exchanged gifts, and talked and laughed about the fact that Mr. Hashimoto used to like to sing "Home on the Range." In fact, when Betsy and I visited in his home, in 1977, Betsy played it on the piano while he sang. Someone decided that we should all sing it together, and we did, or at least we did our best. The problem was that everyone was crying. We were crying, Mr. and Mrs. Hashimoto were crying, Nakashima-san was crying. Even the television crew was crying!

Eventually, Mr. Hashimoto indicated that he was getting tired, and the reunion ended. We hurried back to our rooms to get ready for the farewell dinner to be given at the **Takaoka Chamber of Commerce**. Our laundry had come back and was waiting for us in the room. This was the second time we had sent laundry and, contrary to reports, having laundry done at the hotel was relatively inexpensive. By now, the gifts we had received had long since filled up the dresser drawer that had been assigned to them, and were spilling over on to the chairs and floor. We had no idea how we could get them home, but didn't have much time to think about it.

The reception at the Chamber of Commerce was another "stand-up" type of affair, given on the top floor of the Chamber of Commerce building. The restaurant there is owned by Kimio Arai, and the food that was provided was excellent. This type of reception is a pretty good idea because it lets everybody mingle and converse with everybody else, even while having dinner. Festivities began, as always, with speeches by the two Mayors, followed by karaoke singing by each of them - with uneven results. During the subsequent karaoke singing, Karen Barker, Kazuo Shihoh and I got hold of the microphones and sang "La Bamba." We were terrible. Nobody cared.

During the reception, at about 7:00 o'clock, Mr. and Mrs. Akira Ogawa came to the Chamber and called at the door. This was by prearrangement, and Betsy and I went out to the lounge for a visit with them, to exchange gifts, and to review and exchange photographs. Ogawa-san, a member of the City Council, had visited Fort Wayne a few years ago, and we had entertained him for part of a day. When I visited Takaoka in 1989, he had taken me to see the

Tonami Tulip Festival, and invited me to dinner at his home, where his wife had served a sumptuous meal.

Altogether, our visit with the Ogawas was probably not more than 20 minutes, but was, nonetheless, significant. The Japanese recognize the importance of maintaining relationships, and will often make an effort to have a "small meeting" with people, even though it may be inconvenient to them to do so. These meetings maintain "contact" and nurture relationships. Americans might think it was necessary to have an entire evening, or at least meet for a meal, and if this weren't convenient, pass up the opportunity to meet. But the Japanese custom is, it seems to me, a wiser one.

This dinner was scheduled to end at 8:00 o'clock, but ran over until 9:00 because, I'm afraid, the Americans were having too much fun and didn't realize that we ought to go home. Anyway, at 9:00 o'clock, the bus finally pulled out from the Chamber of Commerce and, as we crossed the street, Betsy and I waved goodbye to Hisako Tanabe, on her way to get a bus back to her home.

XIII

Sunday morning was the first time, since we arrived in Japan that the alarm woke us up. Betsy and I met Mac and Pat Parker for breakfast, and then went down to the hotel lobby to say goodbye to the departing Fort Wayne delegation. We and the Parkers were staying in Takaoka to do some sightseeing and traveling with the Arais, and had made plans to meet Kimio Arai at 9:45.

The bus with our Fort Wayne friends pulled out and we joined all of the Japanese hotel staff in the hotel driveway, waving goodbye. They were on their way to catch a train that would take them to Tokyo and, from there some would come back to Fort Wayne, while several others continued with a trip to China. China is interesting, but I don't want to go there anymore.

At 9:45, Kimio Arai and his wife Keiko, and Takeo Arai and his wife Nobuko arrived to pick us up. Mac and Pat traveled with Kimio and Keiko in their car, and Betsy and I went with Takeo and Nobuko. Kimio and Takeo had walkie-talkie radios, so we could keep in touch between cars. Good idea.

We were blessed with terrific weather on this trip! It was another beautiful summer day, the first of June, and we started by visiting the town of **Tonami**, which considers itself a rival to Holland as a tulip center. (This was the same area to which Mr. Ogawa brought me in 1989. However, the fields were filled with tulips of all kinds and colors at that time, whereas, by June, the tulip season was over.) Since my visit in 1989, a large, modern building has been built, which serves as a kind of tulip museum, a conservatory where all types of tulips are grown during the off-season, a restaurant and a gift shop. We learned all about the history of tulips, and Pat Parker had a chance to "design" one using hands-on computers.

We left at lunch time and drove to a restaurant called "Factory Volcano," where I enjoyed a really good Italian pasta dish. Everyone else ate the house specialty, a shrimp pasta, in which the shrimp came cooked, whole and unpeeled, and were to be eaten as is. There is a very nice shopping area attached, but we didn't have time to do much looking. Still, Keiko and Nobuko managed to slip into one of the shops and buy two really nifty tee-shirts with tulips on them for Betsy and Pat.

We drove into the mountains through some marvelous scenery, and I was amazed at the engineering that has gone into designing dams, tunnels, overpasses, and mountain roads. It rivals anything we have seen in Switzerland. Eventually, we came to the "GokaYama" area, and the ancient village of Aino-Kura. ("Yama" is Japanese for "mountain.") The village is still occupied and is very much as it was centuries ago. There is a large plaque set in stone indicating that it is now preserved as a part of the World Heritage Foundation.

We explored on foot, and Kimio gave us a lot of background and explanation. We took pictures, Kimio bought some soy "cookies" that were very tasty, and Mac Parker bought a sack of dried apricots. All of the Arais are really good company, full of fun and good humor, and we had lots of laughs. We were even learning a few words of Japanese.

After leaving GokaYama, we proceeded to the town of **Inami** to visit the **Wood Carving Center**. We watched men working with wood for awhile, but the main attraction seemed to be the huge shop which had a tremendous variety of magnificent things made out of wood. I have read that Japan is a "cash society," and, sure enough, this store did not accept credit cards. Even though we were all accustomed to using plastic (it's not like having to *pay for it*), we all bought some things anyway, because they were so unique and well done.

It took about an hour and a quarter to drive back to Takaoka. It had been a great day, and we were tired, but we weren't going to miss the dinner that Kimio Arai had promised us at his Chinese restaurant. It is called *The Jinzhou*, and is located in the shopping mall adjacent to the New Otani Hotel. Kimio had invited his mother and also a woman who is an English teacher from Koryo High School. He had reserved a private room for us, was a congenial host, and the meal was the best food that we had tasted since we arrived in Japan. I said, "Kimio, I have been to China, and I have eaten Chinese food, and you have improved on it a lot!" In fact, it was so good that I could hardly believe that it was Chinese. However,

Kimio told me that he had brought chefs from China who had spent 18 months working with his local chefs, teaching them to prepare Chinese cuisine.

After dinner, our main problem was trying to pack. Betsy and I, and Mac and Pat Parker, were scheduled to head into the mountains for two days and from there we would go by train to Tokyo. We couldn't possibly take our luggage with us, so we each prepared a "shoulder bag" with only enough clothes to get by until we arrived in Tokyo. Everything else was packed up in suitcases to be sent by courier to our hotel in Tokyo to await our arrival. We did our best trying to pack all the gifts we had received (we had some spare room because we had brought gifts with us that we had given away), but there was no way to pack everything. The Parkers had a spare suitcase (also emptied from gifts they had brought), and they had some room for some of our extra items. What was left I planned to ship home by mail.

XIV

Kimio came to meet us at the hotel lobby on Monday morning in order to begin our adventure in the **Japanese Alps**. He brought his own car, plus another car from his company, his wife Keiko, Susan Lane, and one of his company drivers. For the first time, the weather was less than perfect, with clouds and a light rain falling. Betsy and I rode with Kimio and Keiko, and Mac and Pat Parker rode in the other car with Susan Lane and the driver.

Between the Chapmans and the Parkers, we had a mountain of luggage, and our first job was to get it off our hands. We drove across Takaoka to the office of a courier service, where we arranged to have all of our bags (except for the shoulder bags that we would carry) sent on to the Imperial Hotel in Tokyo. Each suitcase was wrapped up in a separate plastic cover and tagged, and we were given receipts. The total cost for sending Betsy's and my luggage came to about ¥5,000, a little under $50.00. Kimio helped us with all of this and it was really easy; however, I wondered if it would have been so easy if we had had to do it on our own, relying on the hotel to make the arrangements.

We also bought a box to ship home the extra gifts that Betsy and I had, and for which we had no room in our suitcases. I had proposed we take them to the post office to be wrapped and shipped, being careful to specify that they were to go on the "slow boat," and not by air freight, which costs a fortune. Keiko volunteered that, since everyone was anxious to get on our way, she would take care of shipping the packages later, and I told her that there would be a special place in heaven for her. (As it turned out, Kimio wound up carrying them to Fort Wayne when he came in July!)

Snapshots

We left Takaoka and drove to the city of Toyama (which was on our way), in order to find the unique ATM machine that would give us cash against our American credit cards. Toyama is a very modern and attractive city with a bustling downtown, and we drove into the middle of it and parked in an illegal spot. We were at the entrance to a glitzy, high-rise department store, and Susan Lane led us in to find the machine, in the center of the building and on the fifth floor. We would never have found it without her!

With Susan's help, we were able to get the machine to use English, but the terminology was still foreign. Fortunately, Susan had used it enough to know how to make it work. I drew out ¥40,000 in order to repay Kimio for expenses he had advanced for our trip to the mountains, and another ¥40,000 in order to have some cash for our travels. My notebook has the following comment: "We are *flush*!"

We traveled on toward the mountains to our first destination, the **Museum of Traditional Japanese Art**. When we pulled up in front of it, I could see that Kimio was perplexed, and soon discovered why. This was a Monday and the museum (like museums everywhere) was closed on Monday. What to do?

Betsy and Howard Chapman at the "traditional" tea ceremony.

While the rest of us wandered around the exterior grounds, Kimio went down the road and found an ancient building that turned out to be a place where one could obtain tea served in the traditional Japanese manner. After some negotiation, Kimio persuaded the hostess to do that for us, and we went into a room with virtually no furniture and a fire burning from a square hole built into the middle of the floor. There were tatami mats placed around for us to sit on and a huge black metal pot suspended over the fire from the ceiling. The entire building was like a small museum.

Our hostess proceeded to boil the water and then made and served tea for all of us. She passed out crackers, cookies, and small, pickled vegetables. It was absolutely fabulous and I explained to Kimio the meaning of the English word "serendipity." When life gives you lemons, Betsy said, make lemonade.

XV

We set off again, driving for quite a while, until it was past lunchtime and we stopped at a Japanese version of a fast food restaurant. It looked very much to me like an "oasis" that we build along our toll roads. When we entered, there was a large window along an interior wall displaying plastic models of all of the items available on the menu. One makes his selection, goes to the cashier and tells her what it is, pays for it, and then has a seat at a table. The waitresses take orders for beverages and eventually bring the food when it is ready.

Susan Lane sat at our table and gave us some insights into choosing and eating various Japanese dishes, and also into other Japanese customs. We learned about her experiences living and studying in Japan, and her hopes for the future. Her job in Takaoka would be over by the beginning of August, and she had interviewed for a new job in Tokyo. Susan is mature beyond her years and had been a great help to all of us. I told her that I would call her parents when we got home to Fort Wayne and let them know how well she was doing.

After lunch, we enjoyed a long but spectacular drive into the mountains, eventually arriving at **Shomyo Falls**, the highest and most scenic waterfall in Japan. We took the car up the mountain as far as we could go, and left it in a parking lot. We bundled ourselves up, because it was cool and a light drizzle was falling. We were already above the snow line, and we had a considerable hike ahead of us, all uphill, to get to the viewing area where we could best see the falls. Fortunately, all of us were athletes!

Perhaps because of the weather, or perhaps because it was a Monday, there were only one or two other people in the area on this day, which caused me to reflect on the contrast between this place and the mobs of people at Kiyomizu Temple in Kyoto. The mountains here are comparable to the most rugged mountains I have seen, including the Rockies and the Swiss Alps, and the scenery is simply stunning.

After completing our climb, we spent about a half hour looking at the Falls and taking photographs, and then walked back to our waiting cars. Although the drizzle continued throughout, there was never enough rain to amount to anything or to bother us in any way. As we drove back down the mountain, we stopped for tea at the Himalaya Restaurant, a log-cabin kind of place, very similar to structures built at lodges and fishing camps in the American Northwest. We were the only customers. We had been together long enough that everyone was beginning to loosen up and we really had a lot of fun.

We still had to drive quite a while, climbing most of the time into higher and higher mountains, until we came to the town of **Tateyama**, and the Tateyama International Hotel, where we would spend the night. It is a very large resort with extensive facilities for parties (especially weddings), several places to eat, gift shops, a bar and Karaoke room, and communal baths. It is quite nice and, we learned, the Emperor and his wife have stayed there. I was glad that it was so big, in view of the fact that five busloads of school children, in their early teens, had arrived just ahead of us and were pouring into the lobby. Each bus had the name "Ryobi" on the side, next to a drawing of a bunch of grapes, and beneath everything the words "Dear Friends."

Each hotel room furnished a robe and slippers for each guest, and people were already beginning to appear in these, walking through the lobby and other parts of the hotel toward the baths. The gift shop was immediately jammed with school kids, all of whom seemed to be buying everything in sight.

The hotel is very popular for Japanese weddings, and has an entire section devoted to this. There is a large office area, with several rooms, and fully modern equipment, devoted to nothing but arranging and conducting weddings. There was a large fancy wagon, to be drawn by a horse, which would transport the bridal couple. There were display cases full of all kinds of elegant gifts that the families could buy for the invited guests, and there was a wide variety of wedding clothes. There were clothes that could be rented for the bride, groom, attendants, ushers, and I don't know who else. There were mannequins on display, modeling some of them. It is customary in Japan for all of the guests to receive gifts, whereas the guests, in turn, make presents of cash to the parents. Weddings cost *a lot*, and the usual custom is for each family to pay one-half.

Our room had a marvelous view of mountain and forest. The outside air was fresh and there seemed to be a feeling of total peace. However, when we went downstairs for dinner, we learned that Kimio had spoken to management and had moved us and the Parkers to different rooms. The reason was that he had discovered that our rooms were directly above the Karaoke Room, and that people would be there, drinking and singing, into the wee hours.

Kimio allowed us to take a vote as to which restaurant we would choose for dinner, and we wound up choosing the Japanese style restaurant (although

Howard L. Chapman

I do not, personally, remember having a chance to vote). We had the choice of sitting at tables (Western style) or on the floor (Japanese style). Neither we nor any of the Japanese customers seemed to be choosing the floor. By this time, I had lost my inhibitions about being frank with respect to the subject of food, and simply announced, "No raw fish." There were, of course, lots of other things to eat, and, between Kimio and Susan, we had no trouble picking out meals that we enjoyed.

After dinner, Keiko and Susan returned to Takaoka with the company car and driver, and Kimio stayed at the hotel with us. Our new rooms were furnished in the Western style, but with several Japanese "touches," and with the same advantages of scenery, air, peace and quiet, as the first rooms. We slept fine.

XVI

In retrospect, Betsy and I, and Mac and Pat Parker, have agreed that Tuesday, June 3, 1997, began one of the more extraordinary days of travel that any of us have ever experienced. We left at about 9 a.m. with Kimio Arai to begin the **Tateyama-Kurobe Alpine Trek.** An all-day journey that, we calculated, would involve ten different modes of transportation before we arrived at our destination that evening. We were in Tateyama, on one side of a range of mountains in the Japanese Alps, and we were to go over, through and across Mount Tateyama, across the Kurobe Dam, then over, through and across another mountain, eventually reaching our hotel for the night in the city of Matsumoto.

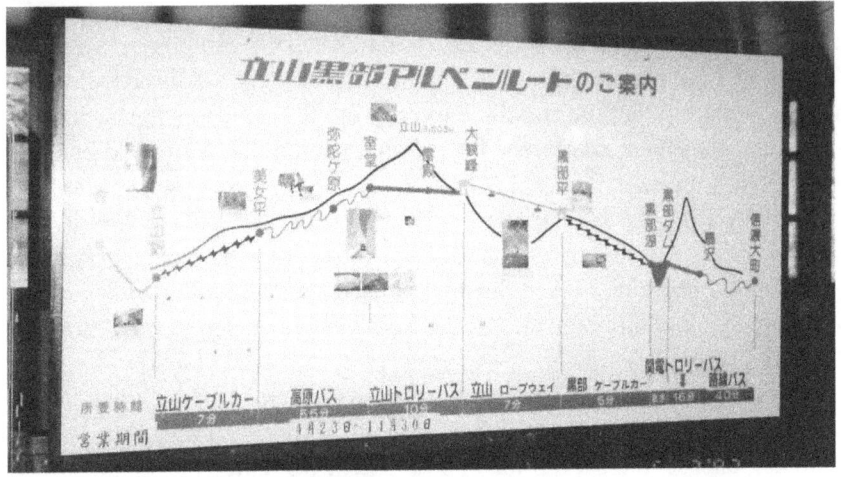

This map, at the railroad station, depicts the journey up across the mountain, down the other side, across the Kurobe Dam, through another mountain and, eventually - after "ten legs" - on to the town of Matsumoto.

Snapshots

Here is a list of the ten modes of transportation:

1. Automobile - Kimio's car from Tateyama International Hotel to Tateyama Eki (the name of the Cable Train station);
2. Cable Train - straight up the mountain to a point about halfway, known as Bijo Daira;
3. Bus (the only vehicle allowed) - continuing up the mountain to a point near the top, called Murodo;
4. Trolley Bus - through a tunnel to a point on the other side of the mountain named Daikanbo;
5. "Rope Trolley" (hanging cable car) - halfway down the other side of the mountain to a station called Kurobe Daira;
6. Cable Train - continuing down the mountain to Kurobe Dam;
7. Legs - we walked across the dam, a distance of about a half mile;
8. Trolley Bus – through a tunnel through the next mountain to Ogisawa;
9. Bus - to the town of Shinano Omachi; and
10. Train (Japan Rail) - to Matsumoto.

Kimio prepared us by going over maps, charts and schedules, showing the various steps of the journey, and telling us what to expect. Although the writing on these was in Japanese, Kimio had written everything out in English. In addition, he had purchased coupons in advance to pay for the various parts of the trip. Each stop along the way, we would need to find the appropriate ticket booth and exchange a coupon for a ticket. This would be easy enough, so long as Kimio was with us, but he would leave us at Murodo. It became quickly apparent that we and the Parkers were the only non-Japanese on this route, and that there were very few, if any, people that we would encounter who spoke English.

By the time we got off the first Cable Train and got on the bus up to Murodo, we were already well above the snow line, and soon there was lots of snow. At one point, in fact, the bus traveled a distance of about a quarter of a mile with snow on both sides of the road that was *twice as high as the bus*. This was June!

When we got off the bus at **Murodo**, we entered a large stone building that looked like an oversized bus station, with restaurants, shops, ticket counters, and people. At a price of ¥300 each, we rented lockers to stow our bags, bought some coffee and some candy, and set off to walk around the vast, snow-covered area surrounding the place. Even though it was cold outside, it was the middle of the day, and everywhere that people were walking was slushy. It was overcast, with low-hanging clouds here and there (we were well above the cloud level), and the scenery would appear and then disappear, depending on the movement of the clouds.

A bus makes its way through the snow banks to the top of the mountain to begin the "Tateyama-Kurobe Alpine Trek."

At one point we could see a deep, ice blue lagoon, and at another point we could look down a steep, snowy slope to the crater of a volcano, where there were hot springs. Betsy was in her canvas tennis shoes which, by then, were soaked, so the two of us decided not to follow the others down to look at the hot springs. Instead, we went into a small, log cabin style restaurant located nearby, where we ordered coffee, looked at souvenirs, and had a pleasant visit with the waitress, who spoke English. After about 40 minutes, Mac, Pat and Kimio returned from the volcano, and we all trekked back to the main terminal for lunch at the largest of the restaurants. There was an extensive menu and the food was good.

Kimio escorted us to the gate where we would begin the next part of our journey. Once again he went over our itinerary with us. He was to retrace the trip back to Tateyama, retrieve his car, and drive home to Takaoka, so we said our goodbyes as we left to get on the Trolley Bus.

Each leg of this trip was a separate adventure. When we emerged from the tunnel on the other side of the mountain, all of the clouds had disappeared, and the temperature was much warmer. The view from the "Rope Trolley"

Snapshots

was spectacular, looking down to the enormous **Kurobe Dam**, and the huge lake behind it, all surrounded by snow-topped mountains.

View of the Japanese Alps while descending by "rope trolley" to the Kurobe Dam.

When we reached the dam, we were amazed at the feat of engineering that it represents. The dam is wide enough on top for three lanes of traffic, plus sidewalks, with water fairly close to the top of the dam on one side, and with a sheer drop of hundreds of feet on the other side. Lots of facilities for tourists were provided on both sides of the dam. There were several Japanese tour groups, but the four of us were the only foreigners. This is not the kind of thing that one finds on the typical tourist itinerary and would be very difficult for a non-Japanese to negotiate on his own.

We spent a lot of time on the dam, taking in the incredible scenery, looking at sculptures on both ends, watching the people, enjoying the sunshine, and then walked through a tunnel to find the gate for the next Trolley Bus. There was a huge collection of school children, all in uniform, sitting on the floor waiting for the same Trolley Bus, and we realized that these were the same children that had stayed with us at Tateyama International Hotel last night.

After asking directions (with a lot of pointing and sign language) we found where we should stand and wait, except, we were tired and decided to sit on the floor like the kids. They thought this was hilarious and began taking pictures of us, and we took theirs in return. Everybody was laughing. I was concerned that there wouldn't be room for everyone on the next bus (the kids were ahead of us), but when the bus came, it turned out to be a string of several, and there was plenty of room for all.

We just missed our bus at Ogizawa, but the next one had already arrived, and would leave in thirty minutes. Also waiting were the five school buses from the night before, bearing the company name "Ryobi," and the inscription "Dear Friends." They had somehow traveled around the mountains since last night and were there to collect all the school children.

Since we were the first on board, we had a chance to sit in the front of the bus, so that we could enjoy the ride to Shinano Omachi through typical Japanese countryside. No one asked for tickets when we got on the bus, but they were collected by the driver when we got off. I wondered, what would he do if someone didn't have a ticket? They would be getting off anyway, so it wouldn't do any good to throw them off. Would they have to ride back to Ogizawa?

The Japan Rail station was less than a half block from our bus stop and, when we entered, we managed to get the attention of the station master. He didn't speak English, but understood what we wanted when we said "Matsumoto." He ran around the corner of his counter, jabbering in Japanese and pointing to the clock. He steered us to a vending machine, and told us to start pumping ¥1,000 coins into it. When we did so, he began pushing buttons, and tickets came out. He then pushed us out onto the platform and pointed at a train that was waiting at a platform on the other side of the tracks. We figured out that this was our train, but weren't sure how to get there, and began going in all directions like headless chickens, until he began yelling and pointing to a stairway that led to an overpass. While we galloped up the stairs and over the crossway, he began to shout across the tracks at the conductor standing next to the train, presumably telling him to hold the train for us. In my experience, Japanese trains never wait for anything, however, this one did, and we dashed, stumbled and careened onto the platform and through the doors which snapped shut right behind us. As our train pulled out, the station master was standing there waving, with a big grin on his face. What a good guy!

Another pleasant train ride. We were concerned that we might not realize where we should get off, but we met a congenial young Irishman, sitting across the aisle, who told us that he was going to Matsumoto and, in fact, to our same hotel, and would be happy to help us get there. He has worked in Japan for some time, and his name is Brefney O'Donovan. How Irish can you get?

The Hotel Buena Vista is *very nice*. In fact, **Matsumoto** seems like a very pleasant town, modern and clean, with mountains rising all around.

Snapshots

The coffee shop at the hotel is called "Chit Chat." At dinner, our waiter started to seat us at a table near some smokers, but then he looked at me and asked, "Do you hate smoke?" I said yes, and he moved us to another part of the room, where we had a very good meal, including an excellent grilled filet of sole.

After dinner we called Kimio Arai at his home in Takaoka, to let him know that we had come through our day unscathed, and to tell him what a fabulous experience it had been.

XVII

TOKYO

It was Wednesday, the 4th day of June, and Betsy and I were up early to take a walk, despite overcast skies and an occasional light rain. After breakfast at the "Chit Chat," we left with the Parkers for the Japan Rail station, to catch our train to Tokyo. We already had our tickets, which we showed to this person and that, until we came to the proper track, and figured out where our coach, car #8, would stop, at 9:54 a.m., exactly. Sure enough, the doors for car #8 opened right in front of us, and we found our seats on another clean, beautiful train, an "express," that would arrive in Tokyo in about two and one half hours. We brought our morning copy of the "Japan Times," and, by now, we had figured out how to buy hot coffee on the train. We were to get off the train at Akihabara Station, and change to the Yamamoto Line. I had asked Susan Lane to write all this out in Japanese, so that when we came to Akihabara Station, I could show the paper to people, who would point us in the right direction.

When we eventually got to **Tokyo**, there was a light rain falling, and we decided to take a taxi to the Imperial Hotel, where we arrived at about 1:00 o'clock p.m. The Imperial is an excellent hotel. It is a successor to a hotel that has been in Tokyo for decades and, in fact, Mac Parker had been at the Imperial when he was in Japan in the 50's. As soon as we registered, the clerk recognized our names and sent a bellman off to get our luggage from storage, and had it sent to our rooms. What a great system!

We spent a little while unpacking and settling in and luxuriating in these new surroundings and then went for lunch at the hotel coffee shop, named "Eureka." My hamburger cost ¥2,000, but it was a good hamburger.

In the lobby, I was able to buy a current copy of the *Herald Tribune*, the first one I had seen since we left Kyoto. The Dow Jones Industrial Average was at 7312; there had been various upheavals and atrocities in Africa; Timothy McVeigh had been convicted of the Oklahoma City bombing; the Chicago

Bulls had won the first game of their series against the Utah Jazz (the Bulls eventually won the championship); and the city of Hong Kong was turbulent in anticipation of the transfer of power, on July 1, 1997, from the English to the Chinese. The Socialists had elected a new government in France (the French need to contemplate China), and, in Washington, D.C., witnesses who were called to testify in the campaign finance hearings were taking the Fifth Amendment.

The four of us took a walk in Hibiya Park, right across the street from the Imperial Hotel. There were shops selling incredible flowers and some kind of a promotion going on in front of a tent that had been set up in a clearing. A Japanese lady came out of the tent and gave each of us a small cellophane sack with some kind of candy in it, and then took pictures of us. Why, we don't know.

We made a note of two restaurants that looked good, the Matsumotoro Grill and, above it, the Cafe Du Bois. We walked on to the Ginza district, which turned out to be much different from what I had expected. For me, "Ginza" always conjured up an image of a kind of seedy, unsavory area, something like Times Square in New York City. It is just the opposite, being more like a combination of North Michigan Avenue in Chicago and Park Avenue in New York, crowded, but clean, orderly and safe.

We stopped in for a beer at a little walk-up restaurant. A man at the table next to us helped the waitress understand that we were only ordering beer, even though the food looked pretty good. We examined the menu on the table, which included several amusing English translations of menu items, our favorite being the "Ethnical Cod." We wound up having a late dinner back at the Imperial Hotel, and were in bed at 10:00 o'clock. It had been a long day.

XVIII

Thursday was to be the last full day that Betsy and I would be in Japan, while the Parkers were staying one more day. Before we left the United States, we had made arrangements through JTB for the four of us to take an all-day trip to Nikko, an area that is both scenic and historic, but a long way from Tokyo. We would be picked up at the hotel by bus at 7:40 in the morning, and returned at 8:00 p.m., and the bus ride would be about 2½ hours in each direction. Betsy and I had been there twenty years ago and decided that we would rather spend the day sightseeing in Tokyo, and Pat Parker decided not to subject her back to the long bus ride. Mac, undaunted, went to Nikko.

The food at the Imperial Hotel is extremely expensive, but it *is* good. Pat joined us for breakfast, and, as the three of us planned our day, I was reminded of that song from "Cabaret":

Snapshots

"Fiddlee Dee Dee Dee-e, two ladies;
Fiddlee Dee Dee Dee-e, two ladies;
Fiddlee Dee Dee Dee-e, and *I'm the only man here*."

After breakfast the three of us went to the hotel concierge to get maps and advice about shopping and sightseeing. We started at a "one-hour photo shop," intending to leave all of my film to be developed. The word "Japanese" has almost become synonymous with the word "camera," so we were surprised to learn that they could not develop the film and produce 4x6 prints in less than two days. On the other hand, we did find a disposable camera that we had been looking for. Fort Wayne friend Marcia Laker had told us about a new camera made by Konica, available only in Japan, that makes sepia prints, so that new pictures look old-fashioned. We bought one to take home to Marcia and two more for ourselves. Hopefully, the folks in Fort Wayne would be able to develop the film properly.

Following our maps, we walked to the large area of parks and buildings that is called The Imperial Palace and found **The Imperial Gardens**. Admission is free (at least it was this day); however, one still had to go through a gate and receive a plastic admission "ticket," and then return it when leaving. Each "ticket" is written in English on one side and in Japanese on the other.

The Imperial Gardens are gorgeous, and we stayed a long time, wandering through them, sitting on shaded benches, and just soaking up the calm beauty of the place. They were not crowded, and the people that were there were interesting: old men with cameras on tripods; well-dressed ladies with parasols; and beautiful children. We passed a couple sitting on a bench with a one-year old girl heartily eating sushi. Perhaps that's the answer - start young. The place is immense and we had no possibility of seeing it all. We could not have seen it all if we had spent all day trying, but we began to get hungry and decided to look for a place for lunch.

While en route to the photo shop, we had passed a restaurant called "Pronto," which we later learned was a part of a chain. We went back there, and it turned out to be a real find for people like us. They sold good sandwiches and other recognizable food, and you could pick out what you wanted. There was a display case selling individual cups of Haagen Daz ice cream, with a variety of flavors (including "Green Tea"). They even had fresh baked goods, coffee, beer and other beverages, and everything was relatively inexpensive. (In Japan, "relatively" is always an operative word.)

We finished lunch and headed for the Takarazuka Theater for a 1:00 o'clock curtain to see a show called (I think) "Keikyu." I thought that some of the actors seemed a little strange and, at intermission, I found out why when Pat and Betsy told me that the entire cast was women. (99% of the audience was also women.) The show was a musical about Hollywood in the 1930's, and was terrible, but would have been even worse in English. Nonetheless, we learned, every performance is packed, and standing room is sold at the back of the theater. The first act lasted an hour and a half, but seemed longer. Even though the show was worth seeing as a cultural experience, at intermission, we left.

It was 3:00 p.m., a sunny, warm day, so we decided to walk to **Tokyo Station**, one of the largest and most famous railroad stations in the world. On the way, we passed shops and restaurants selling food of every ethnic variety, and shops with all kinds of merchandise. One, owned by FILA, was selling an entire line of apparel with the logo "Excitement and Performance." Tokyo Station is, indeed, huge and, on this day, had its annual display of bonsai, all grown and nurtured by employees of Japan Rail.

We decided to take a taxi back to the Imperial Hotel, and gave ourselves a couple of hours to bathe and rest before gathering in the lobby at 6:00 for drinks in the Lobby Bar. It's a neat space, and we thought that the entire scene seemed very glamorous.

The three of us headed across Hibiya Park to Matsumotoro Grill for dinner. We first looked in at the fancy French restaurant upstairs, but they had turned on the air conditioning and the place was like a refrigerator. Besides, the prices were a lot higher, and the Matsumotoro Grill looked fine.

It was a pleasant evening and we were able to get an outdoor table and enjoyed a good meal. We strolled back to the hotel at about 8:30, and Betsy and I proceeded to pack and get to bed early for our departure tomorrow.

XIX

Everyone slept well Thursday night and woke up Friday morning feeling rested, and we knew that jet lag was just about whipped. Meaning, of course, that it was time to go home. We had made arrangements to be picked up by "Limousine Bus" (translation - "bus"), which took *one and one-half hours* to get to Narita Airport. And this was on a day with light traffic. Narita is a nice airport with lots of good shops and restaurants, and the only down part of this whole story is that we had to fly home on Northwest Airlines, which someone told us has been dubbed "Northworst" by its frequent passengers.

All in all, we were glad to be home, but, the trip had been a memorable one. All we had to do now was start making preparations for the delegation, headed by Kimio Arai, which would be coming to Fort Wayne from Takaoka in early July!

Snapshots

(THIS IS THE SCHEDULE PROVIDED BY THE TAKAOKA SISTER CITIES COMMITTEE)

FORT WAYNE DELEGATION SCHEDULE
DETAILED

DATE	TIME	EVENT AND PLACE
May 29th (Thurs)	9:39 a.m.	Depart Kyoto Station (Raicho 15. Car #3)
	12:25 p.m.	Arrive Takaoka Station
		*Met on platform by Mayor, Deputy Mayor, Treasurer, City Assembly Chairman, Superintendent of Education, Chair and Vice-Chairs of International Association.
		* Bouquets presented (Received for delegation by Mayor Helmke and Mr. Delobbe)
		* Leave in cars and bus for Hotel
		(Mayor Helmke in Mayor Sato's car)
		(Mr. Delobbe in Dr. Kitmaura's Car)
		(Other delegation members on chartered bus)
	1:40 p.m.	Gather in Hotel Lobby
	1:50 p.m.	Depart Hotel (transportation same as above)
	2:00 p.m.	Arrive City Hall
		1. View Sun Dial
		2. Welcome from City Hall Staff
		3. View 1st Floor Showcase, Stained Glass Window
		Go to 8th Floor
	2:15 p.m.	Official Visit to Mayor Takashi Sato
		• Mayor Helmke Address
		See chart for seating, please stand when your name is read
	3:00 p.m.	Visit ends. Move to City Assembly Building
	3:05 p.m.	Official Visit to City Assembly Chairman, Masahior Ejiri
		• Mayor Helmke Address
	3:45 p.m.	Visit ends. Return to Hotel
		-------------- Free Time ---------------
	6:45 p.m.	Gather on 4th Floor of New Otani Hotel
	7:00 p.m.	Mayor's Welcome Dinner Party
		• Delegation will enter together and take seats according to separate chart
		• Mayor Helmke Address
	8:30 p.m.	Party ends
May 30th (FRI)	8:21 a.m.	Gather in Hotel Lobby
	8:30 a.m.	Depart Hotel
	8:45 a.m.	Sightseeing at Zuiryuji Temple
	9:30 a.m.	Tea Ceremony
	10:00 a.m.	Depart Zuiryuji Temple
	10:10 a.m.	Arrive Hotel

	10:45 a.m.	Gather on 4th Floor of Hotel
	11:00 a.m.	Sister Cities 20th Anniversary Ceremony
		Stage - - Mayor Helmke, Gabriel Delobbe, Mary Ball Brant, Ladonna Huntley James, Howard Chapman
		*Mayor Helmke, Mr. Delobbe Addresses
		Exchange of Gifts (Lacquerware Panel from Takaoka)
	11:50 a.m.	Closing
	12:00 p.m.	Sister Cities 20th Anniversary Reception
		• Former Chair Mary Ball Brant Address
	1:30 p.m.	Reception Ends
		-------------- Free Time ---------------
	5:00 p.m.	Dinner (3rd Fl. Japanese Restaurant, "Tsumama" or 14th Fl. "Four Seasons" Western Restaurant – Dinner Tickets)
	6:10 p.m.	Gather in Hotel Lobby
	6:15 p.m.	Depart Hotel
	6:25 p.m.	Arrive at Takaoka Culture Hall
	6:30 p.m.	View "Fort Wayne Today" Photo Exhibit
	7:00 p.m.	Freimann Quartet Concert 20th Anniversary Concert
	8:40 p.m.	Depart Culture Hall of Hotel (by bus)
MAY 31st (SAT)	8:45 a.m.	Gather in Hotel Lobby
	9:00 a.m.	Depart Hotel
	9:05 a.m.	Arrive Kojo Park
		Hotel – Kojo Park – Manyo Drive – Manyo Historical Museum – Lunch – Amaharashi Coast – Takeda Residence – Hotel (Accompanied by International Affairs Staff)
	3:30 p.m.	Arrive Hotel
		-------------- Free Time ---------------
	6:10 p.m.	Gather in Hotel Lobby
	6:15 p.m.	Depart Hotel
	6:25 p.m.	Arrive Chamber of Commerce Building Restaurant
	6:30 p.m.	Farewell Party Sponsored by Takaoka Chamber of Commerce
	8:00 p.m.	Closing
	8:10 p.m.	Depart for Hotel by bus
JUNE 1st (SUN)	8:50 a.m.	Gather in Hotel Lobby
	9:00 a.m.	Depart for Takaoka Station by bus
	9:05 a.m.	Arrive Takaoka Station
	9:27 a.m.	Depart Takaoka Station for Tokyo (Hakutaka 5)

Chapter 11

WALES & SAILS

I

This was a hard trip to prepare for. First, a week in cool, damp Wales, then, another week in warm, sunny Greece. We started out in London, spending two nights at the very agreeable Claridge's Hotel. On the day we arrived, September 9, 1998, we felt good enough in the afternoon to visit the Queens Gallery, located at Buckingham Palace. It's a stodgy but interesting old place that is used by the Royal Family to display, from time to time, various parts of the Royal Art Collection. This particular exhibit was called "Quest for Albion."

The most imposing work was an odd, sprawling portrait of Charles II, painted shortly after his restoration to the throne. The portrait was interesting to me because I had just finished reading Ian Pears' *An Instance of the Fingerpost*, set during that period. We also admired a Holbein portrait of Sir Henry Guildford, which, though well done, looks very much like lots of other Holbein portraits, including the portrait of Thomas More, a copy of which my law partner, Otto Bonahoom, has prominently displayed in his office.

Next door to the Queen's Gallery is the Royal Mews, where the Royal Stables are located. The place also serves as a garage and storage area for all of the fancy carriages that royalty use on ceremonial occasions, and has become something of a museum.

The London Underground is still hectic and crowded, but also fast, efficient, and got us back to Claridge's very easily. We walked to the cafe Le Richoux on South Audley Street, where we were among the few patrons who looked British. We can recommend the steak and mushroom pie, and the shepherd's pie. Getting in the custom of Europe, we ordered a bottle of water for the table. In some countries, if you don't want carbonated water, you order it "without gas." Ours, however, was described (very British) as "delightfully still."

Back at Claridge's, we tried to stay awake as long as we could, and I read the current copy of the *International Herald Tribune*. One cannot properly travel in Europe without reading it at least three or four times a week. Kenneth Starr, the Independent Prosecutor, had just delivered his report on President Clinton to Congress. He delivered it in an armored van! Ominously, the Russian economy is reported to be in a state of near collapse. On the lighter side, St. Louis Cardinal baseball player Mark McGuire had tied Roger Maris' home run record at 61.

II

Jet lag is a funny thing. We got up on Thursday morning, had breakfast, and then went back to bed and snoozed until nearly noon. When we got up, we called our British friends, John and Jean Campion, and reached Jean. It was confirmed that John would "collect us" at 11:00 a.m. on Friday in order to begin our trip with them to Wales. We had very little past experience with Wales, but Jean assured me that it was quite civilized, and that the hotels would accept our credit cards.

We decided to spend the rest of Thursday ambling about, starting with a walk to Kensington Park, and then south to the Four Seasons Hotel. It was a nice day, and walking seemed like just the thing to do, to a point. When the weather started to get cloudy, we grabbed a taxi to Harrod's, and arrived in a downpour. The taxi driver was very thoughtful, and found a place that we could get out of the cab and enter the store under an awning.

We found a restaurant in Harrod's called The Georgian Restaurant, but also found that it offered only large meals. On the other hand, the Terrace Restaurant, which is just along the outside of The Georgian Restaurant, offers a lighter menu and turned out to be very pleasant.

After lunch, more meanderings, which took us through parts of Brompton and Chelsea, where we found lots of pleasant little restaurants and shops. After resting on a bench across the street from Royal Marsden Hospital, we decided that we had walked enough, and took the tube back to Claridge's. Here are a couple of things I like about Claridge's: (1) the front lift has no buttons, but is operated by a pleasant gentleman in full regalia, very much resembling a British militiaman from the Colonial era; and (2) the settings for the shower are "hot-cold-tepid."

Snapshots

We tried to book a table for dinner at The Ivy, but it was totally booked. The concierge said that The Ivy is one of London's most popular restaurants, and he recommended a place called "Avenue" on St. James Street, saying that it was "comparable." Well, the food and service are okay, but the decor is super-chic modern, featuring bare walls, big crowds and lots of noise. Next time, if The Ivy is full, we will try Rules.

That evening, before turning in I wrote myself a reminder that, on checking out Friday morning, I would also book a room at Claridge's for July 15-20, 2000, when the American Bar Association will again be meeting in London.

III

John Campion picked us up promptly at 11:00. John, a barrister, has recently retired from his law practice, but seems to be thriving and looked as fit and energetic as ever. It was a lovely sunny day, but I suddenly didn't feel well, for no apparent reason other than (probably) jet lag. At Campion's home, I went upstairs and took a nap for an hour and a half, after which I ate a little tea and toast and was able to travel. The major disappointment was missing one of Jean Campion's marvelous lunches including (according to Betsy) a salmon salad, ice cream and fresh fruit.

Jean Campion, John Campion, Betsy Chapman, Howard Chapman. About to set off on an adventure in Wales.

We set off on the motor way, headed toward Oxford. In England, traffic moves on the left side of the road, and I was very happy that John was going to be doing all the driving. Our first stop was at Burford, where we took tea at "Huffkins Renowned Tea Room." It was very nice, and Jean assured us that they would not use the word "Renowned" in their name, if it were not deserved.

We passed through Cheltenham, a pretty place with interesting Georgian architecture, extensive gardens, and Cheltenham Ladies College. Our destination was Malvern Wells, and we made our way (on a very narrow road) up a considerable hill until we reached The Cottage in the Wood Hotel, a private inn that is owned and operated by the Pattin Family. It is wonderfully picturesque, with a fine view out across the town and valley. As is often the custom in England, we ordered a drink in the lounge, and a lady came and took our order for dinner. After awhile, she came and told us that "your table is ready." The dining room was full, and the guests were well dressed, including jackets and ties for the men. Although I was still not quite up to snuff, I felt well enough to eat dinner, and to report that the food at this establishment is quite good.

IV

It is hard to explain why a person would sleep well for two nights, and then wake up at 1:30 a.m. and require a sleeping tablet to go back to sleep. When I awoke again, I saw Betsy sitting in a chair reading. "What time is it?" I asked. "9:30!" Well, I was embarrassed to be so late, but the Campions were, as always, very patient and, as it developed, John discovered that he had a problem with one of his tires and would require a little extra time to change it.

It was another delightful day (although John and Jean reported that it had rained earlier), and the view from the inn was perfect. After John changed his tire, we snapped a couple of photographs, and we set off through the glorious countryside, headed for the border with Wales.

The Campions told us that they always traveled with their "Good Food Guide," and it came in handy right away. They had originally planned for us to stop at Ludlow for lunch, but because we were late getting away, we stopped at Brimfield. John remembered the Roebuck Inn, which turned out to be very good indeed, the only mishap being a glass of red wine spilled on Jean during lunch.

Our destination after lunch was Powis Castle, in Wales, but not far from the Welsh border. It originally dates to somewhere around the year 1200 A.D., and current ownership can be traced to approximately the year 1587.

The castle is perched on a rock above extensive garden terraces, and has an excellent collection of paintings and furniture. It was originally built by Welsh princes, and was later the ancestral home of the Herberts and Clives. The gardens are extraordinary, with giant flowering trees and entire terraces in bloom with a variety of flowers. The weather had cooled off and clouded up, and there was off and on rain, but we were dressed for it and didn't really mind the weather. Powis Castle and its gardens really ought to be on everybody's itinerary.

As soon as we entered Wales, we began to see signs written in both Welsh and English. At the Powis Castle Gardens, we passed a group of school boys jabbering away in Welsh, our first chance to hear it spoken. It makes absolutely no sense, either to listen to or to try to read it. The written words do not sound anything like they look. Although the Welsh language was in decline for a long while, there is now a conscious effort to preserve it as a living language. It would certainly be useful in the event of a military conflict, because there would be no need whatsoever to encode and decode secret messages!

From Powis Castle we set off across the incredible Welsh countryside, sparsely settled, very green, and occasionally dotted by stone villages, shepherds, and stately homes and castles. Eventually, we arrived at Bontddu Hall, our hotel for the next two evenings. It is perched high on a hillside with a commanding view over the wide estuary of the Mawddach River, not far from the open sea.

The picturesque and charming Bontddu Hall, our first hotel in Wales.

We arrived in a pouring rain, and were glad to see a cheerful fire, and a beautiful dining room with windows all along one side, taking full advantage of the view. After freshening up, we retired to a lounge area where we enjoyed a glass of wine while we ordered our meals from the menu provided, and then were pleasantly rewarded by an excellent meal. Jean Campion is Welsh, and once knew some of the language, but says that she has lost much of it over the years. She told us a little bit about her childhood growing up in Wales, including the fact (which a visitor might guess) that her mother always reminded her to carry a raincoat whenever she went out, at any time of year. Her childhood included the World War II years, as was true for all of us, and we enjoyed sharing our reminisces of that time.

My journal notes say "Jean and John continue to be charming company," and Jean even managed a wry smile at the evening's only misfortune, when a waitress, clearing the table, spilled a dish of vegetables down her back. We agreed that this was, apparently, just her day to be spilled on, and it was just as well that it was time to retire. The rain continued well into the night, which made it a perfect night for sleeping.

V

The International Herald Tribune does not publish on Sunday, and so, at breakfast, we were given copies of the Sunday *London Times*. Clinton/Lewinsky is still the big story, receiving as much press in England as in the United States, and is also the prominent news on television here. Several Democratic candidates have expressed anger with President Clinton, and think that he will hurt the Democratic Party in the November elections. The same news reports indicate that Clinton enjoys high public approval ratings in various opinion polls, which raises this quandary: If Clinton is so popular in the polls, why are other Democrats afraid that he will hurt them?

We enjoyed a pleasant, sunny but cool morning as we set out for the town of Harlech, and Harlech Castle. The castle was originally built by Edward I in the late 13th Century, is in amazingly good condition, and continues to present a very formidable appearance. It was, in fact, used as a fortress until the Civil War, and was the last Royalist stronghold to fall in that conflict.

We climbed the stone steps in one of the towers to the very top, pulled our coats well around us, and took a bracing walk around the parapets. There was a strong wind off the Irish Sea (Ireland is about 100 miles to the West), and one can sense that it is usually cold and windy here. Far below, toward the sea, one looks over a golf course, and there were people out playing. Betsy, holding her coat tightly closed around her neck, said, "It's a five club wind."

Notwithstanding what seemed to us like a harsh climate, the area does

Snapshots

boast beautiful, wide beaches, and is a popular summer resort (out of season and not particularly crowded when we were there). In the gift shop at the Castle entrance Betsy purchased a tape recording of a Welsh male choir. The Welsh are famous for their love of singing, and are known to be good singers.

The next part of our travels took us through marvelous seaside scenery to the village of Portmeirion (where the pottery comes from). It is not an authentic Welsh village, but rather was created in Italianate style during the middle of the 20th Century. It was worth walking through, perhaps, but very "touristy," and crowded. John Campion and I agreed that it was something of a bore.

We had come to Portmeirion because the "Good Food Guide" recommended the Gwesty Portmeirion Hotel as a fine place to eat. Perhaps it is, but if so, it is the only fine place to eat at Portmeirion, and was totally booked. The man who seemed to be in charge said, "You have to book at least a week in advance if you want to have lunch here."

Fortunately, we had a fall back. We retraced our steps through the town of Talsarnau to a country inn called Hotel Maes-y-Neuadd. Serendipity! It is a lovely, secluded place, created of stone masonry, with beautiful gardens, including a *wall* of enormous hydrangeas. We were a little concerned that we might be too late for lunch or that the place might be fully booked, but in the event there was room for us, and we had a fine (if too big) lunch. A large group nearby turned out to be a Welsh family celebrating a birthday, and the interesting blend of faces, dress, languages and dialects provided entertainment to go with the meal.

Driving on to Dolgellau (pronounced Doll-geth-ly), we stopped to visit Cymer Abbey, a small but interesting ruin of an abbey which, like all of them, went to pot after the "dissolution." The "dissolution" occurred when Henry VIII decided to convert from Catholicism, and confiscated all of the property of the Catholic Church. The Abbey ruins seemed to be part of a farm, and one pays a small fee to enter. Seeing no one around, but following a sign, we went to the door of the farm house, rang the doorbell, and made the payment arrangements with the lady that answered. There is a chain fence along one side of the Abbey, and a sheep farm on the other side of the fence. Two men were very busy with the sheep, and it was interesting to listen to their conversation in Welsh.

Dolgellau turned out to be a very attractive and picturesque Welsh village, constructed of the gray stone so prevalent in this area, and evoking a feeling of going back some 50 years in time. The good news is it has become a favorite tourist stop. The bad news is it has become a favorite tourist stop. On a Sunday afternoon, however, it was very quiet. We watched a few folks sitting in front of the Royal Ship Hotel, sipping beer. We walked to the old historic bridge and passed the ever prominent rugby fields. Jean Campion told us that rugby football is very popular in Wales. It is to be differentiated from "soccer," which is a shortening of "association football" (although the British now simply say "football").

It was a pleasant drive back to Bontddu Hall, and John observed that, contrary to a certain foreboding on his part, the sun had been shining all day long. This scenery would be wonderful, even on a cloudy, rainy day. In the sunshine, it is spectacular! (Bontddu, by the way, is pronounced "Pohn-dee.") Betsy and Jean rested while John and I took a walk up the mountainside. We walked for about 30 minutes, which I would not usually find very taxing, except that this seemed like a 30-degree grade. I found it a lot easier going downhill.

Our hotel room had an interesting shower. In fact, I have never seen one like it. The controls for the shower are separate from the faucet to fill the tub. You turn one knob clockwise and water comes on, and the more you turn, the hotter it gets. Once you have found a temperature you like, you turn another knob in order to adjust the volume of flow. As is often the case in Europe, there was no shower curtain, and the shower itself was attached to a flexible tube. Handy in some ways, but one has to be careful not to make a mess.

At eight o'clock, we joined the Campions once again in the "green room" for a drink, ordered our meals, and had another fine supper. As if on cue, the rain began again shortly after we returned to our rooms, in order to provide another great night for sleeping.

VI

As we went to breakfast on Monday morning, there was a light rain still coming down, and it was chilly enough outside that I could see my breath. John found a garage in the town where he was able to buy a replacement tire, and we started off to wind our way back to Richmond, with our first destination to be for lunch at a place called "The Griffin." For the first time, John's "Good Food Guide" had led us astray (John pointed out that it was, after all, three years out of date). The rather smoky pub was functioning, but the dining room at The Griffin was not open for lunch, so we set off for the next choice, the "Three Cocks Hotel" in, where else, the town of Three Cocks, only to learn that it was serving nothing but sandwiches.

After inquiries, Jean suggested that we go across the street to the "Old Barn Inn." She had been inside and came back to report, "It's a little bit basic, but the lady is a homely sort, and says she can do a proper lunch." All of this turned out to be true. Three of us had the traditional English fish 'n chips, and

John and I each had a "pudding." John says that, in England, all desserts are "puddings."

I grew up in the town of Monmouth, Illinois, about 30 miles east of the Mississippi River. I was therefore glad to learn that we would stop at the English town of Monmouth, near the border of Wales. It is located at the mouth of the Monnow River. Now a bustling town, it was the birthplace of Henry V, whose statue can be seen on "Agincourt Square." Jean went shopping for supplies for an evening supper, while Betsy and I bought postcards and stamps to send to all of our family who had grown up in Monmouth, Illinois.

Our last scheduled stop was at the ruins of Tintern Abbey, built centuries ago along the River Wye by monks belonging to the Cistercian Order. Revered by Wordsworth, painted by J.M.W. Turner, it is still in very good condition, even though despoiled after being taken over by Henry VIII at the time of the dissolution, and is well worth a visit. After exploring the Abbey, it was time for tea before setting off on the long drive back to London, mostly on the motorway.

Reflecting back over the entire journey, I wondered how on earth one could possibly tour Wales in any way other than what we had done, i.e., by automobile and with knowledgeable people. I suppose that there are organized tours that go to Wales, but for our part, we have been spoiled.

We got back to the Campions' home in Richmond after dark, watched the news, and presented John and Jean with a stained glass panel inspired by a Frank Lloyd Wright design, and brought from the Art Institute of Chicago. Jean served supper, and then Betsy and I re-packed.

England in one suitcase, sailboat clothes in another.

VII

Tuesday morning, the Ides of September, dawned grey and wet. We ate breakfast and were sorry to have to say goodbye to our good friends and traveling companions. John Campion drove us to Heathrow Airport, where we boarded our flight on British Air to Athens.

We had made arrangements to be met in Athens by Hellenic Tours (owned and operated by Christos Katsavas), and to be transferred to the sailing ship Phoenix, at Alimos Marina. Hellenic Tours was there, and so was Betsy's sister, Fran LeMay, who had also brought a driver and car. Since Fran's driver knew where the boat was and how to find it, and had plenty of room, we elected to go with her, which turned out to be a good idea, since the boat was a little bit hard to find. The Alimos Marina is really huge, seems to have hundreds of boats, and requires a little local knowledge for maneuvering.

Before leaving the airport, we changed our English pounds ($1.70 =

Howard L. Chapman

£1) for Greek Drachmas ($1.00 = 280 GDr.) I also bought the current issue of the *International Herald Tribune*, and the latest *Time* magazine. Most of the news was about the Starr Report, with some politicians now saying that, perhaps, a "censure" of President Clinton would be the best idea, rather than impeachment. The Dow-Jones Industrial Average was at 7,945 and the NASDAQ at 1,655. The Chicago Bears and the Indianapolis Colts were well on the way to losing seasons; Sammy Sosa of the Cubs had caught Mark McGuire (each with 62 home runs); the Russian Parliament had twice rejected Boris Yeltsin's choice for Prime Minister; and Iran was threatening to invade Afghanistan.

The Phoenix was tied up, stern-to, on the outer edge of the marina, where we joined Betsy's brother, Dick Waterfield, Marni McKinney, and Fran's husband, Art Swanson. It is an absolutely beautiful sailing ship, belonging to Betsy's sister, Fran. The crew included Steve Graham, the Captain, Carter Wilbur and Margherita Murer. Before we got on board, we got our first lesson in seamanship (at least as far as this sailboat is concerned) which is, no shoes on board. All of our shoes were deposited in a basket near the aft of the boat.

It was really fun to once again get settled into a sailboat, on yet another "Phoenix." (Betsy and I were on a sailing trip in the Great Lakes a few years ago on a somewhat smaller "Phoenix," with our friends the Hobbses and the Halls.) We spent a while familiarizing ourselves with the light switches, drawer latches, heads and shower and, by then, it was dark. Betsy, Fran and I joined Dick and Marni for a walk to the end of the marina seawall, where we had a spectacular view of Piraeus, and Athens behind it, lit up across the bay. There was a car parked at the end of the seawall, and as we were gazing at the view, Dick began to sit on one of the fenders, only to see lights go on in the car and a certain amount of stirring around. It turned out that there was a romantic young couple parked in the car, and they had been a little bit startled when Dick sat on the car. Fortunately, they laughed and we laughed, and the lights went out again.

Back on board, we enjoyed our first meal on the boat, served on deck in the open air, under clear, quiet, star-filled Greek skies. Salad, pasta, wine and bread, it was to be the first of many good meals prepared by Margherita.

After dinner, we all gathered in the saloon with Steve, our Captain, who had laid out lots of charts, and had a conference on where we should go tomorrow (and thereafter). It was pretty much like the Tower of Babel, with several of us quoting from a variety of guide books, and I went to bed without knowing what had been decided. As a matter of fact, I never did find out what had been decided, and I suspect that nothing was decided, but that didn't keep us from sailing off for the Cyclades Islands the next morning.

VIII

We all slept in, with the exception of Marni. We got up to learn that she had not only risen early, but she had run all the way to the airport and back. **Good grief!**

If you were to try to describe a beautiful sunny day, this was it. Carter served breakfast on deck, and, at 11:00 o'clock, the Phoenix sailed out through the breakwater into the Aegean Ocean, heading south. There are two excellent pairs of binoculars kept on deck, and we could easily make out the Acropolis in the distance.

It would be just about as easy for me to fly a jet airplane as to operate and sail the Phoenix. The instrument panel looks pretty much like an airplane cockpit, and I don't know anything about sailing anyway. The crew, of course, was marvelously efficient and, in a short while, had the sails up, and we enjoyed several hours of pleasant, quiet breezes, time for reading, crossword puzzles, conversation and photographs. At one point, Carter gave us the one piece of disheartening news - the ship had run out of "American" coffee. They had apparently made some efforts to find some in Athens, but weren't able to do so. We would have to make do with espresso. My journal notes say, "How deprived we are!"

We sailed near the Temple of Poseidon, an impressive ruin at Cape Sounian, placed on top of a high cliff jutting out into the sea, and highlighted in gold by the afternoon sun. With our binoculars, we could see that there were lots of tourists at the Temple, and some of them were looking at us. *We* were not jealous of *them*.

As the afternoon wore on, the wind failed, the sails came down, and we shifted to power. Carter brought everyone soft drinks, and the conversation, naturally, turned to the current difficulties of Mr. Clinton. I opined that it would be best all-around if he would resign, but Dick thought that he should stay on.

With plenty of light left, we reached the Island of Kea, a kind of "by the way" island that was absolutely charming. We anchored in a harbor and Steve took us in the Zodiac to a small cluster of buildings on shore. (The Phoenix tows a Zodiac, or "dinghy," which is really a pretty good boat, with a 50-horsepower outboard motor. When going across the Atlantic, or in heavy weather, the Zodiac is strapped on the front of the boat.)

From the sea, the towns and villages on the Greek Islands look like cubist paintings. Houses tend to be square or rectangular, built very close together or on top of one another (going up a hillside), and are universally painted bright white, except for the occasional blue dome of a church. The little village we visited on Kea was no exception. When we arrived at the dock, we were met by some local men who helped us tie up, and then tried to persuade us to visit their taberna, or, in the alternative, encourage us to take their friend's taxi "up into town."

There probably is a nice town on the island, but we never got to see it. Instead, we decided to take a walk in order to get some exercise after a day on the boat, and to get a closer look at the people and their homes. Dick and I went in one direction, Fran, Betsy and Marni in another. When we returned to the harbor area, we found a store whose sign, written mainly in Greek, included the word "supermarket." The friendly proprietor spoke nothing but Greek, but was happy to let me browse around the store and, sure enough, I found some coffee for sale, which looked to me like it might be okay. When Steve Graham came back in the Zodiac to pick us up, I took him into the store and showed it to him, and he agreed to try it. The label was written entirely in Greek, except for the name "Jacob's Mein Mild 'Or." With Jacob's Mein Mild 'Or in hand, we headed back to the anchored Phoenix, where Margherita was getting dinner ready.

An absolutely gorgeous evening, we dined on deck with candlelight, the lights of the little harbor in the distance. We had a salad of lettuce, tomatoes, white beans and onion, followed by a main course of veal scaloppini and ratatouille. We were already getting spoiled by the food! It was a spectacular sky, and the Milky Way has never been closer. Okay, so I plagiarize from the beer ad, but my journal says, "It just doesn't get any better than this."

IX

Do they have bad weather in these islands? The little harbor was dazzling in the morning sun, where breakfast was served on deck and, to the surprise and delight of all of us, Jacob's Mein Mild 'Or turned out to be great coffee!

I am not sure when the decision was made, or who made it, but somehow it was decided that we would sail today (Thursday) to the Island of Siros, a/k/a Syros. We were finding that the names of all of these islands could be spelled two or three different ways, depending on which map or book you were looking at. When they said we would be going to Siros, I had Steve get out the chart so that I could see the course, and I noticed that we would pass an island called Nisos Yiaros. On the chart, there is a dotted line around it, and a legend that says, "**<u>Prohibited Area. See Note</u>**."

Away we sailed, enjoying the day, when, on the horizon, we saw a convoy of seven or eight Greek Navy ships, some destroyers, some light cruisers, and one or two gunboats. They were passing directly perpendicular to our course and, all of a sudden, a gunboat turned and came right toward us, and then a voice came over our radio, calling for our Captain. Steve answered and we were able to hear the Greek naval officer tell us to set a particular course and to hold it for thirty minutes or until further notice. No explanation and no choice!

The new course took us parallel to the convoy, and moving in the opposite direction. After about a half an hour, we were clear of the last of them, and got word over the radio that we could return to our original course. Then, we watched as they sailed along the coast of Nisos Yiaros, and *started firing live ammunition at it*! There were helicopters in the air, big guns blazing, lots of noise, and it was quite a sight.

Now I understood why Nisos Yiaros is marked "**Prohibited Area**" on the charts. The Greek Navy uses it for artillery practice! You sure wouldn't want to make a mistake and anchor there for the night.

Our "temporary escort" by the Greek Navy.

Once clear of the Greek Navy, we sailed on into Siros without incident, and anchored at the dock in a small village called "Finikas," which turns out to be Greek for "Phoenix." (Very few of the harbors or marinas in these islands seem to have individual piers for the boats to berth, and they typically tie up "stern to," meaning that the boat needs to back in, tie the stern up to the dock, and leave an anchor off the bow to maintain the boat's position.) Siros is one of the most populous of the Cyclades Islands with 20,000 inhabitants. Its main city, Ermoupoli, is a thriving town built around an excellent deep water anchorage, and we decided to see it.

After making arrangements to meet Art and Fran later for dinner, Betsy, Dick, Marni and I found a taxi and took the thirty minute ride into the center of Ermoupoli, and had the driver let us out in the middle of the waterfront. Like all of the towns and villages we saw in these islands, it was both pleasant and clean. It has a beautiful square with a wide, marble-tiled walking area around the Town Hall, constructed of local stone. All around this square are modern shops, cafes and restaurants, with lots of outdoor tables for dining or simply relaxing with a cup of coffee or a glass of wine.

Marni had a guidebook that recommended we visit the Cathedral of Agios Giorgios. She said it was "a little way up the hill," and we should just walk up there. We began the ascent, going up one flight of stone steps after another, along narrow walks, and passed many cats but very few people. Once or twice, Marni stopped someone and asked directions to the Cathedral, and the people kept pointing up.

Well, it turned out that the Cathedral is *on top* of the area known as "Ano Syros," and it was a *long* way up. We decided to abandon that particular goal, and struck off in a different direction (this time *horizontal*) until we found another recommended church which, while attractive, was closed. We did, however, find a small hotel nearby, and went to their second floor, outdoor terrace cafe, where the view over the town and harbor was lovely, and where we were able to buy Mythos beer.

We had arranged to meet Art and Fran at 8:00 o'clock at a restaurant called "Lilis," which was so far up on Ano Syros, that it was almost as high as the Cathedral we had been planning to walk to earlier. We needed a taxi for two reasons: first, because the entire journey was almost straight up; and, second, because it is the kind of place we would never have found on our own. Sitting high above the city, looking over the harbor, we found Fran and Art already waiting at an outdoor table, admiring the lights of the city, and watching the ships going in and out of the harbor.

As a group, we ordered salads, bottled water, wine, olives, cheese and bread. Foreign menus are usually an adventure, so three of us decided to have the "Chicken Special," which came in a large crockery bowl, with lots of cheese. Hot and good. When it came time to leave, the waiter advised us that the restaurant, to our surprise, *did not accept credit cards*. We scrambled around to come up with enough cash among us to pay the tab, but no one seemed too concerned. Our congenial attitude may have been partly due to the wine.

The restaurant called two taxis to meet us and take us on a *wild* ride back down the mountain, through the town, and across the island, to our boat in Finikas. Steve and Carter were waiting for us and piped us aboard (although they didn't really have a pipe). I had a little time to devote to reading the novel *Lucky You*, the newest book by Carl Hiassen which is, by the way, hilarious.

X

I was up early on Friday, got dressed and took a walk along the peaceful harbor, where some of the local people were up watching the sunrise and enjoying their morning coffee and conversation. It was the beginning of another gorgeous sunny day and the sun popped up over a hill as I walked. I got back to the boat just as Marni was returning from her morning run. At 8:00 o'clock we cast off. Carter brought in the anchor, Margherita closed all the ports, between them they brought in the fenders and the gangplank, and Steve set a course for Mykonos.

Betsy Chapman, Fran LeMay and Marni McKinney, under sail on *The Phoenix*.

Mykonos is one of the best known of the Greek Islands, and a tourist favorite - for good cause. It has a stunningly attractive main town located right at sea level, it has superb sandy beaches, and within a few minutes' boat trip lies the island of Delos, which is one of the great archeological sites of the world. (Mykonos attracts more than 750,000 visitors a year.)

The sails went up, the motor was turned off, and everything seemed perfect. After about five hours we sailed into the main harbor of Mykonos, but were told that there was no room to tie up at the dock. However, we could try again after 4:00 o'clock. We went to a nearby anchorage, anchored the boat in the crystal clear water (Art went swimming), and then Steve drove Dick, Marni, Betsy and me into the main harbor on the Zodiac.

Having been cleaned out at last night's restaurant, our first goal in town was to find an ATM where we were able to get some cash. Dick and Marni went on to an office of the local telephone company so they could call their respective offices and retrieve their voice mail, while Betsy and I found a newsstand and I bought the current *Herald Tribune*.

We wandered around the town, which has very upscale shops, and then strolled back to a sidewalk cafe to find Art and Fran. More wandering and more shops produced only a small amount of shopping, but I did pick up some cheese crackers and some Pringles (sour cream and onion) to take back to the boat. Meanwhile, Steve and Margherita had gone to the local market, and we saw them coming back loaded with bags of groceries.

By late afternoon, the town had gotten very warm and also very crowded. Lots of large ferries come to Mykonos, as well as virtually all of the cruise ship lines. At one point, I counted four large cruise ships anchored offshore, all funneling passengers into the town. The crowds were getting out of hand, so I made my way back to the dock (which seemed to be away from most of the activity) where the Phoenix was tied up. Fran and Betsy went off together to explore the medieval city, and walked all the way to the striking row of five windmills which greets all incoming ships, a landmark familiar to Mykonos visitors.

We didn't feel like swimming there in the harbor, but the showers felt

The waterfront at Mykonos.

good, and Margherita rewarded us with another delightful meal, served on deck. After dinner, I walked back into town to see if I could find a copy of *USA Today*, and ran into Dick and Marni. The three of us went into a jewelry store, where Dick and I each purchased a gold necklace with a Greek Key design. Marni got hers at once, and Betsy got hers at Christmas. Dick and Marni wound up staying in town until after Midnight, reporting lots of attractive cafes and night spots.

XI

We had decided to spend most of Saturday tied up at Mykonos, get up early, and take the ferry to the island of Delos. One *has* to take the ferry to Delos, since private boats are prohibited. The passage cost 1800 GDr per person, and took about 30 minutes after leaving Mykonos. A heavy rain storm came up as we were half way to the island, and everyone scurried below deck to try to keep dry.

We docked at Delos during a pause in the storm, and Betsy and I, together with Dick and Marni, made a dash up the hill to the archeological museum, one of the very few buildings on the island that is open to the public. We made it there just in time, because a huge thunderstorm with hail came charging up the hillside after us and seemed to almost follow us in the door. We later learned that Fran and Art had found a shelter in some of the ruins, but many of the other tourists had simply gotten soaked.

The entire island of Delos is, in reality, a museum, covered with ruins of ancient buildings, mosaics, and ancient statuary. Even with the poor weather conditions, it was full of tourists. We all enjoyed seeing it (after the storm passed), despite being cold and wet; but, it would be nice to go back and visit it again in better weather.

The ferry took us back to the main town of Mykonos, built around a big, horseshoe harbor, with many marinas, cafes, and shops. We stopped at the newsstand where I was able to get the newest *Herald Tribune*, and then walked back to the Phoenix. The crew was rather agitated over the fact that the boat had gotten knocked about a little bit during the storm, and had experienced some (although apparently slight) damage. To compound problems, an enormous ferry boat had entered the harbor and dropped its own anchor across ours, so that we could not leave until it left. The ferry finally did leave at about 3:00 o'clock, and we left soon after, on a rather cloudy and windy afternoon. Because of the weather, Margherita and Carter served us lunch in the saloon. Contemplating the storm, the boat being jostled about in the harbor, and the damage, Steve said he was "glad to get out of there. It's not the sea that is dangerous, it's the crusty parts around the edges."

We were able to proceed, mostly under sail, until we reached our next destination, the island of Paros. Dick handled the wheel for part of the time, and did not strike any rocks or other boats, nor did we run aground. Whew!

Dick Waterfield at the helm with help from Marni McKinney.

It was late when we got to Paros and found the Port of Naousa. Steve anchored the boat in a quiet cove nearby (I say "quiet," but my journal notes say "like a tomb"). There were a couple of sizable resorts on the beach, but they were closed for the season. We had the cove to ourselves, except for two other sailboats anchored in the distance. Again, because of the cool weather, we had dinner below deck, snug, warm and well-fed.

XII

By morning, the weather had cleared, and the sun was bright and warm once again. Steve loaded us into the Zodiac and transported us into Naousa. This being a Sunday morning, I expected the town to be dead, but it turned out to be very lively with several shops and cafes open, fishing boats active on the dock, and a lot of hustle and bustle. Betsy and I walked all through the town and really enjoyed it. It is clean and sparkling, and the activity around the fishing boats with men piling up enormous piles of nets, provides entertainment. We walked up a considerable hill to the largest church, but found it closed (why at 11:00 a.m. on a Sunday?). On the way down the hill we stopped at the Hotel Fotilia, a small place with fourteen rooms. Not only is this town my favorite of all the places we visited, but this small hotel is one of the most charming I have ever seen.

Back in the harbor area, we visited some shops, bought a few things for the boat (cookies, Pringles, napkins and paper towels), and then relaxed at an outdoor cafe for cappuccino and hot chocolate. On the way back to the boat we met Steve and Margherita, again loaded down with provisions. Margherita's arms were full of cartons of eggs and she told us that she had purchased all of the eggs that the store had!

Once back on board, we raised anchor and set sail for the Island of Ios. We had more good sailing and lots of chances to watch the huge ferries going from island to island. My journal notes say, "Lunch *en route* - on deck. What a life. Crew has been terrific!"

After lunch, Dick advised that he had brought along all the written material necessary to have a meeting of The Waterfield Foundation. Since all of the directors and officers were present, we gathered around the table on deck and had our formal meeting. It was a full-fledged business meeting, and we accomplished as much as would be accomplished at any other meeting, but I can't recall ever enjoying a meeting as much as this one. We need to find a way to do that more often!

We were not able to drop anchor at the main harbor in Ios because it is a rather small harbor with heavy ferry traffic. However, we found a small cove nearby that had a beautiful sandy beach and only one house on the hillside. Fran, Art and Betsy took the Zodiac back to look over the main town while I went for a swim. The water was fabulous. When we had anchored, I found Steve standing on the bow of the boat looking down into the water. He remarked that, although we were in 27 feet of water, it was possible to plainly see the anchor and chain lying on the bottom.

The Zodiac group returned just before dark, full of excitement because they had encountered the sailing ship of TV personality, Geraldo Rivera, anchored at Ios. Geraldo was on board and Art had taken the opportunity to tell him that Bill Clinton is not a nice man. Fran and Betsy had gone to the ferry office in order to check on schedules, but had absentmindedly left their shoes on the Phoenix. They returned with information and sore feet.

Dinner on deck once again, with our first chance to try a local Greek wine called "Retsina." Once is enough. We had contemplated sailing the next day to visit the island of Santorini, but Steve had learned that, because of the depth of the harbor, there is no suitable mooring place for the Phoenix. No way to drop an anchor, so, if we wanted to see Santorini, we would have to find another way to get there. In other words it would be by ferry.

XIII

It was a little bit cool on Monday morning, but the sky was clear, and the bright sun made it warm enough to eat breakfast on deck. All six of us loaded into the Zodiac with Steve and went to town to catch the hydrofoil ferry to Santorini.

When at rest in the water, the hydrofoil looks more or less like a football on water skis. Ours was painted yellow and black and, once it gets going, sits just above the water on its skis. This allows it to go faster than a conventional boat. From a distance it looks like a big bumble bee, only uglier. On the inside, it resembles a third world airplane, dirty, dark, noisy, and showing absolutely no signs of maintenance. The hydrofoils are popular, nonetheless, because they travel so much faster than the regular ferry boats, and in our case, would get to Santorini in only 45 minutes. It was crammed with people and overwhelmed with luggage, most of which was piled around in heaps. Forty-five minutes was plenty.

The island of Santorini, which is also sometimes called Thira, was formed by a volcanic explosion that occurred approximately 1450 B.C. The eruption may have been the cause of the demise of the Minoan civilization, which seems to have disappeared at about the same time. The island presents quite a spectacle as one approaches it from the sea. Vertical volcanic rock cliffs climb straight up into the air, forming a partially broken circle (the former crater), which has now become the harbor. On top, there are villages that look as if they are about to spill right off into the ocean. Looking at the sheer rock cliffs around the harbor, it is easy to understand why boats cannot easily anchor here. Unless, of course, their anchor chain is a couple of hundred feet long!

Our hydrofoil docked at a ferry landing called Athenios, a sleepy place that becomes a temporary madhouse each time a ferry arrives. Taxis took us to the tourist town of Thira, a long trip, mostly straight up. Since we had no better plan, we told the taxis to drop us at the Arresana Hotel, which is right across the street from the Atlantis Hotel. Both, by the way, are excellent hotels. The town is full of white buildings, cafes, jewelry shops, newsstands, and a variety of stores selling tee-shirts and jim-cracks. It is also crammed to the gills with tourists.

All of the restaurants seemed to be of the open air variety, which was too bad because it was cool and very, *very* windy. We selected the Archipelago Restaurant, where Dick and Marni chose a table on the edge, with a fine view looking down over the crater, and a steady wind. The rest of us sat at a sheltered table close to the back wall, where we had a

Snapshots

view of the wind blowing Dick and Marni around. The food, anyway, was fine, and we used the opportunity to try some traditional Greek dishes. Saganaki (fried cheese), cucumber and tomato salad, and souvlaki, which is a shiskabob made with veal. (There seemed to be a lot of sheep grazing around on these islands and we wondered why there were not more lamb dishes on the menus we saw.) Amstel, the Dutch beer, seems to be popular in Greece, and it is always reliable. Our only problem was that we had way too much food.

We decided to go our own ways after lunch. I started by wandering around through the crowded shopping areas. It wasn't long before I had the sensation, "I've been here before." Indeed I had - tourist traps everywhere. I went to a newsstand, bought the *Herald-Tribune*, and went back to the lobby of the Atlantis Hotel to relax and read.

At four o'clock we gathered by prearrangement and took taxis back down the mountain to the ferry dock. There was no hydrofoil scheduled back to Ios, so we took the jumbo-size, traditional type ferry. This was a journey which required two hours. I stood on deck as the ferry entered the harbor at Ios, and saw Steve in the Zodiac, heading for the dock to meet us. I took off my cap and waved and, to my amazement, he was able to pick me out and waved back.

We paused at the ferry office in Ios to gather hydrofoil and ferry schedules and to plan our departure for tomorrow. Dick, Marni, Betsy, and I had scheduled a flight from Santorini to Athens on Olympic Airlines, which meant that we had to figure out a way to get back to Santorini in time to make the plane. We learned that there was no room on the hydrofoil tomorrow, leaving only the 2:00 p.m. ferry, the same boat that we had just gotten off. Having no options makes choosing easy, as we decided on the 2:00 p.m. ferry.

On the way back to the Phoenix, Steve said that he had been busy all day "looking after business." With modern technology, including a satellite phone and a computer, he gets both e-mail and fax transmissions, and can communicate anyplace quite easily.

Back in our quiet cove, we ate dinner on deck, and then repacked our bags for tomorrow's ferry trip back to Santorini (we would be carrying our luggage with us). For the first time, there was "weather" during the night and, at one point, I heard Steve let out more anchor chain. "What a treat," I thought, "to have a crew that's responsible for everything." With all the wind, there was a lot of motion through the night, but we all seemed to sleep just fine, anyway.

XIV

We had a leisurely morning ahead of us and I was up early, which gave me a chance to sip a little coffee and chat with the crew. The wind was gone, and we had a sunny, lovely day.

After breakfast, Betsy, Fran and I all went swimming, while Carter took Dick and Marni waterskiing behind the Zodiac. Toward noon, we hauled anchor and motored to the town on Ios where the ferry docks, and tied up the Phoenix at the dock. We enjoyed lunch on deck, the last of Margherita's good meals, and Fran and Art presented Betsy, Dick, Marni and me with "Phoenix" tee-shirts. The four of us hauled our luggage to the ferry landing to meet the 2:00 p.m. ferry (which arrived at 2:45), hassled our bags on board, and settled in for the two-hour trip back to Santorini. One of our guidebooks describes the Greek ferries as "chaos," reminding us that "chaos" is a Greek word. In addition to a huge mob of people, this ferry was stuffed with one big truck and an assortment of other vehicles, and mountains of luggage. On the plus side, the weather was better and the trip much smoother than it had been the day before.

At the dock in Santorini we found a cab driver who insisted he could take all four of us and all of our luggage to the airport which, in fact, he did. (Much of the luggage had to be tied on the roof.) The airport is on the other side of the island, where the slope of the mountain gets close to sea level. It is a fairly decent airport, but was almost completely deserted when we arrived. In fact, when the taxi let us out, I was concerned that the place might be locked up. Our eventual Olympic Air flight to Athens lasted one hour, went on time, and was very comfortable.

I have one regret about Santorini and our entire trip and it is this: there is a wonderful archeological site at Akrotiri on Santorini, and we didn't get to see it. To be honest, I really didn't understand what it was or where it was until we were back in Athens, and by then it was too late. Next time.

We were met in Athens by our friends from Hellenic Tours, with a minibus large enough to handle all four of us and our luggage, and transported to the Athens Hilton Hotel. This hotel, by the way, is not up to snuff, and not nearly up to its price.

It was dinnertime, and the four of us, Dick, Marni, Betsy and I, took a taxi to Milton's Restaurant in the Plaka, a part of the old section of the City of Athens. The Plaka is a fascinating and delightful place with no motorized traffic and thriving at night. Milton's turned out to be an excellent restaurant, located on a bustling corner, where we sat outdoors and watched the incessant activity. It was nearly midnight by the time we finished dinner, but the evening was fine, and we walked back to our hotel. Betsy and I said goodbye to Dick and Marni, who would be catching an early Lufthansa flight home in the morning.

XV

Having breakfast in the hotel room gave us a chance to enjoy the view over the city with the Acropolis in the distance. At 10:00 o'clock we were met in the lobby by our guide, Antoni, provided through Hellenic Tours. Antoni is a small, fit, greying man with glasses, who speaks excellent English, and is extremely well-read and articulate. Although he seemed overly serious, he also was a splendid guide for our one-day sightseeing tour of Athens.

There are two main things that the tourist must see in Athens, the first being the Acropolis, and the second being the Archeological Museum. "Acropolis" means "high city," and nearly every Greek town has one. The Acropolis in Athens is, however, the most famous. There seems to be no way to get to the top other than to walk, a long steep climb, and that's what we did.

Half way up, Antoni lead us away from the path to an area that allowed us to look out over the Agora, or town center, the ancient City of Athens, now below us. While we stood there, Antoni gave us a history lesson. We were looking at the place where Plato and Socrates lived, wrote and taught. It is a place once inhabited by all the great Greek philosophers, writers, poets and statesmen.

Nearby, we stopped at an enormous rock monument, with a bronze plaque commemorating the fact that this was the spot where Saint Paul addressed the Athenians. Some of them were upset at his talk about "one God," and were threatening to eject him from the city. This is where he addressed them, and persuaded them to let him stay, a speech which converted some, including Dionysus, and began the eventual conversion to Christianity in this area. The speech is recorded in *The Bible* in *Acts of the Apostles*, Chapter 17.

We continued our climb up the wide stone path until we reached the top, where the ancient Greeks built their temples to the gods, including the incredible Parthenon. There are chunks of stone and marble on the ground all over the place, but also evidence of an enormous reconstruction project underway. There are huge scaffoldings on many of the buildings, and we watched men doing meticulous work at restoration. On the one hand, we heard jokes claiming that this reconstruction and renovation has already been going on forever; still, it would be fun to see the progress ten years from now.

Howard L. Chapman

Betsy and Howard Chapman at The Parthenon in Athens.

Looking at the Parthenon, Antoni told us how much of it was destroyed by Venetian cannon fire when the place was occupied by the Turks in the middle of the 17th Century. The cannonballs (the marks can still easily be seen) hit the stone pillars, and the resulting sparks ignited caches of gunpowder, resulting in huge explosions. It makes one cry to think about it. These buildings had survived pretty much intact for centuries until only 330 years ago. By then, people should have had enough sense not to knock them down!

We left the Acropolis, still on foot, and Antoni lead us down another route through the Plaka. The upper part is full of restored homes that are quite expensive, and quite nice, although I think it would be distracting to live in a place that is always prowled by tourists. In the lower part of the Plaka, among the cafes and shops, Betsy and I chose a taberna for lunch, and Antoni left us for an hour.

When we reconvened, we drove to the Archeological Museum, and Antoni spent nearly three hours showing us the high points. Some areas are crowded with wonderful gold objects, others with statuary, and others with murals. Today there are many more ancient stone statues than bronze in the world's museums; however, originally, most statues were made in bronze. Unfortunately, most of the bronze sculpture was melted down during the medieval period and used to make cannons. The few good bronze statues that survived are usually those that were lost at sea, or buried under volcanic ash, and later rediscovered. It was at the Archeological Museum that we saw the enormous exhibit about Santorini, and realized how much is there, and how much we had missed. Antoni was appalled when we told him that we had wasted our time on Santorini in the town of Thira.

On the way to our car, I bought a large bottle of water to take back to the Hilton hotel, at a cost of about eighty cents. A very small bottle cost $5.00 if purchased at the hotel. My journal says, "Is there any scam more shameless than the hotel mini-bar?"

After a long day, we were tired, had dinner in the hotel, and packed.

XVI

In the military, a really, really early wake up time is called "zero dark hundred." That's when Hellenic Tours met us in the hotel lobby, and escorted us to the airport for our flight to London on British Air. British Air, by the way, disappointed throughout, with poor service, little courtesy and cramped seating.

By contrast, the American Airlines representative in London turned out to be an absolute gem. (This is not a reflection on the Brits. The AA attendant was English!) She helped us get our bags rechecked, and rearranged our schedules so that Betsy and I could travel home on the same flight, and reach Fort Wayne three hours earlier than we had planned.

Wales and Sails. All in all, one hell of a good time.

Chapter 12

TEPID WATERS

I

I am not sure why anybody would keep a log of a winter cruise in the Caribbean, let alone take the time to write a journal about it. Maybe it is because I kept the notes while we were doing it, and can't stand to see them go to waste. On the other hand, you, dear reader may go to some of these places, or Betsy and I might revisit them. In either event, a journal will be nice to have.

Betsy and I flew from Fort Wayne to Boca Raton, Florida on January 21, 2000, to gather up our warm weather clothes. We were to join the *Yorktown Clipper*, a "small" cruise ship operated by Clipper Cruise Line, headquartered in St. Louis, Missouri. The boat would be leaving from the Island of Grenada.

On Saturday, the 22nd, we had time for lunch at my favorite lunch place, the Tin Muffin Cafe in Boca Raton, and then our friend and apartment manager, Phil Pingel, drove us to the Miami Airport to catch a 4:55 p.m. flight on American Airlines, nonstop to Grenada. Miami Airport is well described as a zoo! It is overcrowded chaos, a place where all flights are overbooked, where everyone is concerned about crime, where airline personnel are harassed and harried, where nothing is organized in a sensible way, and where every check-in counter has a long line. No one selects this airport by choice.

We were planning to meet Gene and Marcia Laker, and Jerry and Margaret Nolan, who were coming from Fort Wayne to connect on the same flight out of Miami. However, we looked for them in vain. The flight boarded, "wait list passengers" got on, and we sat on the plane watching the last boarding stragglers. I said to myself, "Get on the plane, Gene!" But they didn't.

Grenada is farther south than you might think. It's a three-hour flight from Miami and, to aggravate the situation, you also lose an hour in crossing a time zone. We arrived in the dark and were met by personnel from the Clipper, who gathered our bags and then stuffed us (along with other passengers) into tiny vans. Once all of the seats were full, the aisle was filled with "jump seats," and more passengers were crammed in. No one could have gotten out, no matter what happened. There is no Americans With Disabilities Act or OSHA in Grenada!

Our arrival at the ship turned out to be a depressing experience. Betsy and I had traveled with the Clipper Cruise Line some years earlier and found it to be very pleasant. This time, the cabin seemed, well, neglected. My journal notes say, "El aire condicionando no funciona." The air conditioning didn't work, and the windows were sealed shut.

I went up two decks and spoke to the Cruise Director, a young man named Zach Feldman, who said he would send "the engineer" to our cabin to see about the air conditioning. A half hour later, a man appeared with a screwdriver, and began to tinker with the air conditioning controls, only to have most of them fall off the wall. "We will work on this," he said, and left.

II

Despite the stuffy room, we slept pretty well, and when we woke up, we found a "bulletin" had been pushed under the door during the night. In addition to other intelligence, it advised us that breakfast would be served from 7 a.m. until 8:30 a.m., at which time it would "close." It was already 8:15 a.m. When we traveled with Clipper the last time, meals were available at almost all hours of the day or night. Another disappointment - but we did make it in time for breakfast.

Later, we attended a briefing session in which three onboard "naturalists," Linda Whitman, Ignacio Rojas, and Gregor Williams, talked about things that we would be doing during the week. Mainly, they promoted a number of "excursions" that we could sign up to do, all at an extra cost.

By now, we were anchored in Chatham Bay at Union Island which, so far as I ever learned, is not owned by anybody. Chatham Bay is uninhabited, with no sign of any buildings at all, and only an occasional private sailboat was to be seen. Even though there was a lot of wind, it was a very lovely, sunny day. At the appointed time, Betsy and I joined other passengers on the Sun Deck, where Linda Whitman and Ignacio Rojas distributed snorkel equipment which included masks, tubes and fins. Since I am near-sighted, I had brought my own mask, with prescription glass.

The Yorktown Clipper has two tenders, which they call "DIBS" (an acronym). Each of the DIBS holds one crew member and 16 passengers, all of whom must wear a life vest when being transported between the ship and shore. At the moment, one DIB was defunct, so the other was doing double (tedious) duty, chugging back and forth.

Along the coastline in Chatham Bay we found marvelous snorkeling, with more kinds of undersea life than one could catalogue. One large fish simply lies on the bottom, looking like sand, and waiting with its mouth open for its lunch to swim in; a millipede, about 6-8 inches long, goes through life crawling about on a big rock; and there are lots of sea urchins (don't step on them). Betsy had done some snorkeling before, but didn't feel that she really had the hang of it; however, this time, she seemed to do fine, and we really enjoyed it. I resolved to get her a prescription face mask before we do it again. We didn't know it then, but this was far and away the best snorkeling we would encounter during the week.

We got back to the ship in time for a late lunch. My journal notes, commenting on lunch, are not complimentary. One of the attractions of taking a cruise is that the food will be measured on a scale of "excellent" to "fabulous." On this trip, the food was "nourishing" to "appetizing." Betsy, however, says that she thought that the food was "quite good." She is easy to please.

We sat during lunch with a couple who had been on the Yorktown Clipper the prior week (doing our trip in reverse), and had startling things to tell us. First, they had been required to spend an extra day at the beginning in St. Kitts because a very large number of passengers had been unable to get to the boat by departure time. Then, all three of the ship's generators went out, so that all passengers were sent ashore for the day. As a result, the Island of Nevis was dropped from the schedule. Finally, some kind of illness swept through the ship during the middle of the week, sickening half of the passengers and crew, most of whom stayed sick for two to three days. When the ship returned to Grenada (just before we got on), it had been evacuated and fumigated!

I looked up Zach, the Cruise Director, who seemed to be pleasant and well-meaning. "Where," I asked him, "are our friends, the Lakers and the Nolans." "They are expected." he said, "later today." I went to the railing and looked around and saw nothing but deserted island. How in the hell would they get to Chatham Bay?

It was a beautiful afternoon, and we took advantage of it as a time to nap, read, catch up on my journal, and work the crossword puzzle provided on a daily basis by the ship. I was reading "Crimes of the Century," a documentary by Gilbert Geis and Leigh Bienen. It was sent to me *gratis* by the Northwestern University School of Law, and I suspect that Leigh Bienen is related to Henry Bienen, the President of the University.

At 4:00 o'clock we went through the compulsory fire drill, common on all passenger ships. Everyone put on their life jackets and stood in the hall outside their cabins. Afterward we went to the Orientation Lounge where we heard more sales pitches about up-coming tours. We decided to sign on for a trip to a place called Anse Chastenet in St. Lucia on Tuesday. Also, in a conversation with Zach, we learned that, by some miracle, the Lakers and Nolans had come on board, although we didn't see them arrive.

One of the advantages of a Clipper Cruise is that it is always casual. One exception was the "Captain's Welcome Aboard Party," where I and a majority of the other men on board wore a blue blazer. At last, we got together with the Lakers and the Nolans and heard their travel saga.

All of their flights had been arranged by Clipper Cruise Line, but the connections were unrealistic. The first leg was supposed to take them from Fort Wayne to a connecting flight in Cleveland, and was booked on an airplane that Jerry described as a "flying cigar." The plane would not start for an hour, while the passengers froze on board. Of course, they missed the connection in Cleveland, and were sent on to Philadelphia and from there to San Juan, Puerto Rico, where they arrived at night. There were no flights out of San Juan to Grenada, or anywhere else, until morning and, to make things worse, there were no hotel rooms available in the city because of a "fiesta" that weekend. They sat all night in the San Juan Airport and, as a final blow, all of the electricity and plumbing in the airport went out, and stayed out, for most of the night.

The next morning, American Airlines got them on an "island hopper" flight to Union Island, where they chartered a boat to take them around to Chatham Bay, where they joined the Yorktown Clipper.

The moral: Never, ever, let the cruise company determine your air schedule. Second moral: When taking a cruise, go to the point of departure a day early. (Maybe that should be moral number one.)

Anyway, the Captain, Daniel Ahrens, greeted us at his Welcome Aboard Party, and we never saw him again until the night before we left the ship.

There was still no air conditioning in our cabin. In fact, there were no longer any controls for it (they had fallen off the wall and apparently been taken away by the stewardess). At our request, the "engineer" appeared again with his screwdriver, and said we had no air conditioning because we were "at the end of the loop." Still, he said, we should at least have controls on the wall. Fiddling with them would presumably make us feel better. Even though he promised to again "look into it," he never returned, even after we asked a third time. We learned to live in light clothing.

The itinerary called for the ship to travel at night, and it left Union Island at 4:00 a.m., through rough seas. My bunk was under the window, and the curtain swung back and forth, hitting me on the head. We didn't get much sleep.

III

When we got up on Monday morning, we were anchored at the Island of Bequia (pronounced "bek-way"). The Clipper has an advantage in being able to put in at a small island like this, where larger ships are unable to visit. We docked at the pier (the Yorktown Clipper draws only 8.5 feet) where frantic commercial activity (and noise) went on all day long. On the other side of the same pier was a large freighter that was being unloaded and, at the end of the pier, the island ferries and taxis docked to load and unload passengers and produce.

We, the Lakers and the Nolans (the "Fort Wayne Six") went ashore after lunch to explore, having elected to skip all of the tours. Betsy and I had originally signed up to take a power boat to a small island called "Mustique," but the seas were too rough, and it was canceled. Bequia does not offer much to the tourist (perhaps because not many tourists come), but it is a pleasant place, with nice people, who did not pester us to buy things.

After about an hour of walking, the Lakers and Nolans went back to the ship, while Betsy and I went walking along the coast in the other direction. We found and explored a typical island church, and some interesting shops. I bought a batik with a brilliantly colored hummingbird on a blue background. We eventually brought it back to Boca Raton where we had it framed, and hung it in the kitchen. We kept wandering until the sidewalk ended, but were able to walk along the edge of the water until we came to a pleasant restaurant and bar, where we sat at a table under a palm tree and drank Hairoun, the local beer. Not bad. It was quite nice sitting there, looking across the small harbor packed with private boats. We got back on board in time for a nap before dinner, after which we all headed to bed early.

The ship left Bequia at 1:00 a.m. for St. Lucia, through very rough seas, and corresponding curtain-whapping. None of the Fort Wayne Six got seasick, but there were reports of many who were not so fortunate.

IV

At St. Lucia, we docked at the town of Soufriere, a small place that was hit hard a few months earlier by Hurricane Lenny. Betsy, Gene Laker and I had signed up to go snorkeling and joined a group from the ship that went by taxi to Hotel Anse Chastenet, traveling up and down steep hills over a very narrow road, through thick jungle. Betsy and I had been in St. Lucia once before, and it rained for an entire week. It was raining this day also; nonetheless, I am advised by some that there are times when it does not rain in St. Lucia.

The snorkeling site was very good for its purpose, with a large, roped off "conservation area" in the middle of the water, where there was a coral reef and a lot of fish. This hotel caters to scuba divers, has a couple of buildings full of scuba equipment, and runs a boat shuttle to and from diving sites. Even though the rain continued most of the time, it was warm, and not unpleasant in the water.

When we finished snorkeling, the three of us went into the restaurant and sat down to order a sandwich or a coke, but the numerous waitresses ignored us for about 40 minutes, until it was time to leave. We didn't mind, because the restaurant was dry and under roof (without walls) and, when we got back to the Yorktown Clipper, it was lunch time.

While we ate lunch, the ship traveled around the Island of St. Lucia to Rodney Bay and anchored offshore. By now both DIBS were working, and they began carrying passengers to the beach. We were met by naturalist Gregor Williams, who is a native of St. Lucia, and who escorted some of us (including Betsy, Gene and me) up the steep hill to visit Fort Rodney. According to Gregor, this area was the scene of an important navy battle between the French and the English during the American Revolutionary War. There is a good view from the top of Fort Rodney, but it is a little precarious going and coming, with a handrail at the very top that was loose. Gregor picked up a flat stone and tried to pound some of the nails back in. Meanwhile, Margaret, Jerry and Marcia went to walk, perchance to swim, along the beach below.

Dinner was preceded by an "Island Party" on the Sun Deck, where a local three-piece band performed and a modest but tasty buffet was served. The waiters and waitresses appeared in colorful island shirts, and Gene Laker wore his new tee-shirt advertising the charms of Bequia. I had a pleasant chat with naturalist Ignacio Rojas who told me that tomorrow he intended to take time off to "go to the Internet."

After dinner, a movie, "Runaway Bride," with Julia Roberts and Richard

Gere, was shown, but Betsy and I were too tired to stay up and watch it. The boat sailed at 10:00 in the evening and once again encountered very rough seas, and flapping curtains. I decided to take a Dramamine pill and slept with no problems.

V

Wednesday, January 26, 2000, was spent on the Island of Dominica and I liked it very much. Even though I have heard and read of political turmoil there, it seemed very clean and friendly to us. It has a population of 75,000 people and no international airport. The ship anchored offshore, and the DIBS took us to the dock, where the Clipper provided taxi service into town. Betsy and I followed Ignacio Rojas to the "Corner House," located on the second floor of a building at the corner of the main intersection. It is owned by "Mike," a young (25 years or so) Canadian expatriate who keeps a very tidy establishment, consisting of four rooms furnished in assorted ways, and with a New Orleans-style balcony running around the outside. He has a kitchen adequate to prepare and serve "diner" food, and also sells beer and soft drinks.

More important, in one of the rooms, Mike maintains three computers linked by DSL lines, with access to the Internet. I logged on to AOL, picked up my e-mail and sent some, and Betsy did the same. The big news for us was that our son Steve's friends, Mark and Twana Williams, of Birmingham, Alabama, have a girl! Finally, after three boys! For the use of his computers, we paid Mike $2 U.S.

A note about money: The U.S. dollar is used everywhere in the Caribbean, and there is no real need to carry other money. In addition, there is a currency called the Eastern Caribbean, or "E.C." which, at the time, was being traded at about two for a dollar. It probably wasn't worth that much. I noticed that whenever we paid for anything with dollars, we always got our change in E.C.

When we left the Corner House, we walked up the hill into town where we visited a very nice Catholic Church, but also began to feel quite conspicuous. Nobody else looked like us, and people began approaching us asking for money. It was not threatening, but we weren't comfortable. One rather exotic looking young man came up to me and asked if I would give him a hug and, when I declined, he invited me to dance. Betsy and I decided to head back to the ship for lunch.

During lunch, our friends told us about the Island Tour they had taken that morning. They had had a very nice experience, and were also quite well pleased with the Island of Dominica.

Snapshots

Jerry Nolan was interested in my experiences at the Corner House, and the two of us decided to shuttle back to town and take a cab there. Jerry wanted to get his own e-mail, and I realized that I had not taken the opportunity to check out any news. While Jerry picked up his mail, I logged on to CNN, then to Fortwayne.com. Much of the national news had to do with the forthcoming Super Bowl between the St. Louis Rams and the Tennessee Titans. On the Fort Wayne front, I was happy to learn that the Post Office will open a branch near us, at Time Corners, to replace the one that closed when Keltsch Pharmacy closed its store there.

Jerry and I spent so much time at the computers that we missed the 3:00 o'clock taxi-bus back to the dock, so we paid Mike $6 for our computer time, and bought two bottles of the local beer ("Kubuli"). We sat on Mike's balcony, and watched "life on Dominica" in the streets below. Later, we had time to explore the area, where we found a very nice hotel with a waterfall in the lobby, and browsed through an impressive jewelry shop called "Columbian Emeralds." It had very attractive merchandise, but very unattractive prices.

Back at the ship, the Chapmans, Lakers and Nolans gathered in the Orientation Lounge to drink Jerry's martinis and catch up on our respective days. Each evening, during the cocktail hour, a woman came through with a huge tray of freshly baked cookies, and soon became one of the most popular people on the ship. Then there were lectures, with Zach Feldman talking about tomorrow's trip to the Island of Nevis, and Gregor Williams talking about the history of Nevis.

When they were stranded overnight in the San Juan Airport, the Lakers and Nolans had met Hal and Peg Sutton, of Rockford, Illinois, who were part of a University of Michigan alumni group on the ship. The Suttons had also been the victims of an air schedule devised by the cruise company. Lovely folks, they joined us at dinner, and Jerry did his best not to mention the fact that Indiana University had beaten the University of Michigan in basketball on Tuesday night by a score of 85 to 50.

The best part of dinner was dessert, when Bananas Foster was served. Later, there was another movie opportunity, "For Love of the Game," with Kevin Costner; however, we had sailed from Dominica at 7:00 p.m., and by 9:00 p.m. we had passed from the leeward of the island into heavy seas, and were rocking and rolling. Going to bed seemed like a better choice. (Margaret Nolan gave me some rubber bands on Wednesday night, which I used to tie up the curtain in such a way that it would swing above me, but not hit me in the head. It worked, and I was grateful to Margaret.)

VI

We woke up at Nevis. It is a small island with a population of only 9,000 people. Christopher Columbus thought that the clouds around the peak in the middle looked like snow, so he called it "Las Nieves," (Spanish for "The Snows"), which became Nevis. The capital is Charlestown, but the Yorktown Clipper anchored at Pinney's Beach, where the DIBS shuttled passengers back and forth so that they could spend the morning swimming or walking on the sand. Some people even played a sort of "Cricket," and it was, all in all, very pleasant.

The principal landmark on Nevis is an enormous, super-luxury, Four Seasons Hotel, which had barely opened when it was leveled by Hurricane Lenny in November of 1999. It was now closed and "being renovated." We walked down to look at it, and it was really a mess. I have been told, since, that Four Seasons will not operate it in the future. If it does indeed get renovated, it will be operated by some other company.

Back on board during lunch, the boat sailed around the island to the town of Charlestown and docked at the shore. We walked to the Museum of Nevis History, which is a replica of the house where Alexander Hamilton was born (on Nevis) in 1755 and which contains artifacts and objects relating to his life. Somehow, he made his way to the United States, became aide-de-camp to George Washington, and was the first Secretary of the U.S. Treasury.

Later, Jerry found a store that sold Cuban cigars, but also found that they charged a price of $18 per cigar. He left them there. I, on the other hand, discovered a $5 pair of swim goggles to take back to Boca Raton for use in the pool, so that I wouldn't get chlorine in my eyes. (They leak. You get what you pay for.)

There is a chain of stores throughout many of the islands called "Island Hopper," and the one at Nevis had many nice things, including a large wooden rooster, which Marcia Laker bought to take home to Fort Wayne. Gene declared that it is "gorgeous." (He said that several times.)

Nevis lies only two miles across a channel from the Island of St. Kitts, the last stop on our itinerary. The trip across, to the city of Basseterre, took only two hours, but that was enough time to work the daily crossword puzzle, read a little, and catch a nap before dinner.

After dinner, we retired to the Orientation Lounge for entertainment by the Maple Leaf Band, a local calypso group consisting of eight musicians. All of them played steel drums, but managed to effect a sound that replicated several different instruments. This was followed by a fashion show displaying dresses and accessories from a local store at a place called "Romney Manor," with models that work at the store.

VII

Our final day in the Caribbean, Friday, January 28th, was to be spent on St. Kitts, and we started the day with a tour to The Fortress on Brimstone Hill. Our taxi driver/guide was a local man named Ken Hendricks, who told us that he has three children and six grandchildren, all of whom live in England. Here in St. Kitts, as throughout the Caribbean, all traffic drives on the left (English) side of the road.

I was astonished at the size of the Fortress. It is an enormous, stone structure built on top of a steep mountain, with lots of cannon sticking out in all directions. We learned that it is more than 300 years old, is 780 feet above sea level, and covers over 40 acres. The British and the French fought here often. In fact, according to Gregor Williams, they fought more battles here than at any other place in British or French naval history.

After a steep climb to get to the top, we were able to see other islands in the distance, where ammunition and guns were shipped from Europe during the American Revolutionary War. From there, privateers took them to Washington's army, often under the protection of the French navy.

On the way back, Ken Hendricks told us that sugar cane is the major export of St. Kitts, and that unemployment here is low. I asked him about the "political boss" of St. Kitts who had been featured recently on the television show "60 Minutes." Ken said that this man is "rumored" to have been shot, and "nobody knows where he is."

We stopped at Romney Manor, once a sugar cane plantation and now the home of Caribelle Batik, the same folks who gave us the fashion show on Thursday night. They had a very nice assortment of island fashions; however, two large cruise ships had anchored that morning, and the place was overrun with tourists. Still, we bought a few things.

Betsy and I had earlier signed up to go on a snorkeling tour during the afternoon, but decided to cancel because of the very rough seas. Spending four hours out there on a small catamaran held little appeal.

Instead, The Fort Wayne Six walked into town and explored the shops. After an hour or so, we hired a taxi to take us to see the Ocean Terrace Inn, a resort hotel built on the hillside of old Fort Thomas, with a panoramic view of the city and a pleasant patio. Several of us, accompanied by an employee, toured the grounds and visited a couple of the rooms (which were very modern and quite nice), and then we gathered on the patio for a leisurely libation, enjoying the view. We found our taxi driver waiting, as promised, to take us back to the ship.

That evening, there was a farewell party, and the Captain miraculously reappeared. Where had he been this entire week?

VIII

In retrospect, we had a good time on this trip. Good weather with some interesting things to do and places to visit. We were grateful, of course, that Marcia, Gene, Margaret and Jerry finally made it to the ship to join us. It would not have been nearly as much fun without them.

Saturday morning was time for disembarkation, a time when the Yorktown Clipper staff began to look upon us as "former passengers." Breakfast was "closed" early, and all of us were told to vacate the cabins ahead of our departure time so that the crew could begin preparing for the next arrivals. There was an elaborate system of luggage tagging and passengers departed at various times to the airport for flights home.

Since Betsy and I were traveling back to Miami, rather than to Fort Wayne, we separated from our friends, and caught a late-morning American Airlines flight to San Juan (about one hour), arriving right on schedule. When American booked us on this trip, they apparently overlooked the fact that we would need to clear Customs in San Juan and, by the time we did, we, and everyone else on our arriving flight, had missed our connections.

We joined the long line at the American "Customer Relations" desk to be re-booked, and finally got on a 4:00 o'clock flight to Fort Lauderdale. I was relieved. *This was considerably better than spending the night in the San Juan Airport!*

Chapter 13

RED WINE AND PASTA

I

For two or three years, Betsy had wanted to take a trip to Tuscany. I think it started when she read the popular Frances Mayes book, *Under the Tuscan Sun*. The opportunity came along in the form of a trip sponsored by Indiana University, focused in and around the City of Cortona. The I.U. group left on September 27, 2000, but Betsy and I decided to go a few days early to revisit Florence, a place that has always ranked very high in our nostalgia ratings.

We started from Fort Wayne and flew to Chicago on September 23, 2000, and spent our "layover" time at the American Airlines lounge at O'Hare Field. A couple of good things happened. First, I found that they maintained computers with Internet access for passengers, which allowed me to pick up e-mail and send some (including a thank you to Pat Parker, who had taken us to the airport in Fort Wayne). After I finished that, I went over to the television set and found that Northwestern and Wisconsin were playing football and were in double overtime. To the amazement of everyone, Northwestern won! I hoped that this was to be an omen for the rest of our journey.

After a pleasant, non-stop flight to Rome, we met our driver from Auto Europe who took us on to Florence. We had considered spending these days in Rome, but this was the year of the "Jubilee" celebrated by the Catholic Church and Rome was rumored to be over-crowded. It was a warm, sunny day, and the Tuscan countryside on the drive to Florence persuaded us that this trip was a good idea. Once there, we registered at the Grand Hotel, a pleasant hostelry overlooking the Arno River.

After getting checked in, we felt good enough to go for a walk and were soon dismayed at the huge numbers of people in the streets. We walked to the Duomo, and found a line stretching out the door and around behind the back of the church, disappearing down a side street. A person standing near the front said they had been in line for about 1-1/2 hours. Because it was Sunday, many things were closed; however, one could still see the Baptistry, with its famous doors sculpted by Ghiberti, described by Michelangelo as, "Fit to be portals to heaven."

We tried to get a bite to eat at "Gilli" cafe, but were ignored for so long that we finally got up and went across the piazza to another cafe. We sat there for 45 minutes, until a waiter came to the table and apologized, saying "The kitchen closed about 20 minutes ago."

There were two American women sitting near us having the same problems, and they suggested we all go to the Piazza de Signoria, and try yet another place, but by now it was three o'clock, and most kitchens were closed. We settled on a "snack" place which turned out to be all right: sandwiches of tomatoes and mozzarella cheese on a bun. Everyplace we looked, we saw huge throngs of people. We had avoided Rome because of the crowds!

Florence was, and is, a wonderful place to walk, and we spent about an hour and a half doing just that, coming back to the Grand Hotel feeling tired. After a little vegetable soup, we went to bed at 8:00 o'clock, waking at midnight and taking a pill ("Ambien") to get back to sleep for the night.

II

Monday morning was another glorious, sunny day, and Florence was still as beautiful as we remembered it. The easiest place to have breakfast was right there at the hotel and it was good, except that I had forgotten how terrible European coffee is! One needs to order a pot of hot water, and mix it half and half, even when the waiter says he is bringing "American coffee."

A person should not attempt to travel in Europe without a daily copy of the *International Herald-Tribune*, and the Grand Hotel was good enough to furnish a copy to us. We settled into the hotel lounge with it and spent a pleasant 45 minutes catching up on things. The big news in the United States was the presidential race between Vice President Al Gore and Texas Governor George W. Bush. There were also elections going on in Yugoslavia, and suggestions that President Milosevic might actually lose. The Olympic games were in process in Australia; the Clintons were letting campaign donors sleep in the White House in exchange for contributions; and the Chicago White Sox were about to clinch their division championship.

Florence is a tourist city, full of architectural and historic sites, and many museums - but a lot of them are closed on Monday. A little research told us that the Medici Chapel was one place that was open, and we walked there and were pleasantly surprised to find only a five minute line to buy tickets. It was very hot standing in the Italian sun, so we were glad we didn't have to stay too long.

The history of the Medici family is astonishing. They ruled Florence for over four hundred years, were fabulously rich, and built extravagant tombs as fit their station. The "new" chapel, housing the later family members, is ornate, extravagant and unpleasant, even though fascinating because of its sheer size and sumptuousness. The earlier tombs, however, containing the graves of the original Cosimo D'Medici and his son, Lorenzo (who became Lorenzo the Magnificent), are exquisite and beautiful. This will come as no surprise when you realize that the design and sculptures were done by Michelangelo.

The Medici Palace was another place that was open on Monday. They had a pretty good system there: You went up to the entrance and bought your ticket, which had an entry time stamped on it. You then could go to shops or other attractions in the area until your entry time came, at which time you entered the Palace without any wait at all. We used our "interval" to see the Medici Library, which was close by, but turned out to require climbing four flights of stairs. It was hot! (Once up there, we discovered that there is a well-concealed lift.)

The Medici Palace was once filled to the brim with one of the world's great art collections, but most of the art has now been removed to other places in Florence. Still, for students of history, it is an exciting place to visit, and it is interesting to see how a rich family lived six hundred years ago.

When we left, we decided to walk to the Piazza de Signoria for lunch and, as we walked past the Duomo we noticed - no line! We made a beeline for the door and were just barely edged out by a group of Japanese tourists; but, we still got right in and had a chance to go through this incredible church. We had been in it before, of course, but one forgets. The amazing Dome, designed and built by Brunelleschi, is still astonishing, and I got dizzy looking up at it, finally settling back against a wall in order to maintain my balance. While it is a fine cathedral, the exterior remains its most interesting part and, of course, the Dome is the landmark of Florence.

Another "Monday Open" site is the Palazzo Vecchio ("Old Palace"). Before entering, we found a pleasant sidewalk cafe on the opposite side of the Piazza where, for once, both food and service were good. The Palazzo Vecchio is one of the oldest structures in Florence, and embodies so much history that several books have been written about it. It was once the home of the Medici; Cosimo the Elder and Savanarola were both imprisoned here; and a plaque in front marks the spot where Savanarola was burned at the stake. It is a wonderful museum, and I have since learned that a number of tour itineraries overlook it. They should not. However, be warned: There are lots of stairs to be climbed, and no elevators.

Back on the street, there were still great crowds of people, but by now the shops had reopened (after the "siesta"), and that seemed to take some of the pressure off. We strolled across the fabled Ponte Vecchio ("Old Bridge"), chock-a-block with jewelry shops, and found a small token to bring home for Pat Parker as a reward for taking us to the Fort Wayne airport: an apron with a reproduction of the torso of Michelangelo's "David" on the front.

We learned a lesson that will be of benefit to anyone who visits Florence: Always get a reservation for dinner. We had seen a pleasant restaurant called La Profeta near the Grand Hotel and assumed we would be able to get in if we went early; however, by 8:00 p.m., it was already full. Our hotel concierge called another trattoria named "Il Gobbi" on the Via Porcellana. The Via Porcellana is a street, but in the United States we would call it an alley, and one would not enter except as a part of a large group. Still, Il Gobbi turned out to be a delightful restaurant with excellent food.

The Italian lira was trading at approximately 2,200 lira to the dollar, which takes a little getting used to when trying to figure out how much things cost. Therefore I failed to notice, when the waiter brought my credit card receipt, and it wasn't until I got back to the hotel that I realized, that I had been charged 737,000 lira instead of 73,700 lira. I enlisted the help of the hotel concierge who called Il Gobbi and spoke to the owner, and I then walked back to the restaurant to resolve the problem. The owner was apologetic for the "mistake," but said it was too late for him to reverse the charge. He suggested that I simply "contest" the bill when it came. I looked him in the eye and said I had a better solution: He should just give me the difference in cash and, after a moment or two of reflecting, that is what he did. I suspect that he was influenced by the fact that the concierge at our hotel (who had sent us to him!) had become involved in the discussion.

The Grand Hotel has a pleasant lounge where a man was playing the piano, so we stopped for a little "gelato" and hot tea before heading up to bed. At midnight, of course, we were still awake, but Ambien rescued us once again.

III

The Uffizi Gallery is one of the best known museums in the world. Combine that fact with the enormous multitudes of people that throng

Snapshots

Florence and it is not surprising that the Gallery has a steady, three-hour line waiting to buy tickets to get in. It is possible, however, to buy tickets five days in advance, with a time of entry stamped on them, which allows you to go around the line and enter at that time. The entry tickets have to be paid for (not refundable) at the time you make the reservation. We had contacted the concierge at our hotel a couple of weeks early, and arranged for him to get us reservations to enter at noon on Tuesday, permitting us to spend a leisurely morning with a late breakfast and the *Herald-Tribune*.

Upon arrival at the Uffizi Gallery, we saw the line snaking down one side of the building, making a "U-turn," and then coming back up the other side; but, we also found the separate door for those with reservations. While we waited for our entry time, we watched the people posing outside the museum who pretend to be statues. They cover themselves in white or gold makeup, stand on a box or a bucket, and keep very still until someone drops money into a hat on the ground in front of them. Then, they move in a jerky fashion, like robots or mechanical people, and the first time you see one, it is pretty comical. The idea seems to have caught on, because we saw about twelve of these "statues" at various places in the courtyard of the museum. Unfortunately, some of the "statues" were "off duty" at the time, and they were sitting on the steps chatting with their friends or eating their lunch, all the while covered with makeup, and this kind of ruined the effect that the others were trying to accomplish.

There was a small knot of people with reservations waiting to get into the museum at the same time we did. We entered with that group, flashed our "reservation" card from the hotel, and proceeded up the stairs to the gallery. There is no air conditioning in museums in Italy, and it was hot. The gallery turned out to be at the top of five enormous flights of stairs, with the cumulative effect equivalent to climbing to the seventh or eighth floor of an office building in the United States. There are two very small elevators (four passengers), but one was broken, and the other had a large sign saying "for handicapped access only." We arrived at the top totally winded and covered with perspiration, and came to the final admission point where a young Italian woman asked for our tickets. I showed her the reservation card from the hotel, but she insisted that we were supposed to have "tickets." I told her we had paid for our tickets when we made the reservation and she said, "Yes, but you have to pick up the tickets at the time you enter, downstairs." I tried to argue with her. I explained that the concierge had told us that his reservation card was all that was needed to get in. It was all to no avail, and the large group gathering behind us began to get restless. Betsy found a bench to sit on, and I traipsed all the way back down to the lobby, got the tickets, and then huffed and puffed my way back up to the gallery. When I reached the top, for the second time, I felt like I ought to plant a flag! My journal, reflecting on this experience, says "!!?!#>?&^A%%!!»*^A\\!!!"

Betsy and I sat for about 20 minutes on the bench while I recuperated, and then went in to see the Uffizi Gallery - at last. It has some remarkable treasures - things really worth seeing - Botticelli, Da Vinci, Michelangelo, perhaps six or seven such items. But the huge majority of art in this Gallery is a broken record stuck on monotonous religious themes and boring portraits. The things that are worth seeing are not worth the egregious hassle to see them. I subsequently learned from a local guide that "Uffizi" is Italian for, "Pain in the Ass."

When we left the Gallery, we were well into lunchtime, but could not find the trattoria we had seen the day before. We wandered along through the phenomenal crowds, which reminded us of no place so much as Shanghai, China, until coming to a restaurant which featured a "menu of the day" translated into English to include "horse d'oeuvre," "savage lettuce," and "Florentine creeps." After waiting 30 minutes to be noticed by the waiter, we managed to get lunch; however, the food was more or less as the menu indicated.

I was exhausted, having been totally worn down by the Uffizi Gallery, and we went back to the hotel to rest, write some postcards, and update my journal. I was personally rather grumpy about the way that the day had been going; but my journal reflects the following: "Betsy says to be sure to say that we like Florence."

We had last been in this city in 1971, when we came by train from Rome and stayed overnight. It was a glorious place then, and we had always planned to come back and spend more time. On that trip, we had visited a good restaurant by the name of "Sabatini," and found that it is still going. We made a reservation for that evening, and arrived by taxi at 7:30 p.m. We were the first people to enter the restaurant, and the waiter told us that they did a very successful business serving American and Japanese tourists at these "early" hours. Sure enough, about forty Japanese tourists came in shortly after we were seated and, within another 10 or 15 minutes, the restaurant was full, all Japanese and Americans.

Sabatini is still expensive, but still good. It was fun to walk in, recognize the place, and have the memories come back. It was at Sabatini that I had complimented the waiter on the coffee, and he had puffed himself up and said, "It's Maxwell House!" It was a pleasant evening, and we walked back to the Grand Hotel.

IV

We were learning that taxis are a (relatively) inexpensive way to get around Florence, and on Wednesday morning we took one from the hotel to the Pitti Palace. It is huge, magnificent, beautiful, full of art - and to our surprise, was not very crowded. One must, unfortunately, climb a great many stairs in order to see it (no elevators), but it is not nearly as bad as the Uffizi Gallery. How did people cope when they actually lived in places like this?

A tour of the Pitti Palace starts with the area called the Palatina, which is where the magnificent art collection is seen. It is overwhelming. Art covers the ceilings and the walls. There are frescoes, tapestries, paintings of all kinds, Great Masters. Titian, Tintoretto, Rubens, Van Dyke, Raphael. Sometimes there will be an extraordinary masterpiece on a wall containing 30 other paintings, two or three of which may also be extraordinary masterpieces.

While the Uffizi Gallery has a handful of blockbuster works, the Pitti Palace is, in my opinion, far more impressive, and much more entertaining.

After seeing the Palatina, we toured the Royal Apartments, which are interesting, but not much different from many such places we have seen in Europe. In fact, as Royal Apartments go, these are fairly routine, with the exception of one large room with an astonishing ceiling covered with carvings, paintings, gilt and mirrors. A large circular mirror, lying flat, has been placed waist-high in the center of the room so that people can look down into the mirror and see the ceiling, without craning their necks.

The Pitti Palace also has a large and elaborate Silver Museum, and we walked through, but by now we were becoming sated with culture. I said to Betsy, "My jug is full."

It was a warm, bright, sunny day, and we walked out the back of the Palace and into the Boboli Gardens, which would be even prettier if one did not have to walk uphill to see them. Fortunately, at the top of the hill, there is a very nice outdoor cafe, which affords a fine view over the City of Florence. Having done all that climbing, one feels entitled to enjoy the view! It was a nice place to sit and have sandwiches and iced tea.

After lunch we wandered back out through the Palace, and down the street to the ancient Ponte Vecchio, and from there to the shop at the Uffizi Gallery. The streets along the way were jammed with people and it was reminiscent of the Tower of Babel. We heard every language imaginable.

Despite my grumbling about the Uffizi Gallery, we had found that it contains a really fine shop, and we went in to buy several items, including some attractive ladies watches (one of which was for Betsy). The watches and several other valuable items were in glass display cases in a separate room from the main shop, unattended, but protected by locks on the display cases. I asked one of the clerks to go into the room and unlock one of the cases so I could show her what I wanted. Once she found out what I wanted, she reached down below and pulled open an (unlocked) drawer, filled with the same items on display in the case above!

When our shopping was over, we walked to the Bargello Museum, said to be one of the nicest museums in Florence, but we were too late - it was closed. This presented a good excuse to stop at a cafe, buy some bottled water, and look over our map.

Back at our hotel, I discovered that it contains a private room where guests can use computers with internet access. Betsy and I checked our e-mail, and sent a few messages, and I had the hotel concierge call Auto Europe to confirm that a car and driver would pick us up the next morning to take us to Cortona, where we would join the Indiana University group. There was still time to read the *Herald-Tribune*, before heading to dinner at a trattoria called "Garga." "Garga" turned out to be all right. Good food and service, but with the atmosphere of a madhouse. Constant din.

It was a little hard to sleep that night. About 20 people in their late teens and early 20's decided to hold an all-night party on the street below our window. There was a little balcony-like area that projected from the street out over the river there, with a couple of benches, and it made a good place for them to congregate. Fortunately, we had earplugs with us. I got up at 5:00 a.m., and the kids were still going at it; however, it started to rain at about 7:00 o'clock, and they finally left.

V

On Thursday morning, our driver, Paolo, from Auto Europe, appeared on time, and drove us once again through the lush scenery of Tuscany, to the city of Cortona, a drive of a little over one hour. Cortona is a medieval village which perches high on a mountain, overlooking the Chiana Valley.

The Indiana University travel group would be staying at the Hotel San Luca, but would not arrive for several hours. The hotel, built into the mountainside, is a little different from your usual hotel in that the elevators go from the lobby down, rather than up. Our room was on floor number 5, being five floors down from the top. The hotel rooms are small, but adequate, and we had a balcony with a breathtaking view out over the valley. Because the tour group had not yet arrived, the hotel was pretty empty, and we had a chance to get acquainted with Mariano and Massimo, who seemed to take turns running the front desk. We were expecting our friends, Bill and Suzanne Hall, and Cliff and Elaine Shultz, to arrive with the IU group, and Massimo told us that we all had adjoining rooms on floor five. It was lunchtime, and Mariano recommended that we visit the Trattoria la Grotta in town.

We thoroughly enjoyed our first walk into the village of Cortona. The buildings are ancient, and there are some tourists, but it bears no resemblance to Florence. Trattoria la Grotta is tucked into an out-of-the-way corner where you would never find it unless you were looking for it. It is friendly and picturesque, with excellent food, and a lot less pricey than the restaurants in Florence. After lunch, Betsy went back to the hotel room for a nap, and I walked again into town, found a table outside a "pasticceria," where I ordered a latte, caught up on my notes, and worked the crossword puzzle from the morning's *Herald-Tribune*.

At 5:30 in the afternoon, the IU tour bus arrived and the group gathered on the terrace of the hotel overlooking the valley. The valley of the Chiana River is called "Val di Chiana," and the area is famous for wine, food and scenery.

From the Hotel San Luca, looking over the Val di Chiana.

The tour brochure made a special point of telling us that the Hotel San Luca boasted one of the best restaurants in the area, "Tonino," with fine food and a spectacular view. This was true. As it happened, however, we did not have our dinner in Tonino, nor did we ever eat any of our meals in it, but instead were put in a rather sterile, dark and under-ventilated dining room on floor 3 (three floors down). We dubbed it "The Sterile Room." The food was pedestrian, but it was great to see the Halls and the Shultzes, and to catch up on everything with them. Our Fort Wayne friends, Dick and Marcia Adams, and Max and Holley Hobbs, have often traveled with us, but were unable to come this time, and we all commented that we missed them.

The bathrooms at the Hotel San Luca are tiny. A person could sit on the commode, brush his teeth in the sink, and take a shower, all at the same time. The first time we used the shower, it was a real adventure. A lot of planning went into it. There was no electric plug for my razor in the bathroom, and the pillows on the beds were huge, and hard as rocks. We improvised pillows for the night, got out the Ambien, and turned in for the night. Nobody said it would be perfect.

The next morning we gathered in the Sterile Room at 7:30, and learned that breakfast would be a cold buffet. It was cold, but fresh and well done. Two very important gold stars for having stewed prunes and decent American coffee.

The tour was conducted by an organization called "Alumni Holidays," and the tour guide was an Italian woman by the name of Natazia. A young, energetic person, she proved to be very competent, pleasant and helpful throughout the week.

At 8:30, Natazia gathered us in a lecture room on floor three and gave us some information about the plans for the coming week. Then she introduced an English ex-patriate named Lyndall Passerini, who has lived in Cortona for over 20 years and is, in fact, a genuine Countess. Ms. Passerini gave a historical lecture, telling us that Garibaldi had united the various states of Italy about 150 years ago. Thus, every town has a "Piazza Garibaldi," and, sure enough, that is the name of the square in front of the Hotel San Luca. In the year 217 B.C., Hannibal overran the Romans at the Battle of Lake Trasemino and, she said, when we look over the valley from our balconies, we can see Lake Trasemino in the distance.

She gave us an abbreviated history of Tuscany, illustrated by slides. The earliest recorded inhabitants were the Etruscans, followed by the Romans, and then the modern Italians. The famous Renaissance painter, Fra Angelico, did some of his work in Cortona; Santa Margherita lived there and is entombed in a cathedral on the top of the mountain; and the artist Signorelli was born there.

When the lecture was over, Ms. Passerini led us on a walking tour through the village, with a visit to an ancient church, a visit to the Teatro, a stop at the Museo, and discussions about numerous shops and boutiques. (Part of the movie *Life is Beautiful* was filmed in Cortona, and the Teatro was one of the locales.) We passed a newsstand and I happily purchased the morning edition of the *Herald-Tribune*! We learned that postage stamps are purchased at tobacco shops, and that coffee is purchased at pastry shops.

After lunch, we boarded a tour bus and headed into the countryside to visit the Trerose Winery. "Trerose" means "three roses." We were shown vineyards, machines that make wine, and huge vats where it is aged. The best red wine of this area is called *Vino Nobile* (wine of the nobility), and we were taken to a room where we all had a chance to taste some and, if we wished, buy a few bottles. Since there was no way to ship it, the only other course would have been to carry it home on the airplane, so nobody bought any so far as I noticed.

The locale of our evening meal was changed to the "Wine Cellar," another area of the Hotel San Luca which, while windowless, nevertheless had a little bit of atmosphere, and was more pleasant than the Sterile Room. It was Friday, and fish was the entree. After we finished eating, the Fort Wayne Six (Chapmans, Shultzes and Halls) strolled back into the charming village. Shops stay open late in Italy, and Suzanne bought a nice plaque with a reproduction of the famous Fra Angelico painting of the Annunciation of Christ. We had seen the original in the Museo that morning.

It had been a cloudy and cool day, and by 9:00 o'clock it began to rain. Shopkeepers hurried to get their merchandise out of the street and back into their stores, and we made our way back to our hotel. Once there, Betsy and I once again improvised pillows for the night, and retired.

VI

Saturday dawned grey, cool and windy, and people broke out their sweaters and jackets for our excursion to the town of Montepulciano, a name that derives from the fact that it is located on a mountain top, and its ruling Roman family was named Pulciano. *En route*, we passed several villas, with entrances lined with candle cypress, the tall, graceful trees that are indigenous and common in Tuscany. Natazia told us that we would be dropped off at one end of town, wander through it, and reconnoiter on the other side a couple of hours later. The bus was only able to climb the narrow streets to a point approximately halfway up to the center of town, and we went the rest of the way on foot.

Our guide pointed out the home of Poliziano, who had been a close friend and ally of Lorenzo de Medici, and a patron of the artist, Botticelli. The main square (piazza) is dominated by a huge church with no facade (the front is left unfinished), and we were told that the town simply ran out of money, and never finished it. As in most Italian towns, the central piazza also features a Town Hall with a large clock, and a "Palazzo," being the home of the town's ruling family. The town well was situated next to the Palazzo, since control of the local source of drinking water was important to keep the ruling family ruling.

We now began to follow our maps through Montepulciano and saw the wisdom of Natazia's plan: it was all downhill. It is another charming Italian village, full of intriguing shops, cafes, and wonderful, medieval homes. We stopped at the Cafe Poliziano, and while we were having coffee, Suzanne Hall decided that she wanted to buy a painting that we had seen in a shop on our walk. Bill Hall set off back up the hill to find the shop and buy the painting, but didn't return. After a while, we began to get anxious (among other things, we were all supposed to be meeting the bus pretty soon) so Suzanne and I walked up the hill to the shop. The painting was still there - but there was no sign of Bill. The clerk was busy, but we finally got her attention, only to find that she spoke very little English. Fortunately, a fellow customer was able to help us interpret, and explained to the lady why we were there. She recalled that Bill had come to buy the painting, but that this particular shop did not accept credit cards, and Bill had not had enough cash.

I had enough cash, so we purchased the painting (it seemed to take forever to get that done!), and then began racing back down the hill toward "Cafe Poliziano," looking for Bill and the others. Meanwhile, Betsy had seen Bill wandering about and had run after us to try to tell us that he was not lost after all, but then she lost track of us. Eventually, we all came together at the appointed meeting place, but were late, the bus had had to move, and it was raining hard. Still (bless the Italians), nobody seemed to be very concerned, the bus made a circuit around the block, and everybody was content.

It was getting late, but Natazia wanted us to see a famous old church in Montepulciano. The bus could not get closer than about a block and a half, so we got out and walked through the rain, only to find that a wedding was in process, and the officiating priest made it clear that our tourist crowd was not at all welcome. (Can't say I blame him.) We turned around and headed back, through the rain, to the bus.

I had had the foresight to put the morning edition of the *Herald-Tribune* into my bag, and took the opportunity to catch up on the news. The Olympic Games were in process in Australia; Denmark had voted "No" to the Euro; Milosevic had lost the election in Yugoslavia, but was resisting getting out; Pierre Trudeau, former Prime Minister of Canada, was dead at 80; truckers in Europe were blocking highways to protest high gasoline prices; and Bush-Gore continued to be a "tight race."

After lunch at Hotel San Luca, we gathered in the lecture room to hear an Englishman, Martin Atwood, present a lecture on the Etruscans, the earliest

Snapshots

inhabitants of Cortona. At 3000 years, it is a city older than Rome and was, in fact, overrun by the Romans. Mr. Atwood pulled down the blinds and began to show slides, and I felt rather sorry for him. Most of the group was sleep-deprived (jet lag), had been up early, out all morning in the rain, eaten a huge lunch, and then settled into their chairs when the lights went out. Nearly everyone went to sleep, and I left, found Natazia, and explored various ideas with her for things Betsy and I might do on Tuesday. (More on that later.)

The evening meal was served again in the Wine Cellar, followed by our (now traditional) long after dinner walk. When you leave the Hotel San Luca and turn to the right, rather than to the left, you enter a very large park, with a restaurant in the middle of it, and we walked there to find out if it would be a good place for the six of us (Chapmans, Halls, Shultzes) to have dinner on Monday night. Since Monday was going to be my birthday, we had decided to go someplace outside the hotel. The park was lovely, but it turned out that the restaurant was closed on Mondays.

VII

On Sunday, we arose to greet a rainy, grey sky, ate breakfast at Hotel San Luca, and boarded the tour bus at 8:00 o'clock to travel to the City of Perugia. There, we divided into two groups, each with our own local guide.

Perugia was once governed by the Bagniolli Family, which got into a dispute with the Pope, resulting in the "Salt War," further resulting in the destruction of the city. To make a statement, the Pope leveled all buildings above two stories, filled the entire lower two levels with dirt, and built a military fortress on top. When Italy later became united, the Peruginos tore down the Pope's fortress and built a new town where the old fortress had been. Recent excavations below the "new town" revealed the original two levels that the Pope had filled with dirt, and they have been carefully excavated, making what is now called "Underground Perugia." It was discovered when it was decided to build escalators to take tourists from the lower levels of the hillside up the considerable climb to the town. Now, it is a labyrinth of walkways, shops and restaurants. In addition, they actually did build the escalators, so that we were able to get off the bus, onto the escalators, travel through "Underground Perugia," and come out in the "new town."

It is a delightful place, but not quite so delightful in a pouring rain. Because it was Sunday, the shops were closed, and there was only one cafe that we found that was open. Our guide recommended that it be utilized for coffee and restrooms.

There was some sort of musical event being celebrated in Perugia while we were there, although I was never clear on exactly what it was. One indication of this event was discovered when we entered a huge building full of pianos, brought from around Europe. The building also contained gorgeous paintings on the walls and ceiling, but presented a hazard to pedestrians who could enter and leave only by means of very steep, slippery, stone steps, without handrails.

The rain seemed to become even heavier, and I encountered a man on the street who came from Bangladesh, and was selling umbrellas at $10 apiece. I bought one, and was mighty glad to have it. I also offered to buy one for Betsy, but she insisted on keeping the small, totally battered "Totes" umbrella that she had brought from home.

We came to a Sunday flea market where I saw a man cadging "donations" for the battle against AIDS. People were asked to sign a book of some kind, were given a button to put on their collar, and asked to give money. I realized that I had seen this same man, his girlfriend, and their stand, at a busy street corner in Florence the week before. It is my guess that this is how they make their living. There was also a lady in the flea market selling pillows, and I bought one to replace the cement sack masquerading as a pillow that had been furnished by the Hotel San Luca. We imagined the maids at the hotel, conversing among themselves, and saying, "Isn't it strange how all these American tourists like these big, hard pillows?"

From Perugia, we traveled to Assisi, and stopped at a tourist restaurant called "Ristorante Paradiso," a pink and white stone building obviously designed to handle tours. After lunch, we again divided into two groups, each with a separate guide, and commenced walking through yet another lovely Tuscan city - pounded by a driving rain. Our local guide insisted on walking in the center of the street, stopping in the middle of the weather, gathering the group, and telling us at length about the various sites along the way. Her English was not very good anyway, and most of us decided that we did, in fact, have enough sense to come in out of the rain. By the time we got to the Basilica of Saint Francis, many of us wandered off on our own.

The Basilica is very large, very lovely, and very impressive. It is built on two levels, with a large church on the first level, and another large church below. In addition, it is blessed with a marvelous art collection although, unfortunately, much of it was damaged in an earthquake a few years ago. It is worth a trip to Assisi just to see the Basilica of St. Francis, and many do come just for that purpose.

Even with the heavy rain, and even though it was a Sunday, the city was jammed with tourists. Bill Hall and I decided to strike off in search of a gelateria. On our walk to the Basilica, we had seen one approximately every 50 feet; however, now that we were looking for one, there weren't any. We did find a cafe which, although it had no ice cream, did sell latte. This cafe was tiny, and had only three small tables. At one table, the owner and his wife were playing cards; at a second table their daughter and grandson were watching; and Bill and I sat at the third, the smallest of all, with only two chairs. In a moment, Suzanne, Betsy, Cliff and Elaine all came into the cafe, and indicated that they would also like to order something. Although the owner got up to serve them, none of the family offered to let anyone sit at either of the other two tables. Wandering down the hill to the bus we did, at last, find a place selling ice cream, and found that most of the Indiana University group was already in there.

The drive back to Cortona took us through beautiful, rolling Tuscany, and there was an occasional glimpse of sunshine. Dinner was, once again, in the Wine Cellar. Red wine had been served at all of the evening meals, and had become quite popular with all of us.

When we walked into town that evening, we passed a bar called "Route 66," which advertised a computer with internet access. Bill, Cliff and I wandered in and found the computer in the basement. It cost 5,000 lira for twenty minutes of access, which normally would have been plenty of time, except that this was a terrible computer. It would not accept AOL screen names, some typed letters did not appear, there was no "send" button, and it kept jumping back to the opening screen, demanding that we log in once again. By the time our twenty minutes was up, we thought we were getting the hang of it, but decided that it wasn't worth investing another 5,000 lira.

Ever since he arrived, Cliff Shultz had been trying to learn how to say the number of his hotel room (85) in Italian. Each time he tried, it came out different. Mariano, at the front desk, knew perfectly well, of course, what room Cliff and Elaine were in. This evening when we came back to the hotel, Cliff walked to the desk and said something like, "Ontonto Carnova." Mariano looked at him for a few seconds, and then handed him his key.

VIII

Since Monday was my birthday, and since I had my new pillow, I decided to sleep in, and didn't wake up until 9:00 o'clock. Betsy had gotten up earlier for the morning lecture. I wandered into the town and bought the *Herald-Tribune* and *USA Today*, brought them back to the hotel, and had continental breakfast in the bar. I enjoyed the morning, but learned that I had missed a really good lecture by Martin Atwood.

After lunch, we again boarded our tour bus for our scheduled visit to the City of Siena. The morning had been cool and dry, but the rain began coming down just as we started getting on the bus. The ride gave me a chance to catch up on the news. Israelis and Palestinians were rioting; the Bush-Gore debates were imminent, and "the outcome will decide the election;" and Northwestern beat Michigan State in football!

At Siena, we once again divided into groups, and our group was led by an Italian lady named Donatella, a small, vibrant, cheerful woman in her 50's. She spoke clearly and loud enough to be heard, was humorous and animated (like all good Italians), and succeeded in holding our interest despite the rain.

Siena, typical of Italian cities, has an elaborate cathedral, full of art. There are horizontal black lines on white marble that encircle the interior, and Betsy and I were reminded of the Mosque that we had seen in Cordoba, Spain. Donatella pointed out a small work, a statue of St. Paul by Michelangelo, and impressed us with her knowledge of art. This piece was full of energy, and made all the other statuary in the place look crude. Donatella had enough sense to realize that people in our group were getting "churched out" after several days in Italy. I think someone could make some money by sponsoring a tour called "Italy Without Churches."

The most striking feature of Siena is the Piazza del Campo, the giant square in the center of the city. Every year there is a horse race, called the "Palio," that is run around the circumference and people come from everywhere to watch it. Natazia told us that the Piazza begins to fill with people before dawn and, by the time the race starts in mid-afternoon, there is no room to turn around. "If you scratch your head," she said, "you will not be able to put your arm down." On our visit, however, the Piazza was relatively empty, largely because of the continuing downpour. Betsy and I found a cafe with tables in front that were sheltered by oversized umbrellas. Betsy was disappointed that they did not serve hot chocolate, but hot tea was comforting.

There was still plenty of time for all of us to wander about the Piazza del Campo, and we visited a shop called Ricciarelli, where Betsy was able to buy some of the almond cookies that are traditional in Siena. We also bought a videotape about Siena for our son John, but I was doubtful that it would work on our American equipment. It continued to rain and, by now, Betsy's umbrella was a total shambles, really nothing more than a few spokes; however, she still refused to let me buy her a new one. "We have," she said, "only two more days in Italy."

On our way back to Cortona, Natazia led the group in singing "Happy Birthday" to me. This made sixty-six of them. The Hotel San Luca was sponsoring "pizza night" for our group dinner, and the guests would have an opportunity to watch how it was made. The Fort Wayne Six, however, had already planned to go to dinner at Trattoria la Grotta, where Betsy and I had such a nice lunch on our first day in Cortona.

Snapshots

The owners and staff at la Grotta are lovely people and, knowing it was my birthday, started us off with a bottle of sparkling wine "on the house." The Bruschetta Pomadora was again fantastic, and was followed by pasta, veal and vegetables, together with an ample supply of the local red wine. I had learned to say *"senza aglio,"* which means "no garlic" in Italian.

Betsy gave me my birthday present and, no matter how hard I tried, I could not act surprised, since I had pointed it out to her at a shop in Florence. It was a tee-shirt with the flag of Italy on the front. I then opened cards from everyone, including a hilarious one from Marcia and Dick Adams that Betsy had brought from home. When they sang "Happy Birthday," a young man at the next table turned and said "Hey, it's my birthday too. That's why we are here!" It was a husband and wife with their son and his wife, and it was the son who was sharing the birthday with me.

We had a really good time, and stayed late - so late, in fact, that the gelaterias were all closed. Before going back to our hotel, we walked to the edge of the Piazza di Garibaldi and spent a few moments looking out over the Val di Chiana. A clear night sky full of twinkling stars, but with lightning in the distance behind the hills. A nice moment to remember, and a nice finish to a birthday.

IX

On Tuesday, October 3, the tour group was scheduled to spend the day in Florence. Since Betsy and I had been there for four days already, we decided to do something on our own. After consultations with Natazia and Lyndall Passerini, we had worked out an itinerary, and arranged for a car and driver for the day. At 9:30, we met Claudio Albherghini ("Mr. Taxi"), and his Chrysler Voyager van.

Our first stop was the town of Pienza and it turned out to be an unexpected treasure. Much of the central part of the town is restricted to pedestrians, so Claudio let us out at the edge of the "walking zone," and we walked into the main piazza.

Pienza was the birthplace of Pope Pius II who, in 1459, decided that it should be renovated in his honor. He had the center of the town torn down, and employed the best architects of the time to design and construct the amazing Pius II Square, around which are built the Piccolomini Palace, the Borgia Palace, and a fine Renaissance cathedral. It is all still there, just as it was!

We started by visiting the cathedral which, for once, had exceptionally good light in the interior, mainly because the windows face to the South. Next door we entered the Piccolomini Palace, now a museum, and known as the "Palazzo di Papa" (the Pope's Palace). Inside, we met a pleasant young lady who acted as a guide. There were four people in the museum at the time, us and an Italian couple, so the guide alternated between English and Italian. I was amused at her comment about the four-poster, canopied bed in the Pope's bedroom. "It is not original," she said, "only a reproduction." It was made in the 16th Century!

Pienza is simply a lovely place. There is a fine hotel there, and it would be a pleasant spot to spend a couple of days. Ever since our visit to Montepulciano, we had been hearing about Pecorino cheese, for which the area is known, and which was prominently displayed in every shop. Betsy felt it would be inappropriate for us to return to Indiana without some, so we bought a chunk and took it with us. Claudio had a small refrigerator in the back of his van, but I was not too confident about how the cheese would "travel" with us after that. The weather was sunny and pleasant, and we wished we had allowed more time for Pienza.

Our next stop was a town called San Quirico D' Orcia, where we visited yet another grand church, and some very nice gardens. We were beginning to get hungry, and Claudio recommended that we have lunch at an isolated castle *cum* hotel, in the countryside on a hilltop called Castello Ripa d' Orcia, along the shore of the River Orcia. We soon got off the paved highway and went bumping along for a half hour on a dirt road. "The best way to see Tuscany is on the dirt roads," Claudio said. It was a pretty drive, but we found out when we got there that the Castello did not serve lunch.

Claudio knew of another restaurant in a tiny place called Bagno Vignoni, not far away. He called the restaurant on his cell phone, was told that it was closed that day, but was also told that the owner had another restaurant, "La Parata," that would be pleased to serve us.

Bagno Vignoni exists because of the hot springs there. The Medici family built extensive baths, and the waters were long reputed to have curative powers. It is a village of only a few hundred people, but is, by all appearances, very prosperous. La Parata turned out to be a very good restaurant. Our waitress spoke no English, and the menu was in Italian, so we did our best in guessing what to order, and had a very good lunch of salad, bread, Spaghetti Bolognese, verdura (vegetables), and grilled cheese. (We later learned that there was another waitress who was English. Why she was not assigned to us remains one of life's mysteries.)

During the meal, a young American man came up to our table and said "I'm Matt Miller. Don't I know you folks from Lake Wawasee?" He is the son of Pat and Mike Miller, our Fort Wayne friends, and it turned out that they, as well as Matt and his wife, were on a bicycle riding tour through Tuscany and had stopped at this restaurant for lunch. Pat and Mike, who had been eating at an outside table, came in and we had a great reunion. All of us were totally amazed that we encountered one another in such a remote place.

After lunch, the sun disappeared and the rains returned. Claudio came into the restaurant with our jackets and umbrellas, and told us that it was time to leave to visit the cathedral at Sant Antimo. On the way, we passed through vineyards. We noticed that, at the end of each row of vines, roses were planted. Claudio explained that roses are subject to many of the same diseases as grapes, but are less resistant. The farmer watches the roses and, if the roses die, he knows that there is something wrong with the grapevines that need attention.

It took about thirty minutes to drive to the massive stone cathedral and monastery known as Sant Antimo, sitting alone among the Tuscan hills. The Monks that originally established it chose that location, in part, for its isolation. Now, however, there is a sizable parking lot and there were a number of cars, as well as a couple of tour buses parked there. It is extremely well preserved and, on this gloomy, rainy afternoon, conveyed a definite air of mystery. The French Monks who still live there have recorded their chants, and these are played at a low volume throughout the cathedral whenever it is open. The effect is quite impressive.

The rain finally stopped as we were driving back to Cortona. Claudio parked outside our hotel, and hooked up a device that permitted him to communicate, by satellite, in order to register a credit card charge for the amount we owed him for the day. Claudio had been terrific and, after we returned to Indiana, I wrote an article about him for the Fort Wayne News-Sentinel, and have attached a copy at the end of this journal.

The rest of our group would not return from Florence until later. Betsy had the beginnings of a cold and elected to go to the room to rest. I walked into town and made a stop at an ATM machine for some cash.

Dinner that evening was in the "Sterile Room," a buffet. It would sustain life. After dinner, Cliff Shultz, Bill Hall and I took our walk, while the others went to the lecture room to meet some local residents, a young couple that owns a jewelry shop in Cortona.

X

The next morning, we gathered in the lecture room for a presentation by Lyndall Passerini on "Modern Italy." Many people in the group slept in, and a number were fighting various maladies caused by the persistent cool, rainy weather, and as a result, the crowd was sparse. This was unfortunate, because she was very articulate and interesting. She told us that, for Italians, life focuses on the family, and the current trend is to have only one child per family, because of the high cost of living. Being an only child makes them spoiled and demanding, and many families get into debt trying to provide a lifestyle for their child that "keeps up with the Joneses." The Church, she said, is struggling, and active participation is down dramatically. Also, as most of us knew from reading the newspapers, Italy has a serious problem in dealing with immigration.

After the lecture, the ladies went to a cooking class presented by the chef of Ristorante Tonino, our hotel's "famous restaurant" (it would have been nice if our tour group had eaten there just once!). Cliff, Bill and I went for a walk and decided to go up the mountain to the Cathedral of Santa Margherita, which seemed to be straight up and about five miles in distance. Even though it was grey and cold, our jackets soon came off; however, we did make it to the top. It is a very attractive church, and the mummified remains of Santa Margherita are displayed in a glass case at the front. Cortonans are quite serious in referring to her as their "protector."

Lunch was served in the Wine Room, and Betsy made it to lunch even though her cold was getting worse. We were served some of the dishes that had been "taught" in the morning's cooking class. Someone observed that the size of our group had shrunk. This was to be the last day of the Indiana University Cortona tour, and several people had departed to other destinations, including Florence and Aix en Provence.

The afternoon was "at leisure," but the weather was crummy. Betsy elected to stay in bed and rest, while I walked into town, bought a copy of the *Herald-Tribune*, sat with a latte at a cafe, and then shopped and bought some souvenirs. The local equivalent of the Chamber of Commerce was giving away posters with a reproduction of Fra Angelico's *"Annunciation,"* and I picked up one to bring home, frame, and hang in the foyer. Several people from our group were at the jewelry shop owned by the young couple they had met the night before. Someone said, that evening, that the shop was doing a "land office business" with the owners' new IU friends.

The Halls and the Shultzes wanted to see Bramasole, the home of Frances Mayes, and now a tourist attraction because of the popularity of her book. Betsy and I had been there on Tuesday with Claudio, so we did not join them. They were fortunate enough to have Claudio as their driver, and told us later that they had enjoyed a very fine afternoon with him, and he had shown them quite a number of interesting things, in addition to Bramasole.

I went to the lecture hall on the third floor (which was deserted at that hour) and turned on CNN in order to watch the second Bush/Gore debate. After watching, it was my impression that the debate was a tie. If Bush had a vulnerable point, it was on the issue of abortion. All of the polls showed that Bush lagged Gore among women voters, and abortion seemed to be the principal reason.

Natazia had instructed all of us that we would be expected to give tips for the hotel staff and for the bus driver. The driver, Paolo, had been with us the entire week. His wife and daughter followed the bus in a car, and while we were visiting various cities, we would see the three of them together from place to place. Natazia told us that no tips were expected for her or for any of the lecturers. Each of us put the appropriate amounts in an envelope, and deposited them with Natazia, who would handle the distribution.

Betsy was feeling pretty poor with her cold, and did not come upstairs to the lobby for the cocktail party that preceded the final, farewell dinner. It wasn't exactly a "cocktail" party, since it featured only red or white wine. There were a number of tasty *hors d'oeuvres*, however, and I gathered a few up and took them to Betsy to eat in the room. The *hors d'oeuvres* were good enough that Betsy decided to make the effort to come upstairs for the farewell dinner, served once again in the Sterile Room. My notes say, "Whatever happened to Ristorante Tonino?" Anyway, the food was pretty good.

After dinner, everyone gathered in the lecture room for a "graduation" exercise. The IU representative for the trip, Stefan Davis, announced that all of us had passed! Some of us did some skits, read poems, or sang songs, either individually or as a group. I recited a poem that I had written for the occasion:

"Roses are red, as red as can be;
Assissi was wet, and so were we."

It received polite applause. Cliff Shultz also gave a presentation which consisted of him pretending to ask for his room key in Italian. He asked for it three or four times, each one different.

The rest of the evening was occupied with packing, and it was obvious that there were a number of things that Betsy and I would leave behind. Natazia said it would be all right to leave them on the bed in the room, and that she would let the maids know that they could have them. These included: an unopened bottle of Maalox that I had bought at a local drugstore when I thought I might need it; an unopened bottle of champagne that had been given to us by the Grand Hotel in Florence; travel kits that American Airlines had given us, containing such things as toothbrushes and eye masks; and one unopened bottle of "Acqua Minerale - Senza Gas." Even though the stuff was supposed to be distilled water, it still tasted funny.

By the way, Betsy and I drank the tap water throughout our trip to Italy and never had any digestive problems of any kind.

The IU tour group was scheduled to leave at 7:15 in the morning (!) for a three and a half hour bus trip to Rome to catch the flight back to the United States. Betsy and I were on a later flight, and arranged for Claudio to pick us up at 9:00 o'clock (much more civilized), and he had us at Rome Airport by 11:20 in the morning. Betsy was still feeling lousy, but at least we were on our way home. The connections from Chicago to Fort Wayne were poor and uncertain, so the Fort Wayne Six spent a relaxing night at the Doubletree Suites Hotel in Chicago, and arranged to return to Fort Wayne the next day.

We had a good time. I recommend the food. I recommend the wine. I recommend the company!

The Newspaper Article About Claudio Alberghini

"Globalization is what is new."
Thomas L. Friedman, The Lexus and the Olive Tree."

The city of Cortona, the guidebook says, sits "implacably on the side of a mountain, where it has been for more than 3,000 years. Its historic and archaeological roots can be traced back to the Etruscans, and the city that stands there today is, largely, Medieval. Cortona is in Tuscany, in the North Central part of Italy, and was recently brought to the attention of the literary world in a best-selling book-by Frances Mayes, *Under the Tuscan Sun*.

Although tourists are beginning to discover Cortona, it is still safe from the hordes that infest such places as Florence, where elbow room is the rarest of commodities. In the evening, you can wander into the old town square and sit outside at a cafe, sipping cappuccino, and enjoy the passing parade. There is such a cafe, in fact, in front of the old Teatro, which was used as a locale for filming parts of the recent popular movie, "*Life is Beautiful*." The grocer, the baker and the florist shops are still more prominent than the boutiques and gift shops. All of which is to say that, when in Cortona, it is very much possible to feel oneself back in another age.

Until, that is, you need a taxi.

There are three taxis in the city, and one of them is owned and operated by Claudio Alberghini, also, according to his business card, called "Mr.Taxi." It was our good fortune to encounter Claudio when our schedule called for us to require a car and driver for a day, and our hotel referred us to him. A young man who, in this country, could be taken for a linebacker in the NFL, he turned out to be congenial and good natured, fluent in English, reasonable in price, and entirely accommodating to our schedule.

Claudio drives a new Chrysler van, and it is apparent that he is successful at what he does, which includes driving customers all over Tuscany. It is, however, his use of modern technology and communications that differentiates him from so many of his competitors. His cellular telephone has a permanent cradle next to him in the van, and he has a headphone attachment that allows him to use it while keeping both hands on the wheel.

Did we want to visit a museum in Pienza? With a call, he knew in two minutes if it was open, and what hours. "Where to have lunch?" There is a service that gives the names of restaurants in various towns. A couple of calls secures a reservation at a good one in a remote town called "Bagno Vignoni" where, incidentally, we encountered good friends from Fort Wayne! Were we thirsty? A small refrigerator in the van is stocked with several bottles of Evian water.

Finally, returning to Cortona, it was time to settle up with Claudio. "Do you want to pay by credit card?" he asked. Since tourists don't carry much cash, this would be extremely convenient, but how could he negotiate a credit card transaction? He opened his trunk, took out a device the size of a small laptop computer, plugged his cell phone into it and ran our credit card through. Communication, of course, was by satellite. In less than a minute, he had a confirmation from the credit card company, and his machine printed out a receipt. This transpired in a parking space in the Piazza di Garibaldi on a mountainside in Cortona, Italy!

A couple of days later, we engaged Claudio to drive us to the airport in Rome. On the way, he called a national telephone number and gave them our route, and, received a report on all traffic conditions and possible problems along the way. There is, he says, a national center that continuously gathers and assimilates this data from all over the country.

Should you be traveling to Tuscany, I heartily recommend Claudio. With the proper software (Macromedia Flash Player), you can check out his Internet Web site at www.magictuscanytours.com, and he can be reached at his e-mail address, mrtaxi@tin.it. We have corresponded with him, and he says he checks his e-mail every morning.

Fort Wayne News-Sentinel
November 10, 2000

Chapter 14

OH, CANADA!

I

My wife, Betsy, and I have been traveling to Stratford, Ontario, for the Shakespeare Festival every year since 1969, so I decided that it was about time to record a journal of the event. In the year 2000, we were prevented from going during the summer (our usual time) because of Betsy's illness; however, we rescheduled the trip for October, which was also convenient for our friends and traveling companions, Max and Holley Hobbs. In addition to being good company, the Hobbses also owned a Chrysler Town & Country van, which made a very comfortable means of getting there. At their suggestion, we added Niagara-on-the-Lake to our itinerary, to be visited after Stratford.

We left Fort Wayne at 9:00 o'clock in the morning and drove to Port Huron, Michigan, where we hoped to have lunch at a restaurant recommended by Cliff and Elaine Shultz. Cliff was unable to remember the name of the restaurant, but had said that, "You can't miss it. It's right there when you come in to town." Fortunately, the night before we left, Elaine called and gave us the name, the "Pilot House." Once in Port Huron, we went to a gas station, called the place, made a reservation, and got directions. (The United States mint was in the process of putting out new quarters, honoring the various States of the Union. Each year, five new state quarters were being issued. The pay phones in Port Huron would not, however, accept them, and we wondered if this boded ill for the entire vending machine industry.) The Pilot House turned out to be very nice, on the water, with good food, and not expensive; however, it is not easy to find. It is 7 miles east of downtown!

After lunch, we crossed the Blue Water Bridge into Canada, and made our obligatory stop at the tourist information center in Sarnia, just on the other side of the bridge. There we were able to change American dollars for Canadian dollars, and obtain a free map of Ontario. (The American dollar fetched $1.50 Canadian dollars.)

The October foliage on the drive to Port Huron had been beautiful, but we were all made more aware of it once we crossed into Canada. For some reason, it was particularly outstanding, and reminded me of the autumns of my youth in Monmouth, Illinois.

Stratford has managed to achieve an interesting balance between a rural Canadian community and an English village, with enough tourist facilities to keep it pleasant, but without acquiring the vestiges of a tourist trap. I have been told that there are zoning restrictions that affect much of the town, and are designed to keep new construction or alterations to existing buildings in a style that blends in. The Avon River dissects the center of the city, and it has been dammed up to create a large lake, with a wonderful park encircling it. The lake is a recreation center, with paddle boats and canoes, and has a permanent population of ducks and graceful swans. A number of picnic tables and benches are sprinkled about the park. There is a nice, semi-private golf club here, and some of my best golf memories are from Stratford.

The plays at the Shakespeare Festival are performed by a repertory company, with major artists occasionally brought in for particular roles. The largest theater, the Festival Theater, is perched on a hillside that overlooks the park, and the Avon Theater is in the middle of downtown. The third theater, the Tom Patterson, also near the park, tends to feature the more *avant garde* productions, introduces younger members of the company, and is a little too rustic for my taste. (Still, we have seen some good things performed there.) Every season features three or four of Shakespeare's plays, and a full program of other works, as many as 12 or 14 in a season, ranging from classic drama to modern musicals.

We arrived at the Queen's Inn by dinnertime, and Max's fancy equipment on his van showed elapsed driving time from Fort Wayne of 6.2 hours. It was Monday night, meaning no theater productions were going on, and the downtown was amazingly quiet. Even some of the restaurants were closed.

My notes for the journal say, "It is great to be in Stratford!"

We set our watches ahead one hour to account for the time change, settled our luggage in our rooms, and walked down Ontario Street to Fellini's Italian restaurant, which was still busy even though it was already 7:45 p.m. This was our first visit to Fellini's, and it turned out to be very good. We had never seen it before, but learned it has been there for six years. The bruschetta appetizer is delicious, and enough for a full meal, the Chicken Caesar Salad was also good, and the restaurant follows the pleasant European custom of making wine available by the carafe. During the meal, Holley looked a little bit downcast, and finally admitted that she had just broken a tooth! She would look for a dentist the following morning. At least it was a Monday night. That kind of thing always seems to happen to me on a Friday night, when there will be no dentist in his office for two days.

Some of our friends claim that every time I check into a hotel, I change rooms. In fact, we did on this trip, for the usual reason that the first room only had one bed in it. It turned out, however, that Max and Holley also changed rooms and, on Tuesday morning, we found that they were ensconced in the "Dome Suite" on the third floor. It seems that their prior room, on the second floor, was directly above the room where the Rotary Club met at 6:00 a.m., and began its tradition of singing songs. Besides, the noise and smells from the hotel kitchen managed to come into their room through the registers. The Queen's Inn is acceptable, but Stratford really needs a quality hotel.

II

We went for breakfast at a restaurant called "Features," where the waitress encouraged us to try the "Two Dollar Special." This consisted of two eggs, two pieces of bacon, two pieces of toast, and coffee - for $2.00! Pretty good, and just what I needed. (I had brought along my own can of prunes.)

On the way to the restaurant we noticed that the town was full of high school students. When we entered, there were teenagers (nearly all of them smoking) jamming most of the tables, and a man at the next table offered me the "house newspaper." It must have been read by a great many earlier diners, because it was soaked with grease. Being a Canadian newspaper, there was no news anyway. Holley, meanwhile, was able to locate a dentist, who repaired her tooth, and she seemed quite satisfied with his work.

There was time after breakfast to walk to the picturesque Courthouse and the nearby pharmacy. Next, we made our customary visit to the Rheo Thompson Candy Shop, where the best candy in the world is sold. I bought my usual pound of chocolate-covered nuts. (Rheo Thompson now has competition, for the first time, from a new place called the Rocky Mountain Chocolate Company.)

Max and Holley ate lunch in the hotel pub, but Betsy and I skipped lunch in order to go to the Festival Theater early. The Festival Theater, just a pleasant walk from downtown, has a large gift shop and we possessed a substantial gift certificate as a result of our summer purchase of play tickets which we could not use. One way or another, we managed to spend the entire amount of the gift certificate, and a little more.

Stratford has a charming custom: just before curtain time, a quartet of musicians with long-stemmed trumpets enters the lobby and plays a fanfare to let the audience know that they should go into the theater and take their seats. Each year, we get a little bit of a chill when we hear it for the first time.

We learned why there were so many high school students in town. It was a Tuesday matinee, and they were bused in from all around as a field trip to see *"Hamlet."* The theater, which has a capacity of 2500, was completely full, and two-thirds of them were these high school students. As it turned out, an actor named Paul Gross was in the title role, and he seems to be a television star in Canada, appearing on a program called *"Due South."* He is young and handsome, and all of the teenage girls acted as if he were a rock star. When he made his curtain call, the noise was deafening, as they stood on their seats, bouncing up and down, hugging each other and squealing. Nonetheless, he gave a credible performance.

Betsy and I have seen *"Hamlet"* many times, and I never get tired of it. Besides, every time I see it, I see or hear something I had missed before. As someone has said, the entire play is "filled with clichés." It has poetry, murder, history, sex, revenge, ghosts, pageantry and philosophy. We have seen only one truly bad production, and that was, surprisingly, by the Royal Shakespeare Company, in Stratford on Avon, England, where Hamlet appeared for most of the play wearing Brooks Brothers pajamas. The Company at Stratford, Ontario, has better sense, and this entire production was strong and well done. We enjoyed it very much.

The day had been misty and cool and when we exited the theater at 5:30, a heavy fog had set in. After an acceptable, if not memorable, dinner at a restaurant called "The Old Prune," we made our way back to the Festival Theater for a truly marvelous production of *"Fiddler on the Roof."* *"Fiddler"* is a musical adaptation of the short stories of Sholem Aleichem, who chronicled life in Jewish villages in Russia at the turn of the twentieth century. It combines the considerable talents of Joseph Stein (book), Jerry Bock (music), and Sheldon Harnick (lyrics), with the genius of the original New York director, Jerome Robbins. In recent years, Stratford seems to produce Broadway musicals that are better than they were on Broadway, and we find ourselves asking each other, "Where do they get these performers?" Neither Max nor Holley had seen *Fiddler* before and they were charmed by it.

III

The next morning, Betsy and I decided to go back to "Features" for the "Two Dollar Breakfast Special." This time, there were no high school kids, and plenty of empty tables. There were also lots of newspapers available on the counter, but it turned out that they were all from the day before.

After breakfast, we went to one of the local banks and got some Canadian dollars out of an ATM. I really wasn't very short of cash, but I still giggle at the experience of pushing buttons on a machine and getting money in a foreign country. There was time to do a little more shopping (Stratford has quite a number of very nice stores), and we made an effort to save all of the receipts in order to get a refund of the "goods and services tax" ("GST"), which can be done at the time a non-Canadian leaves the country.

We joined the Hobbses at the Pub in the Queen's Inn for lunch. Afterward, we checked out of our hotel rooms, loaded our stuff into the van, and walked to the nearby Avon Theater to see the two o'clock matinee, Oscar Wilde's "*The Importance of Being Earnest.*" The Avon is functional, but it is not as impressive as the Festival Theater, nor as much fun; however, we read an announcement to the effect that a thirteen million dollar renovation of the Avon will take place when the 2000 Season closes. (The Stratford Festival season runs from the middle of June until the first week in November.)

"*Earnest,*" in its better known form, is a three act, hilarious comedy. All of us had seen it on a previous trip, at which time the venerable William Hutt, the legendary Canadian actor, portrayed the part of Lady Brancaster (in drag, naturally), and received national press coverage as a result. Last August, the city of Stratford renamed the Waterloo Bridge, near downtown, as the "William Hutt Bridge." Mr. Hutt is still at Stratford, although he did not appear in any of the plays we saw. On the other hand, William Needles, an actor who has been at Stratford for as long as we can remember, did have a role in "*The Importance of Being Earnest,*" as the butler. He seemed a little bit frail, both on stage, and when we saw him on the street after the play.

The Stratford production that we saw this time was the four act version (here compressed into two acts) that Wilde had originally written, with dark overtones of homosexuality and social recrimination. The manuscript was discovered in 1953 in an attic in New Jersey! It still has plenty of laughs, but every once in a while the audience is brought up short, especially those who know the other version. It was, in other words, the kind of theater experience that keeps bringing us and many thousands of others back to Stratford year after year.

When we left the Avon theater, we walked back to the parking lot at the

Snapshots

Queen's Inn, got into the van, and began our drive to Niagara-on-the-Lake. Because it was getting late, and dark, we decided to "dine" at a McDonald's restaurant *en route*. For some reason, the road from Stratford to Niagara-on-the-Lake is always confusing, especially at night. I agreed to drive, on condition that Max ride up front and navigate. The entire trip was complicated by some of the densest fog I have ever driven in, which made both driving and navigating that much tougher.

IV

I have described Switzerland as "Disneyland for grownups." The same might be said of Niagara-on-the-Lake. It is nestled into the peninsula where the Niagara River enters Lake Ontario, and still has much the same feeling that must have existed there 100 years ago. It is immaculate, and has excellent hotels and restaurants, quaint streets and buildings, fine parks and waterfront, and miles of pathway along the Niagara River for walking or bicycling. Unfortunately, it also has tour buses, and the passengers tend to clog the main street; however, they usually leave by dinnertime.

The major attraction for us has always been The Shaw Festival. As in Stratford, there is a permanent repertory company, performing at three different theaters, and featuring a variety of dramatic and musical works; however, the emphasis is on the works of Shaw, and no Shakespeare is ever done. Although they do not, in my opinion, achieve the standards that Stratford sets, they are very good indeed.

Arriving in the evening, we checked in to the Prince of Wales Hotel. On our last trip, the hotel was in the process of renovation. It was closed and being completely overhauled. It reopened on July 1 (Canada Day), 1999. The lobby is ornate, maybe a little too ornate, maybe even a little bit kitsch, but I like it. Max Hobbs thinks, "They've ruined the place," but not me. The rooms were wonderful, beautifully furnished and decorated, with plenty of space. What's more, all of the brand new plumbing worked properly (this is no small consideration). In addition, it was absolutely quiet.

Max and I went out for a walk. The audience was out in front of the Royal George Theater for the first intermission, and the ice cream shops were still open. We walked all the way to the Oban Inn, and both opined that we had never seen the town so quiet. This was very different from past visits in the summer season.

There was a little time to look at the newspaper before bed. The Canadian papers were paying scant attention to the Bush/Gore election race. *USA Today* had a lot of coverage, which was quite plainly biased in favor of Gore. The political polls reported that it would be a close race, but no one seems to believe the polls any more. The World Series was in progress, the Yankees vs. the Mets, but it was pretty one-sided in favor of the Yankees, and not interesting enough to watch at bedtime.

V

Breakfast Thursday morning in the Prince of Wales dining room was quite elegant. It was like a fancy New York Hotel, but cheaper. Betsy and I went for a long walk on a beautiful Fall morning, stopping at the Oban Inn, where we made a reservation for dinner the following night. There was practically no wind and Lake Ontario was as calm as I have ever seen it. Autumn had not advanced nearly as far here as further inland, presumably because of the moderating influence of the lake. As a result, all of the flowers were still in full bloom and in all their glory. Most of the leaves were still on the trees, but turning. It is truly a delightful town.

While Max and Holley bought lunch at a delicatessen, Betsy and I went to the "Epicurean," where one goes through a cafeteria line, and then can sit at tables in a garden in back. The weather had gotten warm, and it was very pleasant.

Our 2:00 o'clock matinee at the Royal George Theater was a J. B. Priestly work called *"Time and the Conways,"* a family drama set in the years prior to World War II. Priestly was a very British, middle class socialist, and both his plays and his philosophy have become dated. This play was well staged, well directed and well-acted. It is just not a very good play. As Warren Buffett said, "If a thing is not worth doing, it is not worth doing well."

After the play, Holley decided to head back to the hotel to rest and to skip dinner and the evening play. Betsy, Max and I went to Giordano's Restaurant, at the Gate House Hotel which is, logically, located on Gate Street. We have eaten there from time to time in prior years, and it has always been good.

The 8:00 o'clock evening show, Thornton Wilder's *"The Matchmaker,"* was at the Festival Theater. (Yes, Niagara-on-the-Lake also has a "Festival Theater.") The setting is New York City in the '30's, but the play owes some of its inspiration to Shakespeare's *Midsummer Night's Dream*, with a pair of young lovers fleeing their elders in the "forests" of Manhattan. The musical *"Hello Dolly"* is based on *"The Matchmaker."* Much of the action takes place in a restaurant called "The Harmonia Gardens," which seems to be very much like the former "Luchow's," where Betsy and I dined back in the '60's. The lead role was played by Goldie Semple, who Betsy's father would have described as, "An old campaigner." She had to be in her 50's, but still was very attractive and wonderful on the stage.

I once had a role in *"The Matchmaker"* when it was staged at First

Snapshots

Presbyterian Theater in Fort Wayne. I played the part of the barber, who makes only a brief appearance in the first act, and I had agreed to take the role on condition that I would not be required to hang around the theater for curtain calls. Betsy and I made a special effort to watch during the curtain call and, sure enough, the barber didn't show up this time either.

On the walk back to the hotel, we all agreed that it was a good production of a good show. When we got back, game 5 of the World Series was on, but there was a sense that the Yankees would win. They did, and won the series four games to one.

VI

On Friday morning, it was pleasant to have breakfast again in the Prince of Wales Hotel dining room. Our table was located in the "greenhouse" section, where the walls and roof are glass. The trees and flowers around the outside are spectacular. After breakfast, Betsy and I walked again, but this time down side streets and through new neighborhoods, mainly choosing those blocks that had sidewalks. I was interested to note that there are a number of places where old houses were torn down and new houses were being built. Not elaborate, expensive houses (as at Lake Wawasee, in Indiana, for instance), but simply new houses of the same size and style as the houses that were there before.

There is one store in Niagara-on-the-Lake that we always visit, "Greaves." They make and sell jams and jellies that are wonderful, and we always stock up. My favorite is the combination of strawberry and rhubarb, but by October, we were told, they were sold out. We did get some cherry preserves, blueberry jam, and cranberry sauce. They won't last long. Every few years we make the mistake of having lunch at a restaurant called The Buttery, and this was our year. At least it sustained life through the matinee.

Whereas Shakespeare is the focus at Stratford, here it is George Bernard Shaw, whose life spanned 94 years, from 1856 to 1950. It is hard to believe that he died that long ago, but we were reminded of it when we read that, in 2001, his works will come out of copyright. The one Shaw play that we saw on this trip was *"The Doctors Dilemma,"* performed at 2:00 o'clock on Friday at the Festival Theater. Shaw did not like doctors, and this play is a hilarious lampoon of the medical profession. (One chronicler says that, in this play, he has divided doctors into three categories, the fools, the frauds and the murderers.) Shaw is difficult, and this company invariably does it well. There was a good audience, and the show was appreciated. One of the advantages of coming here is that it is one of the few places where one can see the works of Shaw performed, and performed competently.

Between shows, we honored our dinner reservation at the Oban Inn, another revitalized and renovated hostelry, which continues to have a fine kitchen.

The evening performance, at the Royal George Theater, was a musical called *"She Loves Me,"* which had only limited success when it first was produced, and for a very good reason. It is a shallow, ho-hum piece of fluff, with pedestrian music. Still, the cast worked hard, and had good voices, and it was a pleasantly entertaining evening. So long as you did not expect too much.

VII

On Saturday, we left Niagara-on-the Lake at 9:00 a.m. (EST) and drove pretty much straight through to Fort Wayne, about eight hours driving time. We did allow ourselves a stop at the duty free shop on the Canadian side of the Blue Water Bridge, where we accomplished: 1) a rebate of most of the GST we had paid in Canada; 2) purchase of Bombay Gin and Canadian Club Whiskey at very low prices (Max bought single malt scotch, which is probably the best bargain of all); and 3) exchange of our remaining Canadian currency into US dollars.

Another good Canadian theater trip. That makes thirty one in a row.

Chapter 15

A STIRLING EXPERIENCE

Vitznau

If Disney were to build a theme park based on Switzerland, the first hotel would be modeled on The Parkhotel Vitznau on Lake Lucerne. It is a fairyland castle in a fairyland setting. Betsy and I arrived from Fort Wayne on a warm Saturday afternoon, August 18, 2001. We had barely made our plane connection in Chicago on Swissair, and did not really expect that our luggage would be on board. But, when we landed in Zurich, we found that our bags had made the flight also, and we thought good thoughts about Swissair. Old reliable. Little did we suspect that, within a few months, it would be bankrupt, and leave passengers stranded all over the world!

Our Swiss friend, Thomas Duermueller, had sent a car and a driver to meet us, and he whisked us from Zurich airport down to Vitznau in about an hour and a half. A summer Saturday on Lake Lucerne is perfect for relaxing on the balcony and watching the swimmers, the boats and the pedestrians. In fact, you might just say it's perfect.

As always, I had my current copy of the *International Herald-Tribune* (without which one cannot travel) to help pass the time. The PGA golf tournament was in progress; the Chicago Cubs held a slim lead in the National League Central Division; there was fighting in the Mid-East, the Balkans, several places in Africa, Sri Lanka, and other places besides. George W. Bush was the President of the United States, but the Democrats had recently taken over the Senate, and everything political was a struggle. (James Jeffords, the treacherous and venal senator from Vermont, elected to office as a Republican, had decided to switch parties and shift the balance of power in the Senate from the Republicans to the Democrats.) The U.S. economy had been slumping, and the news presented a tedious list of the latest layoffs. The Dow Jones Industrial Average was at 10,240, and the NASDAQ had sagged to 1,867.

From our hotel balcony, we watched a ferry boat pass by, with the name "Schwyz" on it. It is one of several that traverse Lake Lucerne, with one of them arriving and leaving at the Vitznau Station every twenty minutes or so. A wedding had taken place somewhere around the lake and, at about 5:30 p.m., a large boat arrived at the hotel dock with the wedding party, come to celebrate and hold the reception at the hotel. There was a piano set under a tree near the lake, tables with umbrellas and lawn chairs, and people sipping beverages. The music found its way up to our balcony. What a spot.

At eight o'clock we made our way to the outdoor restaurant, a magical setting overlooking the lake, and everything about the evening was perfect except that I ate too much. The best entree on the menu is "Veal Zurich Style with Rosti," and it is a lot of food. I knew that, but I ordered it anyway, and ate it all. After dinner, Betsy was chagrined when she weighed herself on the bathroom scale. "How can anybody be weighed," she said, "in stones?"

Sunday morning was a lovely day for a long walk along the shores of the lake, to what we thought was a hotel, but turned out to be a Swiss school for hotel management. We had planned to have a cup of coffee there, but were directed, instead, to an outdoor restaurant on the lake, just across the street. I am sorry to keep going on like this – but what a place! Flowers, swimmers, bikers, hikers, and a lake with water that is like crystal.

We walked back to the Parkhotel Vitznau, where the concierge gave us maps and information about the area. It took about ten minutes for us to walk into the little town of Vitznau, where we boarded the ferry boat "Schiller," and cruised along until we arrived at Gersau. Sunday afternoon is quiet anywhere, and it didn't take long to explore Gersau, which is another idyllic little village, set among the mountains on the lake. We wound up at a small cafe near the ferry boat station, found a table outdoors, and had some ice cream while we waited for the ferry boat "Callia" to take us back to Vitznau. There is another hotel in Vitznau, called "Vitznauer Hof," which looks very nice, and is given four stars under the Swiss hotel ranking system. One would never choose it over the Parkhotel; however, Parkhotel closes for the season in November, and Vitznauer Hof would make a good substitute during the winter months. We strolled back along the lake to the Parkhotel for a nap, a shower, and to write postcards to send to friends in Indiana.

Zurich

After a night of thunderstorms, Monday morning was cloudy, but the hotel was pleasantly quiet, since many of the guests appeared to have left following the weekend. Our driver picked us up at 11:00 o'clock and drove us to the Hotel Baur Au Lac, located in the heart of Zurich. Once settled in a room, we hurried off to *Sprungli*, everyone's favorite cafe, for lunch. The waitress invited us to "share" a table with two willing if not eager young women, and a very pleasant Swiss lady helped us understand the menu (all in German). *Sprungli* also has a huge candy store, bakery, pastry shop, and all around sweets establishment on the ground floor on the BahnhofStrasse, Zurich's main street. We thought about shipping some candy home, but the clerks told us that they did not ship any candy until cool weather.

There was time for a walk through the Old City, before heading back to the hotel to get ready to go out for dinner. Betsy had brought an American hair curler which, of course, only worked on 120 volt current; but in Europe, the electric current is 240 volts. We explained the problem to the hotel Concierge, and he gave us an "adapter" which, he assured us, would solve the problem. An adapter is not the same as a "converter." It simply changed the shape of the plug, and I should have realized this, but didn't. When Betsy plugged it in, the hair curler promptly melted. We went back to the Concierge with this news, and he recommended we go to a shop called "Kilian," where a new hair curler could be purchased. Since it had begun to rain, we retained a taxi, drove to Kilian, and found a new hair curler, but it wasn't cheap. CH90 (90 Swiss francs) and CH20 for the taxi.

At 6:30 p.m. our car and driver took us from our hotel on a 40-minute drive to the Town of Baar, where Thomas Duermueller and his wife Renate live. It was still raining, so Thomas came out to meet us with an umbrella, and I told him that it was first time I had ever seen him without a business suit. His home is a part of a group of town homes with a main living area on the upper floor and bedrooms below. The decor is very Swiss, modern in style, elegant, attractive and comfortable.

For dinner, Renate had fixed veal Zurich style with rosti. Hers was even better than the meal we had enjoyed two nights earlier at Parkhotel Vitznau! She also served greens and tomato salad, bread and cheese, and wine. I made a serious effort not to repeat my mistake of overeating. After a lovely evening, our driver took us back to the hotel. Jet lag was still a problem, so a sleeping pill (Ambien) was welcome.

Tuesday morning, I asked the desk clerk if we might move our room to one of the rooms overlooking the river, and was told that this could be done later in the day. We then walked to the nearby office of Thomas Duermueller, met him, and also met his assistant, Sybylla. We spent some time going over business affairs, had a tour of the facility, and then went to lunch at Carleton Restaurant, an excellent place for lunch, which offers dining indoors or out. As he often does, Thomas presented Betsy with a box of "pralines" from *Sprungli*. In Switzerland, a box of "pralines" is what we would call a box of chocolates. When we got back to the hotel, we made the switch to the new room, overlooking the river.

That was a mistake. Hotels in Zurich are prohibited, by city ordinance, from using air conditioning (presumably as an ecological measure). Our original room at the Baur Au Lac had been located on the north side of the building and therefore got no sun. The new room, overlooking the river and thus unshaded, faced west, and was a hot box. As soon as we went into the room, this was obvious, and I went back to the front desk and asked to move back, but the clerk said they had already sold our other room, and we could not go back to it. I called Thomas, and asked him where we could go to find air conditioning, and he suggested we move outside the city of Zurich to the Dolder Grand Hotel. After some phone calls and intervention by Thomas, we arranged to move the next day. We spent the rest of Tuesday afternoon and evening walking through the Old City section of Zurich, browsing in the shops and being amazed by some of the prices. Admittedly, these are upscale shops, but, at one of them, I priced a rather ordinary man's belt at over $600.00. Americans don't realize how reasonable clothing is in our country. The Hotel Baur Au Lac has a lovely outdoor dining room, surrounded by a garden, and that evening Betsy and I had a light meal of salad, soup and sandwich. Our room, unhappily, was like an oven all night long.

Dolder Grand

Wednesday was another sunny day and we spent the morning with breakfast, repacking to move out of the Baur Au Lac, settling the room bill, returning the "electric adapter" which had melted Betsy's hair curler, and arranging for a taxi. A taxi in Zurich is a little bit different than a taxi in New York City. It is a black Mercedes sedan, driven by a man in a dark suit and tie, and usually has classical music playing in muted tones through the sound system. Our taxi ride up the mountain to the Dolder Grand Hotel was nostalgic. In 1969, Betsy and our son, Steve, and I had come to Zurich, and stayed at the "Waldhaus Dolder," a sister hotel. We had arrived there on the morning that Neil Armstrong walked on the moon, and everybody loved Americans. The picturesque place we stayed in has now been replaced by an extremely ugly cement building (still called the "Waldhaus Dolder").

Snapshots

The Dolder Grand (higher up the mountain) is still the same as we remembered it from 1969. That is, it is still magnificent, and still absurdly expensive; but, Thomas had wheedled us a very favorable rate. It is a hotel to rival any in the world, with luxurious accommodations, located high on a mountain, overlooking the city and Lake Zurich. In addition to air conditioning, the Dolder Grand offers tennis and a 9-hole golf course. In the room, the television brought in CNN, BBC, Bloomberg, and NBC Super Channel, as well as numerous European channels.

After lunch, we decided to start walking along the many miles of footpaths that go through the woods in the area. In 1969, we had visited the nearby "Wellenbad," a huge swimming pool and park, open to the public. Every so often, it creates big waves at one end that roll to the other, and swimmers can play in the "surf." It is still there, but requires that one pay an entrance fee. We persuaded the ticket taker that we only wanted to go in and have a look, and she waved us through the turnstile. It was a hot day, and there were lots of bathers and, for the most part, it was as we had remembered it.

We left the Wellenbad and began walking through the woods, but every path seemed to go only uphill. The woods are thick and expansive, and the trees are enormous. Once full of bears and other wildlife, they are now populated by hikers, joggers, and horseback riders, and benches are placed at convenient spots along all of the paths. After getting lost a couple times, we retraced our steps and found our way back to the hotel.

We called the maid and asked her to take away the *duvets* on the beds, and replace them with sheets and blankets. Everyplace in Switzerland people sleep with these thick "comforters" that feel wonderful for about 90 seconds, and then leave you feeling as if you were sleeping in a sauna. The term "Swiss Bed" means that you have sheets and blankets, instead of the traditional Swiss *duvet*. Go figure.

We went to the hotel business center, where computers were available, and we checked our e-mail, looked at the current news, and also checked the Fort Wayne website to see what was going on at home. The Federal Reserve Board had once again reduced interest rates, and the Israelis and Palestinians were talking peace while effectively at war. An e-mail from my brother Bruce told us that he and Sarah were about to celebrate their 25th wedding anniversary. I remember the wedding very well. I was the best man.

That evening, we took the five minute automobile trip to the Sonnenburg, once a hotel and restaurant, but now the international headquarters of an organization known as FIFA, which is to soccer what PGA is to golf. The old hotel that Betsy, Steve and I visited so many years before has been torn down, and a new building has been erected with offices and guest rooms for

FIFA officials and guests. The public restaurant, however, has been retained, located on a huge, outdoor veranda with spectacular views.

We were not eating in the public restaurant, however, but were scheduled to meet Thomas and Renate at the FIFA private restaurant indoors. We had a lovely meal, wine, view, and company. We would be leaving Switzerland the next day. Before heading back to the Dolder Grand, we thanked Thomas and Renate profusely for the delightful visit that we had experienced, and said our goodbyes.

When we got back to our hotel, we noticed several burly men with blue suits, obviously carrying pistols under their jackets. They were patrolling the public areas and halls, and asking people not to use certain elevators. Upon inquiry, we learned that they were all private bodyguards employed by "some Prince from the Middle East." We later saw the Prince in the dining room at the head of a very large table of people, several of which were apparently wives and children. Because our room had a large balcony with a great view, we placed an order to have breakfast delivered in the morning by room service, took our sleeping pills, and retired.

A car and driver took us to the Zurich Airport on Thursday morning which was yet another warm and sunny day. Air travel in Europe is considerably different than in the United States, and can be confusing, and we were very glad to have our driver park the car, bring the bags, and help us get checked in for our British Air flight to London, and then on to Scotland.

Stirling

We were met at the airport in Edinburgh by a very competent Scotsman by the name of Bob McLauchlan, who drove us to the town of Stirling, and the Stirling Highland Hotel, where we would join an Indiana University alumni group organized and traveling under the auspices of a company called Alumni Holidays International ("AHI").

We found our hotel room to be small, stuffy, clean, and comfortable. There were two moderate-size windows, and we opened both of them as far as they would go, and left them open all the rest of the time that we were in Scotland, with the result that the room was, for the most part, rather airy after that. We must have been favorably impressed overall, because the notes in my journal say, "LOVE THE SCOTS!" There was a large clock tower about a block from our room, and we heard it strike loudly, and thought we would be awakened every hour, on the hour, until we got used to it, which would take approximately one week; however, we found that they shut it off at 9:00 o'clock in the evening, and did not start bonging again until 8:00 o'clock the next morning.

Snapshots

Most of the Indiana University group had arrived ahead of us and, by the time we had checked into the room and made our way downstairs to the group meeting place, orientation was already in process. It was conducted by the AHI representative, a very comely and very Scottish lass named Anne Allman. (Well, she seemed very Scottish, but we later learned that she was born in England.) We received IU identity tags, an updated itinerary, and some literature about Scotland, and places we would visit during the coming week. There was also biographical material about some of the lecturers that we would be hearing.

When the orientation was over, we greeted our Fort Wayne friends, Bill and Suzanne Hall, and Cliff and Elaine Shultz, and arranged to be together for the "Welcome Dinner." There was entertainment provided during the meal, with bagpipes, a couple of comedians, some Scottish girls doing some kind of a dance that involved swords, and an Irish jig. We were astonished at the energy of the entertainers! The menu for our first meal was billed as traditional Scottish fare, and included "haggis, neeps, and tatties." Don't ask.

Betsy's European-style hair curler, acquired with much difficulty in Switzerland, would not fit the Scottish electric plug. Fortunately, Suzanne Hall had brought a set of electric adapter fittings from home, we were able to fit one into a wall plug, and then plug the Swiss hair curler into that.

Friday morning began with a lecture by a Scot named John Harrison, a freelance historian and writer. He discussed the history of Scotland and its (seemingly perennial) struggles against England. We learned about William Wallace, played by Mel Gibson in the movie "Braveheart," who was in power in Scotland for only one year, from 1297 to 1298. If he had quit after the battle of Stirling Bridge, instead of staging raids into the north of England, he probably would have survived for a longer time. (Harrison says the movie "Braveheart" is mostly fiction, and ought to be ignored.) Later, Robert the Bruce came to power and defeated the English at Bannockbum. He did much better, holding power for a total of 23 years until his death in 1329.

After the lecture, we met our AHI "local guide," a lady named Babs Edgar, who I would guess to be in her forties, and who had a very lively sense of humor. We all boarded a bus and headed up the hill from our hotel to Stirling Castle, which was one of the major fortresses by which the Scottish held off the English or, alternatively, the English kept control of the Scots. We were amazed at the size, grandeur, and wealth of history surrounding this castle. (The Stuarts made it their court and power base.) It is as imposing as any castle we have seen anywhere, and several of us wished we could spend a couple of days just exploring it.

Howard L. Chapman

Our tour next saw Stirling Bridge, scene of the William Wallace victory, and the William Wallace Monument. The monument is a mammoth obelisk erected on top of a hill outside Stirling, and is visible for miles. At the base of the hill there is a visitor center, a parking lot, and a path that leads up the hill to the monument. And, at the foot of the path, there is an oversized statue of - Mel Gibson! He is dressed in his "Braveheart" costume, with one fist in the air, and "Freedom" inscribed on the pedestal. Babs told us that tourist admissions have tripled since the movie came out. Our last stop was the famous battlefield at Bannockbum, where King Robert the Bruce defeated the English to gain Scottish independence in 1314. There is an impressive statue of the King, sitting atop his horse, preparing for battle.

After lunch, Bill Hall went back up the hill from the hotel on foot (no small feat) to try to find his sunglasses, apparently left at the castle. Betsy and I, Suzanne, and the Shultzes walked from the hotel to the town of Stirling, which was a very pleasant walk, being entirely downhill.

Stirling, the ancient capital of Scotland, is now a delightful town of about 45,000 people, with plenty of shops and restaurants, and no obvious evidence of poverty. We purchased postcards and stamps, and I secured a current copy of the *International Herald-Tribune*. NATO forces were struggling to keep the peace in Macedonia; Beijing admitted that China has an AIDS epidemic; America's economy was slumping; and Democratic congressman Gary Condit had given an interview with newswoman Connie Chung in which he insisted he "did not kill Chandra Levy."

Walking back to the Stirling Hotel was all uphill, but not as bad as we had expected. We met Bill Hall coming from the other direction, and learned that his quest for sunglasses had been unsuccessful. (They were later discovered, buried in Suzanne's purse.)

At 4:00 o'clock we assembled for a question and answer session with four local Scots, all interesting folks, and all with different backgrounds. They were happy to give their opinions on everything from Scotland's economy to the royal family, and after the session, they joined our group in the hotel pub, and then stayed for dinner, each sitting at a different table in order to continue the conversations. By this time, we were favorably impressed with the food at the Stirling Highland Hotel.

After dinner, the AHI Hoosier Travelers group was offered a viewing of the film "Rob Roy," in the theater at the hotel, and I watched a few minutes, but was too sleepy to stay long. Besides, it didn't show much promise. Instead, I went looking for a hotel housekeeper. I had been trying to secure a rubber mat for our bathtub. It was very slippery, and I thought I might have a chance to catch one of the housekeepers in the evening.

Snapshots

Mary Queen of Scots

On Saturday morning we started the day with another lecture by John Harrison, and he was just wonderful! We covered the Stuart dynasty, Mary Queen of Scots, and Bonnie Prince Charlie. The name "Stuart" started with a man called "Walter the Steward," which then became Stewart, which was in turn changed to Stuart by Mary, Queen of Scots, who preferred the French spelling. Mary must be one of the most tragic figures in all of history. She became Queen of Scotland at the age of one week, spent much of her adolescence in France, and should have stayed there. Instead, she came to Scotland, and because of one problem after another, spent much of her remaining life in a series of prisons, and was finally executed by Queen Elizabeth. (Harrison referred to Queen Elizabeth as "the original power dresser.")

The town of Stirling figures very prominently in the story of Mary, Queen of Scots. The town walls were built in the 1540's, and Mary both lived and was imprisoned, at various times, in Stirling Castle. In 1558, with Elizabeth on the throne, and John Knox, the Protestant evangelist, in the pulpit, the issue of entitlement to the crown heated up. If it could be determined that Elizabeth was illegitimate, Mary would have a good claim; but she was Catholic, and partial to the French, which didn't sit well with the Protestant Scots or the English.

At the age of six, Mary had been sent to France to be married off to the son of the French King, Henry II, and Catherine de Medici. Married at fifteen, she was widowed when her young husband died less than three years later. She returned to Scotland and made a bad marriage with Henry Stewart, Lord Darnley, for whom she bore a son (James). Mary may have had too close an attachment to a handsome young Italian named Rizzio, and Darnley may have been unhappy about it. In any event, Rizzio was murdered in Mary's antechamber. Sometime later, Darnley himself was murdered, and Mary may have been complicit in that. Shortly thereafter, she married the murderer, the Earl of Bothwell. Many in the Scottish nobility became upset with her, and she was forced to flee for her life.

Mary tried to escape to England and naively went to Elizabeth seeking protection, but Queen Liz slapped her in captivity for 19 years, eventually having her head cut off. Maybe Mary had the last laugh: her son, James, was crowned James the Sixth of Scotland, and later also crowned as James the First of England, thus uniting the two crowns, and providing the "United Kingdom" that we know today.

Our lecturer, John Harrison, also talked about Prince Charles Edward, son of the exiled King James III, and known to history as "Bonnie Prince Charlie."

Charlie and his followers (the "Jacobites") hoped to regain the throne for the House of Stuart. In 1745, he landed in Scotland and raised an army to fight the English, came south through Stirling and captured Edinburgh, and started to proceed even further south, but eventually fell back to Stirling and took over the castle. The English laid siege to the castle, but the siege failed. In 1746, however, the English defeated the Jacobites at the Battle of Culloden Moor, which was followed by the savage slaughter of Scots by the English in the Highlands, and was the last land battle on British soil. By the end of the 1700's, Scotland was pacified and "content."

The Lochs

We were content also, this being a gray and chilly day, to don our sweaters and jackets, board our bus, and head for the "Bonnie Banks of Loch Lomond" which is 23 miles long, full of fish, picturesque and serene. On the way, we stopped the bus and climbed a hill to take a look at the Trossachs mountains and scenery. It was cool and dry, and we gathered for a group photograph. We journeyed on to Luss, a hamlet of 300 people, for lunch at the "Lodge on the Loch," built in 1992. This is "Rob Roy" country, and our guide, Babs, gave us more history as we walked through the village, marveled at the burgeoning flowers along the walks and surrounding every house, and took in the history and beauty of Loch Lomond.

It didn't take too long, after we left Luss, to arrive at Loch Katrine, a tranquil lake lying in the heart of the Trossachs. Today, it provides drinking water for the city of Glasgow, and no boats with engines are allowed, except for rescue ships and one tourist boat, the "Sir Walter Scott." Scott, the famous Scottish poet, was the author of "The Lady of the Lake," and this was the "Lake." Near one end of the Loch is Glengyle House, birthplace of Rob Roy MacGregor, also immortalized as "Rob Roy" in Scott's writings (and in the visually gratifying but otherwise disappointing movie).

We had a little time before our boat, The Sir Walter Scott, would set forth on our cruise of Loch Katrine. So I got in line at a small shop to buy an ice cream cone. A little girl in front of me came away from the window, tilted her cone, watched the ice cream fall on the ground, burst into tears, and went to the back of the line, with assurances from her father that she could get another one.

Once we had our ice cream, we got in line to board the Sir Walter Scott. Betsy and I were late getting onboard (waiting in line to buy ice cream), but Cliff and Elaine Shultz had managed to save seats for us. It was just as well, because the boat was packed and, once out on the water, the temperature dropped very noticeably. The tourists all put on their coats, but the Scots seemed quite comfortable in shorts and tee-shirts. The trip on the boat from one end of Loch Katrine to the other took about one hour. The weather was fine and it was a delight.

As our bus traveled from place to place, our guide, Babs, pointed out places of interest and gave us lectures on the history, culture, and people of Scotland. We saw one large, flat area along the side of the lake, where the clans gathered in the old days, wore their tartans, displayed their weapons, swore their allegiances, and competed in feats of strength (the precursors to the "Highland Games.") As we traveled back to Stirling, Babs played some music over the bus loudspeaker, inspiring and appropriate as it was the theme from the movie "Rob Roy." Before dinner, I walked into town and made reservations for Betsy and I, the Halls and the Shultzes, at Olivia's Restaurant for Monday night.

At dinner that night, there was general consensus that the hotel continued to provide unusually good meals, especially when taking into account that it was in a group setting. Stirling seems to have been made for walking, and after dinner, several of us went out for a stroll. Although it was rather cold outside, our hotel room, with the windows wide open, stayed just cool enough for comfortable sleeping.

A Scottish Sunday

Sunday morning was warm and sunny, and we walked uphill from the hotel, toward Stirling Castle, to the Church of the Holy Rude, a famous and historic Presbyterian Church. It was here, in 1567, that James (thirteen month old son of Mary, Queen of Scots) was crowned James the Sixth, King of Scotland, during a service at which John Knox preached the sermon. The Presbyterian Church is The Church of Scotland, but not many people go to church, Presbyterian or otherwise. Our guide, Anne Allman, told us that the Scots use their churches mainly for "hatches, matches, dispatches, and festivals."

The Shultzes and Halls joined us for church, together with Bob and Mary Jane Compton from our Hoosier Travelers group. I later learned that Bob was a fraternity brother in college with my good friend, Fort Wayne attorney Lindy Moss. After the service, we had an opportunity to chat with Rev. Coull, the pastor, and learned that he had lived in the United States and had served at a Presbyterian church in Atlanta, Georgia.

We returned to the Stirling Hotel in time for our first lecture on Scottish literature, by Professor Owen Dudley Edwards, born in Dublin, Ireland, but now a Professor at the University of Edinburgh. It would be appropriate to say that his dress, appearance, and demeanor were eccentric, ☺, but his knowledge of history and literature was astonishing. Thoroughly versed in Robert Louis Stevenson, Sir Walter Scott, and Bobby Burns, he could spout Lochinvar for several minutes at a time, and knew U.S. history as well as I did. He was a wonderful, entertaining speaker, although his politics are obviously bright red.

After lunch, Babs continued to educate and entertain us as our bus headed to the City of Perth, to visit Scone Palace (pronounced "Scoon"), the home of the Earls of Mansfield. Once again, we passed the Stirling Bridge, and the William Wallace Monument, now becoming a familiar sight, and the Royal Hotel, where Charles Dickens once stayed.

The day was truly gorgeous, and Betsy and I had our turn to sit at the front of the bus, and to talk with Babs and the bus driver, Roddie. In the United Kingdom, people drive on the left, and the driver sits on the right. Our driver, Roddie, was right in front of our seats. He had a chair that was on some kind of bellows that bounced up and down with every bump in the road, so that his head bobbed up and down as much as a foot or more, as if he were riding some great horse. Babs explained to us that this was intentional, and designed to protect his back by acting as a kind of shock absorber.

We traveled past the famous Gleneagles Resort and Golf Course, where a tournament was going on, and the day continued to dazzle us. The sky was brilliant blue, with Georgia O'Keefe clouds, and I remarked that Montana has nothing on Scotland when it comes to a Big Sky. As we drove, Babs told us that the real Macbeth wasn't such a bad guy. In fact, he had been a good king of Scotland for 17 years, and was killed by Malcolm, not out of revenge, but out of avarice. She thinks that Shakespeare gave Macbeth a bad rap. In my opinion, the whole history of Macbeth is too cloudy to be sure of what really happened; however, there can be no question but that Shakespeare took plenty of poetic license. Anyway, I'm glad that he did.

Perth is an "upmarket" town of about 42,000 people, with lots of shops, gray stone buildings, and showers of flowers. It sits abreast the River Tay, the longest in Scotland. In 1599, John Knox preached the Reformation here, and was instrumental in establishing the Protestant Church as a power in Scotland.

The Palace of Scone is very impressive, surrounded by marvelous grounds and gardens, and full of priceless antiques and history. Mary was crowned Queen of Scots here. The palace was awarded to David Murray, who became Earl of Mansfield, and his descendants, as a reward for helping King James the Sixth as an infant, protecting him from conspirators. The "Stone of Destiny" (which was known to us as the "Stone of Scone") was located here until 1296, when King Edward I took it to London to symbolize English domination of Scotland. It was returned to Scotland in 1997, and is now located at Edinburgh Castle. Scone Palace has an actual size replica on the lawn near the palace. (I told Babs that, while having tea in London, I had once been served a "scone of stone." She gave me a polite smile.) The present Earl and his family still maintain private apartments, but the main floor of the palace, and the grounds, are open to the public from April 2 until October 2 of each year.

We learned that Queen Victoria once came to visit Scone Palace. They spent two years preparing for her visit, and she stayed one night, leaving nothing behind except a pair of white gloves, which are still kept on display on the bed in the room where she and Albert slept.

Visiting these family estates is one of the best things to do in Britain. Taxes on property are heavy and, in order to avoid having to sell their properties, the owners put them into trusts which qualify as charities. As a benefit, the public gets to come and visit. All of them have at least one restaurant, and gift shop. I separated from our group a little early, in search of a cup of coffee, wandered into the gift shop, and found a large assortment of souvenirs tailored to families with Scottish ancestry. "Chapman" was among them, and I bought some coasters, refrigerator magnets and key chains, all with the "Chapman Coat of Arms."

Our last stop of the day was the Glenturret Distillery, where single malt Scotch Whisky has been made (often illegally) since 1775. It gets its name from its location, in the "Glen" of the Turret River. Although it still makes and distributes Scotch, it is now primarily a tourist attraction. We had a tour of the place, an explanation of how the liquor is made and bottled, and then were escorted to a large room for "tasting." Each chair had five glasses in front of it, and each glass had about one ounce of Scotch: Twelve Year; Fifteen year; Eighteen Year; "High Proof;" and Malt Liqueur.

A few of us drank all of the samples, some drank three or four of them, and most of us drank at least two. Afterward, our spirits were very high, to put it mildly. We gathered outside the gift shop, and I led a conga line back to the bus. We must have been pretty good, because some other tourists in the parking lot began photographing us.

On the trip home, our AHI guide, Anne Allman, talked about tips - what would be expected. The "recommended" tips, upon completion of the tour, were: £7 per person for Roddie, the bobbing driver; £11.5 per person for Babs; and £11.5 per person, to be divided among the hotel staff. This worked out to approximately $90 per couple. In the U.K., there are "pounds" issued by the Royal Bank of Scotland, but they are, in fact, interchangeable with British pounds.

Anne also told us that the movie *"Mrs. Brown,"* starring Judy Densch, would be shown in the hotel theater after dinner for those who were interested. Betsy and I had seen it, and it is a pretty good movie, about Queen Victoria after the death of Prince Albert, and her relationship with a Scotsman, "Mr. Brown." Anne also told us that on Wednesday, which is scheduled as a "free day," we would have the option of signing up for a tour to St. Andrews at an additional cost of £35 per person. The Chapmans, Halls, and Shultzes told Anne that the six of us had unanimously decided to sign up. By now, she was referring to us as "The Select Six." This was better, at least, than the moniker given our group by Fort Wayne attorney Dick Baach when the six of us were in Harrogate, accompanied also by Dick and Marcia Adams. Dick Baach had called us "The Gang of Eight."

After dinner, Cliff Shultz, Bill Hall and I decided to walk into the town of Stirling, where we found an ATM machine operated by the Royal Bank of Scotland, and I was able to withdraw (the daily maximum) of £200. Cliff also tried to withdraw money, but the machine told him he was using the wrong pin number. We went to a different bank and tried the machine there, but Cliff got the same news. The steep walk back uphill to the hotel, in the brisk Scottish night, prepared us for a good night's sleep.

Edinburgh

Monday was scheduled as an all-day excursion to Edinburgh, Scotland's main city. Betsy and I had been there in 1974, and enjoyed it immensely. It is still a treat. On the way, somebody referred to our "bus," and Anne Allman told them, in no uncertain terms, that it is a "coach," and not a "bus." A "bus," she said, "is the vehicle that stops at the corner to pick you up, and carries you into town."

The trip "by coach" from Stirling to Edinburgh Castle took about 1-1/2 hours. It was here that Mary, Queen of Scots, gave birth to James the Sixth (later to become James the First of England). He was born in the tiny room that we had seen on PBS in a video entitled "The Royal Mile." It refers to the one mile of highway in Edinburgh, leading through the center of the city up to the castle.

The castle is massive, and would be impregnable against medieval weapons. We spent quite a lot of time exploring it, including that "tiny room." Betsy's curiosity was even greater than mine. She kept exploring, while I went to the coffee shop, bought coffee and a Danish pastry, and found a seat outdoors in the sun. Our guides, Anne and Babs, and Roddie, the bobbing driver, got there ahead of me. I noticed that they had a routine. At each stop, they would "turn loose" the group, and then gather at the closest coffee shop. They would time their visit to the "loo" about three minutes before the next

Snapshots

scheduled bus departure. Since theirs was a routine born of experience, I decided that I would follow it also.

I still had time to check out the castle gift shop, where I found key rings for all birthdays. Mine said that people born on October 2nd had "good communication skills; are sometimes gullible, but can be trusted to keep a secret; and do not like to be 'pressurized'." There was also a list of celebrities born on that date, including Mahatma Gandhi.

When we left Edinburgh Castle, our coach returned down the "Royal Mile" to the University of Edinburgh for another lecture by the eccentric leftist, Owen Dudley Edwards, covering Scottish literature and politics from the Seventeenth Century to the present. We were ushered into a great hall, surrounded by busts of prominent Scots. One of them, Simpson, invented the use of chloroform for "midwifery." At the time, some doctors and clerics objected to the use of anesthetic during childbirth, saying that pain was a "natural and essential" part of the birthing experience. Within a short time, however, Queen Victoria gave birth, and insisted on using it, and after that, there were no further objections heard.

Other "famous busts" included Sir Walter Scott, Johnson's Boswell, and a physician named Watson, who was the model for "Dr. Watson" in the Sherlock Holmes novels. The Professor told us that we were not far from the Elephant Cafe, where J. K. Rowling wrote the Harry Potter books. He was quite outspoken in support of independence for Scotland, and raised an interesting question: If Scotland becomes independent from England, who gets the oil in the North Sea? On the subject of Scottish justice, he told us that Scottish juries have three options for verdicts in criminal cases: guilty; not guilty; and not proven. Otherwise, his message was highly political, and can be summed up as: "left is good - right is bad; Scots are good - English are bad."

After the lecture, we were taken to the Carlton Highlands Hotel, where we were served a very good lunch. Afterwards, having time on our own, Betsy and I walked with Bill and Suzanne Hall to Holyrood Palace, another former home of Mary, Queen of Scots, and still used as a palace by the British Royal Family. The Queen's private apartments are located on the third floor, but we were permitted to tour the "Royal Apartments" on the second floor. Betsy and I had tried to visit Holyrood Palace in 1974, but were not able to do so because, at that time, the Queen was in residence, and it was not open to the public. I promised Betsy that we would visit it on our next trip to Edinburgh and, as you can see, I was as good as my word.

This was a "bank holiday" in Scotland, so there was no *Herald-Tribune* for purchase. This made no sense to me, since the *Herald-Tribune* is not published in Scotland, and I could see no reason why it would not be for sale just because of a local holiday. But it was not. Nonetheless, I was able to access a computer at the Crowne Plaza Hotel, where I used my Visa Card and obtained 15 minutes of computer time at a cost of £3. I checked my AOL e-mail, and sent a thank-you note to our friend Thomas Duermueller in Zurich. By way of "news," I was able to learn that Tiger Woods had won the NEC Invitational Golf Tournament, after a playoff with Jim Furyk; and that Sammy Sosa had hit two home runs as the Cubs beat the Cardinals.

On the way back to Stirling on the coach, bobbing Roddie played a CD on the sound system, the "Edinburgh Tattoo." On arrival, "The Select Six" headed into town. I had reserved a table at Olivia's Restaurant, in downtown Stirling, for that night. The food was only fair, and service was nowhere in evidence. Still, it was fun for the six of us to get out on the town and have dinner at a Scottish restaurant. It also made us appreciate the restaurant at the Stirling Highland Hotel. When we left Olivia's Restaurant, we walked further down the hill to the Royal Bank of Scotland, where I retrieved cash from the ATM machine. Both Bill Hall and Cliff Shultz were in need of cash for the expected tips, but neither were able to access the local ATM's. Accordingly, I became the "bank" for all of us.

That evening, when Betsy and I returned to our hotel room, I checked to be sure that our maid had, as requested, left the rubber mat in our bathtub. There were no "grab bars," and no "friction strips" on the bottom of the tub, so it was really dangerous. We had learned to open the bathroom door before getting in or out of the tub, because the doorknob gave something to hold onto, and provided balance. Sure enough, on Tuesday morning, we learned that Cliff Shultz had slipped and taken a fall out of the tub and onto the floor of his bathroom. To his relief and amazement, as well as the rest of us, he did not suffer any great injury.

The Highlands

Tuesday began early, with an 8:00 a.m. departure by coach for the Scottish Highlands. The ultimate destination was the City of Inverness, far to the north, but the real point of the day was the trip itself, riding through the spectacular Highlands scenery. Our guide, Babs, provided commentary as we traveled along, and our first stop was only one and a half hours after we departed; however, it was a really neat stop, in the village of Tyndrum. There is an establishment there, apparently created for tours and large groups, called "The Green Welly Stop at Tyndrum." Its symbol is a large, green Wellington boot.

There was a very good restaurant, another area serving lighter food, a

Snapshots

large souvenir shop, a newsstand with all of the current magazines and papers, a section selling candy, toiletries and sundry items, an "outdoor" shop with mountain climbing, hiking, boating and similar equipment, and, finally, an area devoted to fine Scottish woolens and other apparel, as nice as we had seen anywhere in Scotland. After a snack, there was heavy-duty shopping, and I purchased a blue woolen sweater. I would also have bought a small, cut-glass decanter and matching glasses, except that the clerks told us they could not be shipped because of possible breakage. (I think they are missing something here. Betsy and I once purchased a very fragile decorative bowl in Delft, Holland, and had it shipped home with no problem.) During the conversation with the clerks, we learned that "Whisky" is what Americans call Scotch. "Whiskey" ("ey" on the end) refers to Irish Whiskey. American whiskey is not spoken of.

The Highlands scenery was breathtaking, and Babs continued educating us about the history of Scotland, occasionally pointing out a historic locale where one clan slaughtered another at various times in the past. At one spot, Glencoe, the Campbells pretended to be house guests, and then conducted an underhanded attack on the MacDonalds. It was an episode so scurrilous that most of the MacDonalds left Scotland and came to America to establish restaurants.

At Rannoch Moor, we had a chance to get out of the coach for a photograph opportunity, and marveled at a lone hiker trudging through the wilderness in the distance, pack on his back. Babs told us that the Scottish flag is the St. Andrews Cross, white on a blue field. But they also seemed to have another flag, the red "rampant lion," on a yellow field. We learned that the thistle is emblematic of Scotland because barefoot Vikings, attempting a sneak attack on sleeping Scots, stepped on thistles, and their outcry alarmed the Scots and saved them.

Lunch was served at a woolen mill at a place called Spean Bridge. Nearby, we passed the monument at the "Well of the Seven Heads," where seven decapitated heads were once displayed. Scotland does, indeed, have more than its share of blood and guts.

We reached a place named Fort Augustus, at the southern end of Loch Ness. There is a canal there joining two lakes, by means of a series of locks. (The locks between the lochs?) Mainly, we spent an hour walking around in the rain, wondering why we were there. I later figured out that we were killing time so that we would not be too early for our train from Inverness, returning to Stirling.

As might be expected, our guides had a considerable spiel about the Loch Ness Monster and, as we drove along the edge of Loch Ness, we were all told to keep a careful eye out in case she appeared. Along the banks, we stopped for a "long distance view" of Urquhart Castle, a ruined medieval castle that was presently inaccessible (except on foot) because of construction of a new visitor center. Under better conditions, the group would have gotten off the coach and walked downhill about one half mile to see the ruins; however, it was raining hard, and there was a unanimous vote to skip it. As a result, we drove directly on to Inverness, and arrived with one hour to kill before the departure of our train.

The weather was not conducive to exploring Inverness; however, we really had no grounds for complaint. This was the only day that we had noticeable rain during our week in Scotland, and Scotland is known for its rain. The Royal Highlands Hotel, a pleasant place, is next to the railroad station, and we found a table where we could sit, order hot chocolate, and pass the time.

The railroad station was spartan, and there were no American newspapers for sale, which I thought was unusual for a railroad station. An indication of the typical weather in Inverness could be seen on a permanent sign outside a coffee shop that says, "Come in, have a coffee, warm up."

Ours was the 4:50 train called "Inverness to Glasgow," and Stirling was scheduled as the eleventh stop. As soon as the train left the station, it stopped for no apparent reason. The voice of the conductor could be heard over a loudspeaker, but it was unintelligible. The train sat there for *over an hour*, and we eventually learned the reason: someone had started to run across the railroad tracks in front of the train, and then darted back safely to the side; the train engineer was unnerved by this, and declared himself "unable to continue;" under union rules, he was entitled to go home for the day, and the train had to sit there until a replacement engineer could be brought in.

There was a food cart that came down the aisle, but ours was the last car on the train, and by the time the man with the cart got to us, he had nothing left except peanuts, orange juice, and shortbread. It was a long time until dinner.

St. Andrews

Wednesday was to be the last day with our Indiana University tour in Scotland, and "The Select Six" had all signed up to go to St. Andrews, rather than spend a free day in Stirling. This was a day off for the AHI guides, Anne and Babs, and also our driver, Roddie the Bobber. There were about 20 of us on the St. Andrews trip, and we were introduced to a guide-for-the-day, Christina, and a new driver, Sandy. (For some reason, Sandy did not seem to bob as much as Roddie did.)

En route to St. Andrews, Christina picked up where Babs left off, with history and humor. "Scotland," she said, "has nine months of winter and three months of bad weather." In the old days, the town of Stirling had been on the route of an annual cattle drive, and every year farmers drove approximately 30,000 head of cattle right through the town. In order to get to market, they had to cross Stirling Bridge, which was a toll bridge in those days, and was referred to by the town fathers as "a fine earner." We passed through the town of Dollar, and I only mention it because it looked very prosperous and attractive, and would be well worth a visit on another trip.

We made a comfort stop at the "wee village of Falkland," with immaculate homes, multitudes of flowers, and (this day at least) sunshine. There was time in Falkland for a walk, and I bought some bottled water at a little shop. We passed a house with a fenced-in yard, and a large collection of exotic birds. The owner of the house came out to talk with us, and explained that he raises "show pigeons." Apparently, it is strictly a hobby, and he earns no money from this. Although Falkland seemed like a delightful place, Christina told us that most residents commute to jobs in larger cities, since they "cannot make a living in Falkland."

The road took us through idyllic lowlands countryside, dotted with sheep and cattle, and attractive little farms. We also passed Loch Leven. There is a castle on an island in the middle of the lake, and Mary, Queen of Scots (bless her heart) was once a prisoner there. While there, she had been forced to sign papers abdicating her crown in favor of her son, James the Sixth. Later that same afternoon, she miscarried twins fathered by her third husband. It was said that, "she began the day badly, and then it fell away."

After seeing it on television on many occasions, it was great fun to see "Royal St. Andrews," which includes five golf courses, where golf has been played since the 1350's. We visited the Old Course Hotel, and walked along the Old Course fairways on Holes Number 17 and 18, where we observed a few foursomes as they hit their shots.

After a short walk into town, we found "The Doll's House," a restaurant that had been recommended to us by our guide, Christina. Sure enough, it was a lively place, with friendly Scottish service, and good food. Judy Bauman, a member of the IU group who now lives in Minnesota, joined "The Select Six" for lunch.

Next, we stopped in a bank where I obtained £100 from an ATM, and then got 10 one-pound coins from the bank teller. This must be a rather common request, since she had a drawer full of little plastic bags, each bag containing ten one-pound coins.

We visited the cemetery and the ruins of the ancient cathedral, and Bill Hall and I set forth to climb the tower. Unfortunately, there was a turnstile in the doorway, and one could not pass without inserting a token. We had no idea where one might purchase such a token, so we gave it up, and all strolled back into the city to explore the shops. Nowhere is a town so devoted to anything as St. Andrews is devoted to the game of golf. Shops in great abundance sell everything imaginable related to golf, and nearly everyone on the streets is dressed for golf. Bill and I found a place that sold ice cream cones, bought one, and then later found a place with an ice cream cone machine. The machine made and sold cones, and also talked to you when you bought an ice cream cone from it.

We visited the Golf Museum at the "Old Course," and bought some souvenirs, and then prepared for our trip back to Stirling. I had brought along a box of *Sprungli* "pralines" that our friend Thomas Duermueller had given us before we left Zurich, and we passed them around. There were just enough for everyone on the coach to have one. There was a short stop in the town of Dundee, where we saw Scott's ship, "Discovery," and marveled at how wide the River Tay is at this location. Returning, we passed one last time the view of Stirling Castle, on a promontory in the distance, and the Wallace Monument, now familiar but still dramatic sights. These sights were perhaps more dramatic now that we knew something about them.

That night, AHI conducted a "graduation ceremony" before dinner, and Anne Allman gave each of us our "diplomas," together with individual bookmarks with "Scotland" written on them. Each of us then was called to the front of the group to describe our "high point of the trip." Betsy said that her high point was the opportunity to visit Holyrood Palace, in Edinburgh, after waiting 27 years to do it. When my turn came, I said that Holyrood Palace was also my high point, after hearing Betsy talk about it for 27 years. Suzanne Hall was most impressed by the beauty of the Highlands, while Cliff Shultz said that the high point, for him, was when he spotted the Loch Ness monster. He was the only one who saw it.

Finally, the entire group lined up along the wall with a sign that read "Hoosier Travelers," and had a photo taken. Anne Allman did the photography, and she had to take pictures with about fifteen cameras, since so many people in the group wanted one. After another good meal, we returned to our rooms to pack for departure next day, and I was relieved to get through one last shower without falling out of the tub.

On to London

It was Thursday, the 30th day of August, 2001, and we got another opportunity to experience Scotland's famous rain. Most of the Indiana University group got up early for a bus that took them to the airport in Edinburgh, for a flight back to the United States. Betsy and I had the luxury of a later start, and were picked up at Stirling Highland Hotel at 9:30 by our old friend, Bob McLauchlan. He drove us to Edinburgh in ample time for our 11:30 train, but we would have been at sea in figuring out what to do, had it not been for Bob. He parked, and left us in the car while he went to find a "trolley," then loaded our luggage and led us to the first class lounge. (In Europe, the difference between a first class and a regular coach railroad ticket is not all that much, and is well worth it, especially if you are traveling any distance.)

The lounge was very attractive and clean, and certainly would rival the customer lounges that airlines maintain at airports. A hostess met us, found us a table, and brought tea, coffee and cookies. Later, she arranged for a porter to get us, handle our baggage, and take us to our train. On the way to our coach, we passed a luggage car, and the porter gave our bags to a man in charge, who gave us baggage claim checks, again, just like on an airplane.

We had reserved "places" (not "seats"), and they were very comfortable, with a table between us. As soon as the train left Edinburgh, a young lady in a uniform came by offering tea and coffee, and gave us menus which described the food that would be available should we choose to eat lunch "at our places." The conductor was also a woman and, when she came by to collect our tickets, told us she could book us for lunch in the restaurant car at 1:00 p.m.

One becomes spoiled with trains in Europe. We relaxed to enjoy the ride, and I perused my current copy of the *Herald-Tribune*. News items included: a boat full of refugees from Afghanistan was anchored off Christmas Island and the Australians were refusing to allow them entry, nor would Indonesia; the U.S. Open Tennis Tournament was underway, and the British press was full of stories about local boy Tim Henman; and, the stock market still was in decline, with the Dow Jones Industrial Average down to 9919, and the NASDAQ at 1791. One article discussed the fact that the European Community would begin using the Euro on January 1, 2002. The design of the new Euro Notes had just been announced, and the *London Times* was highly critical, saying that the new designs are "dull" and "soulless." The 500 Euro Note, they said, "displays what might be a block of council flats." (The English, you may recall, elected not to adopt the Euro.)

After a pleasant lunch in the restaurant car, we arrived at Kings Cross Station in the heart of London, and calculated that the entire journey from Edinburgh had required four hours and thirty minutes. As soon as we stepped off the train, a porter popped up and called us by name, advising that he would help us obtain our luggage and get us into a taxi. Once he had loaded our bags onto his cart, he took us to a side entrance of the station "to avoid the queue," where we hired a taxi and set forth to the Stafford Hotel.

We had been to the Stafford before, and hope we will go again. It is quiet, small, pleasant, and has one of the best locations in London. The concierge recommended Green's Restaurant, which was an easy walk, and a good recommendation. On the way back to the hotel after dinner, it began to rain, but Betsy and I had our umbrellas, and we just walked through it, doing our own rendition of "Singing in the Rain."

The Tate Modern

On Friday morning, we walked to the underground station and bought all-day transit passes for £4 each. We then took the tube from the Green Park Station to Southwark on the Jubilee Line, and from there walked to the Tate Modern, an "art gallery" that is affiliated with the original Tate Gallery. It was once a great warehouse, located along the River Thames, and has been totally renovated. The top floor has a large open space with a fine view across the river, with St. Paul's Cathedral in the background. We went there first, found the coffee shop, and secured a table by the window. From there, we could see the new pedestrian footbridge that would someday serve the Tate Modern from the other side of the river, but "someday" seemed to be a long way away. The bridge was supposed to have been finished in time for the celebration of the Millennium, but "it started to sway." They are still working on it. Nearly all of the art that is on display at the Tate Modern is total rubbish. If it were taken out of the gallery and put up for sale in a flea market, they would wind up throwing most of it out. I doubt there would even be an attempt to sell it.

The building itself is interesting, however, and is worth one visit in order to see the architecture. The artist Juan Munoz created an enormous sculpture at the entrance, utilizing a series of elevators ("lifts"). He had died unexpectedly the week preceding our visit, so the "lifts" were not operating "as a tribute to his memory." Doesn't that seem backward? Wouldn't he have preferred that they be operated, as a tribute to his memory?

We left the Tate Modern in the rain, and passed the newly restored Globe Theatre. We debated whether or not to go in for a tour of it, decided against, and walked on across Southwark Bridge to the Mansion House tube station. Since we had our raincoats and umbrellas, we only got soaked from the knees down. I bought the Friday *Herald-Tribune* at the tube entrance, and we caught a train back to Green Park, and then went for lunch at Richoux, one of a chain of tearooms done in Victorian decor, with passable English food. We had soup and "rarebit," which came with a salad.

I decided to go all out, and have "elegant rarebit," which meant that it included grilled tomatoes and bacon, which I shared with Betsy.

Snapshots

The Stafford is not too far from the Ritz Hotel, and across the street from it, on Piccadilly, is Boots, the chemist. It is good to know about Boots. Their stores are scattered all over London. The lower level sells sandwiches and other snacks, offers film processing, and has a public loo. We went there to leave our disposable camera to have the film developed. There was time to stroll through the high-rent district: Tiffany, Laurent, Vuitton, etc., and the Burlington Arcade. It was an area we had visited 25 years ago and had not been back since.

Mamma Mia

Returning to the Stafford, we found a hotel computer, and were able to pick up our e-mail, and send a few messages of our own. We had a small meal in the bar at the hotel (we split a club sandwich), and then left by taxi for the Prince Edward Theater. We had tickets to see *"Mamma Mia,"* with an 8:30 curtain.

The Theater District was a terrible zoo, with crowds of people spilling out of bars, others drinking on the streets, drunks all around, an insufferable din. Our taxi crept through the traffic, and the shoulder to shoulder pedestrians, including many who were homeless, some on drugs, shady types of all kinds, in an atmosphere of porno shops, and general sleaze. We remarked that it was even worse than Times Square had been before Rudy Giuliani became Mayor.

The theater was huge and sold out. *"Mamma Mia"* is a musical based on the songs of the rock group ABBA, four Swedes who were popular in the 60's. About half the crowd seemed to be cult followers of ABBA, and they ate up the show. But the fact is, it is a good show, and the music is a lot of fun. The cast for this production was pedestrian and the music was amplified to such a level that we stuck Kleenex in our ears. But, the ultimate compliment, I bought a CD of the original cast recording on the way out.

After the show, the chaos in the Theater District was worse than ever, it was hopeless to try to find a taxi, and we decided to walk back to the Stafford. On Shaftesbury Avenue, a young drunk tried to grab my cap, and then pointed and yelled at me, but when I glared at him he just turned around and walked away. Other than that, the walk back was uneventful.

A Good Day in London

We enjoyed sleeping in on Saturday morning, and having a pleasant breakfast in the Stafford dining room, where we read the *London Times*. We had received a phone call from our friends, Jean and John Campion, and made arrangements for them to pick us up on Sunday for an excursion.

Howard L. Chapman

Neither Betsy nor I had ever toured Buckingham Palace. I am not sure just how long there have been public tours there but, in any event, we had never been. One can secure tickets in advance at £9 per person, and we got tickets that would let us enter at 11:45. That gave us time, before entering, to watch The Changing of the Guard in front of the palace, which is still a dazzling spectacle, and which still attracts enormous crowds every day.

It seemed as though the line of people waiting to enter the palace was endless, but we got in rather quickly. It was fun for Betsy and me to go through the Art Gallery, because that had been the scene of the play "Single Spies," starring Prunella Scales, which we had seen in London some years ago. (Ms. Scales, in the role of the Queen, engaged in a dialogue on art with the actor playing Anthony Blount, the notorious spy.) The palace is beautiful, and well worth a visit. We learned that it is now open for two months during the summer, and closed for the rest of the year. On our prior trip to London, we had gone through the Queen's Gallery, a separate art gallery that is attached to the palace, but it was now closed for renovation and expansion.

All of this tourism, of course, helps to cover the freight that the people of England pay in keeping up the royal family. Thinking to do our part, we stopped for a while at the palace gift shop, but did not buy anything. Nearly everything that was for sale had "Buckingham Palace" printed on it.

After leaving the palace itself, a visitor is permitted to walk through the extensive gardens outside, and we marveled at the giant holly bushes that were several times taller than we were. We thought of our friends, Suzanne and Bill Hall, who are such inveterate gardeners. They should see these holly bushes.

A taxi took us to Fortnum and Mason, a London tradition. It is a large store with some of the most interesting inventory that one can find anywhere. There are two or three restaurants, but the best one is the Patio Restaurant, where one can look over the main floor of the store, and watch all the activity, while having lunch. When we finished, we spent about 30 minutes exploring the place, including its spectacular deli section. The deli includes, among other things, such items as Scotch Eggs and Apple Pork Pie.

The weather was good, so we decided to take a walk. First, we went down to St. James' Palace (residence of the Prince of Wales), then into St. James' Park (pausing to listen to a brass band), then on to Buckingham Palace, and around the circumference of Green Park, and back to Piccadilly. We stopped at a shop called "Poet et Manger" (must be French), and bought sandwiches and fruit drinks to carry back to the Stafford for dinner. There was time for a little nap, a chance to update my journal, a review of the *Herald-Tribune*, and even a check of e-mail on the hotel computer.

Snapshots

We arrived at the Duke of York's Theater for a 7:30 curtain, to see something Irish called "*Stones in His Pockets*." I cannot describe whether it is a comedy, a drama, or simply somebody's bad dream. Once inside, I realized that we had been to the Duke of York's Theater before, and it is a fire trap. You walk down from the street level, two narrow flights of stairs, to a theater that has no air conditioning. The play featured two male actors, who assumed multiple roles and, I think, had Irish accents.

Again, there was no hope of finding a taxi after the play, but walking back to the hotel was not such an attractive option. England had just beaten Germany in a World Cup soccer match, and the streets were full of obstreperous, drunken soccer thugs. We ducked into the Leicester Square underground station, and got a train back to our hotel.

The Campions

At 10:00 o'clock on Sunday morning, our friends John and Jean Campion, collected us at the Stafford, and we set off in their car for Cliveden. This day, September 2, 2001, was the 5th anniversary of the death of Princess Diana and Dodie Fayed, whose father owns Harrod's Department Store. When we passed Harrod's, all of the window displays had been taken down and replaced by wreaths of white flowers on plain green fabric, and huge piles of fresh flowers had been strewn along the sidewalk, in commemoration of their (or at least Diana's) death.

I am always glad to have John Campion doing the driving when we are with them in England. Driving on the left seems to get more daunting with age. It was not easy to find Cliveden, but John was a good navigator and, after a drive of about an hour, we arrived. We left the car in the "Car Park," and walked approximately ten minutes through the gardens to the main house. Since the sky looked ominous (and it was England), we carried raincoats and umbrellas with us. We came to a glass building housing the Conservatory Restaurant, which offered coffee "and." The four of us sat down at a table to pore over our guidebook and maps of the grounds of Cliveden.

Betsy and I met the Campions for the first time in 1985, when we came to England to attend the annual meeting of the American Bar Association. The ABA and the London Bar Association had "matched us" with them, and we have been wonderful friends ever since. Sitting at the little restaurant gave us a chance to catch up on what had been happening in our respective lives, and those of our children and grandchildren.

"Cliveden" derives its name from the great chalk cliffs over the Thames River along the West side of the property (Cliv-den is pronounced as in "shiver"). It is a grand estate that has been the home of various families among English aristocracy, beginning in the late 1600's. In 1942, Waldorf, 2nd Viscount Astor, presented the buildings and grounds to the National Trust and, since 1984, Cliveden House has been operated as a hotel. The Viscount was married to an American woman, Lady Nancy Astor, the first woman to sit in the British House of Commons. She was often quoted in her day, once saying, "I married beneath me. All women do." When invited to one of her parties, Winston Churchill asked how he should come. "Why don't you come sober, Mr. Prime Minister?" she said. The family maintained connections to the United States, as is evidenced by the hotel in New York City, known as "The Waldorf-Astoria."

There are a series of gardens, each with its own character, featuring roses, topiary, statuary, water gardens, a formal parterre, and walks through the woods, or along the banks of the river. The present house, which is the third on its site, was built by the architect, Charles Barry, for the Duke of Sutherland in 1851.

We strolled around the vast grounds, and wound up at the main house, now a hotel and dining room. The buildings are reserved only for guests of the hotel, although visitors can purchase National Trust Tours and obtain a tour of some of the house. Those with restaurant reservations qualify as "guests." Since John Campion had made reservations (weeks in advance) for lunch at the restaurant in the main house, we were able to have the run of the place, until the time that our reservation came up. We enjoyed a very elegant, very tasty and very expensive meal there. After lunch, we moved to the "Great Hall" for coffee, followed by more strolling about the gardens, including a marvelous view over the Thames River from the famous cliffs.

We motored back to the Campion's home on the edge of Richmond, had more time to talk, and to see their very English and very pleasant garden. Jean fixed what she called "a light meal," and then John drove us back to the Stafford. I was astonished that he could do it in 30 minutes! The Campions technically live in London, but it is about as far out on the edge of London as one can get, and they think of themselves as living in the village of Richmond.

Home

Monday, our day of departure, was Labor Day in the United States, but just another Monday in England. We arrived in plenty of time to check in for our American Airlines flight back to the States. It had been fun. We preceded, by eight days, the attacks on the World Trade Center and the Pentagon.

Chapter 16

Shamrocks

Patsy

This was our second trip to Ireland with Patsy Malone. Patsy has a travel business that she started in 1996 for the purpose of taking American tourists to Ireland, and showing them *Ireland Behind the Scenes*. It would be tempting to break here and write a biography of Patsy, but that will have to wait for another occasion. Suffice it to say that she is a *grande dame* in every good sense, and a very amazing lady. During our first trip with her, in 2004, we had spent some time in Dublin, and other places in central Ireland, and the rest of the time in the northern part, including the six counties which continue to be a part of the United Kingdom. This time, we would revisit Dublin and some of the other areas in the central part, and also some new areas in the south. Our long time and wonderful friends for many years, Dr. William Hall and his wife, Suzanne, were going to be on the trip with us.

We flew on Aer Lingus, the Irish airline, with a nonstop flight from Chicago to Dublin, leaving on August 23, 2006. Airline service between Chicago and Fort Wayne, Indiana, has become so unreliable that it made sense to drive from Fort Wayne to Chicago to make the flight, and for this purpose we enlisted the help of Bill Weber, who had a van large enough to take all four of us and our luggage. On the way, we stopped in Chesterton, Indiana, and Bill purchased an "I-Pass," which is a transponder that allows the vehicle to pass through all the toll gates in Indiana and Illinois without having to stop and pay. The transponder cost $10.00, and there was another $40.00 to buy an allotment of "tolls." As often seems to be the case, traffic was at a standstill on Interstate 294, with several long waits, but we still managed to get to O'Hare Airport in ample time, followed by a smooth check-in with Aer Lingus.

There had been a recent terrorist plot discovered in Great Britain, which involved the use of liquid explosives to be smuggled onto airplanes. It was the intention of the terrorists to destroy ten airplanes traveling from London Heathrow to the United States. As a result, a new security rule had gone into effect which prohibited any "liquids or gels" in carry-on baggage. This meant that passengers could not carry on a bottle of water, a stick of deodorant, or a tube of toothpaste. Laptop computers, cell phones, electric razors, and so forth, could still be carried on.

Once through security, we had time to kill in the "Premier Club Lounge," where we read the paper and talked over our itinerary for the coming trip. Bill, Suzanne and I all took "Airborne," which is a tablet, dissolved in a small amount of water, and then drunk, like Alka-Seltzer, to ward off colds and other bugs encountered on airplane flights. It must have worked, because none of us caught a cold. (As it happens, Betsy did not catch a cold either, even though she did not take Airborne.)

The airplane left the gate at the designated moment of departure, was ushered into a long line of planes waiting to take off, and trundled slowly along for 1-1/2 hours before being allowed to leave. The pilot announced that this delay occurred because "the wind has shifted," and all the flights had to be redirected to other runways. With the delay, we arrived in Dublin at nine o'clock local time and were met by two very courteous drivers sent by Patsy Malone to fetch us, one driver for the Chapmans, and one for the Halls. Despite its reputation for chilly, wet weather, Dublin greeted us with clear skies and warm sunshine.

Driving into Dublin, we were impressed, once again, by all of the colorful doors on the homes and offices that we passed. Bright hues in every color you can think of. Our driver told us that there was great excitement over the upcoming Ryder Cup matches to be played in a few weeks at "The K Club" (Kildare Hotel and Country Club) on the outskirts of Dublin. Betsy and I had stayed at The K Club in 2004, and I had a chance to play the Arnold Palmer course, where the Ryder Cup matches would be played.

We arrived at the Merrion Hotel, which is blessed with a marvelous location. One can walk to many of the things a tourist comes to see. The hotel consists of four restored town houses, one of which was once the home of the Duke of Wellington, and contains one of Ireland's foremost collections of contemporary art. It is an absolutely first-class hotel, and Betsy and I had a pleasant suite, facing to the West. We discovered that Patsy had provided us with a bottle of Canadian Club Whiskey (for me) and a bottle of Beefeater Gin (for Betsy), a large bowl of fresh fruit, a box of chocolates, and a display of fresh flowers. The sun made the room warm, so we opened the windows to cool the room, showered, and took a much needed nap.

Being energized, we decided to venture out with two goals: find an ATM to buy some Euros; and, replace my electric adapter plug which had gotten broken in transit. In the lobby, I asked the concierge where I could buy a replacement for the adapter, and he reached down behind his desk, took one out and gave it to me. He said I could have it and keep it, with no charge! From there, we went around the corner, found an ATM, and bought a supply of Euros. I was again delighted by the fact that one can be in a foreign country, find a machine on the sidewalk, put a card in it, and be rewarded with local currency.

Returning to the Merrion, we went to the lounge and ordered soup, brown bread and coffee. At 4:00 o'clock, Bill and Suzanne joined us, and the four of us went for a walk. Stephen's Green is only a short distance from the Merrion, a perfectly lovely urban park, full of flowers in August, and well used by families at all times of the year. We made our way to Grafton Street, a pedestrian shopping area, crowded with people; saw the famous statue of Molly Malone; and then walked to Trinity College, but were too late to view the Book of Kells. During our walk, we passed the Shelbourne Hotel, once "Dublin's finest," but now closed and being completely renovated. We were told that the owners were quite disappointed that the renovations would not be completed in time for the Ryder Cup.

We and the Halls changed into finer clothes and made our way to the Penthouse Suite of the Merrion to meet our fellow travelers. The Penthouse Suite is difficult to access, and we had to go to the hotel lobby and have a staff person escort us there, which included a special key to operate the elevator that would take us. The suite has two stories, and as we entered on the lower level, Patsy Malone met us on the stairs, as radiant as ever, with big hugs for Betsy and me. The scene was repeated once we got upstairs when we met Chris Allen, the incomparable driver, guide and friend, who would once again accompany us.

We were introduced to Dr. and Mrs. Marshall Grunwald (Marty and Sandi) of Elmhurst, Illinois, and Mr. and Mrs. George Strong (George and Annsley) of LaCañada, California. We learned that the Grunwalds were also repeat travelers with Patsy. Next we saw Don and Rosalie Jordan, who had been with us on the trip with Patsy in 2004, and once again greeted old friends with handshakes and hugs. Six of the ten travelers would be going with Patsy for the second time which is a good endorsement, I thought. My first overall impression is that this trip is going to be a lot of fun, and this group is going to be very compatible. That turned out to be accurate.

The upper floor of the Penthouse Suite at the Merrion has a large balcony that looks out over the hotel courtyard and beyond, and we gathered there with champagne and canapés to watch the approach of evening. At 8:00 o'clock we went down to the restaurant, where a private room had been set aside for us. Called "Restaurant Patrick Guilbaud," after the owner, it is renowned for award-winning cuisine and service, and has two Michelin stars. There are no other two-star restaurants in Ireland. In fact, only approximately 1900 restaurants in the world have one star, only about 90 have two stars, and there are only some 28 of them with three stars.

Patrick Guilbaud himself came into the room, was introduced by Patsy Malone, distributed special menus for the event, and told us a little bit about the course of fare that evening. As the meal was served, he came in with each course in order to tell us a little bit about it, and to describe the wine that was being served with that course. Patsy gave each of the five traveling couples an engraved glass memento, commemorating the fact that this was the tenth anniversary of the founding of her company, *Ireland Behind the Scenes*. Then jet lag overtook me, I skipped dessert, and went upstairs to bed. Betsy came later, and told me the next day that I had missed a wonderful dessert; however, I think I would have fallen asleep in my chair if I had stayed. One problem with jet lag, of course, is that you wake up in the middle of the night and have trouble getting back to sleep; however, Ambien is a modern solution for that.

The following morning we were scheduled to walk a distance of less than a block, meet a Member of Parliament, and tour Leinster House, the Irish Parliament. We were to gather in the lobby at 10:00. I woke up at 7:00 o'clock, saw that Betsy was sound asleep, and decided I would nap a little longer. The next time I looked at the clock it said 10:00 a.m.!

I called the concierge in the lobby and asked him if Patsy was there which she was. She was gracious when I told her we were just waking up and would not make the Parliament trip. She advised us to go ahead and have breakfast and said she would collect us at 11:30 in front of the hotel. She also gave me Chris Allen's cell phone number so we could check up on them if we had any questions, or needed to reach them.

Breakfast came by room service, together with the current edition of the *International Herald-Tribune*. One cannot travel without it. The news was depressingly familiar: conflict in the Middle East, war between Israel and Hezbollah, and the formation of a U.N. peacekeeping force to patrol the border between Israel and Lebanon. It occurred to me that this had been the main topic of news during every trip abroad that I could remember.

Desmond Guinness

At 11:30, we met in front of the Merrion and boarded our private coach. There was lots of room as the coach seated 37, and there were only 12 of us, counting Patsy and Chris. Chris's seat was equipped with a microphone that allowed him to tell us things while he drove and, as we went on our way, he gave us bits of Irish history and pointed out points of interest, including the Guinness Brewery, the home and statue of Oscar Wilde, and large manufacturing plants of Intel and Hewlett Packard, which, between them, employ over 15,000 people.

Ten years ago the Irish government revamped its tax structure and passed several laws that were accommodating to business and, as a result, the country is booming. For decades, people have left Ireland for other countries, especially for America, in search of work. Now, they are moving back to Ireland because of the employment opportunities that are there. Predictably, there is some grumbling about immigrants who do not work, especially Nigerians. We observed that the Merrion hotel staff was from places as diverse as Lithuania and India.

We were on our way to the town of Leixlip, and Chris remarked at all the traffic. In particular, we went over a new "super highway," the M50, which, he said, has become a "big parking lot." Sure enough, trucks and cars were lined up as far as we could see in both directions, and barely moving.

Well into the town of Leixlip, we came to the stone archway over the gate indicating the entrance to Leixlip Castle, the home of Desmond Guinness. He is a descendant of the Guinness Brewery family, and his mother was Diana Mitford, one of the four "Mitford sisters" who were so well known during the early part of the last century. Desmond has snow white hair and electric blue eyes, is attractive, bright and witty, and really ought to have a biography of his own. He greeted us in the foyer with a choice of champagne or peach juice (or a mixture) and then invited us to the drawing room to see a slide presentation on his work on behalf of the Irish Georgian Society. He founded the Society some years ago for the purpose of acquiring and preserving great Irish houses of the Georgian Period and many of them have been saved from the wrecking ball through his efforts. One of them, Castletown (which we visited in 2004) was purchased by him in order to save it, and then given to the Irish Georgian Society. Renovation is "slow going" he said, because only private money is being used.

After seeing and hearing about the work of the Society, we were joined by Desmond's wife, Penny, and his son Patrick and family, who met us for lunch in the dining room. Desmond sat at our table and entertained us with his conversation on antiques, art, and architecture. At Leixlip Castle, he has hosted many celebrities, from Mick Jagger to Jackie Onassis.

The marvelous lunch included salmon, Irish potatoes, vegetables, and red and white wine. Dessert was an apple pastry accompanied by a dollop of clotted cream. Desmond has servants to tend the castle and serve the meals, and lauded his "cook" whom, he regrets, grows old (as does he and I, I thought to myself).

After lunch, we were given a tour of the castle and an opportunity to use "the facilities." I had noticed a book about Diana Mitford, with a painting of her on the book jacket. While poking around the castle I also saw the original of that painting and could not help but note that it looked as if she had been painted nude, and then had a few filmy lines added to give the suggestion of a gown. She had been, quite obviously, a stunning woman.

On the drive back into Dublin, we passed over Road M50 and it was still totally clogged with jammed traffic. I joked to Chris that I recognized one of the trucks that I had seen when we passed over it the first time.

Number 10

After rest and reconnoitering at the Merrion, we were off at 6:45 to "Number 10," a name which is derived from its street number. It faces the River Liffey and, from the street, does not appear to be remarkable at all. However, it has been superbly restored, decorated and furnished as an 18th Century Georgian town home. There is no sign to indicate what it is, simply the number "10" in gold numbers on the black door. It was built in 1745 for Lord Belvedere by architect Richard Castle, and was purchased in 1998 by John Lynch, the current owner.

Because he would be joining us at dinner and drinking during the evening, Chris Allen had recruited his friend, Vinny, to drive the coach. Vinny deposited us at the front door of Number 10 and, as we entered, we were greeted by three tuxedo-clad gentlemen who offered to take coats and umbrellas, and proffered champagne, cocktails or soft drinks. John Lynch soon joined us and began showing us the house and telling us about it. The first thing that strikes the modern visitor is the fact that this house is substantially lit by candlelight. Although it is fully wired for electricity, and has some electric lighting in places, most rooms are lit by candles. In one room I counted 40, and stopped counting. Even the chandeliers are lit by candles, just as they would have been 250 years ago.

The house contains an excellent collection of Irish antique furnishings and a mixture of classic, contemporary and modern art. As John Lynch took us through, it seemed that every painting, every piece of furniture, had a story.

Snapshots

Most items were antiques, except for several gorgeous rugs that John had made especially for each room.

When we entered the dining room, I kicked myself for not bringing my camera, because it was one of the most beautiful tables I had ever seen, easily seating the 12 of us. The meal was delicious, and the service was impeccable.

After dinner, Patsy asked all of us to go upstairs to a drawing room, where she had "a surprise." When we got there we found comfortable seating with coffee and sweets, and a lovely Irish soprano by the name of Naimh Murray. She is an attractive and cheerful blond, was wearing a green cocktail dress, and was accompanied by her brother, Ronan Murray, on the piano. She entertained us with a variety of music, including traditional Irish songs and modem selections. She has a legitimate soprano opera voice, and we were all bowled over by her performance.

Gardens, Houses and Theaters

On Saturday morning we were greeted by another lovely day and were off at 10:00 o'clock (a civilized hour) to visit the home and garden of Helen and Val Dillon. Helen Dillon is a well-known gardener and author of garden books, who hosts a weekly television show on gardening, and is said to be "the greatest gardener in all of Ireland." Their home and garden is a Mecca for visiting garden enthusiasts. Betsy and I had been there with Patsy in 2004, and I knew that Bill and Suzanne Hall would be delighted (they are avid gardeners).

We were met at the door by Val Dillon, Helen's husband, who led us into the house and gave us a brief history. Of course, all of us were peering out the picture window at the incredible garden outside, and eventually Val said, "Well, I seem to have run out of things to say to you," and took us out into the garden. He told us that the garden is maintained by three people: him, his wife, and a woman who comes by five days a week. The main thing, he said, is to constantly be "deadheading." At one point he reached over and picked a snail off a plant, saying, "Oh, you naughty boy." He dropped it on the ground, and stepped on it. He told us that he has killed about 30,000 snails in the garden over the years. Before we left, all of us had to visit the seashell bathroom, a bathroom in the house in which the walls and ceiling are totally covered by a variety of seashells, arranged in striking geometric patterns.

We traveled on to Woodbrook House near the town of Bray, and the home of Sir Marc and Lady Cochrane. It is an 18th Century house with 19th Century additions, and furnished with interesting art and antiques. A large former opera house on the grounds is now used for auctions and, we were told, there are antique auctions held there regularly. The Cochranes were not there to greet us, and we were met and shown through the property by Sir Marc's "secretary," who had also been the secretary for his father, and had worked for the family for over 32 years.

It was time for lunch, and we drove to the village of Glasthule, to find the small but popular seafood restaurant known as Caviston's. The restaurant is really tiny and only seats about 24 people, and because the food is so good, it is always full. They serve people at specified times and seatings, and Patsy had arranged for the 12 of us to have lunch. Glasthule is on the Irish Sea, and this day was celebrating a "cultural festival," with the result that the town was crowded. Chris left us at the door of Caviston's and then drove off to find a place to park the coach, returning to join us for a delightful lunch including oysters, prawns and crab.

Back in Dublin at the Merrion Hotel we rested, packed for the departure the next day, and I got on the hotel computer to check e-mail. I also looked at the local news from Fort Wayne to see what was going on at home. Betsy and I decided to skip dinner (after the large, late lunch at Caviston's) and instead ate some of the fruit and chocolate truffles that were in our hotel room.

At 7:15 we met Bill and Suzanne Hall in the hotel lobby and took a taxi to the Abbey Theatre for a performance of *"The Importance of Being Earnest,"* by Oscar Wilde. We have seen it before, and know the play. It was a dismal performance. The director apparently decided to rewrite parts of it, and to make his production unique, with the result that it was simply bad. Marty and Sandi Grunwald left at intermission; we, and the Halls, left during a break shortly thereafter. There are plans to build a new Abbey Theater, and to move the production company there, and a controversy exists as to whether or not to preserve the current theater building. In any event, they will have to do better with their plays. Betsy and I went there in 2004 and endured another stinker then. (The next morning we learned that the Jordans and the Strongs had gone to the Gaiety Theater to see *"Riverdance,"* and thought it was spectacular.)

County Kilkenny

On Sunday morning our bags were collected from our room and stowed on the coach as we left Dublin (and also the Merrion Hotel, sigh - it had been wonderful).

Chris drove us through Dublin, telling us about points of interest, and giving us a little history now and then, and ending at Phoenix Park, located on the outskirts of the city. The Dublin Zoo is located there, as is the residence of the President of Ireland (currently Mary McAlesse), and also the American Embassy. Chris advised that there is very little security at the home of the President of Ireland, lots of it at the American Embassy.

Snapshots

We also learned from Chris that this was a big day for Gaelic football, Dublin vs. Mayo, the winner to go to the championship game. This sport is enormously popular in Ireland and is something of a mixture of soccer, rugby, American football, and maybe parts that don't fit in any of those. Chris proudly displayed his cap, which said "The Dubs" on the front.

At the end of a long road in Phoenix Park we came to Farmleigh, a grand mansion located on an estate of 78 acres, and once owned by Edward Cecil Guinness, the first Earl of Iveagh. It was purchased by the Irish government in 1999, and is now used as the official residence for visiting heads of state, and for holding high level meetings of government. We were met at Farmleigh by a good-natured, rotund Irishman by the name of Dennis, who provided a private tour of the house, including the parts currently used by visiting dignitaries and not seen by public tours. The last official visitors were the Prime Minister of Japan and his entourage. We visited the bedroom he used, which is still furnished as it was 100 years ago, except that it now has a television set - and no chamber pot.

Chris Allen and Patsy Malone.

Leaving Farmleigh and Dublin, we drove for about two hours to the town of Kilkenny, a quaint and attractive town that was bustling, surprisingly so for a Sunday. I remarked that "dun" and "kil" appear in a lot of Irish names. Chris explained that "dun" is Gaelic for "castle," and "kil" is Gaelic for "church." We were to spend the afternoon in Kilkenny on our own, and Chris dropped us off in front of the castle. The castle was probably interesting, but we didn't go in. Betsy, Bill, Suzanne and I were hungry, and decided we had seen enough castles for the moment. Instead, we went across the street to a large, two-story building called "The Design Center," where, at Chris's direction, we found an upstairs restaurant, serving cafeteria style, with really good food and huge portions.

After eating too much (this was getting to be routine), we left the restaurant and browsed through The Design Center, where a variety of beautiful Irish crafts and goods were for sale, especially woolens, ceramics, and glassware. We resisted the temptation to buy something and instead strolled through town on the main street. Most of the shops were open and there were crowds of people. A man with a microphone was doing an imitation of Bing Crosby to raise money for a local charity, and seemed to be having some success.

When we left Kilkenny it was only a short drive to Thomastown and Mount Juliet Conrad, a lovely hotel located on a 1500 acre estate, overlooking the River Nore. It is a magnificent Georgian mansion, named by the Earl of Carrick for his wife, Juliana, also known as Juliet. Guests can entertain themselves with golf, fishing, biking, horseback riding, hiking, croquet or the spa. The hotel has thirty-two guest rooms, but very few with two beds. We specifically requested two beds and, perhaps as a result, found ourselves in a pleasant suite with a view across the river and meadows beyond.

Don Jordan, Bill Hall and I hurried to join Chris Allen at the hotel bar, adjacent to the golf shop, to watch the Dublin - Mayo "football" match. It was being played in Dublin, before a crowd of 90,000 fans, and was totally packed, as was this particular bar, with vocal fans shouting for both teams. We all had "a glass" and watched the second half which, unfortunately for Chris, resulted in a victory for County Mayo. It was interesting to see how good-natured the losing fans were, and Chris commented that it would be fun to be in County Mayo just then, where everyone would be "ecstatic."

I also checked, as a matter of interest, the cost to play golf at the Mount Juliet course: €64 for greens fees, €40 to rent clubs, and €45 for a cart. The euro, at the time, was worth US$1.28.

While Bill, Don, Chris and I were watching football, Betsy and the others were taken on a tour of the house and grounds at Mount Juliet Estate. Later, in our room, we sampled the wine, candy and fresh fruit that had been provided to us by the hotel, which tided us over until a late dinner at Kendal's Restaurant, located in the same building as the golf facilities. Unlike our dining experiences on this trip so far, food was no better than ordinary and the service was poor.

Nicholas Mosse

On Monday morning, another warm, sunny day, we decided to have breakfast in the hotel restaurant, and then left for a nearby small factory known as Jerpoint Glass. Once there, we met the owners, who told us a little bit about glassmaking, and took us into the factory where we watched glassware being made. I couldn't help but wonder if they could operate their business if they had been subject to OSHA. Their adjoining shop had an interesting assortment of their products, including paperweights, at a cost of €27.50 for a small one. We didn't buy any. Too much weight.

Shortly after leaving the glass factory, we pulled into the parking lot at Jerpoint Abbey, a ruined abbey now open to the public, and clamored around in it, taking photographs, and enjoying the gorgeous weather.

We proceeded to the Nicholas Mosse Pottery and Country Shop, near the town of Bennettsbridge. I confess that, when I saw this on the itinerary, I thought, *"Oh no, not pottery."* What a pleasant surprise it turned out to be! We met Nicholas Mosse, who founded the business from scratch, now employs 60 people, and ships his pottery throughout the world. He is most gracious, explained the pottery making process to us, and took us through the various production stages. Most interesting to me was the penultimate stage, where designs are applied using sponges—thus the name "sponge ware." (I assume that the final stage is the firing of the piece.) To my surprise, I found that I was very much interested and actually learned something watching a pile of clay be transformed into a gorgeous finished article.

On the second floor we discovered a very nice restaurant, and Patsy had reserved a table for all of us. She had selected a menu in advance, and we sat down and enjoyed a fine lunch served by very cheerful (as always) Irish waitresses. Later, in the shop below, I found myself purchasing several items of pottery to be shipped back home. Now that I am home and sit here writing this, I wish I had bought more.

Nicholas Mosse and his family live on a large estate called Kilfane Glen and Waterfall Garden, and we went there and were met by his wife, Susan Mosse, an old friend of Patsy Malone. (Patsy's connections in Ireland are astonishing.) Susan was on her way to an appointment, but she gave Patsy the key to "the cottage," and said we could go ahead and explore on our own. We entered acres of jungle and deep woods, with monster rhododendrons, a large maze with a circus mirror, a sprinkling of interesting sculpture, and lots of paths going in various directions. Patsy led us along one of them, down a steep hill, then up a steep hill, then down a vertical green spiral staircase to a cottage nestled at the base of a large waterfall. When the Mosses purchased

Howard L. Chapman

the property, they did not know that the cottage or the waterfall were there. A friend read about them in some archival source and mentioned it to Nicholas Mosse at a party. The cottage had been covered by growth since 1830. When they rediscovered it, it had simply been "abandoned."

The cottage and the grounds around it have been completely renovated, and it is now a very nice two-bedroom guesthouse, completely modem and with all amenities (and no shortage of tableware!). Patsy used the key to let us in and we explored the cottage. When we left, we used steppingstones to go across the creek and take a different path back to the coach.

We returned to Mount Juliet Conrad late. Betsy and I went directly to the golf shop and got putters and golf balls, and tested the 18-hole putting course. It is designed to send every putt into the water. Three putts on a hole is a good score on any hole, although I did make a hole-in-one during the course of the game. A little rain fell, but we kept playing. In Ireland, if you are going to play golf, you can't be worrying about a little rain, or, as the Irish say, "a soft rain." After about 12 holes on the putting course, we caught up with the Grunwalds and Patsy, but couldn't keep playing because we had agreed to meet Bill and Suzanne at Kendal's Restaurant for dinner.

Patsy had recommended that everyone go into Thomastown to eat on this evening, but no one did. We should have taken her advice. Instead, Betsy and I met Bill and Suzanne at Kendal's and once again, had a so-so meal.

When we got back to the hotel, I located a hotel computer and checked on our e-mail. We had been concerned about our good friend Ginne Christoff, who was having knee surgery at Mayo Clinic shortly after we left. We were glad to get e-mail messages from friends Pat Parker and Lee Vann telling us that Ginne was doing well. I was also able to obtain a hotel copy of the *International Herald-Tribune*, and learned that, despite a cease fire, Israel and Hezbollah continued to skirmish. France, who brokered the cease fire, had then balked at furnishing troops to enforce it; however, they received so much criticism for this that President Chirac had changed his mind and said that France would contribute up to 2,000 troops to the U.N. peacekeeping force. In other news, an American named Karr, apprehended in Thailand, claimed to have been the killer of Jon-Benet Ramsey ten years ago, but few people think he actually did it. There was much anticipation of the Ryder Cup, to begin at the K-Club on September 22nd, and American players had begun to arrive in Ireland. Tom Lehman was the American Ryder Cup captain.

We did most of our packing before going to bed, but were perplexed about what to do with the unopened bottle of wine that the hotel had given us on arrival. We finally decided that we would take it with us.

Snapshots

Ballymaloe

On Tuesday morning we left at 9:00 o'clock, early for us, on our way to the Village of Shanagarry, in County Cork, to visit the famous Ballymaloe Cookery School and Gardens. We drove for a couple of hours, through beautiful countryside, while Chris talked to us about the history of Ireland, and the background of the problems between the North and the South, which the Irish call "the troubles." At present, the two areas are at peace, but it is an uneasy peace. There seems to be little doubt that at least some of the more militant Irish nationalists are determined to unify the country and drive the British out, one way or another. Listening to the history, it is not hard to see why so much animosity remains.

At about eleven o'clock we made a stop at the pretty seaside town of Dungarvan, where we availed ourselves of the facilities at Lawlor's Hotel, notwithstanding a sign that said "Toilets for Hotel Guests Only."

We traveled on to the Ballymaloe Cookery School and Gardens. All of the buildings and grounds give the impression of being well maintained and in excellent condition. We entered through a very nice shopping area (and bought a couple of items, including a bib for our grandson Danny) and then continued into an open courtyard where a pleasant lady served us tea, coffee and a variety of pastries. She then showed us into the demonstration room/classroom where we met the owner, Darina Allen, whom I liken to the Irish version of Martha Stewart (without the scandals). She has written on cooking, has a television show, and has appeared in many countries on television. She also operates the cooking school which, during most of the year, has 58 students who come from all over the world. (Her website is: cookingisfun.ie.)

The demonstration room had seats for about 100 people facing a large cooking surface, and a mirror, placed above it at an angle so that the audience can see what is happening directly below on the stoves and cooking areas. Darina handed out recipes for the dishes she was about to prepare, and some other cooking-related information. She then prepared the meal while we watched, explaining as she went, and it was clear why she would be successful on television. She is pleasant, attractive, likeable and well-spoken. She started by making a loaf of soda bread, and I privately resolved to make some myself when we get home. The meal preparation lasted between 2 and 2-1/2 hours, during which time her husband, Tim Allen, snapped some photographs.

Patsy had come to Ballymaloe in the past with groups, but it had always been at a time when students were there and classes were in session. Because we came during a vacation recess, we had an opportunity to actually see Darina prepare a meal.

And here is the best part: after watching the preparation, we all adjourned to a dining room where, joined by Darina and her husband Tim, *we got to eat it*! It may have been the best meal we had in Ireland and that is saying a lot. Darina sat at our table and told us that her classes, comprising 58 students, usually represent a dozen or more nationalities and about 25% to 30% of them are men. They range from total beginners, learning to boil water, to professional chefs. There are dormitories "on campus," and about 85% of the students live there with the rest commuting. A twelve week cooking course cost €8,775, and dormitory accommodations could be included for an additional €115 per week (for a single room).

Darina Allen demonstrates cookery while preparing the lunch that we would later get to eat!

Indulge me while I tell you what was on the menu: White soda bread with scones of various kinds; pea and coriander soup; glazed loin of bacon (not properly named, in my opinion, because it was a very excellent pork dish); shanagarry pepper and tomato stew; scallion champ (which means mashed potatoes, only better); a summer green salad with Ballymaloe French dressing; and Cullohill apple pie.

After lunch, one of the staff members showed us around part of the grounds, where much of the produce used at the school is grown. They grow most of their own vegetables and also keep chickens, and thus get the

Snapshots

freshest of eggs. We learned that the daughter of Darina and Tim had been married a few days ago, there on the grounds, and workmen were still taking down tents, lights, and other items from the wedding. It must have been an enormous event, from the looks of things. Also on the grounds was a gazebo, the interior of which is lined with seashells in geometric patterns, created by the same woman that created the "loo" at the Helen and Val Dillon home in Dublin. We were told that most of the shells were obtained locally, although some had been brought in for special parts of the design.

We all agreed that the Allens, like Mr. and Mrs. Mosse, were genuinely nice people, happy to see us, and obviously fond of Patsy Malone.

Leaving Ballymaloe, we drove to the seaside village of Kinsale, where Patsy and her husband, Lou Malone, had once lived for a year. It is a "postcard town," with many fine restaurants and shops, but, apparently, not any particularly fine hotels. Patsy felt we should have the opportunity to see the town and we stayed overnight at Perryville House, which she described as an upscale bed and breakfast. We were met by the owner who immediately offered us champagne and helped get everyone settled in their rooms. The place was comfortable but very much in need of an elevator. Betsy and I had to climb up to the third floor. Fortunately, we are both athletes!

Patsy had arranged for us to have dinner at a restaurant known as "Fishy Fish Cafe," but they canceled our reservation for vague reasons. Patsy was perplexed and unhappy, but called a friend who owned another restaurant, "Toddie's," which is a very good place. We had a nice meal, a nice time, and a nice evening. Betsy and I, and the Halls, left at 10:30 to go back to Perryville House and go to bed. The others lingered on for about another hour.

Kenmare

Wednesday brought the first rainy day, this time for real. The rain looked like it would last for a long time. "Well," Chris Allen told us, "you wouldn't have all this green, would you, if we didn't have the rain. I mean, it just wouldn't be Ireland."

Anyway, we got our raincoats and umbrellas and walked into Kinsale, where I was able to buy the *International Herald-Tribune* and also *USA Today*. We strolled up and down a few streets, but it was too wet to do much more. The group convened at 11:00 and we set off into County Kerry. Because of the rain, Patsy offered a choice between a good, fast, but less scenic road or a bumpy, slow but scenic road. I said "less bumps," but others wanted bad road and scenery, and that view prevailed. There was a lot of rain and fog, and there were times when Chris complained about the visibility, or rather, the lack thereof.

Howard L. Chapman

We began going through some rugged country and the road was narrow and harrowing, with many steep drop-offs along the side. I did not remember that Ireland had such imposing mountains. Betsy, Bill, Suzanne and I discussed our memory of our trip to Inverness, Scotland, and remarked that this scenery was very reminiscent of that. Eventually, however, the weather cleared, and we got to see some of the fabulous views, including valleys, seaside, inlets and mountains. Sometimes all at once.

Eventually, we arrived at the town of Bantry, on Bantry Bay, for our scheduled lunch at O'Connell's Restaurant. Rain descended again, and we left promptly after lunch for the town of Kenmare, and our destination, the Park Hotel Kenmare. It is a grand old lady, very well kept, and lovingly furnished and maintained. Betsy and I had a large suite with a view over the estuary, and we invited Bill and Suzanne to come join us, both to see the view, and also to drink the wine that we had been carrying with us from Mount Juliet Conrad. We observed that the tide was out when we arrived, and a white boat in the estuary outside our room was resting on the bottom.

When we broke up, Betsy and I went to the golf shop and made a Friday tee time. Then, following instructions from the lady at the golf shop, we followed a path to a stone wall which had an opening big enough for us to slide through, and wander into the town of Kenmare. It seems that all Irish villages and towns have quaint streets, picturesque shops, an abundance of pubs, and cheerful, friendly people. We entered one of the shops named "Quill's," and I bought a golf shirt. I had not intended to buy a golf shirt, but they were selling these particular shirts for €9.90, and I couldn't resist.

That evening was a rare "coat and tie" night. At seven thirty we gathered in the hotel bar and met John Moriarty, the bartender, and Francis Bennett, the hotel owner, both of whom are (of course!) old friends of Patsy. "John pours a good drink," she told us, and she was right. In fact, he poured me such a "good drink" that I carried most of it with me into dinner and never did drink more than half of it.

The group was not scheduled to dine together that evening, so Betsy and I joined Bill and Suzanne Hall and entered the dining room at 8:00 o'clock, where we received a nice meal and had a chance to catch up on our respective impressions of the trip so far. Good food and good company. We were enjoying ourselves.

After dinner, I checked e-mail on the hotel computer, which I found to be located in a phone booth just off the lobby. I learned that our friend Ginne Christoff had left the hospital and was at a rehab center in Rochester, Minnesota; that one of the younger attorneys was going to leave our law firm; and that the Chicago White Sox were struggling to hold on to a wild card spot in the American League. That night, for the first time, I decided to sleep through without any Ambien, and got by okay, arising at 8:30 without the benefit of an alarm clock.

The Grandeur of County Kerry

The following day provided us with "Irish weather." In other words, it was intermittent mist - sun - fog - sun - rain - sun. When the sun was out in full force, it was hot, but that never lasted long. At breakfast in the dining room, we continued to be impressed by the quality of service at Park Hotel Kenmare. On this occasion, a delightful young waiter persuaded us to try "black and white pudding." I asked him what it is, and he said, "If I tell you what's in it, you won't eat it. But just try it, it's lovely." So we did, but I was neutral. It was okay, and might taste good if I was really hungry; except, at this point in the trip, I doubted that I would ever be hungry again. (I never had the courage to inquire as to the ingredients of black and white pudding.) We weren't scheduled to depart the hotel until 11:00 o'clock, which allowed for a pleasant, leisurely morning.

Soon after we left, we entered Killarney National Park, and were amazed at the natural beauty of the place. I would say that the scenery compares well with anywhere I have been. It does, of course, feature narrow roads with steep drop-offs. A woman coming in the opposite direction stopped her car, flagged us down, and told Chris that there had been "a crash" up ahead, and there would not be enough room for our coach to get past. Chris was polite and said, "Thanks, we'll chance it," and off we went.

There were sheep everywhere, including on the road, and it was simply necessary to avoid them. They had paint splotches on their backs and sides in various colors, which allow their owners to identify them. We also came across a herd of wild goats living along the side of a rocky hill. Eventually, we reached the site of the auto wreck, where a police car, ambulance and tow truck were all in evidence, with a long line of cars in each direction. For some reason, the policeman in the road waived us on and we got through without any time lost at all. The passenger side of the windshield on the wrecked car was badly cracked, and we hoped it had not been caused by the head of a passenger. The car had a big letter "L" in the windshield, which meant that the driver was a "Learner."

As we traveled on, the scenery continued to amaze me. We stopped at a place called "Ladies Viewpoint," which is so named because Queen Victoria and "her ladies" stopped there once to admire the view. Think about that for a moment - Queen Victoria was so important that they named a place simply because she stopped to look at the scenery!

Howard L. Chapman

Howard Chapman and Patsy Malone.

Within Killarney National Park is Muckcross House, located on Muckcross Estate, consisting of 11,000 acres. Like so much of Ireland, it was once owned by the Guinness Family, and is now owned by the Irish government. It is a huge house, with many interesting antiques and works of art, and a guide began to take us through; however, midway through the tour, Chris Allen, Don Jordan and I "bugged out" and went to the visitors' center. We just got there before a heavy rain started and were glad to find a comfortable place to sit down and enjoy a cup of hot coffee (Betsy and I had visited Muckcross House during our first visit to Ireland with Gene and Marcia Laker in 1979).

Even though it was raining hard when we entered the visitors' center, by the time twenty minutes had elapsed, the sun was out, and people were eating outside. Irish weather! We observed that there were a lot of crows on the grounds, very large birds, and "No Crow Feeding" signs among the outdoor tables. After their tour, the rest of our friends got there, and there was time for everyone to shop before we headed back, via a different route, to Kenmare. Betsy, Bill, Suzanne and I went walking into the town of Kenmare, visiting the shops and, of course, purchasing a copy of the *International Herald-Tribune*. Back at our hotel, we sorted out laundry, nibbled complimentary chocolates, and finished the wine that was left from the previous day.

Patsy had arranged for all of us to have dinner at "Packie's Restaurant" at nine o'clock in the evening; however, Betsy and I felt that this was later than we wanted to eat, and we advised Patsy that we would eat "on our own."

Instead, she contacted the owner of Packie's, a gentleman by the name of Martin Halliser, and arranged for us to go at 7:00, and to have his same menu, a "tasting menu," that had been prepared for our group. As usual, Patsy had gone the extra mile for "her people." On the way to Packie's, Betsy and I stopped in The Lime Tree Restaurant and made a reservation for us and the Halls for the following evening.

Packie's Restaurant turned out to be excellent. "Excellent" really isn't a sufficient adjective, but it will have to do. We had a marvelous dinner, and passed our friends on the street coming to dine as we were heading home - umbrellas up – looking forward to an early bedtime.

Golfers

Friday morning marked the first day of September, and we slept in (8:40!). During breakfast in the lovely dining room, Betsy discovered that she did not have her purse, and thought she had left it in the lobby the night before, hanging on a doorknob. Panic! I went to the office and made inquiry and, sure enough, they were holding it. Nothing was missing.

At ten thirty, Betsy left with Patsy, the Jordans, Grunwalds and Halls. Patsy had arranged both a minivan and also a car. The drivers of the two vehicles turned out to be husband and wife - newlyweds.

At eleven o'clock I joined Chris Allen, George Strong and Annsley Strong at the Kenmare Country Club, where we rented clubs and "trolleys." There were no riding golf carts (called "buggies" in Ireland), and you either carried your clubs or pulled them behind you on a "trolley." The greens fees were €45 and it cost 2 more euros to rent a trolley. The golf course is very hilly, with a lot of steep up and down climbs. The weather changed every ten minutes, including periods of mist and occasional light rain, but I was comfortable with a turtleneck shirt, a sweater, and, when it rained, a windbreaker.

We didn't keep score, and had a really good time. Maybe golf would be better if nobody ever kept score. Anyway, in reflecting, I would guess that Chris and I shot in the high 80's or low 90's, which wasn't bad, at least for me, considering some of the worst putting ever seen by mankind.

The Kenmare golf course scenery is marvelous. We would climb up a hill to the next tee and then look out over the fairway across water, sometimes with mountains in the background. On the fourteenth hole, a real squall blew up and we hunkered behind a waist-high wall with some overhanging trees behind it. With the wind coming from the other direction, it furnished adequate shelter. Chris broke out a flask and some tiny cups and we had "a drop" to warm us up. I felt pretty good after that, but went five over par on the next three holes.

After play, we four golfers gathered in the hotel bar "for a pint." George and Annsley Strong treated us to "sandwiches and salad," since there had been no place to eat on the golf course, and we had had no lunch. Patsy and Betsy showed up about twenty minutes later, and we regaled one another about our day.

At 6:45 we met the Halls in the hotel lobby and set off for "The Lime Tree Restaurant." Pretty soon, the other six travelers in our group appeared, and we wound up sitting at three tables, all in a row. It was another excellent dinner. The only problem: I ordered "homemade ice cream with hot chocolate sauce," and it turned out to be three scoops! And I ate it all!

Before bed we retrieved our passports from the hotel lockbox and packed. My hang-up bag, purchased at L. S. Ayres twenty years ago for $15.00, has been all over the world, but finally gave out. I hoped, with luck, to nurse it back to Fort Wayne. We arranged a wakeup call and ordered breakfast by room service. Could we possibly, I wondered, want to eat?

Ashford Castle

Saturday promised to be a long "travel day," as we would be driving from Kenmare, in County Kerry, to Ashford Castle, located at the Village of Cong, in County Mayo. Our wakeup call came at 7:00 a.m. (Ouch!), and breakfast was brought to the room at 7:30. At the expense of repetition, I will quote from my notes, "Park Hotel Kenmare has the best service in the world."

There was a heavy rain coming down, but it was intermittent, so we took turns dashing from the entrance of the hotel to get on the coach. As we waited for Patsy Malone (who was settling up with the hotel), the conversation among the group centered on the beauty of Ireland, the amazing compatibility of all of the travelers, and the thorough job Patsy had done in preparing our itinerary.

As we left County Kerry, we were reminded frequently of the impending "Irish football" finals, Kerry vs. Mayo. Green and yellow flags were everywhere, including on cars. (After we got home to Indiana, I tried to find out who finally won, even looking on the Internet, but never could find any information.) The other major Irish sport, hurling, involves men running around in short pants with helmets and sticks, throwing a ball around. The final in that event involved Killkenny vs. Cork, and was to be played on September 3rd.

We passed through the picturesque town of Adare, which was pretty (but not necessarily as pretty as its brochures claimed), and also through the much larger city of Limerick. The river Shannon passes through Limerick, and I was surprised at how wide it is. George Strong used the occasion to recite the following "limerick":

> There once was a lawyer named Rex,
> With very small organs of sex.
> When charged with exposure,
> He said with composure,
> *De minimus non curat lex.*

Thus inspired, Chris discussed the history of Limerick, and Irish history as a whole. He also told us about "the Tinkers," which refers to itinerant bands of people that we refer to in America as "Irish travelers." They tend to "live off the land," take every opportunity to draw government subsidies, and intimidate property owners into giving them payments in order to leave them alone.

Our destination was Bunratty, and "Durty Nelly's Pub," where we would have our lunch. When we got to Bunratty, we had time to shop, and Betsy found a very nice Irish woolen sweater at Blarney Woolen Mills. Durty Nelly's Pub is a well-known tourist spot. Legend has it that a customer complained to Durty Nelly because there was a fly in his beer, and said he wouldn't drink it. She plucked the fly out of the beer and handed the beer back to the customer, who again refused to drink it. She then threw him out, saying, "You won't drink the beer with the fly in it, and now you won't drink the beer without the fly!" The ambiance of the place is quaint and fun, the beer is good, the waitresses are pleasant, and the food is fair. (We have been spoiled.)

It was a long day of traveling, but we finally arrived at Ashford Castle. Leaving the main road, we entered through a huge stone arch, and passed a security guard, to enter the castle grounds. We drove through many acres of surrounding woods and golf course until we reached a stone bridge that crosses a river to the entrance of the castle.

Patsy asked Chris to stop the coach before we got to the bridge, and told us all to disembark, which we did. There, in front of the bridge, was a bagpiper in full regalia, playing "Wearing of the Green." The piper *led us across the bridge*, to the entrance of the castle itself where, to our amazement, most of the Ashford Castle staff, including the Manager, were lined up, standing at attention, to greet us. Patsy turned around and beamed, "A tenth anniversary surprise." It was very nice, and I think all of us were choked up a little bit. In my case it was, in part, because I always get choked up when I hear bagpipes; but more so, I think, because it was such a fine moment for Patsy.

A staff member took us to our respective rooms. Ours was a lovely suite with a fine view over Lough Corrib, Ireland's largest lake. There was no air conditioning, the room was warm, and the windows would only open by about one foot. We did find an electric fan, which we turned on, opened the windows as much as we could, and then called housekeeping for a luggage rack and some soap. Once again, fresh flowers, wine, and a box of chocolates had been provided for us.

Welcome in our honor (and especially in honor of Patsy Malone) at Ashford Castle.

Ashford Castle has 350 acres of grounds. There are 72 bedrooms, 5 state rooms, and 6 suites - each individually designed and distinctive. Guests have the opportunity to play golf, ride horses, fish, try falconry, archery, clay pigeon shooting, cycling, hiking or jogging. There are horse-drawn carts, known as "jaunting carts," available to carry guests about the grounds. There is also a spa, a large pub and conference facilities. Ashford Castle is a five-star hotel, brimming with fine art, antique furniture, suits of armor, and enormous fireplaces. The 1950's movie "*The Quiet Man*," with John Wayne and Maureen O'Hara, was filmed in the vicinity, and we had an opportunity to see many of the sites that were used on location. During the filming, of course, the actors and actresses had stayed at Ashford Castle.

At six o'clock we walked back across the bridge through a fine mist to board the "Lady Arduilaun" for a cruise on Lough Corrib. The boat has two covered rooms, one of which contains a bar, and an upper deck for outdoor

Snapshots

viewing; however, the rain became steadily heavier, so there wasn't much interest in being up on deck. The only other passengers on our cruise were a group of nine young Irish women who were having a "hen party." One of them was soon to be married. They were in their late 20's or early 30's. and were an attractive, jolly and rowdy bunch, who turned out to be a lot of fun. Before we cast off, Patsy introduced us to her son, Jeff Malone, who had just arrived from Shannon Airport, having flown from California. Jeff is a handsome bachelor in his 40's, and immediately caught the attention of some of the "hen party" girls.

The boat cruise on Lough Corrib is operated by Patrick Luskin, whose father started the business years ago. Patsy first met Patrick when he was a teenager, driving one of the "jaunting carts" on the castle grounds, and they renewed their acquaintance when Patsy brought her first group to Ashford Castle some ten years ago. Patrick was not on the boat during our tour, but would join us for dinner the next night. Instead, we had a substitute skipper, a bartender, and "Martin," who plays the accordion and sings traditional Irish songs.

The rain came down, the bar did a lively business, Martin played the accordion, people sang and danced, and everyone became very friendly. *My Lord - what a party it turned out to be*! It rained steadily for the entire time that we were out on the boat, and no one noticed!

Howard Chapman and Chris Allen enjoying "the cruise" on the *Lady Arduilaun*.

Howard L. Chapman

Back on shore, we took several photographs of us and our new friends, four of whom were sisters named "Malone," including the one getting married. Jeff Malone thought that he had fallen into heaven, and the girls tried earnestly to get him to accompany them for the rest of the evening; however (to the best of my knowledge), he resisted.

We regrouped at eight o'clock in the spectacular main dining room of the Castle. The Grunwalds decided to have a table of their own, and Betsy and I joined the Halls, the Strongs, and the Jordans. Patsy, Chris, and Jeff ate at "Cullen's at the Cottage" restaurant, on the Castle grounds.

Connemara

It is always interesting to travel in a foreign country on a Sunday morning. People were getting out of church, but otherwise, there was very little sign of activity. We started the day traveling in the coach past lovely scenes of Lough Corrib, in a landscape dissected by stone walls and dotted with sheep. Lough Corrib stretches for forty miles and has 365 islands in it, which makes it very picturesque. Inevitably, the main topic of conversation on the coach was the amazing party we had on the boat the prior evening. Although Betsy and I had been through this country before, I had forgotten the rugged beauty of it. There are beautiful mountain ash trees growing wild, old castles, pleasant villages and rugged mountains. There were not many buildings, and Chris told us that development is limited by the government.

We took a detour to drive along Killary Fjord, the only fjord in Ireland, and stopped in the Village of Leenanne, at its terminus, to look at the harbor. There are boats there that will take you on a tour. It is sea water, which means that it is tidal, and we noticed objects here and there in the water which, we were told, indicate that "fish farming" is being practiced. It is controversial, because of the contention that it creates pollution.

Driving through the mountains, we saw peat being cut out of the ground, and stacked along the side of the road. It will be dried and then burned for fuel.

Next we drove along Kylemore Lake, which is gorgeous in itself, but is best known as the setting for Kylemore Abbey, built on a hillside along the shore. It is now a school for girls, operated by nuns, but, we were told, it will be closing in a couple of years. Apparently, there are not enough students to keep it going. Kylemore Abbey presents one of the most perfect photo opportunities a person will ever find, and everyone took advantage of it. When we were at Kylemore Abbey in 2004, it was Spring, and the hillside was entirely purple with rhododendrons - but not in bloom this time.

Still, an unforgettable scene. After a little sightseeing on the grounds, we retreated to the visitor center for "coffee and."

Suzanne and Bill Hall at Kylemore Abbey.

We departed Kylemore Abbey and proceeded to the Village of Clifden, and Mitchell's Restaurant. It was very good the first time we went there, in 2004, and it was good this time. Should we go there again, I would want to remember to order the Cashel blue cheese salad and the open-face fresh crab sandwich.

As we drove away from Clifden, I read, in the *Sunday Independent*, an article about "Today's Birthdays." My eye caught the following: "Desmond Guinness, author and conservationist, is 75." I showed it to Patsy Malone, and she said, "We must call him." She proceeded to ring him up, and when he came on line we all sang "Happy Birthday" to him. Patsy talked with him for some time and later told us that he was thoroughly delighted with being remembered, and by the singing.

We returned to Ashford Castle in time to take a nap, and then Betsy and I went off for a walk. Bill and Suzanne Hall had decided to take a falconry lesson, and we met them on the grounds just as they were coming out. They were absolutely thrilled with the experience, saying that it was unlike anything they had ever done before. The four of us continued walking until we came to a cottage with a plaque on the wall that said "The Quiet Man House - Squire Danaher lived here. 1951." It appears to now be used as a private residence, but has a prominent place in the movie.

In order to check e-mail, I had to get a card at the front desk with a "scratch off" security code. The code allowed me to access a hotel computer. It was also possible to use the Internet on the television set in our room, but there was a charge for it, and I decided to use the hotel computer, for nothing. While checking out the TV in the room, we noticed that "*The Quiet Man*" is available to guests "on demand."

At eight o'clock we walked back over the stone bridge to the restaurant called "Cullens at the Cottage," so named because it is in a thatched cottage. In 2004, our earlier trip, it had been under construction. Patsy introduced us to Patrick and Marian Luskin, and they joined us for dinner. Once I saw him, I remembered that he had been the skipper on the Lady Arduilaun in 2004. Before I could say anything, however, he fixed me with a gaze and said, "We've met before." They have four children, ages 7, 5, 3, and 1, which, I think, gave Marian some interest in our three grandsons, ages 6, 3, and 1. "Oh my," she said, "three boys?"

Shortly after dinner was served, the four Malloy Brothers appeared, and began to set up their instruments. They are local musicians who do traditional Irish singing, and encourage everyone to get into it - which all of us did. I danced with Betsy and with Patsy. This kind of music encourages not only dancing, but lots of clapping and stomping, and went on until well after 11:30. Chris Allen and I sang a duet of "Dublin Can Be Heaven." I include the lyrics here, so that they may be preserved for posterity:

Dublin can be heaven,
With coffee at eleven,
And a stroll on Stephen's Green.
There's no need to hurry,
There's no need to worry,
You're a king, and the lady's a queen.
Grafton Street's a wonderland, there's magic in the air.
There are diamonds on the lady's hands, and gold dust in her hair.
And if you don't believe me,
Just come and meet me there,
In Dublin, on a sunny Sunday morning.

St. Clerans Manor House

Although Monday was to be a "travel day" we didn't have to leave until later in the day. We enjoyed a nine o'clock wakeup call and breakfast in the room, settled our hotel bill, and set off for County Galway. It was Labor Day in the United States, but none of us were conscious of it at the time. We were "immersed in Ireland." We came to the area known as "Connemara," and we were struck by how wild it is. Not mountainous, but hilly, and reminiscent of the moors that we had visited in England.

We stopped at Connemara Marble Company where owner Ambrose Joyce gave us a tour of his plant and talked to us about the business of acquiring marble and producing beautiful objects from it. Naturally, there is a shop, and Betsy and I bought a couple of things in anticipation of the coming Christmas season.

We came into view of Galway Bay, made famous by the well-known song, went through the town of On Spideal, and then through part of the City of Galway known as The Claddagh. It was once an area where trade flourished between the Irish inhabitants and Spanish merchant ships. A number of the Spanish visitors stayed on, and their offspring came to be known as "The Black Irish." Chris continued driving through Galway, pointing out the sights, and giving us a little history of the place, and then let us off at the "bottom" of Shop Street, a pedestrian street that is true to its name, and runs for several blocks. We would be there for two hours, and Chris would pick us up again outside a hotel known as "Jury's Inn."

Unfortunately, the weather did not cooperate. This makes it hard to appreciate any place, but even taking that into account, our impression of Shop Street was: overcrowded, cheap shops, dirty. In no way was this pedestrian street to be confused with pedestrian streets such as we have seen in Vienna or Berlin. Patsy had recommended a fish and chips restaurant called "McDonagh's" for lunch, so Betsy and I, and the Halls, followed her in. While we waited in line, one of the food handlers sneezed repeatedly over the food - and Patsy Malone and her son Jeff wisely left. Unfortunately, we and the Halls stayed and ordered fish and chips. It cost a lot, was barely edible, and left the four of us hoping we would not get sick.

Bill Hall and I went to a nearby McDonalds and got coffee to drink while Suzanne and Betsy shopped. The rain was incessant, and the four of us slunk back to Jury's Inn, only to find that the toilets were locked. We were mighty glad to see Chris pull up with the coach and load us on.

As we drove out of Galway, the Strongs and the Grunwalds and the Jordans all said that they had found decent places to eat. Rose and Don Jordan, however, complained that they were experiencing some kind of "contact skin rash," which they thought they had contracted at Perryville House in Kinsale. All in all, this had not been a very good day so far - but it was going to get better.

After driving a short distance from Galway, we found ourselves in open country once again, and came to a sign indicating the entrance to "St. Clerans

- a Merv Griffin Hotel." The road at the entrance would more properly be called a "lane," and was very narrow. Chris took out a few tree limbs getting the coach in. St. Clerans is owned by the American entertainer Merv Griffin, and he uses it as a home when he is in Ireland. The rest of the time, it is operated as a very upscale country inn, with 12 deluxe guestrooms, an elegant dining room, a drawing room, library, and other smaller rooms. Betsy and I were in the Robinson Suite, named in honor of Merv Griffin's mother (her maiden name was Robinson). It was immediately apparent that no expense had been spared in renovating and furnishing every part of the place.

St. Clerans Manor House.

Our group had St. Clerans to ourselves and, once settled in our suites, we began visiting one another to compare them. Bill and Suzanne Hall were in the Griffin Suite, and it was every bit as grand as ours. Every suite was spacious, with fine windows, exquisite appointments, and every amenity. The Grunwalds were in a suite with a totally different look, but no less dramatic. Jeff Malone had a room to himself, and said he was amazed at how splendid it was. Each room, once again, was stocked with fresh fruit, a box of chocolates, a bottle of wine, and fresh flowers and, at St. Clerans, there was also a decanter of port wine and a plate of fresh cookies. Near our suite, I found a small room with a computer, and used the opportunity to catch up on e-mail.

Everyone dressed for dinner and we met in the drawing room at 7:30 for cocktails before adjourning into the dining room. The table was perfect in

Snapshots

every way - flowers, crystal, candles, and a special menu from Japanese Chef Kuma. The meal was exquisite. All of us were old friends by this time, and there was much joke-telling and general levity. During dinner, Ken Burgin, the Manager of St. Clerans, came into the dining room with a Federal Express package for Patsy. It turned out to be an 8x10 glossy photograph of Merv Griffin, inscribed by him to Patsy, and acknowledging her 10th anniversary trip. She was moved. At the end of the meal, she was presented with a large cake with ten candles, and an inscription that it was "Celebrating *Ireland Behind the Scenes* - Ten Years."

When dinner was over, we all retired to the drawing room, where the bar was open, and a trio of musicians was playing. A small hardwood floor had been laid in front of the fireplace, and two young women in "Riverdance" costumes were seated on one of the couches. Both of them, we learned, had performed in Irish step dancing shows. The pianist, a lady named Carmel Dempsey, is a well-known performer in Galway, and has recorded some of her music. First, the two step dancers gave us a sample of some of the dancing similar to what one sees in "Riverdance." At a close distance, I was amazed at how limber they were. When they kicked their legs backward, they actually kicked themselves in the back. At other times, they were on their toes, like ballet dancers. After they danced awhile, they encouraged all of us to get out on the dance floor and learn some traditional Irish dancing (but not step dancing!).

"Irish "step dancers" performing for us in the
drawing room at St. Clerans Manor House.

At midnight, the step dancer girls left, and a sing-along began, and continued until 1:00 o'clock a.m. Before going to bed, I went outdoors for a couple of minutes, just to see whether I could hear any noise of any kind. It was absolutely still.

Doonbeg

The next morning we had the opportunity to sleep in - however, Betsy and I woke up before eight a.m. It was a sunny day and surprisingly warm, so we decided to take a walk before breakfast. We asked Ken Burgin, the Manager, if we had to eat breakfast by a certain time, and he said, "At St. Clerans there are no clocks." Our walk took us through deep woods, lush fields, and, eventually, to a row of new houses under construction. An Irish woman stopped her car next to us and asked us for directions. She said that it was unusual to see people walking in Ireland this early in the morning, and she assumed we must be local.

Breakfast was as good as would have been expected, and we left St. Clerans at 11:30. We were on our way to have lunch at "Moran's on the Weir," but we were going to be too early. Chris and Patsy decided to stop and let us "wander about" in the tiny village of Clarinbridge, in order to kill some time. Bill Hall and I found a news agent, but no *International Herald-Tribune*. Don Jordan noted Jordan's Bar, and we remembered that we had seen it on our trip in 2004. Bill and I wandered about the streets a little bit, and found Betsy and Suzanne in an antique shop. Suzanne showed us an antique "spongeware" cup priced at €150.

We arrived at Moran's on the Weir, looking forward to a repetition of the fabulous lunch we ate there two years previously. Don and Rose Jordan, who had been with us (and Patsy) in 2004, had finally told Patsy that they would come on this trip, "on condition that we will have lunch again at Moran's." There were 13 of us sitting at one long table in a small room, intended for 8 people. No matter. There was an abundance of "garlic-grilled oysters," open-face crab sandwiches, and a steady flow of beer and wine. We all ate more than our share of oysters, but Sandi Grunwald consumed 16 of them, 12 raw and 4 grilled. For a while, the oysters stopped coming, and Patsy inquired as to why the pause. She was told that the man in the kitchen who was shucking oysters got tired, and took a break!

During the meal, Patsy got a call from Ken Burgin at St. Clerans. Jeff Malone had left his jacket there, and Ken agreed to bring it to Moran's. He said it was on his way home anyway.

As its name indicates, Moran's sits along the banks of a tidal estuary, or "weir." The tide had been out when we arrived, with boats resting on the bottom, but while we were eating, it came in with a vengeance. By the time we left, the entire inlet was full of water.

A steady rain greeted our arrival at Doonbeg, it was windy, and there was an Irish chill in the air. The hotel manager came out to meet us and, during the conversation, Bill Hall told her that we might play golf the next day. She said, "Well, I hope it stays nice for you."

The Lodge at Doonbeg Golf Club is located on the Atlantic Ocean and near the small village of Doonbeg. It is only a few years old, and construction of nearby buildings is still going on. We were told that the intent is to eventually create a village atmosphere. The Lodge itself belies its age - it is new but does not look new. It, and the rest of the facilities, indicate first-class construction and expensive taste. It is only about one hour from Shannon Airport, but one feels quite isolated nonetheless. The golf course was designed by Greg Norman, and lies along 1.5 miles of beach, with ocean views from 16 of the 18 holes. When it opened in 2002, Golf Digest named it the "Best New International Course." It is a true links course, where the wind blows constantly, and I would advise anyone playing it to follow our example, and not keep score.

On the plus side, the Lodge at Doonbeg is absolutely first-class in every way; the seaside scenery is breathtaking; the staff is friendly and helpful; the golf course is beautiful and challenging. On the other hand, it is isolated. If one does not play golf, one can get bored very quickly. The weather must be brutal most of the time, and, let's face it, it is very expensive.

Patsy and her husband, Lou Malone, had once planned to buy one of the condominium units in the Lodge, but later changed their minds. According to Patsy, units in the Lodge were being offered, at the time of our visit, at $2,000,000. We were told that 60% of the club members are Irish and 40% are from other countries, many of them Americans. Patsy remains a member of the Club, and her name is listed on a plaque on the wall as a "Founding Member." Because she is a member, she was able to arrange for all of us to use the "Members Only" part of the Club, primarily the members' bar and dining room.

I met Chris Allen in the bar for a drink before dinner, and he introduced me to Patsy's husband, Lou Malone. Lou had just arrived from Los Angeles via Shannon Airport, and he and Patsy planned to spend another ten to fourteen days in Ireland. My notes say, "Lou is a delightful guy."

Patsy had arranged for us to have dinner that night in the Members Restaurant. Betsy and I ate with Bill and Suzanne Hall and had a good time reviewing all the things we had done in Ireland. We had originally reserved a 9:48 tee time, but I changed it to 11:48, which all of us agreed was a much more civilized hour. The green fees cost €190, club rental cost €30, and the cost for a caddy was €50. It would be an expensive round of golf, but it might be a long time before we had a chance to play Doonbeg again.

Golf at Doonbeg

It was our last day before heading home. We slept late and had a lovely breakfast. When we arrived at the pro shop, Chris Allen, Lou Malone, and Jeff Malone had already teed off, using the 9:48 tee time that Patsy had reserved. Bill Hall and I arranged to use a golf cart, but had to have a caddy drive it. George Strong and Annsley Strong played with us, only they walked. They shared a caddy, who carried one bag and pulled a trolley with the other. Our caddy was a wonderful young man by the name of Michael O'Brien, who told us that he is a five handicap. "I don't mean a caddy five, I mean a real five," he said. He quietly advised us that, once we were out of sight of the Clubhouse, he would be happy to walk, and Bill and I could ride in the cart as we pleased.

Praise the Lord that we had caddies! Without them, we would never have found our way around the course and, if we had, we would have lost even more balls than we did. Besides that, one needs them for local knowledge. For example, one of the greens has a pothole bunker right in the middle of it, and you cannot see it from the fairway. Our caddies, of course, warned us to "hit to the right side of the flag," away from the bunker.

The pot bunkers are impossible. I got into two of them and simply hit the ball backwards away from the green in order to get it out. The rough is no better, consisting of hip-high grass that is bent over and matted down. If your ball goes in it, your caddy will walk to where it went in and "step around," hoping to step on it. When we hit a ball into the rough, the caddy usually found two or three balls, but, more often than not, did not find ours. The scenery, which incorporates the ocean, is breathtaking; however, a stiff wind blew all day, and, when we began, it was cold. Still, there was intermittent sun and I had my second sweater off part of the time. As I said, we did not keep score; however, Bill Hall, George Strong and I each had one birdie during the round. Apart from that, there was no need to discuss scores.

Our suite in the Lodge looked out over Number 18 green. Our spouses and friends were there watching for us, and, when we arrived, came out to welcome us. Our performance on the 18th green did not, however, merit much of a celebration. Bill Hall and I went into the pro shop, thinking we might buy a "Doonbeg" cap, but didn't find any that fit quite right.

We rested and packed and got ready for Patsy's farewell dinner. At seven o'clock we gathered in the Members Drawing Room for cocktails. There was a pianist providing background music, and lots of picture taking. I managed

Snapshots

to take Patsy aside and gave her a check for a gratuity for Chris Allen. He had been a splendid and affable driver, guide and companion throughout.

Dinner was served in the "Billiard Room," where an exquisite meal was presented, complemented first by white wine, then by *Chateaunuef de Pape* (which had been decanted), and finally by port. At the end, there was a cheese course, before dessert. Just as the Jordans had been induced to accompany us by a promise to revisit Moran's Restaurant, Sandi Grunwald had agreed to come on condition that there be a cheese course. During dinner, there was a series of toasts. We heard nice words from Patsy, from Chris, and from George Strong. By this time there was a sincere affection among everyone who had been on the trip. After dessert was served, Patsy was presented with yet another cake to celebrate the tenth anniversary of *Ireland Behind the Scenes*. Of course, all of us were stuffed, and could not begin to eat any cake. (I had pretty much quit with the cheese course.)

Patsy and Chris presented each of the five couples with an autographed copy of Desmond Guinness's book, "Great Irish Houses and Castles." They are wonderful books, beautifully illustrated, and very heavy. They would, however, fit in a suitcase.

As a surprise for Chris, Patsy had arranged for an old friend, Kate Purcell, to perform for us. She plays the guitar and sings traditional Irish songs. When she came in the room, Chris lit up, and said, "Oh - is it Kate?" It is customary, on such an occasion in Ireland, for the audience to sing along; however, none of us except Chris knew the lyrics. Bill Hall requested a couple of songs from her, but she didn't know them.

Chris and I reprised our duet of "Dublin Can Be Heaven," and persuaded George Strong to join us. I furnished him with a copy of the lyrics that Chris had given to me in 2004.

I got tired and trundled off to bed, but Betsy stayed and played the piano - playing songs that the Americans knew and could sing.

The Short Goodbye

Patsy arranged for a van and driver to take Betsy and me, together with Bill and Suzanne Hall, to Shannon Airport to begin our trip back to America. We got up early, finished packing, had breakfast, and then found Chris Allen to say our goodbyes to him. At the beginning of the trip, Patsy had provided us with two bottles of liquor, and we returned the Beefeaters Gin, unopened, and most of the Canadian Club.

Our driver, Connor, arrived and got us to Shannon Airport with plenty of time to spare. Once again, the boarding experience with Aer Lingus was pleasant and uncomplicated; except that Betsy suddenly realized that she had left her raincoat at the Lodge at Doonbeg. I telephoned Chris Allen from the airport, and found that he was already "on the road" to Dublin, taking the Jordans, Strongs, and Grunwalds with him. He agreed to ring Patsy, who was still at Doonbeg, and try to salvage it. (In the event, Patsy did find it and shipped it to Betsy, and it arrived in good shape.)

While we waited to board our flight home, the Halls presented Betsy and me with a souvenir shot glass from Kylemore Abbey - which we will display and use.

Once on the ground at O'Hare Field in Chicago, we cleared customs, and I called JoAnne Weber on my cell phone. She was parked nearby, waiting for us, came and picked us up, and drove us back to Fort Wayne.

Ireland had been memorable. I would recommend it to anybody.

Chapter 17

TAKAOKA REDUX

I

The mayor of Fort Wayne, Indiana, Tom Henry, had been invited to join Takaoka, Japan, in celebrating its 400th anniversary, and eleven of us went along. The delegation included Tom, his wife Cindy, Jerry Henry and his wife Becky, Rick Briley and his wife Lucy, Steve McElhoe and his wife Cathy, Tom Herr, Stan Barker, Toyoharu Tamura, and yours truly, Howard Chapman. This would be my fourth trip to Takaoka, the first having been in 1977, when Fort Wayne and Takaoka made their sister city relationship "official."

We departed from Fort Wayne in the morning on September 9, 2009. When I arrived at the airport, I found Mayor Henry standing in the lobby with a TV crew, being interviewed about the trip and plans to discuss potential economic development matters with Japanese officials and business people. Later he, and some of the others, would travel on to China to pursue possible business opportunities for the city there.

Airport check-in was uneventful, except for my good friend and law partner, Tom Herr. When he took out his passport, he discovered that he had brought his daughter's passport, and left his at home. After the panic subsided, calls finally reached his wife, and she brought his passport to the airport in time. Meanwhile, he and Stan Barker were dealing with an enormous cardboard box containing a gift from Fort Wayne to Takaoka in recognition of their celebration. It was about five feet tall and three feet wide, and fragile.

Howard L. Chapman

They were eventually able to get it checked in, and we all knocked on wood that it would somehow arrive, intact, in Japan.

Tom Herr with the Fort Wayne gift to Takaoka, about to get it checked onto the airplane.

Old friends and loyal sister city backers Gabe DeLobbe and Karen Barker were there to see us off. Both have visited Takaoka, and Gabe has been there five times. For the Henrys, Brileys and McElhoes, this was to be their first trip to Asia. Tamura-san, known to all simply as "T," is a native Japanese now living and working in Fort Wayne, and would be our mentor and inestimable guide.

After a layover in Chicago, we boarded a Boeing 777 operated by All Nippon Airways for our thirteen and one half hour flight to Tokyo. There was currently a concern about "H1N1 flu," and many of the Japanese passengers were wearing face masks. I can recommend the airline. The airplane was spotless and all of the stewardesses were Japanese dolls, who did everything possible to be pleasant and accommodating. At 3:15 in the afternoon (Chicago

Snapshots

time) they turned off the cabin lights and I took five milligrams of Ambien, and rested (not slept) comfortably until seven o'clock. Soon thereafter, we were served a traditional Japanese meal, the highlight of which was "Udon noodle soup."

II

There is quite a time change when one lands in Tokyo. 12:45 *a.m.* in Fort Wayne is 1:45 *p.m.* in Tokyo. Time change is the bane of all modern travelers, causing jet lag and constipation. Further, since we had crossed the International Date Line, it was still Thursday. Our group cleared customs at Narita airport and, after a 45 minute wait, boarded a shuttle bus for the eighty minute drive to The New Otani, our hotel for the night. It was already apparent that we were fortunate indeed to have Toyoharu Tamura to guide us on our way.

The New Otani is a huge hotel, with luxurious Japanese gardens, accessible to guests and enclosed so as to exclude the hustle of the surrounding city. We were all housed in a newer addition called "The Garden Tower" (it overlooks the gardens). Tamura-san had arranged to take several of us to a local restaurant, but I elected for an early meal at the hotel's "Garden Lounge." A very nice club sandwich, Caesar salad and water for "only" fifty dollars. (The dollar had been declining for some time, and one dollar fetched only 86 yen.) Sleeping that night was aided by sleeping pills, but when I woke up at six the next morning, I felt pretty good and ready to face the day.

The breakfast buffet was terrific, and I was able to get a current copy of *The International Herald Tribune*. Civilized travel is not possible if this newspaper is not available. The main story was about the fact that President Obama had addressed Congress in support of his universal health care plan. Meanwhile, the huge box carrying the Fort Wayne gift to Takaoka had spent the night in the hotel lobby, and Stan Barker took care of shepherding it onto our bus and, eventually, onto our airplane to Toyama.

In Tokyo, international flights go in and out of Narita Airport, and domestic flights go in and out of Haneda Airport. The check-in process at Haneda turned out to be very awkward and confusing, with a variation of the "three line" concept. Everything was in Japanese and very little English was spoken. Again, hooray for our guide, "T." Our plane to Toyama was huge, a Boeing 777 that was just as big as our plane from Chicago, and it was fully booked. I was squeezed into a middle seat, and again noticed a high percentage of passengers wearing face masks.

The trip to Toyama took less than an hour and, when we deplaned, we realized that the Mayor of Mirandopolis, Brazil, was traveling on the plane with us. Mirandopolis is another sister city of Takaoka and he, with two interpreters, was also there to join in the 400 year anniversary celebration. A delegation from Takaoka greeted us in the airport lobby, including Mitsuhiro Nakao, and an interpreter. Nakao-san visited us at our home in Fort Wayne several years ago, and handling the sister city visitors seems to be a part of his job for the city of Takaoka. From the moment we saw him, he seemed to be constantly on the move.

There was a bus with ample room for all of us. It was immaculate and modern, and staffed by two conductors/stewardesses/attendants who smiled a lot, talked some (their comments were interpreted), and generally tried to be helpful. The interpreter was a young Englishman from the city of Oxford named Jonathon Perry, who is employed by the city of Takaoka as a part of their international affairs department, and who, we learned, also teaches English on the side. He is fully fluent in Japanese, and would be with us during our entire weekend in Takaoka. He proved to be a very congenial and useful addition.

III

On the way to Takaoka we stopped at a traditional Japanese restaurant, sat on the floor at low tables, and received a wonderful lunch. Even though we sat on cushions on the floor, there were contraptions that slid under the cushions that provided a backrest. I don't know whether the Japanese use them, or if they are just for western tourists. The lunch was typical Japanese fare, and included a beautiful selection of raw fish. Tom Herr happily consumed all of mine. (I shared his happiness, since I wanted no part of it.) As I had learned from past travels, Tom has a cast iron stomach, an endless supply of energy, and requires very little sleep.

When our bus arrived at the Hotel New Otani in Takaoka, the entire hotel staff was lined up at the entrance, applauding our arrival, and welcoming us. Also, there were several old friends, and I had a chance to give big hugs to Hisako Tanabe, and to Kimio Arai and his wife, Keiko. Hisako is a retired English teacher who stayed in our home in Fort Wayne for a month in 1975, when she came as chaperon for ten high school girls. Kimio has visited Fort Wayne twenty times and has been a steadfast backer of our sister city program. He and Keiko have also stayed at our home in Fort Wayne. It was an emotional time for many of us. The notes in my journal simply say - "Wow."

Hotel rooms in Japan tend to be a little smaller than in the U.S., but mine was comfortable. On this visit, I had no trouble turning on the lights. When you enter the room, there is no electricity, and to turn it on, you have to drop the plastic fob on your hotel key into a special slot in the wall. When you

Snapshots

leave the room and take the key out of the wall, the electricity in the room goes off. Very efficient, and no doubt saves the hotel a lot of money.

The bottle of water that I had been carrying in my flight bag had been leaking, so I had to hang things around the room to dry out. With that done, I unpacked, sent out a sack of laundry, and changed into a business suit. Things tend to be formal in Japan. Everyone met in the lobby and boarded the bus to go to the train station to pick up the delegation from the City of Beverley, in the United Kingdom. Beverley is another sister city of Takaoka, and its delegation turned out to consist of one man, a former mayor by the name of Jim Whitfield. He was arriving by train.

IV

Once we had collected Jim, we continued to City Hall. Again, the entire staff of people who work there were on the front steps to greet us, plus a group of young school children who shouted in unison, "Welcome to Takaoka," as we got off the bus. Our group now included representatives from America, England and Brazil, and there were many flags from all of those countries that were waving among the crowd. We stood in front of the building for a while as the children sang songs for us, and then processed into the lobby, passing a large work of art given to Takaoka by Fort Wayne during our visit there in 1989. We worked our way past the usual array of city offices, and then went up some stairs to a meeting in the City Council chambers.

Takaoka Mayor Masaki Takahashi presided, and introduced the members of the City Council. The mayors of Fort Wayne and Mirandopolis, and the past mayor of Beverley, were introduced, and speeches were made by just about everybody, including Stan Barker, on behalf of Fort Wayne Sister Cities International. These were followed by the ritual exchange of gifts among the various sister cities and Takaoka. Mayor Henry presented Takaoka with Fort Wayne's quite large, quite beautiful, and quite spectacular triptych that Stan Barker had husbanded with such care all the way from Fort Wayne. Stan then presented "Wayne the Eagle," a remarkable work of art resembling our bald eagle. It was created by Fort Wayne artist Sayaka Ganz, and is made entirely of found plastic objects, such as an egg beater or a serving fork.

All of us were provided with an extremely detailed schedule of all of our planned activities throughout the weekend. By "detailed," I mean planned down to the minute. This schedule included a one hour "free time break" that afternoon, which we used to rest and freshen up at the hotel before heading off to the Mayor's Banquet, to be given in our honor.

Howard L. Chapman

V

The banquet was held at the Onoya Ryokan. A ryokan is a Japanese inn. This one is set in a lovely and tranquil garden, with the walls pretty much open on most sides. In accordance with custom, all shoes were left at the door, and everyone was provided with slippers. By this time, the representatives from two more of Takaoka's sister cities had arrived from Jinzhou and Liaoning, both in China. The total group, including Japanese dignitaries, was pretty large, using several long tables, and completely filling the inn.

With advance planning from Tamura-san (who overlooks nothing), I was seated opposite old friends Hisako Tanabe and Kimio Arai. Hisako was stunning in one of her kimonos, and Kimio had brought some photo albums filled with old memories. The waitresses were also in kimonos, there were soft lights, and everyone had a nice view of the gardens. Music was provided by two women, one playing a stringed instrument called a *"koto,"* and a man playing a kind of flute called a *"shakuhachi."*

Hisako Tanabe, Howard Chapman and Kimio Arai at the Mayor's Banquet.

The meal began with "hot-pots" that heated what I first thought was cooking oil, but turned out to be a very tasty soup. Courses kept coming. There was seafood, vegetables and assorted other things to eat - and an abundance of beer and sake, the Japanese liqueur. *"Kampai"* is a Japanese toast, the equivalent of "Cheers," and plenty of "*Kampai*!"s could be heard around the room. We reckoned that such a dinner in the United States would cost at least $200 per person. After this really fine meal, there were more speeches and gifts. Kimio, Hisako and I all had gifts to exchange, and I presented Mayor Takahashi with a golf cap with "Fort Wayne Country Club" prominently displayed on the front. With Kimio as an interpreter, the mayor and I had a good talk, and he gave me his assurance that he will look forward to a golf game when he visits Fort Wayne. If that happens, I hope that Kimio comes along, not just to join in the golf game, but to help interpret!

The entertainment and music continued through dessert; however, everyone in the crowd ignored them and kept on talking, and the performers did not seem to mind. In Japan, there is rarely any question as to when a function is over. That is because someone stands up and announces, "This function is now over." That happened at nine o'clock, and all of us returned to the New Otani. I found that my laundry had already been returned, and my room had cooled considerably since the sun had gone down. I set my clock and went to bed. (One hint for the traveler- bring your own alarm clock. Where there is a language difference, hotel wake up calls can be problematical.)

VI

Saturday morning dawned cool and rainy. While I was waiting at the elevator, a strange scene unfolded on the balcony of a building across the street. A woman was clearly in great distress, pounding on the wall, pulling her hair, falling down and gesturing, while another woman seemed to be trying to calm her. At one point I thought that the first woman would actually throw herself over the railing. Eventually, a man appeared in the doorway, barefoot and getting his trousers closed up. The three of them carried on for some time before the man and the second woman went back inside, leaving the first woman curled up in a corner in the fetal position. I went downstairs to breakfast. (Tom Herr later learned from Jonathon Perry that the building in question is a rather well disguised "gentleman's pleasure" establishment.)

The breakfast buffet had quite a variety of dishes, most of which were traditional Japanese and not really appealing to the occasional westerner; however, there were a number of other dishes that were available, and one could have a perfectly good breakfast.

The representatives from all of the sister cities gathered after breakfast in the hotel lobby for a visit to the Zuiryuji Temple. This was my fourth time to experience this but, since each visit was at least ten years apart, I was eager to do it again. It is quite spectacular.

To start with, the Zuiryuji Temple, a Buddhist shrine, is a national treasure. It was first built by Toshitsune Maeda nearly 400 years ago, and consists of seven buildings, all surrounded by splendid gardens and large courtyards filled with large "fields" of fine white stones, precisely raked into a design that will induce tranquility. (One does not walk on the stones.) This morning we were joined by another English speaking guide, Mieko Takeguchi, who would accompany us during many of the events of the next two clays. She told me that she has not visited an English speaking country, and yet her English is excellent.

We were greeted at the main entrance of the temple by a Buddhist priest, Yotsuya-san, who took us from place to place, explaining the history and meaning of things (with Jonathon Perry translating). Eventually we arrived at the central building where we would participate in a tea ceremony. Shoes off! Who should appear to lead the tea service other than Kimio Arai, dressed quite impressively in traditional formal garb! There were also several ladies, all quite attractive in their kimonos. We seated ourselves around the wall of the main room, were given instruction as to the proper way tea is served in a "tea ceremony," and also how the recipients are expected to behave when they receive it. Kimio himself served me, and allowed me to do the "whisking" part of the tea preparation - which is not as easy as it sounds.

After the tea ceremony there was time to visit the beautiful shrine in the center of the building and to rub the anatomy of a seated, life size statue of a man near the entrance. We were told that if your shoulder hurts, you should rub his shoulder, and he will absorb the pain for you. Likewise for aches or pains anywhere else. From his expression, I judged that lots of people had been rubbing him. There was also a nice gift shop, and many of us took advantage of it. We were reminded that credit cards are not as widely accepted in Japan as in the United States, and that a shopper needs to carry some cash.

Steve McElhoe had a small cut-out figure of "Flat Stanley," and several of us had our pictures taken with it. I learned that this relates to a game that American children play in the first and second grade. The object is to see how far Flat Stanley travels, and where he shows up. I suppose there is some prize for having his picture at the most remote location. The rain continued, but it was lighter than before, and our bus was supplied with an ample assortment of umbrellas for us to use - reminding me again that the Japanese are terrific hosts.

When we left the Zuiryuji Temple it was lunch time, and our bus took us to the Chamber of Commerce, which has a restaurant on the top floor, with a nice view of Takaoka. The lunch was served in the familiar lacquer boxes that I have often seen at Japanese restaurants, and Tom Herr informed me that these are called *Bento boxes.*" There was some excellent Miso soup with clams, and steamed rice, and all of the food was fully cooked, which I found to be gratifying.

Snapshots

Our table included Tom Herr, Tamura-san, Stan Barker, Mieko Takeguchi, Nakao-san, and me. I sat across from Nakao-san, who had not stopped moving since he met us at the airport the day before. By the time I had taken a few bites, his meal was gone, and he was off and about the room looking after details for our afternoon tour.

VII

As soon as we were finished with lunch we got back on our bus and made a bee-line for Takaoka Civic Hall, a large auditorium located in Memorial Park. It was the original site of the ancient city castle, and is located in the central part of town. (This was the same location where Fort Wayne's Freimann Quartet performed to a packed house in 1997.) The park itself is worth a visit, with lots of water, swans, and - usually - peace and quiet. Today it was full of people on their way to attend the ceremony at Civic Hall to commemorate the celebration of the 400th anniversary of the founding of the City of Takaoka. Still, since we had to walk some distance from the bus to Civic Hall, we got a chance to experience some of the charm of the place.

When we arrived there, an attendant gathered up our umbrellas and put them all together in one location - which was good, because there was a sea of umbrellas that had already been stashed in the lobby. As it happened, we were behind schedule, and Nakao-san was in a frenzy. The program had already started!

Howard Chapman and Fort Wayne Mayor Tom Henry with the mascot celebrating Takaoka's 400 year celebration.

We were ushered to reserved seats in the front of the auditorium. The place was completely full. There was a man on stage creating music on a keyboard with the assistance of a computerized synthesizer that made him sound like an orchestra. Behind him there was a large screen, and various lights and colorful designs played and shifted in accompaniment to his music. Next, some men in kimonos came on and performed music, songs, and an assortment of chants, and they were followed by someone else in a *"No"* costume, who did a ritual dance.

This was followed by the appearance of two enormous drums with a woman standing on each side of them, and the women proceeded to rhythmically bang the drums. All of a sudden, the stage erupted with what must have been dozens of girls dancing and playing small drums, followed by as many older girls with larger drums on wheels.

By this time the audience was going nuts. I know I was. It was electric. Then, while they cleared the stage, a woman at the side of the auditorium played more music by ringing a large instrument full of bells.

It was finally time for the speeches! Several tables had been arrayed on stage, and it became littered with men in dark suits. Representatives from each of the sister cities were up there, and each was called to take his turn at giving a two minute speech, without the benefit of translation. I had no trouble understanding our mayor, Tom Henry, and Jim Whitfield, the representative from Beverley, England.

At the conclusion, a screen dropped down and there was a movie about the founding of Takaoka, four hundred years earlier. The movie portrayed Lord Toshinaga, riding along on his horse and, to my surprise, he and the horse also showed up the next day, riding in the parade.

On the way out, a couple of thousand "goodie bags" had been assembled, and each of us got one as we passed by. Fortunately, it was no longer raining, as we had to walk several blocks back to our bus, and all of our umbrellas had been collected and *put back on the bus* while we were in the ceremony.

VIII

"Behind schedule" as always, our bus next took us to a downtown building known as "Wing Wing." There is a reason why it is called "Wing Wing," but I was never able to learn what that reason is. Inside, on the ground floor, there was an event going on which included a large number of booths or stalls where crafts were being demonstrated, wares were being displayed, and civic groups were pitching their organizations. There was a big crowd, and lots of beautiful children. Hisako Tanabe was there in charge of one of the stalls; she seems to have involvement in everything. I was happy to learn that she would be with us the next day.

There were rows of chairs set up for the sister city guests, and a microphone. An old friend, Dr. Kitimura, seemed to still have an important position with the Takaoka sister city program, and stood up and made a speech, followed by more speeches, followed by introductions of all of the sister city mayors. During all of this, Nakao-san was buzzing around the room, pretty much a blur. At one point, Jonathon Perry was wowing an audience with yo-yo tricks, but Nakao-san brought him up short and told him to get back to work - whatever that was.

After the speechmaking we had time to mingle and I had a nice reunion with another old friend, Jin-ichi Miyazaki. Jin-ichi has been to Fort Wayne, and we reminisced about our tennis game some twenty years earlier. We caught up on our families, including the sad news that his wife and a daughter had both passed away not long ago. He told me that he would have a prominent position in the celebration parade that we would see the next day, and I promised to look for him. Finally, just before we left, a lady in one of the craft booths managed to palm off funny looking hats on Tom Henry and me, and we were polite enough to wear them until we got outside.

Our bus took us back to the New Otani, where we were already late for the beginning of the Mayor's Reception, which was held in the hotel banquet hall. Before we got there, though, several of us stopped in the lobby to watch a bridal party arriving for a wedding reception in another part of the hotel. Except that they were all Japanese, it could very well have been a bridal party in the United States.

The Mayor's Reception was sponsored by the Chamber of Commerce of Takaoka, which has a sister organization relationship with the Fort Wayne Chamber of Commerce. Food, beer and sake were plentiful and free, and it was no surprise to see that there was another big crowd. There was much networking and exchange of business cards. People were following the Japanese custom whereby you do not pour your own beer (or whatever), but pour it for your neighbor, who then reciprocates.

Japan is very strict about drinking and driving. It is not a matter of blood alcohol content, but rather, did you have any alcohol at all. As a result, partygoers commonly have a relative pick them up, or take a bus or taxi to go home. It is common to see taxicabs waiting outside drinking establishments with two drivers in them. One will take the customer home in the cab while the other drives the customer's car home. Then, both leave in the taxi.

Once the speeches had begun, the food was uncovered and people began to dig in. After the Mayor, a succession of speakers took the podium (many of them politicians). They talked at the top of their lungs, but no one seemed to pay any attention to them at all - and they did not seem to mind. Tamura-san had suggested that we wait and eat later in the hotel coffee shop, so I did. Instead, I talked with a number of old friends, including former Mayor Sato. I also met a man who had hosted an exchange student from Fort Wayne, and a man named Maeda who is descended from the Maeda family that helped to found Takaoka. I also met Mrs. Maeda; however, except for her, the women in our group, and hotel staff, I did not observe any other women at this event. In Japan, business and politics seem to remain very much male domains.

In addition to ignoring the speakers, people also ignored the entertainment that followed. It was mostly stylized dancing in costumes, singing, and assorted music, all of which appeared to have no purpose other than to raise the noise level. All in all, it was a very nice event until, as is the custom, the announcement was made that, "This reception is over now."

Most of the Fort Wayne delegation went downstairs to the coffee shop. Tamura-san had given each of us a coupon to use for the purchase of food. Some of us had grilled ham and cheese sandwiches, while I ordered a "mixed sandwich," which turned out to have egg salad, tomato, lettuce, ham and cucumber. It was good, but required a knife and fork to eat it. Also, happily, it turned out that there was some very good chocolate ice cream available. After dinner, some went with Tamura-san to a private home to watch preparations of a float for the next day's parade; however, I was happy to be in bed by 9:30.

IX

The Sunday morning breakfast buffet at the New Otani had undergone several changes since the day before, with an eclectic mix of Japanese and western food, and I was able to find a boiled egg, a tasty sausage, cereal, juice and some mixed vegetables. At 8:40, all of us (representing the sister cities from America, Brazil, China and England) assembled in the lobby to board our bus for the morning's tours. I again remarked about the exceptional cleanliness of the bus, with clean white doilies on every seat, delicate curtains in the windows, fresh flowers at the front, and a uniformed stewardess.

The highlights of the morning excursion would be the Amaharashi Coast along the Sea of Japan, the new Aeon Mall shopping Center, and lunch at the Sakae Sushi restaurant. On the way out of the city we passed Takaoka's huge statue of Buddha, then drove up into the mountains on a very steep and winding road. We stopped a couple of times at overlooks, where the view was fine but would have been amazing were there fewer clouds. If it were clearer, we would have been able to see the snow covered Japanese Alps in the distance. At the top of the mountain we visited a large monument with

Snapshots

a statue of The Goddess of Mercy, and used the opportunity to take a lot of photographs with the valley below as a background.

After descending that mountain, we climbed another one to the location of a huge bell suspended from the roof of a wooden, open-sided building. In Japanese it is called "*Heiwa no kane,*" the bell *(kane)* of peace *(heiwa)*. There is a great log that hangs close by from the ceiling, and one rings the bell by pulling the log back and then rushing at the bell with it. It makes a lot of noise. When a person rings the bell they will be protected from having bad luck. Needless to say, everyone rang the bell. By this time there was light rain, and some concern for the big parade that was scheduled for the afternoon.

Ringing the *Heiwa no Kane,* certain to bring good luck to everyone who rings it. (It is loud.)

Down the mountain we went, to the Amaharashi Coast. This is spectacular scenery that very much evokes the Monterey Peninsula along the coast of California. We left the bus to walk down to the beach, dodging traffic, and holding umbrellas - because it had begun to rain harder. Again, the weather frustrated our view of the scenery. On a clear day, the Japanese Alps rise out of the sea across the bay. There was a photograph of it at the place where the bus stopped, so at least we were able to get some idea of what we were missing.

Hisako Tanabe had been with us this entire morning, and I enjoyed the chance to catch up with her and to hear about her family. My wife, Betsy, and I had met her husband, Yutaka, and her two daughters, Yoshiko and Yumiko, on our first visit to Takaoka in 1977. Since then, the girls have grown up, and Yoshiko is married with a family and lives in Tokyo; but Yumiko, who has become fluent in English, lives with her family in a town close to Takaoka. We had reunited with Yumiko on our two subsequent visits, and she and her youngest son, Yuji, were scheduled to meet us when our bus made its stop at the Aeon Mall.

The Aeon Mall is very large and is modern in every respect. Most of the stores were familiar names, but there was a generous sprinkling of more traditional Japanese shops and goods. It glitters, and is spotless.

Our schedule said that we would have an hour to spend at the mall; but, we seemed to be always behind schedule and when we finally got off of the bus, we only had about 40 minutes to be there. Yumiko and Yuji were waiting for us at the entrance, and they, Hisako and I headed for the nearby Starbucks, ordered lattes, and all talked as much as we could in the short time that we had. Hisako advised that she still studies English as a student with Jonathon Perry (he says that she is "as sharp as a tack.") Yumiko claims to now speak better English than her mother, but Hisako rejoins with, "Well, I taught her." Yuji, age five, grinned and posed for pictures, and had a wonderful time, even though everything had to be translated for him. In accordance with custom, we exchanged gifts, hugs and tears, and then I had to head back to the bus. Hisako stayed, but said she would rejoin us that afternoon.

Yumiko Kaneko, her son Yuji, Howard Chapman
and Hisako Tanabe, at the Aeon Mall in Takaoka.

Snapshots

At the Sakae Sushi restaurant, shoes are left at the door, and customers sit on mats on the floor, at low tables. Most of us ate sushi with lots of raw fish; however, thanks to the foresightedness of Tamura-san, two of us were served with the "no raw fish special," consisting of vegetables and rice.

X

This afternoon was to be the culmination of the entire weekend of festivities, The Big Parade. We understood that the sister city delegations would first be observers at the reviewing stand, and then would be invited to become a part of the parade itself. By the time we had finished lunch and gotten downtown it was 1:30, and we were already late. All of the streets were blocked, and a great crowd had gathered. If you know how a ship acts as an icebreaker, then you can visualize how Jonathon Perry and Tamura-san led us through the throngs until, eventually, we reached the reviewing stand.

Our seats had been saved, and all the people sitting there welcomed us, with no recriminations about our tardiness. The parade had begun, and a series of school groups were going past, some with very small girls, others boys, others mixed, others older, all the way up to teenagers. All were having a wonderful time marching, playing music, or twirling batons. Many were carrying a variety of objects such as animal figures or flags, or pulling and pushing carts or wagons with displays in them.

The weather had changed completely, and for the first time since we arrived, it was hot. Boiling hot. The Japanese and Chinese on the viewing stand, nearly all men, were wearing dark suits and ties, and sweat was rolling off them. As the parade rolled by, one or two of them got up and left and did not return because -I am sure - of the hot sun. Our Fort Wayne group was all dressed alike in khakis and dark blue polo shirts with a Fort Wayne logo on them, so we were relatively comfortable. I had been foresighted enough to bring a cap and sun glasses, which were invaluable. Jim Whitfield, the former mayor from the city of Beverley, was sitting next to me. He took out his handkerchief, a rubber band, and a piece of paper, and fashioned a cap. He needed it. Anticipating the possibility of rain, I had brought an umbrella and, for a while, I opened it and shared it with Jim.

And the parade kept rolling by. Not only was the size of the crowd enormous, even the parade itself was huge. We later learned that there were more than 2,500 participants *in the parade*! Bands. Singing groups. Dancing groups. Wagons. School kids. More bands. Many of the adult groups were dressed in medieval costumes of soldiers, kendo fighters, samurai and nobility.

And then came the *real* crowd pleasers.

Howard L. Chapman

I had seen the ancient, giant floats before. On an earlier visit, I had even helped to push one in a parade. Still, when the first one came into view, it was arresting. Each float, hundreds of years old, is three to four stories high, resting on two heavy wooden wheels, with more than a dozen men in front pulling, another dozen or more in back pushing, and one more on each side of each wheel, helping to turn them. I do not know how much one of these floats weighs, but it is a lot. To say that they were colorful is an understatement. They were lavishly decorated, and a favored few, in traditional costumes, were riding on them.

The ancient floats parade through Takaoka, accompanied by men and women in traditional costumes.

The entry of the first float was dramatic, but the entry of each one after it was just as dramatic. The first one was pushed to a place in front and to the left of us, and the others entered one at a time into the viewing area and proceeded to line up until, at last, there were seven of them arrayed in a grand row of color and splendor. Meanwhile, row after row of men in costume came into the area, led by my friend Jin-Ichi Miyazaki, who managed to come over to our stand and give us a smile and a bow.

Moving these floats is a laborious and difficult job. The wheels are on fixed axles, and in order to turn a corner, the men pulling and pushing have to take turns lifting and turning the float. I suspect that every parade provides several patients for local orthopedic practitioners.

Snapshots

Eventually, "Lord Toshinaga" himself came riding by, mounted on his handsome horse, and surrounded by an entire retinue of nobles and servants. This seemed to be the signal for the giant floats to begin their journey away from the parade and down a side street. They will be housed, somewhere, until another occasion that justifies bringing them out.

Once the last float had left the viewing area, Jonathon Perry signaled Mayor Henry that it was time for us to join the parade. (It was far from over!) Lucy Briley unfurled a City of Fort Wayne flag, and Jerry Henry did the same with an American flag. They conducted us into the street, and we became a part of the show. Our Japanese hosts had provided each of us with a small American flag to carry in the parade, and had also given appropriate flags to the sister city representatives from Brazil, England and China.

As we proceeded along the parade route, the street was jammed with people on both sides, and every window and balcony was occupied. After a block or so, Hisako Tanabe and two other interpreters stepped forward from the crowd and joined us. Everyone along the way seemed genuinely warm and friendly. As we passed by, they smiled and applauded, and many shouted "Welcome!" Several parents sent their beaming children out to shake hands with us. As we walked, the same thought kept recurring in my mind: "If we had only had sister cities, there would never have been a war."

After we had walked for a half mile or so, the parade made its way into Memorial Park. There is a great meadow there, and all of the parade participants were gathering in groups in front of a large stage. There was going to be entertainment and speeches, and we were told that some or all of the sister city representatives might be called up on stage. Many of us from Fort Wayne found a shady area under a tent and Hisako and I spread out newspapers and sat down.

The Japanese are amazing hosts. Before long, young people were passing through the crowds handing out cans of cold drinks. We had seen a group of American basketball players come by in the parade, and now they came to the tent to get out of the hot sun. We struck up a conversation and learned that they play for a local professional team.

Hisako introduced me to the other ladies who had joined us during the parade. They are all her friends, and are all students of English under Jonathon Perry. After about thirty minutes, it became apparent that we were not going to be called to the stage and, about then, Nakao-san came by and said, simply. "It is over."

XI

Hisako and her friends guided us back to the New Otani Hotel, stopping at the famous Buddha for photos. It was five o'clock, and Tamura-san had provided us with coupons for a Japanese dinner at a traditional restaurant on the third floor of the hotel. Then we were to gather in the hotel lobby at 6:30. The schedule called for us to walk to an area near the train station where we would witness an exhibition called "The Fighting Floats."

I chose to skip the dinner and went to my room for a shower and a nap. I later learned that Tom Herr had used the coupon at the restaurant, and reported a very nice meal. At 6:30 we met once more in the lobby of the New Otani. We were told that the "Fighting Floats" was a very popular event, and that there would be large crowds of people. Accordingly, we were divided into small groups, each with a local translator/guide, and Hisako Tanabe was assigned to escort me.

The Takaoka train station is within walking distance of the hotel, and we set out on foot. As we neared the staging area for the event, we could see that great masses of people of all ages were already congregating. We maneuvered for a viewing spot as close as we could get, but were still a long way from the floats. These were different from the floats that had been in the parade, and looked more or less like two large, square houses on wheels, surrounded on all sides by white lanterns decorated with red calligraphy. The idea, as best as I could understand it, was that each float would have a team of men to power it, and the floats would take a run at each other.

It was ten minutes until seven, and the main event was not scheduled until seven thirty. In the meantime, great ladders were erected nearby, and men were on top performing acrobatics. Americans tend to be about a head taller than the average Japanese and I had no trouble looking over the crowd; however, Hisako could not see very much at all.

I said. "Hisako, it's been a long day, it looks like we'll just be standing here for at least another forty minutes, and I didn't eat dinner. What would you say to just going back to the hotel and getting some Udon noodle soup." She replied that this would be fine. She had already eaten, and the hotel would probably not have Udon noodle soup, but she knew where to go to get some.

We walked back toward the hotel for a couple of blocks, and then went down a flight of stairs to the underground shopping area. Below the downtown of Takaoka, as in many Japanese cities, there is a thriving commercial area full of shops, service establishments and restaurants. Our group had been on such a constant pace since our arrival that, incredibly, none of us had yet gotten down there. Most of the places were open, and Hisako guided us to a traditional noodle shop. It was packed.

Had I gone to this noodle shop alone, without Hisako, I would have starved. Picking out my food was not a problem, since there was a large display outside with photographs of all of the menu items. Getting it was another matter. Hisako found an empty table and had me sit down, and then got in a line of people at a machine that looked like a vending machine, with lots of buttons, and Japanese writing. She put money into the machine, pushed some buttons, and received a ticket. She then went to another line and, when she arrived at the counter, exchanged the ticket for my order which, by then had arrived from the kitchen.

If one eats noodle soup in Japan, it is necessary to eat it as the Japanese do, using chopsticks for the noodles, and drinking the soup from the bowl. It was delicious! Maybe I was just hungry, but I told Hisako that it was the best meal that I had while in Japan. By seven thirty, a lot of the people had left to see the fighting floats. Among the remaining patrons, we noticed the actor who had portrayed Lord Toshinaga in the parade that afternoon.

This meal gave Hisako and me a chance to visit and to finish catching up on lives and families, without any interruptions. We walked back to the New Otani and said goodbye, and Hisako, who does not drive, left for home in a taxi. I took advantage of the opportunity to try to get on the internet, using the hotel computer, but was frustrated by the difference in keyboards and the fact that no one at the desk spoke English well enough to help me. I returned to my room to pack for our departure back to Tokyo, and was happy to be in bed early.

XII

Monday morning was a lovely sunny day, and I was awake and up shortly after dawn. I went for a long walk through the mostly empty city, and it was kind of eerie after two days of large crowds of people. When I passed through the covered shopping street, memories of our first visit to Takaoka, more than thirty years ago, came flooding back. This street was then the center of activity, but now many of the stores and businesses have moved to the Aeon Mall or to the underground city.

When we gathered in the hotel lobby to get on our bus to the Toyama Airport, the entire hotel staff lined up again to see us off and wish us well. Hisako came too, and also Jonathon Perry and many others. In Toyama we ate the box lunches given us at the hotel as we waited to board the Boeing 777 for our return to Tokyo. This time there were plenty of empty seats.

At Haneda airport, in Tokyo, there are shuttle buses to take people into the city, but for some reason there were no more that day, even though it was early afternoon. Tom Herr and Stan Barker had come to Tokyo earlier that morning, so I was on my own to get to the Tokyo Hotel New Otani. Tamura-san (the indispensable) took me to a taxi stand, got me in the right taxi, and told the driver where to take me. *Good thing.* There are two taxi stands that look just alike, except that one of them only takes people to Yokohama! Tamura-san returned to help the Henrys, Brileys, and McElhoes get to Narita Airport for their afternoon flight to China. Meanwhile, my taxi was spotless, with clean white doilies on the seats, and the driver in jacket, tie and white gloves. "Just like New York," I thought.

Toyoharu Tamura (known best to all of us as "T"), our inestimable escort in Japan, and Howard Chapman.

Once I had checked in to the now familiar surroundings of the Tokyo hotel, I found Stan Barker and Tom Herr, and we waited in the lobby for Tamura-san. He arrived later than expected, and I proposed that we skip going out to a restaurant and eat at the hotel; however, Tamura-san had made arrangements for us to meet some others and have dinner at "Ninja" restaurant in the Akasaka district. This sounded too good to pass up.

"Ninja" turned out to be an unusual place, full of dark corridors, torch lights, private dining areas, magicians, and "ninja" waitresses. It had low ceilings, and American guests had to be careful not to bump their heads in getting to their tables. We were joined by Takeo Akatsu and his wife Ako, friends of Tamura-san. We also met Americans Donald Babcock, an executive

Snapshots

with Nisource, and John Sampson, President of the Northeast Indiana Regional Partnership. They were in Tokyo as part of a trade delegation led by Indiana governor Mitch Daniels. Altogether, it made for a lively evening in a congenial group, and with a very interesting and unusual meal.

Tamura-san was scheduled to stay in Japan for a while in connection with the trade delegation, but Tom Herr, Stan Barker and I were headed home. When the hotel breakfast buffet opened, we were waiting at the door. A bus (pre-arranged for us by Tamura-san, God bless him!) took us to Narita Airport. We embarked on the long but restful journey home. It won't be too long before a group from Takaoka will be coming to Fort Wayne, probably in connection with our Three Rivers Festival. I know we will do our best to reciprocate for the hospitality we received while we were visiting them, but it will be a daunting task.

Still, I know we will try.

www.ingramcontent.com/pod-product-compliance
Lightning Source LLC
Chambersburg PA
CBHW031426160426
43195CB00010BB/627